Jewish Literature
Between the Bible and the Mishnah

A Historical and Literary Introduction

George W. E. Nickelsburg

FORTRESS PRESS   Philadelphia

For Jeanne Marie, 'ה אֲשֶׁר בָּה חָנַן אוֹתָנוּ

and Michael John, הַשָּׂר הַקָּטֹן

COPYRIGHT © 1981 BY FORTRESS PRESS

First Fortress Press paperback edition 1987

Library of Congress Cataloging in Publication Data

Nickelsburg, George W   E   1934-
  Jewish literature between the Bible and the Mishnah.

  Includes bibliographies and index.
    1. Bible.   O. T. Apocrypha—Introductions.
  2.   Apocryphal books (Old Testament)—Introductions.
  3.   Dead Sea scrolls—Introductions.   I.   Title.
BS1700.N48   229'.061   80–16176
ISBN 0–8006–1980–3

Printed in the United States of America   1-1980
94   93   92   3   4   5   6   7   8   9   10

Contents

Preface

This volume has been designed primarily as a first introduction to the Jewish literature of the so-called intertestamental period. As such it is intended for college, university, and seminary students, for clergy, and for lay people who have some familiarity with the methods of modern biblical interpretation. At the same time, I hope that my colleagues in biblical studies who have worked with the early Jewish writings in a sporadic and ad hoc fashion may also find the book helpful in focusing on the broad and central issues in this literature.

Certain basic decisions about content and format were necessary. Since this is primarily an inductive work, I have employed the principle "first things first." Thus I have avoided long discussions of technical issues and details and have sought to guide the reader directly into the contents of the individual writings. Further study of particular details and questions can be pursued through the notes and bibliography at the end of each chapter.

A number of considerations have limited the scope of the literature that could be treated. I have discussed the canonical book of Daniel, all of the Apocrypha except the story of the guardsmen in 1 Esdras and the Prayer of Manasseh, most of the Pseudepigrapha (including some works omitted from the collection of R. H. Charles), and a selection of the Qumran Scrolls, which with the exception of the Genesis Apocryphon are treated as a collection in Chapter 4. The Septuagint, the Greek translation of the Hebrew Scriptures, was the Bible of much of the Jewish Dispersion during this period, and the interpretations of these Scriptures reflected in this translation are an important witness to the religion and theology of early Judaism. However, the sheer mass of the evidence has made it impossible for me to include here the chapter that this material deserves. Because of their length, the special problems attached to them, and the extensive bibliographies that have grown around them, I have not treated the works of Philo of Alexandria and Flavius Josephus. The roots of the Samaritan literature and the rabbinic writings are to be found in this period, but again special problems (not the least of which is dating) made it impractical to treat them here.

A decision about the format of the book had to take into consideration two important and complementary factors in biblical studies. Since the writings of early Judaism are literature, one could logically arrange the individual works according to their literary genres. Such an approach would have been the easiest way to proceed. On the other hand this literature was produced in time and space and was conditioned by both. To ignore this historical element is to jeopardize the discipline. I have therefore employed a chronological sequence that runs from the late Persian period to the Second Revolt (ca. 400 B.C.E.–140 C.E.). In some cases this creates problems because we cannot always be sure of the dating of certain works. I have tried to obviate these problems by treating a large number of these works in a chapter entitled "The Exposition of Israel's Scriptures" (Chapter 7). In this chapter and elsewhere, when the date of a writing is questionable the issues and alternatives are presented pro and con. This will allow the student or teacher to use the book in a course that is not structured historically and will facilitate the study of individual books.

Each chapter begins with a capsule history of a segment of the period. These short introductions touch only on matters necessary for a basic understanding of the literature discussed in the respective chapter. Bibliographies at the end of the chapters provide resources for a more detailed study of the historical data.

This book represents the fruits of twenty years of study and ten years of teaching and publishing. Much that is discussed here cursorily I have treated in considerable detail elsewhere. Attention is called to this bibliography at the appropriate places. This prolific cross-referencing is intended as a kind of shorthand rather than as excessive self-citation. I have tried to balance it by reference to the opinions of others, particularly when they differ from my own.

It is my pleasant duty to thank friends and colleagues for their help and encouragement. Norman A. Hjelm, Director of Fortress Press, invited me to write the book. The unfootnoted context of the project has been my work in the Pseudepigrapha Group of the Society of Biblical

Literature and my teaching at the University of Iowa. My colleagues at Iowa, Jonathan and Helen Goldstein, have listened to my ideas, critiqued them, and offered some of their own. From my friend Norman R. Petersen I have learned much about the workings of narrative literature. Parts of the manuscript were read by John J. Collins, Jonathan A. Goldstein, Marinus de Jonge, Ralph W. Klein, Burton L. Mack, Jacob Neusner, Michael Stone, and John Strugnell, who have both saved me from embarrassing errors and contributed helpful and wise suggestions. The manuscript was proofread by my graduate assistants, Gwen Sayler and Melanie Roth. It was edited by Mary Lou Doyle, and most of it was typed by Georgiane Perret. The subject index was prepared by Melanie Roth. Galley proofs were read by my graduate assistant, Richard Grigg. The maps for the book were prepared by Thomas C. Eagle of the University of Iowa Department of Geography and by Mrs. Elsie Tamson. Final responsibility for the contents is of course my own.

I would like to express special thanks for the generosity of the Foundation Compendia Rerum Iudaicarum ad Novum Testamentum of Amsterdam, and the editors of *Compendia,* who have kindly permitted me to use in this book material which I first prepared for a *Compendia* article on Jewish narrative writings, namely, the sections on Daniel 1–6 and the additions to Daniel; Tobit; Judith; the *Book of Jubilees;* in part the *Testaments of the Twelve Patriarchs;* the Genesis Apocryphon; the *Martyrdom of Isaiah;* the *Testament of Abraham; Joseph and Aseneth;* the *Books of Adam and Eve;* the *Biblical Antiquities* (Pseudo-Philo); and the *Paraleipomena of Jeremiah.*

During the five years that I have worked on this book I have received more than a fair share of encouragement, understanding, and loving toleration from my family—Marilyn, Jeanne, and Michael. The completion of the book is my word of thanks. It is dedicated to our children as the transmitting of a heritage, in the belief that beauty and truth and insight are not limited to the confines of canon.

Iowa City, Iowa   G. W. E. N.
July 31, 1980

Preface to the
Revised Edition

This paperback is a slightly revised reprint of the original 1981 edition. Revisions are of three kinds: a few corrections of errata; updated references to literature previously listed as "forthcoming"; and a revision of the original pages 6–7, primarily to include items of general bibliography published since 1980.

I had hoped to make more extensive revisions of the 1981 edition in order to include a few more ancient works and to take into consideration reviewers' suggestions and the rapid development of the discipline. Practical considerations have made that unfeasible at this time. In lieu of such a revision I would like to call the reader's attention to the following items. Two major Qumran works have appeared recently in English translation: Yigael Yadin, ed., *The Temple Scroll*, 3 vols. (Jerusalem: Israel Exploration Society, et al., 1983); Carol Newsom, *Songs of the Sabbath Sacrifice: A Critical Edition* (Harvard Semitic Studies 27; Atlanta: Scholars Press, 1985). In my two chapters in *CRINT* 2:2 (see below, p. 7) I have discussed, in a format similar to the present book, "The Prayer of Nabonidus" and "The Story of Darius' Bodyguards" (1 Esdras 3—4), which fit with the texts in chapter 1 below, and three Hellenistic Jewish poets (Philo the epic poet, Theodotus, and Ezekiel) whose epic and tragic works are excellent examples of Jewish adaptation of "pagan" Greek literary genres. Finally, the bibliographies for the individual texts can be conveniently updated by consulting the chapter bibliographies and the appendix in Kraft and Nickelsburg, eds., *Early Judaism and Its Modern Interpreters* (see below, p. 8).

Iowa City, Iowa   G.W.E.N.
October, 1986

Abbreviations

AASOR	Annual of the American Schools of Oriental Research
AB	Anchor Bible
Adam and Eve	*Books of Adam and Eve* (= *Apoc. Mos.* + *Vita*)
Ag. Ap.	*Against Apion*
AGJU	Arbeiten zur Geschichte des antiken Judentums und des Urchristentums
AnBib	Analecta biblica
Ant.	*Antiquities*
Apoc. Abr.	*Apocalypse of Abraham*
Apoc. Mos.	*Apocalypse of Moses*
APOT	R. H. Charles, ed. *Apocrypha and Pseudepigrapha of the Old Testament*. 2 vols. Oxford: Clarendon, 1912.
Aram.	Aramaic
Asc. Isa.	*Ascension of Isaiah*
b. Ber.	*Berakot*, in Babylonian Talmud
b. Giṭ.	*Giṭṭin*, in Babylonian Talmud
b. Sanh.	*Sanhedrin*, in Babylonian Talmud
b. Yebam.	*Yebamot*, in Babylonian Talmud
BA	*Biblical Archaeologist*
Bar	Baruch
2, 3 Bar.	Syriac, Greek Apocalypse of Baruch
BASOR	*Bulletin of the American Schools of Oriental Research*
B.C.E.	Before the Common Era (= B.C.)
Bel	Bel and the Dragon
BETL	Bibliotheca ephemeridum theologicarum lovaniensium
Bib	*Biblica*
BibOr	Biblica et Orientalia
BJRL	Bulletin of the John Rylands University Library of Manchester

BZAW	Beihefte zur Zeitschrift für die alttestamentliche Wissenschaft
BZNW	Beihefte zur Zeitschrift für die neutestamentliche Wissenschaft
CBQ	*Catholic Biblical Quarterly*
CD	Cairo (Genizah text of the) Damascus (Document). Published by S. Schechter. *Fragments of a Zadokite Work*. Rev. ed. by J. A. Fitzmyer. New York: KTAV, 1970. Translation by Vermes, *Scrolls*, 95–117.
C.E.	Common Era (= A.D.)
1, 2 Chr	1, 2 Chronicles
Col	Colossians
Comm.	Commentary
ConB	Coniectanea Biblica
1, 2 Cor	1, 2 Corinthians
CRINT	*Compendia Rerum Iudaicarum ad Novum Testamentum.* Assen: Van Gorcum, 1974–
CScA	Contributi all Scienza dell' Antichità
CTM	*Concordia Theological Monthly*
CurTM	*Currents in Theology and Mission*
Dan	Daniel
Deut	Deuteronomy
Diss.	Dissertation
DJD(J)	Discoveries in the Judaean Desert (of Jordan). Oxford: Clarendon, 1955–
EBib	Études bibliques
EncJud	*Encyclopedia Judaica*. New York: Macmillan, 1971.
Eph	Ephesians
Ep Jer	Epistle of Jeremiah
Esdr	Esdras
Esth	Esther
E.T.	English translation
Exod	Exodus
ExpTim	*Expository Times*
Ezek	Ezekiel
FRLANT	Forschungen zur Religion und Literatur des Alten und Neuen Testaments
Fs.	Festschrift (jubilee or memorial volume)
Gal	Galatians
GCS	Griechische christliche Schriftsteller
Gen	Genesis

Gen. Rab.	*Genesis Rabbah*
Gk.	Greek
Hab	Habakkuk
HDR	Harvard Dissertations in Religion
Heb	Hebrews
HR	*History of Religions*
HSM	Harvard Semitic Monographs
HTR	*Harvard Theological Review*
HTS	Harvard Theological Studies
HUCA	*Hebrew Union College Annual*
IDB	G. A. Buttrick, ed. *Interpreter's Dictionary of the Bible.* 4 vols. Nashville: Abingdon, 1962.
IDBSup	Keith Crim, ed. Supplementary Volume to *IDB.*
IEJ	*Israel Exploration Journal*
Int	*Interpretation*
Isa	Isaiah
JAL	Jewish Apocryphal Literature
JAOS	*Journal of the American Oriental Society*
Jas	James
JBL	*Journal of Biblical Literature*
Jdt	Judith
Jer	Jeremiah
JJS	*Journal of Jewish Studies*
Jos.	Josephus
Jos. As.	*Joseph and Aseneth*
Josh	Joshua
JQR	*Jewish Quarterly Review*
JSHRZ	Jüdische Schriften aus hellenistisch-römischer Zeit
JSJ	*Journal for the Study of Judaism in the Persian, Hellenistic, and Roman Period*
JTS	*Journal of Theological Studies*
Jub.	*Jubilees*
Judg	Judges
J.W.	*Jewish Wars*
1, 2 Kgs	1, 2 Kings
LAB	*Liber Antiquitatum Biblicarum* (Pseudo-Philo)
Life	*Life of Adam and Eve*
LXX	Septuagint, Greek translation of the Hebrew Bible
m. Abot	*Abot*, in the Mishnah
1, 2, 3, 4 Macc	1, 2, 3, 4 Maccabees
Mal	Malachi

Matt	Matthew
Mic	Micah
Mor.	*Moralia*
ms(s).	manuscript(s)
Neh	Nehemiah
NTS	*New Testament Studies*
Num	Numbers
Numen	*Numen: International Review for the History of Religions*
NumenSup	Supplement to *Numen*
Od.	*Odyssey*
Par. Jer.	*Paraleipomena of Jeremiah*
Phil	Philippians
Pr Azar	Prayer of Azariah
Prov	Proverbs
Ps(s)	Psalm(s)
PsOT	James H. Charlesworth. *The Pseudepigrapha of the Old Testament.* 2 vols. Garden City: Doubleday, 1983–85.
Ps(s). Sol.	*Psalm(s) of Solomon*
PVTG	Pseudepigrapha Veteris Testamenti Graece
1QH	Hymn Scroll. Published by E. Sukenik. *The Dead Sea Scrolls of the Hebrew University.* Jerusalem: Magnes, 1955. Translation by Vermes, *Scrolls,* 149–201.
1QpHab	Habakkuk Commentary. Published by M. Burrows. *The Dead Sea Scrolls of St. Mark's Monastery* 1. New Haven: American Schools of Oriental Research, 1950. Translation by Vermes, *Scrolls,* 235–41.
4QpIsa^c	Isaiah Commentary. Published by J. Allegro. DJDJ 5: 17–27. Translation by Vermes, *Scrolls,* 228.
4QpNah	Nahum Commentary. Published by J. Allegro, DJDJ 5: 37–42. Translation by Vermes, *Scrolls,* 231–35.
4QpPs^a	Psalms Commentary. Published by J. Allegro. DJDJ 5: 42–50. Translation by Vermes, *Scrolls,* 243–45.
1QS	Rule of the Community (Manual of Discipline). Published by M. Burrows. *The Dead Sea Scrolls of St. Mark's Monastery* 2. New Haven: American Schools of Oriental Research, 1951. Translation by Vermes, *Scrolls,* 71–94.
RB	*Revue biblique*
RechBib	Recherches bibliques
Rep.	*Republic*

Rev	Revelation
RevQ	*Revue de Qumran*
RevScRel	*Revue des sciences religieuses*
Rom	Romans
RSV	Revised Standard Version
1, 2 Sam	1, 2 Samuel
SBL	Society of Biblical Literature
SBLASP	SBL Abstracts and Seminar Papers
SBLDS	SBL Dissertations Series
SBLSBS	SBL Sources for Biblical Study
SBLSCS	SBL Septuagint and Cognate Studies
SBLTT Ps.Ser.	SBL Texts and Translations, Pseudepigrapha Series
SBT	Studies in Biblical Theology
SC	Sources crétiennes
Sem	*Semitica*
Sib. Or.	*Sibylline Oracles*
Sir	The Wisdom of Jesus the Son of Sirach (or Ecclesiasticus)
SJLA	Studies in Judaism in Late Antiquity
SPB	Studia Postbiblica
SUNT	Studien zur Umwelt des Neuen Testaments
SVTP	Studia in Veteris Testamenti Pseudepigrapha
T.	*Testament of*
Abr.	*Abraham*
Iss.	*Issachar*
Jos.	*Joseph*
Mos.	*Moses*
Napht.	*Naphtali*
Reub.	*Reuben*
Sim.	*Simeon*
Zeb.	*Zebulun*
TDNT	G. Kittel and G. Friedrich, eds. *Theological Dictionary of the New Testament.* E.T. Grand Rapids: Eerdmans, 1964–74.
TextsS	Texts and Studies
Tg. Neof.	*Targum Neofiti 1*
Tg. Ps.-J.	*Targum Pseudo-Jonathan*
Tob	Tobit
TU	Texte und Untersuchungen
TZ	*Theologische Zeitschrift*
v(v).	verse(s)

Vit. Isa.	*Vita Isaiae*
VT	*Vetus Testamentum*
VTSup	Supplement to *Vetus Testamentum*
Wis	Wisdom of Solomon
WUNT	Wissenschaftliche Untersuchungen zum Neuen Testament
y. Sanh.	*Sanhedrin*, in Jerusalem Talmud
ZAW	*Zeitschrift für die alttestamentliche Wissenschaft*
Zech	Zechariah

SHORT TITLES OF WORKS
FREQUENTLY CITED

Cross, *Library*	Frank Moore Cross, Jr. *The Ancient Library of Qumran*. Rev. ed. Garden City, N.Y.: Doubleday, 1961.
Milik, *Books of Enoch*	J. T. Milik. *The Books of Enoch: Aramaic Fragments of Qumran Cave 4*. Oxford: Clarendon, 1976.
Nickelsburg, "Stories"	George W. E. Nickelsburg, "Stories of Biblical and Early Post-Biblical Times," *CRINT* 2:2, 33–87.
Nickelsburg, "Bible"	George W. E. Nickelsburg, "The Bible Rewritten and Expanded," *CRINT* 2:2, 89–156.
Nickelsburg, *Resurrection*	George W. E. Nickelsburg. *Resurrection, Immortality, and Eternal Life in Intertestamental Judaism*. HTS 26. Cambridge: Harvard University, 1972.
Pfeiffer, *History*	Robert H. Pfeiffer. *History of New Testament Times, with an Introduction to the Apocrypha*. New York: Harper, 1949.
Schürer, *History*	Emil Schürer. *The History of the Jewish People in the Age of Jesus Christ*. Vol. 1. Rev. ed. by G. Vermes and F. Millar. Edinburgh: Clark, 1973.
Tcherikover, *Hellenistic Civilization*	Victor Tcherikover. *Hellenistic Civilization and the Jews*. English translation. Philadelphia: Jewish Publication Society of America, 1959.
Vermes, *Scrolls*	Geza Vermes. *The Dead Sea Scrolls in English*. 2d ed. Harmondsworth: Penguin, 1975.

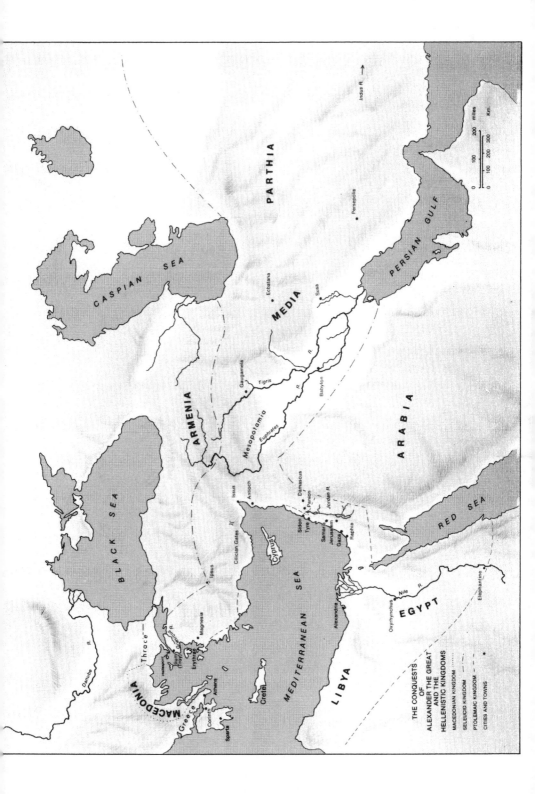

THE CONQUESTS
OF
ALEXANDER THE GREAT
AND THE
HELLENISTIC KINGDOMS

MACEDONIAN KINGDOM ——————
SELEUCID KINGDOM —·—·—·—
PTOLEMAIC KINGDOM ————————
CITIES AND TOWNS •

CASPIAN SEA

BLACK SEA

MEDITERRANEAN SEA

RED SEA

PERSIAN GULF

MACEDONIA

Greece

THRACE

ARMENIA

MEDIA

PARTHIA

ARABIA

LIBYA

EGYPT

MESOPOTAMIA

Danube R.

Sparta
Corinth
Athens
Erythrae
Magnesia
Ilium (Troy)
Ipsus
Cilician Gates
Issus
Antioch
Cyprus
Crete
Sidon
Tyre
Damascus
Panion
Jordan R.
Samaria
Jerusalem
Gaza
Raphia
Alexandria
Oxyrhynchus
Nile R.
Elephantine
Gaugamela
Tigris
Euphrates R.
Ecbatana
Susa
Babylon
Persepolis
Indus R.

0   100   200 miles
0   100 200 300 Km.

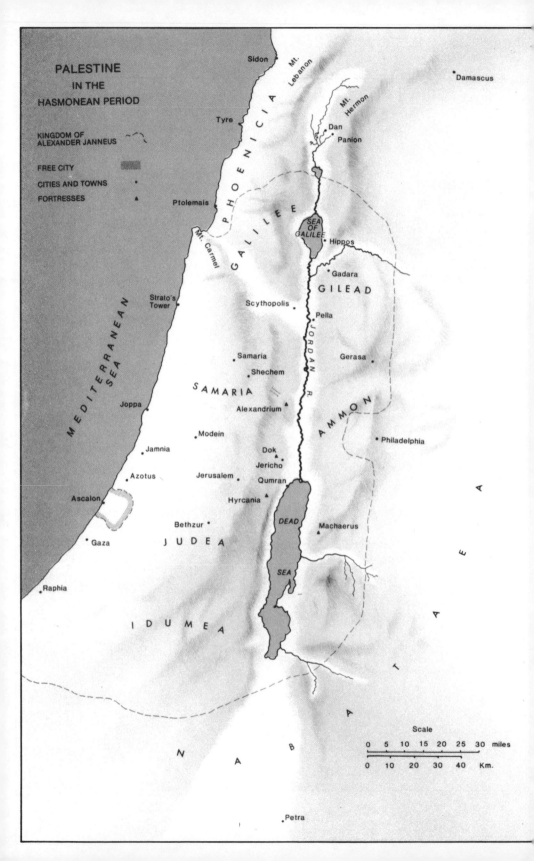

PALESTINE
IN THE
HASMONEAN PERIOD

KINGDOM OF
ALEXANDER JANNEUS

FREE CITY

CITIES AND TOWNS   .

FORTRESSES   ▲

MEDITERRANEAN SEA

PHOENICIA

Sidon

Mt. Lebanon

Tyre

Damascus

Mt. Hermon

Dan
Panion

Ptolemais

GALILEE

SEA OF GALILEE

Hippos

Mt. Carmel

Strato's Tower

Scythopolis

Gadara

GILEAD

Pella

JORDAN R.

Samaria
Shechem

SAMARIA

Gerasa

Joppa

Alexandrium

AMMON

Modein

Jamnia

Dok
Jericho

Philadelphia

Azotus

Jerusalem

Qumran

Ascalon

Hyrcania

Bethzur

DEAD

Machaerus

Gaza

JUDEA

SEA

Raphia

IDUMEA

N   A   B   A   T   A   E   A

Scale

0   5   10 15 20 25 30 miles

0   10   20   30   40 Km.

Petra

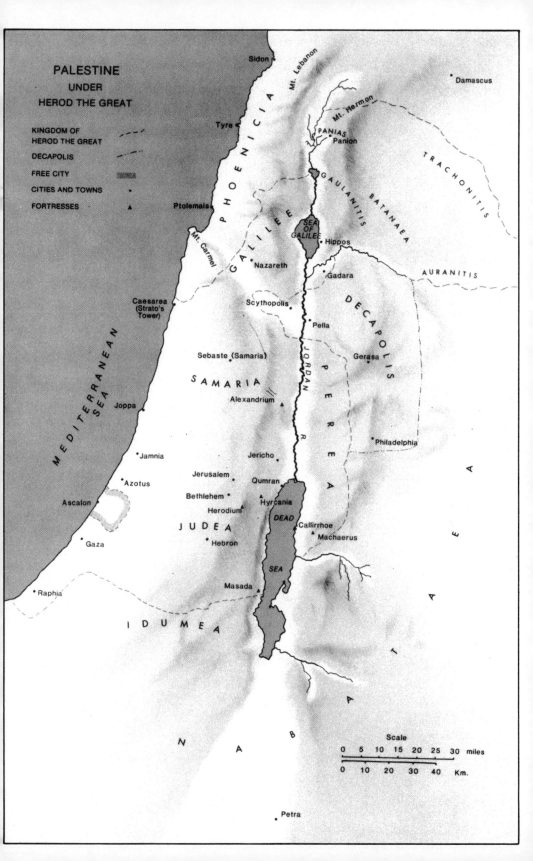

PALESTINE
UNDER
HEROD THE GREAT

KINGDOM OF
HEROD THE GREAT
DECAPOLIS
FREE CITY
CITIES AND TOWNS   •
FORTRESSES   ▲

MEDITERRANEAN SEA

PHOENICIA

Sidon
Tyre
Ptolemais
Mt. Carmel

Mt. Lebanon
Mt. Hermon
Damascus
PANIAS
Panion

TRACHONITIS

GALILEE

GAULANITIS

BATANAEA

SEA OF GALILEE
Hippos
Nazareth
Gadara

AURANITIS

Caesarea
(Strato's Tower)

Scythopolis
Pella

DECAPOLIS

Sebaste (Samaria)
Gerasa

SAMARIA

Alexandrium

JORDAN R.

PEREA

Joppa
Jamnia
Azotus
Ascalon
Gaza
Raphia

Jericho
Jerusalem
Bethlehem
Herodium
Hebron

Qumran
Hyrcania
Callirrhoe
Machaerus

Philadelphia

JUDEA

DEAD SEA

Masada

IDUMEA

N   A   B   A   T   A   E   A

Scale
0   5   10   15   20   25   30 miles
0   10   20   30   40 Km.

Petra

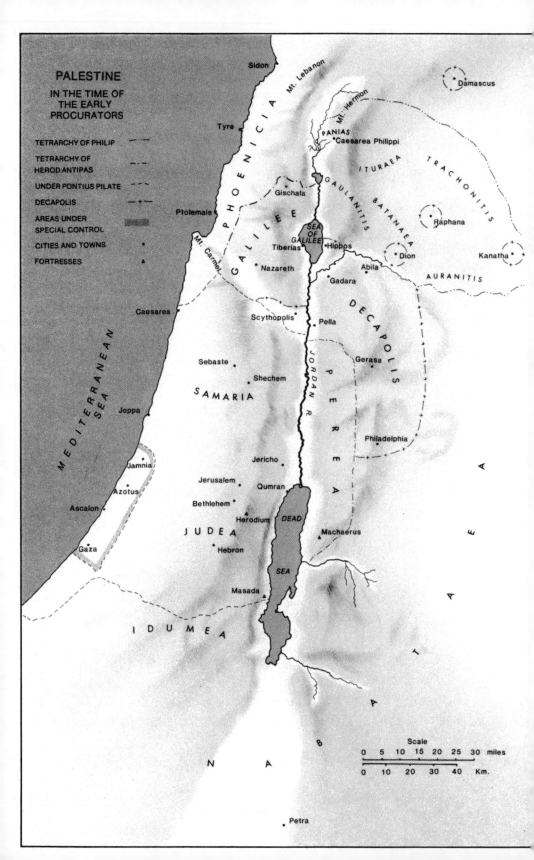

PALESTINE

IN THE TIME OF
THE EARLY
PROCURATORS

TETRARCHY OF PHILIP
TETRARCHY OF
HEROD ANTIPAS
UNDER PONTIUS PILATE
DECAPOLIS
AREAS UNDER
SPECIAL CONTROL
CITIES AND TOWNS
FORTRESSES

Sidon

Mt. Lebanon

Damascus

Tyre

PANIAS
Caesarea Philippi

Mt. Hermon

ITURAEA

TRACHONITIS

PHOENICIA

Gischala

GALILEE

GAULANITIS

BATANAEA

Ptolemais

Raphana

Mt. Carmel

SEA
OF
GALILEE

Tiberias

Hippos

Kanatha

Nazareth

Abila

Dion

AURANITIS

Caesarea

Gadara

MEDITERRANEAN SEA

Scythopolis

Pella

DECAPOLIS

Sebaste

Gerasa

Shechem

SAMARIA

JORDAN R.

P
E
R
E
A

Philadelphia

Joppa

Jericho

Jamnia

Jerusalem

Qumran

Azotus

Bethlehem

Ascalon

Herodium

DEAD

Machaerus

Gaza

JUDEA

SEA

Hebron

IDUMEA

Masada

A
B
A
T
A

N

A

Scale

0 5 10 15 20 25 30 miles

0   10   20   30   40 Km.

Petra

Introduction

The five centuries that spawned the literature which is the subject of this book were times of crisis, transition, and creativity for the Judeo-Christian tradition. At the beginning of the fourth century B.C.E. most of the literature that would later become the Scriptures of the Jewish people had already been written. By the middle of the second century C.E. both rabbinic Judaism and early Christianity had emerged. Both religions claimed to be the heirs of God's promises to Israel and embraced the earlier writings as Scripture. These religions had been shaped, however, by the events and developments that had transpired during these five centuries. Thus the study of early rabbinic Judaism and early Christianity must reckon with this period and with the literature that grew out of it and reflects it.

Fundamental and far-reaching changes shook the Jewish people during these centuries. The Persian Empire fell. Alexander's victories brought Greek language and culture to the East. The persecution of the Jews by the Macedonian king, Antiochus IV, tested the mettle of Jewish faith and threatened to exterminate the religion. After a brief period of independence Palestine bowed to the sovereignty of Rome. New turmoil brought revolt. Palestine was devastated, Jerusalem was destroyed, and the Temple was leveled.

These events and others like them made their inevitable impact on the shape of Jewish life, religion, and thought. Persecution, oppression, and political domination were met with capitulation in some cases, but they also spawned varieties of resistance and the theoretical undergirdings for it: militant zeal and passive resistance; apocalyptic speculations about help from the heavenly sphere and hopes for a human helper, a messiah; speculations about God's justice in an unjust world. The Jewish community divided into parties and groups and sects. In and through this

1

whole process individuals and members of various religious communities wrestled with the events that touched and troubled their lives, and they sought to make sense of them by interpreting their religious heritage and by creating new traditions that spoke with relevance and force to their circumstances. The literature of this period provides us with the evidence and some of the actual substance of this religious, cultural, and intellectual process. Moreover, this literature reveals, in various stages of development, literary forms of biblical interpretation three to four centuries before they emerge in the writings of the rabbis. Thus from almost any viewpoint the literature of this period is crucial to an understanding of the emergence of early rabbinic Judaism.

The situation is basically the same for the study of early Christianity. The seedbed of the church was first-century Judaism. As Jews, Jesus of Nazareth and his disciples breathed this religious and cultural environment and spoke its idiom. They received their Bible from the Jewish community and as it was interpreted by this community. Indeed, the very early church was a messianic movement within the bosom of Judaism, and fundamental aspects of its early history are intelligible only when viewed against the rejection of its messianic views and expectations by the majority of contemporary Jews. Thus in a variety of ways the literature of this period provides an indispensable key for the understanding of the rise of Christianity.

Unfortunately, Christian study of Judaism has often been imperialistic. Its purpose has been to enhance the study of Christianity, and often to do so by contrast. Thus Judaism is mocked up as the dark "background" against which is played the glorious drama of Christian origins. A more appropriate model is that of "roots." To the extent that we shall deal with the issue or imply it, we are interested in seeing how both early rabbinic Judaism and early Christianity sprang from the same seedbed.

The problem of Christians coming to terms with their Jewish roots is particularly acute. Centuries of overt stereotype and polemic and the continued unconscious use of prejudicial concepts and terminology obscure the facts and issues. Consider the following configuration:

B(efore) C(hrist)			//	A(nno) D(omini)
Old Testament	/	Intertestamental	//	New Testament
Israelite	/	(Late) Jewish	//	Christian

The very chronological terminology we employ presupposes a Christian confession, dividing time "before the Christ" and according to the "year of our Lord." Similarly, the application of the term "intertestamental" to the Jewish literature of this period presumes the Christian belief that in Jesus there is a New Covenant (i.e., testament) which has replaced the Old Covenant. Another distinction separates early Hebrew or Israelite religion and theology qualitatively from its Jewish development, and this latter from its Christian successor. On the one hand this distinction sees Judaism as a legalistic or wildly apocalyptic perversion of inspired Israelite religion. On the other hand it fails to admit the profound debt that early Christian faith and thought owes to Judaism. In its more arrogant and blind form it defines the Judaism of this period as "Late Judaism," as if this religion had come to an end with the emergence of Christianity.

In order to avoid these pitfalls and to sensitize the reader we shall employ more neutral terminology. Our chronological determiner will be the common existence of Judaism and Christianity; hence the Common Era (C.E.) and Before the Common Era (B.C.E.). While in keeping with Christian self-understanding we shall speak of the New Testament, we shall refer to the (Hebrew) Bible or Scriptures, imposing no category of oldness on the Covenant which Jews still consider to be viable. Similarly, recognizing the present existence of Judaism we shall speak of the period under consideration as Early (postbiblical) Judaism.

APPROACH AND METHOD

As has already been suggested in the Preface it is this author's belief that literature is rooted in history and is affected by it. Theological conceptions arise not in a vacuum but in response to historical circumstances and events. While it is not always possible to determine these latter, particularly when we are dealing with ancient documents, our relative ability to understand milieu affects our understanding of literature. Thus, granting all the problems, uncertainties, and ambiguities, and underlining the caveat, we have arranged the book historically, we have provided most of the chapters with historical introductions, and we have raised historical considerations when and where they are relevant.

Within this historical framework our subject matter is treated as literature. We are interested not simply or primarily in ideas or motifs or in contents in some amorphous sense but in literature which has form and direction: in narrative which has plot with beginning, middle, and end; in other types of literature which use particular forms and rhetorical devices with consistency and purpose. The critic's task is to find these forms and directions and to interpret them. Not infrequently it is a difficult and ambiguous task. Nonetheless, we invite the reader to search with us for the logic that caused things to be written in the manner and the order in which they were written.

Above all it should be emphasized that this volume is not a substitute for the ancient texts themselves. When we retell a story in brief form our purpose is not to save the reader the trouble of going through the original. Here, as throughout, we offer a possible road map, a grid, an ordering of relationships and emphases as we see them. To some extent we intend this as a prolegomenon for a study of the exegetical *details*. On the other hand our interpretations should be considered as challenges to find more viable ways of reading the texts. The history of interpretation and criticism is precisely such an ongoing process.

An attempt has been made to strike a balance between a study of the parts and a study of the whole. In general the overarching question is: wherein lies the integrity, the wholeness, the thrust of a particular text? At the same time, some writings are more patently composites of earlier, shorter writings than are others. Occasionally these parts are discussed separately. In some cases the attempt has been made to separate levels of tradition, but for the most part this is seen as a task secondary and consequent to the interpretation of the whole.

PROBLEMS AND PERSPECTIVE

The study and interpretation of ancient literature is fraught with difficulties. We must deal first with the time gap. As people of the twentieth century, we are reading the literary products of an age and culture separated from us by two millennia and thousands of miles. Even if we are able to read the texts in their original languages we face the barrier of strange thought patterns and modes of expression. At times even those who have some familiarity with the canonical biblical literature will find themselves in a strange world.

The problems of interpretation are compounded by our individual prejudices and tastes. We have already mentioned false and derogatory Christian presuppositions, which must be neutralized if the literature is to be read fairly and in its own right. Taste presents another kind of problem. Distaste for mythic thought can erect a barrier to understanding it. A preference for clear, logical, conceptualized exposition may hinder the interpretation and appreciation of narrative. Empathy must precede criticism. The critic of literature, like the music critic, must first enter the artist's world and view it from within before criticizing the manner in which it has been expounded or delineated or judged.

Our experience and appreciation of more modern forms of literature may also create difficulties for our study and evaluation of these ancient writings. As one "adapts" to more complicated and "sophisticated" art forms, older forms can seem not only simple but simplistic. The person who has experienced William Walton's boistrous interpretation of Belshazzar's feast may find it difficult to appreciate George Frederick Handel's exposition of the same story. But that is hardly fair to Handel, who wrote in his own time and place and wrote well. Similarly, the artistry of the narrative literature of early Judaism must be judged in terms of its own environment and not in the context of the modern short story or novel.

One important factor that holds together the largest part of this corpus of literature is its common setting in hard times: persecution; oppression; other kinds of disaster; the loneliness and pressures of a minority living up to its convictions in an alien environment. Within this context these writings may be read and appreciated as a sometimes powerful expression of the depths and the heights of our humanity and of human religiousness and religious experience. In them we may see ourselves as we have been or are or might be: the desperate puzzlement of Enoch's decimated humanity; the anguish and then the ecstasy of a Tobit; the courage of a Susanna or a Judith; the defiant tenacity of the Maccabean martyrs; the desolate abandonment of an Aseneth; and the persistent questioning of an Ezra.

Through it all is told the story of a people from whom sprang Jesus of Nazareth and Hillel, Akiba and Paul. Those who live in these two traditions, long ago tragically sprung apart, may find here some commonality. For others the story is recited as part of the human saga, as a source of interest, wonderment, and perhaps enlightenment.

THE CORPUS

The noncanonical literature of early Judaism, which bulks considerably larger than the New Testament, is traditionally divided into five categories. The term "apocrypha" (Gk. "hidden books") was employed by Saint Jerome to refer to those books or parts of books not found in the Hebrew Bible but included in its Greek translation, the so-called Septuagint (Gk., translation by "the seventy"). Jerome included these texts in the Vulgate, his Latin translation of the Bible, together with another popular work, the apocalypse 2 Esdras (4 Ezra). In 1546 the Council of Trent declared all these writings except 1 and 2 Esdras and the Prayer of Manasseh to be part of the canonical Scriptures.

"Pseudepigrapha" (Gk. "pseudonymous writings") is a term applied to other noncanonical Jewish literature.

The Dead Sea Scrolls, or Qumran Scrolls, were found in the late 1940s in caves near the ruins of Khirbet Qumran, by the northwest shore of the Dead Sea. They include all the books of the Hebrew Bible except Esther, several of the Apocrypha and Pseudepigrapha, and numerous sectarian writings composed by a group who lived at Qumran or by related groups.

Two other categories of Jewish writings are tied to known authors. In the mid-first century C.E., Philo of Alexandria composed a large number of exegetical writings and a few treatises in defense of Judaism. In the last part of the first century Flavius Josephus wrote a *History of the Jewish War* of 66–72 C.E. Early in the second century he composed his *Antiquities of the Jews*, an extensive rewriting of the Bible and related traditions, tracing the history of the Jews from Adam to the Herods. Space does not permit us to treat these two large collections of literature.

Although we shall use the terms "apocrypha," "pseudepigrapha," and "Qumran Scrolls," they are problematic for a number of reasons. When we treat these works historically in their own context the canon-related term "apocrypha" is post factum and therefore irrelevant. "Pseudepigrapha" focuses on one aspect of a widely varied group of texts, an aspect that is not their central defining characteristic. It also ignores the pseudonymous nature of some of the Apocrypha (e.g., Tobit and the Wisdom of Solomon) and some canonical writings. The Scrolls, as we noted, are a mixed collection. A more proper literary categorization of these writings would divide them into genres: apocalypses, narrative fiction, testaments, history, and the like.

BIBLIOGRAPHY

Bibliographies on individual works appear following the notes at the end of each chapter and are divided into three sections. The first of these sections cites a readily available translation of the work. The books of the Apocrypha are available in all editions of the Bible formally approved by the Roman Catholic church, in many other editions of the English Bible, and under separate cover. Especially useful is *The Oxford Annotated*

Apocrypha, Expanded Edition (New York: Oxford University Press, 1977), which also includes 3 and 4 Maccabees. The Pseudepigrapha are usually cited according to the new edition by James H. Charlesworth, ed., *The Pseudepigrapha of the Old Testament*, 2 vols. (Garden City, N.Y.: Doubleday & Co., 1983, 1985), which includes many works not found in the old standard edition edited by R. H. Charles, *The Apocrypha and Pseudepigrapha of the Old Testament*, 2 vols. (Oxford: Clarendon Press, 1912). Most of the Pseudepigrapha published in Charles, vol. 2, appear in the handy edition edited by H. F. D. Sparks, *The Apocryphal Old Testament* (Oxford: Clarendon Press, 1984), usually in fresh English translation. The Qumran Scrolls are available in an excellent English translation by Geza Vermes, *The Dead Sea Scrolls in English*, 2d ed. (Harmondsworth: Penguin Books, 1975). The second section of each bibliography lists editions of the works in their original languages or ancient versions, as well as additional English translations. The third section contains a listing of secondary literature, usually in chronological order although general works are sometimes listed before discussions of specific or narrow topics.

A few frequently cited works, listed above on p. xvi, are cited by short title in the bibliographies and notes. Literature listed in the bibliographies is cited by full title in the notes of the respective chapters the first time it appears, and thereafter by short title.

In addition to the bibliographies we have provided, a few general works are worthy of note. Still useful are the detailed analyses of the Apocrypha by Robert H. Pfeiffer, *History of New Testament Times, With an Introduction to the Apocrypha* (New York: Harper & Brothers, 1949). John J. Collins has written two useful introductory volumes, *Between Athens and Jerusalem: Jewish Identity in the Hellenistic Diaspora* (New York: Crossroad Publishing Co., 1983), and *The Apocalyptic Imagination: An Introduction to the Jewish Matrix of Christianity* (New York: Crossroad Publishing Co., 1984). *Jewish Writings of the Second Temple Period*, section 2, vol. 2 of *Compendia Rerum Iudaicarum ad Novum Testamentum* (Philadelphia: Fortress Press, 1984), edited by Michael E. Stone, contains detailed introductory material on the literature treated here, as well as the works of Philo and Josephus, and many others. Volume 3 will be an introduction to the rabbinic corpus. Volumes 3:1 and 2 of the revised edition of Schürer's *History* (Edinburgh: T. & T. Clark, 1986) is an introduction to Jewish writings of the Greco-Roman period that is even broader in its scope than *CRINT* 2:2. For bibliography on the Pseudepigrapha one should consult James H. Charlesworth, ed., *The Pseudepigrapha and Modern Research with a Supplement*, (SBLSCS 7S Chico, Calif.: Scholars Press, 1981). Other and sometimes overlapping bibliography is found in Albert-Marie Denis, *Introduction aux Pseudépigraphes grecs d'Ancien Testament*, SVTP 1 (Leiden: E. J. Brill, 1970); and Gerhard Delling and Malwine Maser, *Bibliographie zur Jüdisch-Hellenistischen und Intertestamentarischen Literatur: 1900–1970*, TU 106² (Berlin: Akademie, 1975). For a concise historical and literary survey of Judaism in this period, the reader is referred to Michael E. Stone, *Scriptures, Sects and Visions* (Philadelphia: Fortress Press, 1980). A detailed history of post-1945 research on early Judaism has been compiled in Robert A. Kraft and George W. E. Nickelsburg, eds., *Early Judaism and Its Modern Interpreters* (Philadelphia: Fortress Press/Atlanta: Scholars Press, 1986).

Prologue:
Exile—Return—Dispersion

When the battering rams of Nebuchadnezzar's army breached the walls of Jerusalem in 587 B.C.E. they effectively opened a new era in the history of Israel and the religion of its people. Three facts dominated Jewish history in the sixth and fifth centuries: the Fall of Jerusalem and the ensuing Exile in Babylon; the Return from Exile and Restoration of the Jewish community; and the continued Dispersion of a large number of Jews. These facts would continue to exert a powerful influence on the lives, thought, and religion of this people for centuries to come. Subsequent Jewish history was postexilic not only chronologically but also in its essence. Thus certain perspectives on the facts and events of sixth- and fifth-century Jewish history, as these perspectives are expressed in the biblical literature of this period, provide us with an interpretive key for understanding the history and literature of later, postbiblical Judaism. In the biblical literature we see the emergence of certain theological conceptions whose paths we can then trace through the literature of postbiblical Judaism.

DESTRUCTION AND EXILE

Tragedy was already a well-established fact of life for the Hebrew people. In 722 B.C.E. Samaria, the capital of the northern kingdom of Israel, fell to the army of Shalmaneser, king of Assyria. Many Israelite citizens were deported to Assyria and Media never to return. In their place the Assyrians resettled foreigners, who intermingled with the surviving Israelite population. Their descendants would reappear later as the Samaritans.

Subsequent Assyrian invasions reduced the southern kingdom of Judah to a vassal state, though Jerusalem, its capital, and the Davidic monarchy remained intact. The collapse of the Assyrian Empire before the rising power of Babylon (612–609) provided Judah with a new overlord. Rebellion was in the air in Jerusalem, but to no avail. In 597 the city surrendered. The royal family and many of the Judean aristocracy were deported to Babylon. Zedekiah was appointed king in place of his nephew Jehoiachin, the reigning monarch.

The events of the next ten years are recounted in some detail in the biographical sections of Jeremiah. Again rebellion flared up. The prophet foresaw disaster and sought to stave it off by counseling surrender. When his advice was rejected Jerusalem fell in 587 to Nebuchadnezzar's army. The city was burned, its walls leveled, and the Temple plundered and destroyed. Zedekiah was blinded and deported. The leading citizens were either executed or exiled to Babylon. Gedaliah, a Judean noble, was appointed governor. Shortly thereafter he was assassinated by compatriots, and his friends fled to Egypt, taking Jeremiah with them. A third deportation to Babylon took place in 582.

We can scarcely overestimate the trauma inflicted by the fall of Judah and Jerusalem. The enormity of the human tragedy will be evident to anyone familiar with the disasters of war. There was also a religious dimension. The people of Judah understood themselves to be the chosen people of Yahweh, who was unique and all-powerful among the gods of the nations. Jerusalem was the site of his Temple, the place where he caused his name to dwell (Deut 12:11; 2 Kgs 21:4), the cultic center of his religion, where sacrifice was offered and where "the tribes go up . . . to give thanks to the name of Yahweh" (Ps 122:4). Little wonder that Jeremiah had to contend with the theory that the Temple was under divine protection from violation (Jer 7:2–15; 26:2ff.). Thus the shock waves resulting from the fall of Jerusalem and the destruction of the Temple are deeply etched into all the contemporary Jewish sources. Moreover, these events became a kind of prototype for similar disasters in the future inflicted by Antiochus Epiphanes (168 b.c.e.), Titus (70 c.e.), and Hadrian (135 c.e.).[1]

Our knowledge about the particulars of life in the Exile is scant.

> Transported to southern Mesopotamia not far from Babylon itself, [the Judean exiles] . . . were . . . apparently placed in settlements of their own (cf. Ezek. 3:15; Ezra 2:59; 8:17) in a sort of internment. They were not . . . free; but they were not prisoners either. They were allowed to build houses, engage in agriculture (Jer. 29:5–6), and, apparently, to earn their living in any way they could. They were able to assemble and to continue some sort of community life (cf. Ezek. 8:1; 14:1; 33:20–21).[2]

Whether the assemblies mentioned by Ezekiel represent the beginnings of the institution later known as the synagogue is a moot question. In any event the exiles had to come to terms with the practice of their religion at great physical distance from Jerusalem and in spite of the annihilation of its cultic center. This religious aspect of life in the Exile is attested in the prolific theological productivity of the period. It was a time for deep reflection upon the tragedy of 587 and its causes, for consolidation of the Israelite religion through the preservation of its traditions, and for nourishing the hope of restoration.

The Deuteronomistic history (Deuteronomy through 2 Kings) received its final form during the Exile. The fall of Jerusalem was seen as the result of the sins of King Manasseh (687–642)—an interpretation quite consonant with the original Deuteronomist's emphasis on sin and punishment. The reversal of this divine punishment of sin would be found in a return to obedience.

The author of the so-called Priestly work was particularly interested in Torah, especially cultic law. He anticipated a return to the homeland and a resumption of the cult.

Closely related to the circles of this author was the prophet and priest Ezekiel. Brought to Babylon in the first wave of exiles, he issued his indictment against the sins of Judah and announced that Yahweh would abandon his sanctuary. Exile was punishment. Nonetheless, the future promised restoration (chaps. 34–39). God would renew the covenant broken by his people's disobedience. He would put sinew, flesh, and skin on the dry bones of those who lay "dead" in the graves of their captivity. He would gather the lost and the scattered of both Israel and Judah, uniting them again as one people under the care of his shepherd, the Davidic prince. Then God would return in his glory and dwell in a new temple (chaps. 40–48).

Return and renewal are the heart of the message of the so-called Second (Deutero-) Isaiah, an unknown exilic prophet whose elegant poetry has been preserved in the latter chapters of Isaiah (chaps. 40–55). His oracles, composed during the latter part of the Exile, breathe hope and optimism. Babylon will soon topple before the army of the Persian king Cyrus. A return to the homeland is imminent. Israel has more than paid for her sins (40:2). Yahweh, the universal king who moves people and history toward his own purposes, is prepared to do a new thing. He himself will lead a new Exodus out of Babylon, across the wilderness, and into the land, where he will again take residence in Jerusalem (40:3–11; 43:15–21). Speaking in eloquent metaphor the prophet bids "Mother Zion"—at once barren, widowed, and divorced by God for her unfaithfulness—to make ready for the return of her dispersed children and the renewed compassion of her estranged Husband (50:1; 52:1–2; 54:1–17).

Integral to his message are Second Isaiah's songs about the Servant of Yahweh. This anonymous figure is depicted in largely prophetic terms. Yahweh presents him as one on whom he has put his Spirit (42:1–4). The Servant describes his prophetic call (49:1ff.). He has received divine inspiration, that he may be the spokesman of Yahweh (50:4–9). His destiny is to suffer and die (50:5–6; 53:1ff.), but suffering leads to victory. Yahweh will vindicate his Servant and exalt him before the kings and nations (50:7–9; 52:13–53:12). The precise identification of the Servant vacillates in Second Isaiah. At times he is explicitly identified with Israel (e.g., 44:1). On the other hand he has a mission to restore Israel (49:6). Quite likely, poetic materials that originally had a personal referent have been applied to the nation as a whole. The last two songs present a remarkable view of suffering, interpreted within the framework of a pattern of humiliation and exaltation, misunderstanding and vindication. Suffering cannot be construed simply as divine punishment for sin. The kings and the nations, who have thus understood the Servant's suffering, view his exaltation in astonishment. They confess that their original interpretation was wrong and that indeed he suffered in their behalf (52:13ff.). This daring interpretation of suffering will later have a profound influence on theologies formulated in response to persecution.

The offices of prophet and king undergo a transformation in the theology of Second Isaiah. Israel, the Servant purified by exile, has as a whole the responsibility to be a light to the nations (49:6). The Davidic dynasty is of little significance. Cyrus is Yahweh's "anointed" (45:1).[3] David is referred to only as "a leader and commander for the peoples," and the Davidic covenant is extended to all Israel (55:3–4).

We have noted how Second Isaiah's metaphors flow into one another. Of a similar order is his easy, sometimes almost imperceptible fluctuation between present and past history and between history and myth. The prophet celebrates a historical fact—the triumph of Cyrus, king of the Persian Empire. Yet as he anticipates the Return to Zion, present events mix with past history. The trek through the wilderness will be a new Exodus. Similarly, his description of the first Exodus is itself not told as straight history. The dividing of the Red Sea was at the same time the conquering of the ancient dragon, the chaos monster (51:9–11), and the passage is an appeal to the divine Warrior to strike out against chaos as he had in the past: "Awake, awake, put on strength, O arm of Yahweh; awake as in the days of old." The triumph of Cyrus against Babylon, Israel's historical enemy, is at the same time the triumph of the divine Warrior against his primordial foe. Similarly, a new Exodus involves a new act of creation when the wilderness will be made "like Eden" (51:3).

There is a finality about the new act of God which Second Isaiah awaits. He anticipates a new age, qualitatively different from the present one. The shape of nature itself will change, as the Creator re-forms the topography of the land, the structures of its water systems, and the growth patterns of its vegetation (40:3–4; 41:18–20; 42:15f.; 43:19–20).

In his use of myth, his portrayal of an imminent future as qualitatively different from the historical past, and his assertion of a coming universal kingship of God over all nature and history, Second Isaiah brings us to the verge of what we shall later term "apocalyptic eschatology." For him the kingdom of God was at hand.

RETURN AND RESTORATION

In 538 B.C.E. Cyrus issued an edict in which he directed the Jerusalem Temple to be rebuilt and its sacred vessels, which had been taken by Nebuchadnezzar, to be returned.[4] Leading a first group of Jewish returnees was the heir to the house of David, Sheshbazzar, the son of King Jehoiachin. Of his activities we know very little. Zerubbabel, his nephew, succeeded him as governor of Judah. Under Zerubbabel's supervision and after considerable delay the rebuilding of the Temple went forward. His colleague was the high priest Joshua, a descendant of Zadok, the Solomonic high priest whose descendants had dominated the Jerusalem priesthood for centuries. The plan of the Temple was that of Ezekiel, and the priesthood was at least predominantly Zadokite. Supporting this group were the prophets Haggai and Zechariah. Haggai predicted that the completion of the Temple would mark the dawn of a new era, and he hailed Zerubbabel, the descendant of David, as Yahweh's "servant," whom he had "chosen" and would "make like a signet ring" (2:23). Zechariah dubbed Zerubbabel and Joshua the "sons of oil," that is, the anointed (and thus divinely legitimated) leaders of the community. In support of the program to restore the monarchy and the Temple the author of the book of Chronicles rewrote the history of Israel, glorifying David, stressing the importance of Temple and cult, and, where possible, relating David to both. The Temple was completed in 515, but in spite of the glowing expectations of Haggai (2:7–9) it was a far cry from the splendid edifice built by Solomon. Thus the hope for a more glorious sanctuary would persist in the postbiblical literature. With the completion of the Temple, Zerubbabel disappears from the historical sources. With him went the presence of a Davidic heir as ruler of Judah. The hopes of Jeremiah and Ezekiel for a restoration of the dynasty would continue to be applied to the future, to an unknown figure whom God would enthrone as his "anointed" king. Meanwhile civil authority would reside increasingly in the high priest.

A very different side of the events of 538–515 is reflected in the anonymous oracles in Zechariah 9–14 (Deutero-Zechariah) and in the last chapters of Isaiah (chaps. 56–66). These latter are the product of an anonymous "pupil" of Second Isaiah, usually called Third (Trito-) Isaiah. The change in mood from Isaiah 55 to 56 is immediately evident. High optimism has given way to disillusionment. The Return did not initiate a glorious new age. The Temple still lay in ruins. The Jerusalem community was split into factions and locked in acrimonious controversy. The one party can be identified with the developing establishment led by Zerubbabel, Joshua, Haggai, and Zechariah. As this group consolidated its power they increasingly excluded from participation in the Reconstruction the Levitic priests, a group with a long history of opposition to the Zadokite priesthood. Deutero-Zechariah and Third Isaiah made common cause with these disenfranchised Levites. Resisting the belief that the end-time could be brought in by a program of restoration and reconstruction, they drew upon prophetic and other mythic traditions of the past, portraying the present in dark colors and depicting the future resolution of this situation as an act of direct divine intervention.

Third Isaiah's transformation of the traditions of Second Isaiah reflects the change in situation and the dire straits in which Third Isaiah sees himself and his group. (1) Second Isaiah described the whole of a purified Israel as Yahweh's Servant, his "chosen one," in opposition to Babylon and the nations. Third Isaiah, reflecting the split in the community, speaks of "the servants" and "the chosen ones" of Yahweh, contrasting them with the wicked of the Israelite community. (2) Whereas Second

Isaiah spoke of the doom of Babylon, Third Isaiah envisions an imminent judgment that will separate the righteous and wicked of Israel. This message is carried in a new oracular form that combines words of doom for the wicked of the community with words of promise for the righteous. (3) Although Second Isaiah used mythic language to describe God's new act he identified that new act with a chain of historical events: the victories of Cyrus, the fall of Babylon, the Return. For Third Isaiah, judgment and end-time lie in the future, and they are depicted almost entirely in mythic, ahistorical terms: the direct intervention of God himself (59:15–20; 64:1ff.; 66:15ff.) and the creation of new heavens and a new earth (65:17ff.; 66:22).

In Third Isaiah we have the primary ingredients for the second-century apocalyptic theology of Daniel and others: an oppressed minority who deem themselves the righteous; the expectation of an imminent judgment to alleviate the present situation; the dawn of a new age qualitatively different from the present one; the use of mythic, ahistorical language to depict these future events.[5]

Third Isaiah's vision of judgment and the creation of new heavens and a new earth were not realized, and the expectations of Haggai and Zechariah were not fulfilled. The Davidic dynasty was not restored. The Temple was completed, but, as we learn from the prophet Malachi, cultic practice disintegrated. The priests grew weary of their duties. They accepted sick and injured sacrificial animals, which the Law forbade to be offered (Mal 1:6–14). As teachers of the Law they caused the laity to sin, and they showed partiality in their legal decisions (Mal 2:1–9). The people were not bringing to the Temple the tithes and offerings prescribed in the Law (Mal 3:8–9). The prophet also rebuked the Jewish men for their intermarriage with non-Jewish women and for their practice of divorce and remarriage (Mal 2:10–16).

This situation provided the context for the appearance of Ezra, "the scribe of the Law of the God of heaven." An official envoy of the Persian king Artaxerxes I, this Jewish priest from Babylon arrived in Jerusalem in 458 at the head of a sizable Jewish entourage.[6] Reacting with great shock to the widespread intermarriage, he called for immediate divorce of foreign women, using the authority of his royal commission to enforce his orders. Two months after his arrival in Jerusalem he gathered the people in a public square and read to them from "the book of the Law of Moses," most likely a penultimate form of the Pentateuch.

Ezra was followed in 445 by Nehemiah, the cupbearer to Artaxerxes I. His principal task was to rebuild the walls of Jerusalem and thus provide the little community with protection from harassment by neighboring peoples. After a twelve-year tenure as governor, Nehemiah returned to the Persian court, only to reappear once more in Jerusalem. During his second stay he enacted a number of reform measures: enforcement of the payment of tithes, prohibition of violations of the Sabbath rest, and once more the dissolving of mixed marriages.

Ezra and Nehemiah found the Jewish people in a state of religious chaos. They must have understood the mixed marriages of Jews and foreigners to be not only a violation of the holiness of God's people but also a threat to their existence as an identifiable people and hence to the continued existence of the Jewish faith. It was this faith that they sought to preserve through their reform measures. Theirs was a task of consolidation around the Law of Moses. In this sense Ezra's public reading of the Law was highly symbolic. Although the Pentateuch did not yet have formal authority as Scripture[7] the work of Ezra and Nehemiah was an important step toward its establishment as the revealed record of God's gracious deeds in behalf of his people and the normative instruction and law for the conduct of their lives. To no small extent the process of consolidation around the Mosaic Law was aided by the royal authority of the Persian king with which Ezra and Nehemiah were invested.

With the close of Nehemiah's memoirs we enter a period of Palestinian Jewish history about which we know virtually nothing. A century later (333 B.C.E.) the rise of Alexander the Great would set in motion a series of events and circumstances whose impact on Jewish life, culture, and religion would rival the influence of the events we have just chronicled.

DISPERSION

The deportation of Israelites in 722 and the Exile to Babylon in 597 and 587 marked the beginnings of a widespread Dispersion of the Hebrew people beyond the borders of their homeland. The precise extent of this Dispersion during the sixth and fifth centuries is unknown. One party of Jews fled to Egypt taking Jeremiah with them (Jer 42–43), and still other Jews were located there at this time (Jer 44:1). We also know of a Jewish military colony at Elephantine at the first cataract of the Nile.[8] Jeremiah speaks of Jews in Moab, Ammon, and Edom (40:11). The exilic and postexilic prophets refer to a Dispersion in all directions (Isa 49:12;

60:4–9; 66:19–20; Zech 8:7–8). It seems likely that part of this Dispersion was caused by migration rather than by flight from Assyrian or Babylonian enemies, although the time, reason, and circumstances for such migrations are unknown.

Prophets from Isaiah to Zechariah expressed their hope for a return of the dispersed people of God. This hope was never realized. The Israelite deportees were evidently assimilated among their neighbors. A sizable and significant number of Jews remained in Babylon. Large numbers continued to live in Egypt. Many Jewish exiles chose to remain in Dispersion long after the restraints of exile had been removed.

Life in Dispersion created problems and opportunities that are the subject of a number of postbiblical writings: How does one practice one's religion in a non-Jewish environment that is often hostile or at least filled with enticements to apostasy? What are the possibilities of converting non-Jews to the faith of the one, true, and living God?

For some Jews of the postbiblical period the Dispersion continued to be a theological problem, and a massive return from the Dispersion, often portrayed in the language of Second and Third Isaiah, became a standard item in descriptions of the end-time.

SUMMARY

The events of the sixth and fifth centuries B.C.E. had a profound and lasting effect on the shape of postbiblical Judaism. (1) The Dispersion transformed the geographical configurations of the Jewish people and opened up new possibilities for the propagation of the Jewish faith to non-Jews. It also moved this religion into a cosmopolitan setting in which rich and complex interactions took place between religion and culture. (2) The codification of legal traditions (the Pentateuch) during the Exile was carried out in part under the belief that the tragedy of 587 was the result of Israel's disobedience to their God and his will as expressed in this Law. The work of Ezra and Nehemiah was a crucial step in the canonization of this Law and its developing centrality in the postbiblical period. (3) The events of the sixth century spawned a literature that, along with the Law, would deeply influence the shape of postbiblical Jewish religion and theology. These writings (Second and Third Isaiah above all) were quoted, paraphrased, and alluded to, and their theological modes of expression, especially the emerging apocalyptic eschatology of Second and Third Isaiah, found new relevance and use in the

dark hours of Jewish history that follow. (4) The destruction of Jerusalem and the Exile meant the disruption of life and the breaking up of
institutions whose original form was never fully restored. Much of postbiblical Jewish theology and literature was influenced and sometimes
governed by a hope for such a restoration: a return of the dispersed;
the appearance of a Davidic heir to throw off the shackles of foreign
domination and restore Israel's sovereignty; the gathering of one people around a new and glorified Temple.

NOTES

1. See below, Chapters 3, 8, and 9.
2. John Bright, *A History of Israel*, 346.
3. "Anointed" translates the Hebrew *meshiah*, a term that the preexilic texts
apply to the reigning monarch of Israel or Judah. Later it became a designation
for a future ruler. Its Greek translation is *christos* (= Christ).
4. The historical sketch here is dependent on Cross, "A Reconstruction of the
Judean Restoration," and Paul D. Hanson, *The Dawn of Apocalyptic*.
5. Third Isaiah lacks the elaborate angelology and the hope of resurrection
and eternal life that characterize much of second-century apocalyptic.
6. There is much dispute over the chronological relationship between the
missions of Ezra and Nehemiah. See Bright, *History*, 374–403. I have followed
Cross, "Reconstruction."
7. H. Orlinsky, "The Septuagint as Holy Writ . . . ," *HUCA* 46 (1975) 94–
96.
8. E. G. Kraeling, "Elephantine Papyri," *IDB* 2:83–85.

BIBLIOGRAPHY

John **Bright**, *A History of Israel*, 2d ed. (Philadelphia: Westminster, 1972)
271–339, detailed discussion of the events between 722 and 587 B.C.E. Peter R.
Ackroyd, *Exile and Restoration* (Philadelphia: Westminster, 1968), general historical and literary introduction. Ralph W. **Klein**, *Israel in Exile: A Theological
Interpretation* (Philadelphia: Fortress, 1979). Christopher R. **North**, *The Suffering Servant in Deutero-Isaiah*, 2d ed. (London: Oxford University, 1956),
the Servant songs and the history of their interpretation. Frank M. **Cross**, "A
Reconstruction of the Judean Restoration," *Int* 29 (1975) 187–201, a historical
reconstruction of the events of the Restoration. Shemaryahu **Talmon**, "Ezra and
Nehemiah," *IDBSup* 317–28, survey of scholarship on the books and the period.
Paul D. **Hanson**, *The Dawn of Apocalyptic* (Philadelphia: Fortress, 1975), detailed discussion of Third Isaiah and Deutero-Zechariah, their historical context,
and their relationship to Jewish apocalypticism. Menahem **Stern**, "The Jewish
Diaspora," *CRINT* 1:1 (1974) 117–83, the extent and nature of the Dispersion
in the first century.

1

Tales of the Dispersion

The Eastern Dispersion (Babylon and Assyria) is the setting for the stories and other texts that we shall consider in this chapter. Because these writings show minimal effect from the revolution begun by Alexander's conquest, it is convenient to discuss them before turning to the Hellenistic period.

DANIEL 1–6

The book of Daniel owes its present form to a Palestinian author who wrote between 167 and 164 B.C.E.[1] For the first half of his book he used a collection of older stories that had already been edited into the form and order in which we know them.[2]

The setting of these stories is the royal court in Babylon during the Exile. The dramatis personae include certain youths of the Judean aristocracy exiled in Babylon and the reigning monarch and his entourage of sages, magicians, and other courtiers. The climax of each story is a demonstration of the unique power and sovereignty of the God of Israel, most often acclaimed by the monarch himself. This demonstration is the result of a contest or conflict between the Judean youths and the monarch or his sages.

The principal hero in these stories is Daniel, whose deeds are central to chaps. 1–2 and 4–6.[3] His ability to predict the future through the interpretation of dreams, his persecution by enemies, and his exaltation to high position in the court are all reminiscent of the biblical figure of Joseph.[4]

The present order of the stories presumes the Jewish editor's interpretation of the four kingdoms in Daniel 2:36–45: Babylon (represented by Nebuchadnezzar and Belshazzar), Media (represented by Darius), Persia (represented by Cyrus, whose accession marks the end of Daniel's activity according to 1:21), and Macedonia (yet to come, from the viewpoint of the stories).[5]

Daniel 1

This chapter is the editor's introduction to the collection.[6] After providing the setting and introducing the heroes (1:1-7) he recounts two incidents that foreshadow the principal motifs and the structure of the stories in chaps. 2-6: (1) Daniel refuses the king's food on religious grounds and requests a vegetarian diet. At the end of the trial period the superior physical appearance of Daniel and his friends vindicates their piety and implies the miraculous power of their God. A similar vindication of the youths' obedience to their God is the subject of chaps. 3 and 6. (2) As to their schooling in the wisdom of Babylon,

> *God gave them* learning and skill in all letters and wisdom; and Daniel had understanding in all visions and dreams. . . . The king . . . found them ten times better than all the magicians and enchanters that were in all his kingdom (1:17, 20).

The demonstration of Daniel's divinely given wisdom is central to the action in chaps. 2, 4, and 5.

Daniel 2

A possible explanation of this chapter is as follows. The present form of the story is the result of a long process of interpretation. In the original version the colossus in the dream represented the Babylonian kingdom, with Nebuchadnezzar symbolized by its head of gold (v. 38) and each of his successors by a metal of lesser value.[7] The point of the story was the disintegration and fall of the kingdom. When the story was revised and reinterpreted during the time of Alexander's successors the four metals came to represent not four *kings* of Babylonia but four successive *kingdoms*: Babylonia, Media, Persia, and Macedonia.[8] The iron no longer functioned as a final and base metal, but being the material of weapons, it symbolized the war and violence of the present time (v. 40). The mixture of clay and iron represented the division of the empire under Alexander's successors, the Seleucids and the Ptolemies. In the next stage of the story the temporary mixture of clay and iron symbolized the marriage of the Seleucid king Antiochus II and Berenice, daughter of Ptolemy II (252 B.C.E.), and the subsequent disruption of the peace brought about by that marriage when Antiochus died in 246.

In the story as it now stands, the colossus, composed as it is of the materials from which idols are made (cf. 5:23), appears to represent the idolatrous kingdoms of the world, which will all be destroyed by the transcendent power of the God of heaven.[9] The power and sovereignty of this God are evident in the contest that pits his servant Daniel against the Babylonian sages. Nebuchadnezzar demands that "the magicians, the enchanters, the sorcerers, and the Chaldeans" reveal the content of his dream, as well as its interpretation. "Impossible!" they cry,

> There is not a man on earth who can meet the king's demand. . . . None can show it to the king except the gods, whose dwelling is not with flesh (2:10–11).

In the kind of unreasoning fury permitted only a monarch, the king orders the annihilation of all the wise men in Babylon, including Daniel and his companions. The Jewish youths pray for deliverance, and the mystery of the dream is revealed to Daniel. His prayer of thanksgiving is an acclamation of his God, whose sovereignty extends over nature and the kings of the earth and who gives wisdom and revelation to the wise (2:20–23). The "exile from Judah" (2:25) is brought before the king. In Daniel's interpretation of the dream he makes the following points: only God can reveal mysteries, and I am his spokesman (2:27–30); Nebuchadnezzar, the "king of kings," rules only by divine consent (2:37); over against the kingdoms of Nebuchadnezzar and his successors, which will be destroyed like the colossus in the dream, God will establish a kingdom that will never be destroyed (2:37–44). Nebuchadnezzar responds by paying Daniel homage and acclaiming,

> Truly, your God is God of gods and Lord of kings, and a revealer of mysteries (2:47).

The dream will come true. The triumph of the God of heaven will become fact.

Daniel 4

The king in the original version of this story was probably Nabonidus, the father of Belshazzar.[10] The narrative line demonstrates the absolute sovereignty of Daniel's God. This note is struck in the opening verses of the chapter, which are a royal edict, addressed to "all peoples, nations, and languages that dwell in all the earth," acclaiming "the Most High God":

> How great are his signs,
>   how mighty his wonders!
> His kingdom is an everlasting kingdom,
>   and his dominion is from generation to generation. (4:1–3)

The story that follows relates the events that led to this edict. The king had refused to accept the sovereignty of the Most High and to admit that he (the king) ruled only by divine permission. In a dream that Daniel interpreted when "the magicians, the enchanters, the Chaldeans, and the astrologers" again failed, the king was told that he would be punished "*till you know* that the Most High rules the kingdom of men and gives it to whom he will" (4:25). The events occurred as foretold, and the king learned his lesson. Reestablished in his kingdom he now issues the universal edict acclaiming this God (4:37). The first-person singular form of the narrative gives the whole the force of a confession of faith.

Daniel 5

The tale of Belshazzar's feast is explicitly linked with the previous story. The king did not learn the lesson taught his father (5:18–21) but arrogantly exalted himself against the Lord of heaven (5:22).[11] The dramatic element in the Danielic stories reaches its high point in this tale. A royal banquet of massive proportions—blasphemous, idolatrous, and rowdy! Then suddenly the ghastly apparition—the disembodied hand etching its cryptic message into the plaster of the palace wall. The arrogant king turns white, his knees knocking in sheer terror.[12] The narrator's pace slackens as he uses a lengthy contrast between the Babylonian sages and Daniel to build up the suspense which is relaxed only when Daniel interprets the writing, uttering the word of doom. The king fulfills his promise to reward Daniel, and then the story moves swiftly to its conclusion. That very night the God "who removes kings" (2:21) brings Belshazzar's kingdom to an end (5:26). The king is slain, and his kingdom is given to Darius (5:30–31). Here alone among the stories in chaps. 2–6 the king does not acclaim the God of the Jews. The acclamation, however, is implicit in the king's investiture and acclamation of Daniel (5:29), which come as a consequence of the revelation which Daniel received from the God whose sovereignty was affronted.

Daniel 6

The king here is "Darius the Mede."[13] We are now in the world of palace intrigues. Daniel's rivals are not Babylonian sages but colleagues among the "presidents and satraps" of Darius's kingdom who hatch a conspiracy against Daniel. The story has parallels and precursors in the biblical story of Joseph (Gen 37ff.), the material about Mordecai in the book of Esther, and the non-Jewish *Story of Ahikar*.[14] The protagonist in these stories is a wise man[15] whose actions arouse the wrath of his enemies or rivals, who then plot his death. He is condemned, but rescued, sometimes at the brink of death, exalted to the highest rank in the royal court, invested and acclaimed, and vindicated of the charges against him. Daniel 6 follows this basic plot line, but with several significant variants. Daniel's wisdom is not stressed here. He is a *righteous* man who obeys his God, knowing that this behavior will lead inevitably to his condemnation but trusting in God to deliver him (6:23). His rescue by miraculous divine intervention vindicates his initial act of obedience (6:16, 20–23, 27) and leads to a royal acclamation of his God.

These variations notwithstanding, the basic structure that we have observed in the other Danielic stories recurs in this story and is especially evident in the king's speeches. As Daniel is cast into the pit of lions Darius says, "*May your God,* whom you serve continually, *deliver you*" (6:16). He returns the next morning and asks, "O Daniel, servant of the living God, *has your God,* whom you serve continually, *been able to deliver you?*" (6:20). When the king discovers that this is the case he issues an edict "to all the peoples, nations, and languages that dwell in all the earth." All in his realm should worship the God of Daniel,

> for he is the living God,
>   enduring forever;
> his kingdom shall never be destroyed,
>   and his dominion shall be to the end.
> He *delivers and rescues,*
>   he works signs and wonders
>   in heaven and on earth,
> he who *has saved Daniel*
>   from the power of the lions. (6:25–27)

Thus Daniel's condemnation was a challenge to the power of the God whom he obeyed, and his rescue is an open demonstration of his God's power, which the king acclaims in an edict demanding universal obedience and worship of that God.

Daniel 3

This is the one story in the collection in which Daniel plays no role. The heroes are his companions, Shadrach, Meshach, and Abednego. Like chap. 6 this is a story of persecution and deliverance, of trusting obedience (3:16–17) and vindication (3:28). As in chap. 6 the king's edicts and speech carry the theme and structure common to the other stories. Nebuchadnezzar issues an edict demanding under penalty of death that *"all the peoples, nations, and languages"* fall down and worship a colossal image (3:6–7). The king verbalizes his challenge of the God of Shadrach, Meshach, and Abednego and construes their imminent death as an ordeal.

> If you do not worship, you will immediately be cast into a burning fiery furnace; and *who is the god that will deliver you out of my hands?* (3:15)

Their subsequent deliverance proves that their God is sovereign. Nebuchadnezzar now confesses his faith in this God and reverses his previous challenge to that faith. He does so first in an acclamation:

> Blessed be the God of Shadrach, Meshach, and Abednego, *who . . . delivered* his servants who trusted in him . . . rather than serve or worship any god except their own God (3:28).

He then issues an edict which negates his first edict:

> *Any people, nation, or language* that speaks anything against the God of Shadrach, Meshach, and Abednego shall be torn limb from limb . . . ; for there is *no other god who is able to deliver* in this way (3:29).

The stories in Daniel 1–6 are governed by a common structure: the testing, the demonstration, and the acclamation of the power and sovereignty of the God of the Jews. The placing of this acclamation on the lips of the monarchs stresses the universality of this sovereignty. *The God of the Jews is God also in the land of captivity, and he is lord over the captors and their gods.* The assembling of such a collection of stories with a common setting in the Dispersion suggests that the collection was made in the Dispersion. Moreover, the use of the same dramatis personae and the uniform structure of the stories suggest a specific function. Their narration of past history serves as an example for Jewish sages in foreign courts and in the service of foreign monarchs.[16] When these courtiers remain faithful to their God he protects them from danger and causes their activities to prosper (chaps. 1, 3, 6). Furthermore, he enlightens them so that they can be his spokesmen in their foreign environment (chaps. 2, 4, 5). The youths' witness to their God is a constant theme in all the stories. A striking result of this witness is the veritable conversion of the monarchs and their unabashed confession of faith in the uniqueness and universal sovereignty of the God of the Jews. This suggests that the authors and the collector of these stories nourished such a hope for their own times and through their own activities.

ADDITIONS TO THE BOOK OF DANIEL

The stories about Daniel and his friends were part of a living body of tradition. Although they were quite possibly of diverse origin they crystallized as a collection in what we call Daniel 1-6. Around 166-165 B.C.E. this collection was supplemented by a cycle of visions ascribed to Daniel (chaps. 7-12), and together they were issued as a single book (see below, p. 90). The older forms of the tradition were, however, not completely lost. The Qumran "Prayer of Nabonidus" was a reworked form of the tradition behind Daniel 4 (see n. 10).

Less than a century after its compilation Daniel 1-12 was itself expanded. The ancient Greek translations of the book included three lengthy additions which served to enrich and enhance the cycle of stories about Daniel and the three young men. Two of these additions are stories similar to those in chaps. 1-6. While the complex history of the traditions in these supplementary stories may have arisen apart from the figure of Daniel, in their present form the stories center on the heroics of Daniel and constitute an integral part of the Greek version of the book that bears his name. The third addition is of a different sort. Here two liturgical pieces (a prayer of confession and a hymn of thanksgiving) that originated independently of the book of Daniel have been integrated into the story about the three young men.

Susanna

This is a story of persecution and vindication in the tradition of Daniel 3 and 6. Susanna is cast in the role of the righteous one, condemned to death because of her obedience to God, rescued by Daniel, the divinely sent savior figure, and vindicated of the charges against her. The story was placed at the head of the Danielic cycle to explain how the young, wise Daniel rose to prominence in Babylon (v. 64).[17] As in some of the other stories the acclamation at the end is directed to the God who saves (v. 60).

Susanna's piety and innocence are evident in a variety of ways in the story. Her name in Hebrew means "lily."[18] She is introduced as a God-fearing woman (vv. 1–4). When she is propositioned by the elders she makes a conscious and explicit choice to obey God (vv. 22–23; cf. Dan 3:17), whom she trusts (v. 35) and to whom she prays for deliverance (vv. 42–43). Throughout, her innocence and piety are contrasted with the wickedness and lechery of the elders (contrast vv. 1–3/5; vv. 20–21/22–23; v. 31/32; v. 56/57). The story appears to have been influenced by the story of Joseph and Potiphar's wife, with the male and female roles here reversed.[19]

The fact that Susanna was not included in the original book of Daniel does not in and of itself prove that it was not part of an early Aramaic cycle of Danielic tales. However, the peculiar contours of the story suggest a later date and a different origin. The old court tale has been democratized. The heroine is not a sage but an ordinary, God-fearing person. Her enemies are not a king or his courtiers but Jewish compatriots. Thus the confrontation between Jew and foreigner, essential to Daniel 1–6, is lacking here. This is basically a story about life in the Jewish community. The setting in Babylon functions only to allow for the presence of Daniel the famed sage of Babylon. The story could have been written anywhere for the purpose of encouraging obedience to God in the midst of the temptations and pressures that arise in the Jewish community. Verses 54–55 and 59–60 contain a wordplay in Greek that *may* indicate composition in that language.[20]

Bel and the Dragon

The structure typical of Daniel 1–6 is here elaborated in a pair of episodes that are inextricably interwoven into a single plot (the conversion of Cyrus) which is resolved only at the end of the second episode.[21]

A. Bel:	Living God	vs.	idol
	Daniel	vs.	priests
	Daniel	vs.	the king

An Ordeal:
Cyrus acclaims Bel
Daniel is vindicated
Priests are killed
Bel is destroyed
King is not converted

B. Dragon: Living God   vs.   dragon
           Daniel   vs.   the king

                 An ordeal vindicates Daniel
                 King is converted

     Daniel and king   vs.   the Babylonians

                 Daniel is sentenced to death
                 Daniel is rescued
                 King acclaims Daniel's God
                 Babylonians are killed

The emphasis of the story is in its explicit and repeated polemic against idolatry. The term "living God" is frequent in Jewish polemics against idolatry, and the present story is a demonstration of the impotence of the Babylonian gods in the face of the superior wisdom of Daniel, the servant of the living God.[22] Cyrus's acclamation is a fitting climax to the story and a natural inference from the action:

> You are great, O Lord God of Daniel,
> And there is no other besides you. (v. 41)

A number of remarkable parallels to Isaiah 45–46 suggest that our story may have developed as a kind of commentary on these chapters of Second Isaiah. There Yahweh addresses Cyrus (45:1), who does not know him but will come to know him (45:3). He is Yahweh; besides him there is no other God (e.g., 45:5, 6; cf. Bel, v. 41). He is creator (45:18; cf. Bel, v. 5). Isaiah 46 begins its polemic against idols with the words "Bel has fallen" (so LXX).

Bel and the Dragon is a delightful, entertaining tale with its own touches of humor: the priests and their families confidently moving about in the recesses of the temple, blissfully unaware of the telltale footprints they are leaving behind; and the dragon bursting asunder from his diet of pitch, fat, and hair cakes. Such humor is typical of Jewish writings that polemicize against idols by mocking them.[23]

In comparison to the stories in Daniel 1–6, Bel and the Dragon appears to be typologically late. The plot is more complex. It has lost its court setting in favor of idolatrous Babylonian paganism in general. Daniel's enemies are not rival sages or princes but pagan priests and "Babylonians." The king's conversion is explicit: "The king has become a Jew" (v. 28). The episode of the lions' den looks secondary to the version in

Daniel 6.[24] The story knows the tradition that Daniel served under Cyrus (10:1; cf. 6:28) and may have been written to provide a conversion story about the last of Daniel's overlords.

The Prayer of Azariah and the Song of the Three Young Men

This addition to Daniel, inserted between 3:23 and 24, consists of a prayer of confession attributed to Azariah (Abednego) and a hymn of thanksgiving placed on the lips of the three young men. These two poetic pieces are joined to each other and to vv. 23 and 24 by some brief narrative prose.[25]

Azariah's prayer is a confession of the nation's sins based on traditional Israelite covenant theology. Its closest parallels are Baruch 1:15–3:8 (see below, pp. 110–11) and Daniel 9:4–19 (see below, pp. 86–87), although these prayers make more frequent and explicit reference to Deuteronomy 28–32. Verses 3–10 praise God, acknowledging that his judgments are righteous.[26] Through their sins the people have broken the covenant and thus deserve to be delivered to their enemies. The author appeals to God's covenantal mercy and to the promise he had made to the patriarchs (vv. 11–13). As God had warned, this promise to create a great nation (Gen 15:5) has been nullified because the nation broke the covenant (Deut 28:62; Pr Azar 13–14).[27] Moreover, the people are without political leadership and prophetic voice, and they lack the sacrificial means to make things right with God (v. 15). Following David's precedent the author asks that their humbled and crushed spirits be accepted in lieu of sacrifice (vv. 16–17; cf. Ps 51:16–17). Thereby he expresses and pleads the repentance that can restore the covenantal relationship (vv. 6–10, 18; cf. Deut 30:1–3). The prayer for deliverance is made explicit (vv. 19–20b) and is followed by a request that their enemies be subjugated (vv. 20c–21; cf. Deut 28:7; 32:41–43) and be made to acknowledge God's universal sovereignty (v. 22)—a constant motif in Daniel 1–6, as we saw in the first part of this chapter.

Azariah's prayer appears to have been a previously existent composition reused for its present purpose. Its insertion here conforms to a typical Jewish literary pattern: deliverance comes in response to prayer.[28] In point of fact, however, the contents of this prayer hardly fit the young men's present predicament. They are more appropriate to the general circumstances of the Babylonian Exile or to the time of Antiochus Epiphanes's persecution of the Jews, that is, the supposed or the real setting of the book of Daniel (see below, Chapter 3). Reference to the cessation of the cult and lack of leadership (v. 15) and to the unjust and wicked king (v. 9) may indicate that the prayer was actually composed during the persecution.[29]

The prose insertion following the prayer forms a transition to the second half of the addition. Verses 23–25 emphasize the ferocity of the fire, thus heightening the miracle, although v. 25 may be an answer to the prayer in vv. 20c–21.[30] Verses 26–27 describe the miraculous deliverance for the curious reader and provide cause for the three young men to sing their hymn of praise.[31]

The hymn divides into four major sections. Verses 29–34 are a doxology to the God who is enthroned in his temple (vv. 31–33), perhaps his heavenly temple (v. 34). The rest of the hymn is a threefold appeal for the whole creation to join in the praise of God. Verses 35–51 are addressed to heaven, its inhabitants and its elements. Verses 52–60 extend the appeal to the earth, its components and its inhabitants, following in general the order of creation in Genesis 1. Having mentioned the last-created beings, "the sons of men," the author now addresses Israel in particular (vv. 61–65). Finally, as a climax v. 66 makes reference to the three young men and the reason for singing the hymn. The brevity of this reference in the context of such a long hymn suggests once again that the author of the addition has employed an extant liturgical work, inserting this verse to make the hymn relevant to its new context.

The hymn cannot be dated with any certainty. Its theme is perennial. The influence of the canonical Psalter is evident in several ways. Its content appears to paraphrase Psalm 148.[32] Its structure, with identical refrain after each line, recalls Psalm 136, and the wording of vv. 67–68 reflects Psalm 136:1–3. The liturgical character of this hymn has not been lost; it is still to be found in Christian hymnals and liturgies, often under its Latin name, *Benedicite opera omnia.*

These two poetic compositions may well have been written in Hebrew, although composition in a Hebraizing Greek is not excluded. In the former case they and their narrative framework may have been inserted into the Semitic form of Daniel from which the Greek translation was made. Alternatively, they could have been translated and inserted into Daniel by the Greek translator of that book.[33]

This long addition has the effect of breaking up the continuity of the story in Daniel 3. On the other hand the sharp contrast between the tone and genres of the two poems serves to underscore the change in the action from disaster to salvation. The poems convert the story from mere narrative to quasi-liturgical drama, eliciting the involvement of an audience attuned to such liturgical tradition.[34]

TOBIT

God is with us, even in the midst of trouble and suffering! This is the theme that the author of Tobit develops in his story about life among the Israelite exiles in Assyria.

The opening genealogy introduces Tobit as a genuine Israelite (1:1-2).[35] The narrative commences with a description of his many acts of cultic devotion and deeds of kindness (1:3-18). Tobit's righteous deeds are precisely the source of his trouble. He is persecuted for burying the bodies of fugitive Jews whom the king has executed (1:16-20).[36] After his restoration to favor, his burial of a dead Israelite results in his blindness and subsequent suffering (2:1-14).

Innocent suffering is not the lot of Tobit alone. Far from his home but at exactly the same time (3:7), a distant relative of Tobit, the young woman Sarah, finds herself in a similar predicament. She has been married seven times, and each of her husbands has been slain on the wedding night by a demon who is in love with Sarah. The author presents the introductions to these two stories one immediately after the other (2:1-3:6; 3:7-15), relating the events in close literary symmetry.

Tobit's piety (2:1-7)	Sarah's innocence (presumed, e.g., 3:14)
His blindness (2:9-10)	The demon (3:8a)
He is reproached (2:14b)	She is reproached (3:7, 8b-9)
His prayer (3:1-6)	Her prayer (3:10-15)

Two righteous people, the victims of senseless suffering and the objects of reproach, in a moment of despondency pray for death as a release.

The author now introduces the third plot, which will resolve the problems raised by the first two. God responds to the prayers by sending his angel Raphael ("God has healed"), who uses Tobias (Tobit's son) as his agent to drive off the demon and to heal Tobit's blindness (3:16ff.). But that is to get ahead of our story.

Presuming that God will answer his prayer by taking his life, Tobit summons Tobias for some "deathbed" instructions:

> Live uprightly . . . and do not walk in the ways of wrongdoing. For if you do what is true, your ways will prosper through your deeds. Give alms from your possessions. . . . Do not turn your face away from any poor man, and the face of God will not be turned away from you. If you have many possessions, make your gift from them in proportion; if few, do not be afraid to give according to the little you have. So you will be laying up a good treasure for yourself against the day of necessity. For charity delivers from death. . . . Do not hold over till the next day the wages of any man who works for you, but pay him at once; and if you serve God you will receive payment (4:5–10, 14; cf. 14:8–11).

The irony of Tobit's words is readily evident given the situation. Tobit commands his son to act as he has acted, and he promises him that God rewards such piety. Yet from Tobit's own viewpoint God has not repaid him in kind, and his deeds of charity have not delivered him from the premature death he now awaits.

A humorous interlude follows. Tobit is seeking someone to accompany Tobias on a journey to recover some money he had deposited in another city. Raphael appears in human guise. When Tobit inquires about his identity Raphael presents bogus credentials (cf. 5:12 and 12:15), and poor blind Tobit joyfully welcomes the angel as the son of a long-lost relative.[37] Then he sends Tobias off to seek his fortune with these words: "Go with this man; God who dwells in heaven will prosper your way, and may his angel attend you" (5:16). He reassures Anna, his heart-broken wife, that "a good angel will go with him" (5:21). The reader can chuckle with the author, for he is aware of the real truth of the words that Tobit has unwittingly uttered.

The heart of the book unfolds the resolution of the plots. Raphael provides Tobias with the necessary magical equipment to drive off the demon and heal Tobit (6:1–8). He informs Tobias of the girl's predicament, but his reassurances move the anxious youth to deep love for the troubled Sarah (6:9–17). The tension builds in chap. 7 as Sarah's parents expect the inevitable tragedy of another dead son-in-law. (In 7:9–10, for "Eat, drink, and be merry, for it is your right to take my child," read "Eat, drink, and be merry, for tomorrow you will be dead"; cf. v. 11, "*for the present* be merry.") Raphael's magic works. The demon is rendered inoperative. Tobit's money is returned. His suffering is alleviated.

His son has married the right kind of wife, and they present him with sons and grandsons. He lives to a ripe old age. Thus the truth of Tobit's instruction to his son becomes evident, and he repeats the moral of the story in his testament (14:8–11). In similar fashion Raphael comments,

> For almsgiving delivers from death,
>   and it will purge away every sin.
> Those who perform deeds of charity and of righteousness will have
>   fulness of life;
> but those who commit sin are the enemies of their own lives. (12:9–10)

The action of the story has proven the truth of these assertions. God has rewarded his pious servants.

For Tobit the way from piety to reward was long and tortuous and led through the valley of deep suffering. It is with this suffering and its resolution that our author is especially concerned. His statement on the subject involves a complex chain of events and the interweaving of multiple plots. Tobias's marriage to Sarah solves the problem of her widowhood, and conversely her widowhood makes her available to be the kind of wife that Tobit admonished Tobias to seek (4:12–15). Moreover, the possibility of Tobias's finding Sarah was provided by the money Tobit had deposited in Rages, by the circumstances which made it impossible for him to collect it (1:14–15), and by Tobit's suffering and his consequent death wish which led him to remember the money and send Tobias off in search of it. Thus each problem contains the germ of a solution for the other. The combination of these plots for the common alleviation of everyone's suffering is not simply evidence of the author's literary genius. It is a literary device by which he creates a portrait of a God who carefully orchestrates the events of history, working them to his own gracious ends. Indeed, this God had "destined" Sarah for Tobias "before eternity" (6:17). Our author presents a hypothetical case, which provides a window into the workings of divine sovereignty that operates in spite of suffering. Although the case is hypothetical the use of the story genre, set in time and place with lifelike characters, asserts the reality of the divine operation in history.

If through the structure of his plots our author suggests *how* God works through suffering, he also addresses himself to the *why* of suffering. Tobit himself provides us with a clue to the author's view:

> For you have scourged me,
>   but you have had mercy on me. (11:15)

"Mercy" and "to have mercy" are the terms most frequently used by this author to describe God's saving activity. This mercy means release from "scourging." But why should Tobit the righteous man be scourged? The lengthy descriptions of Tobit's piety do not imply that he is sinless. His own prayer includes a confession of sin (3:3). His harsh judgment of his wife (2:11–14) and his lapses into unfaith (3:6; 10:1–3) are further indications that our author's righteous man is not a perfect man.

Although our analysis may suggest that Tobit is a treatise on the suffering righteous person not totally dissimilar from the book of Job,[38] we may note one important substantive difference. Whereas the book of Job confines its treatment to an individual, the fate of the nation is of great concern to the author of Tobit, and he speaks almost exclusively of it in the last two chapters.[39] In his earlier prayer Tobit lamented Israel's sin and God's punishment of the nation through plunder, captivity, death, and dispersion (3:4–5). He voiced this sentiment in the midst of a complaint about his own suffering. Now, in the light of his newfound health he utters a hymn of praise to the God who will also save Israel. The Captivity and Dispersion are God's punishment for Israel's sins, but the punishment is not final. Thus Tobit applies the formula "scourge/have mercy" several times to Israel's present situation and future destiny (13: 2, 5, 9; cf. 13:14; 14:5). This formula occurs most frequently in parallel literature in connection with the nation.[40] This suggests that the author's application of it to Tobit's own suffering is secondary and that the problem of Exile and Dispersion and the hope for a regathering of the people are foremost in his mind. This return from Dispersion will have as its focus proper pan-Israelite worship in a Jerusalem rebuilt according to the promises of Isaiah 54 and 60 (13:9–18; 14:5). In his testamentary forecast (14:4–7) Tobit envisages the Babylonian Exile, the Return, the rebuilding of the Temple, and then in the end-time the rebuilding of a glorious Jerusalem and the conversion of the Gentiles.

A key for our understanding of the author's *situation* and *purpose* can be found in the manner in which the book develops Tobit's character and unfolds the events related to his life. Deeply stamped into the early chapters is the senseless suffering of Tobit and Sarah and their families. Their prayers are spoken out of a sense of despair, and they are paradoxical in nature. While God may be addressed and even blessed (3:11) the best one can hope for is death, which brings release from a life that is effectively devoid of the gracious presence of God. Tobit addresses

God as righteous judge and begs forgiveness in the form of quick dismissal from the continual reproach of others. God responds to his and Sarah's prayers in a totally unexpected way. He sends his angel, through whom God "is with" Tobit and Sarah,[41] healing their ills and moving the course of events toward his own gracious ends. When these ends have become apparent Tobit bursts into a hymn of unmitigated praise to the God who "scourges" but "has mercy." The figure of Tobit is paradigmatic in his movement from despair (or rather a vacillation between despair and faith) to doxology. The author is addressing the Tobits of his own time, assuring them of God's gracious presence and activity and calling them to doxology and to repentance and the pious life. In the midst of senseless suffering one may still, like Tobit, assert the justice of God. For the reader Tobit's assurances of an angelic presence are humorous, but they are also statements of the author's belief in the real presence of God in his own time.

The book of Tobit is profoundly doxological in content and tone. In addition to the three hymns of praise there are numerous references (usually exhortations) to the praise of God.[42] When Raphael has revealed himself he commissions Tobit to write a book that has an implicit doxological function:

> Praise God forever. . . . Praise him forever. . . . And now give thanks to God, for I am ascending to him who sent me. Write in a book everything that has happened. . . . So they confessed the great and wonderful works of God and acknowledged that the angel of the Lord had appeared to them. (12:17–22)

The readers are to praise God because even now he is with them and because their future is in his hand. The dispersion of God's people, their absence from "the good land" (14:4), and their inability to gather as a single worshiping community in Jerusalem are a problem of the first magnitude for our author. Yet he exhorts his readers to praise the God who will gather the scattered and bring the nations to worship at his Temple.

Our author also calls his readers to the pious life, as is evident from the several sections of formal teaching (4:3ff.; 12:6ff.; 14:9ff.). The gathering of the Dispersion presupposes repentance (13:6) and the pious life. This piety involves prayer, fasting, almsgiving (12:8), and deeds of kindness to others according to one's ability and station in life (4:7–11), as well as devotion to one's family and the maintenance of one's Israelite identity through endogamous marriage (4:12–13).

Tobit might be called a wisdom novel. Its greater length and more detailed character portrayal distinguish it from the Danielic tales. Both its theme and some of its formal instruction set it in close conjunction with the type of wisdom theology that we shall see in the Wisdom of Jesus the Son of Sirach (see below, pp. 56–64).

The place of the book's writing is disputed.[43] However, several factors seem to point to the Dispersion: Tobit's persecution and reproach by foreigners (1:16–20); the long exhortation to marry within the nation and the incorporation of this theme into the narrative; the continuous concern with the Dispersion and Return.

Within such a context the author's message and purpose may be delineated more specifically. He repeatedly affirms the universal sovereignty of Israel's God and his presence and activity even among the dispersed in spite of distress. He exhorts his people to maintain their identity in the land of their Dispersion. The source of such identity is in the family, in a respect for one's parents, and in the preservation of the purity of the line. Repentance and piety will lead to the gathering of the Dispersion. Meanwhile Israel is to acknowledge God among the nations (13:6), that they might be converted and join in that universal praise of him which constitutes the heart of Tobit's vision for the future. Thus Tobit is remarkably similar to the stories in Daniel 1–6.

The date of Tobit is uncertain. The last historical event mentioned is the rebuilding of the Temple (515 B.C.E.). We may suppose that he wrote before the persecution of the Jews by Antiochus Epiphanes (168 B.C.E.) since the historical summary in chap. 14 makes no reference to it. Many scholars suggest that his reference to "the prophets" (14:5) does not allow a date before ca. 200 B.C.E., when the prophetic corpus was presumably canonized. However, he need not be referring to the whole collection of prophetic writings as we know them, and he does not speak of "the Law and the Prophets" together, thus implying canonicity for the latter.[44] Numerous fragments of the Aramaic original and an early Hebrew translation of Tobit have been found among the Dead Sea Scrolls.[45]

THE EPISTLE OF JEREMIAH

Satirical polemics against idols and idolatry are a developing mode of expression in exilic and postexilic literature.[46] Taking his cue from one such text in Jeremiah 10:2–15[47] and from the prophet's letter in Jeremiah 29, this author has composed a tractate which he alleges to be the copy of another letter Jeremiah wrote to the exiles in Babylon.[48] Beyond this claim in the superscription (v. 1), however, there are no indicators in the text that it is either Jeremianic or a letter.

In the introduction (vv. 2–7) the author tells his readers that they will see gods of silver, gold, and wood carried in procession and worshiped and feared by the Gentiles. Such fear should not possess the Jews. In their hearts they should determine to worship the Lord, whose angel is with them to witness their thoughts and requite them.[49]

Following this introduction are ten sections of unequal length (vv. 8–16; 17–23; 24–29; 30–40a; 40b–44; 45–52; 53–56; 57–65; 66–69; 70–73) in which the author heaps up arguments and evidences that demonstrate that idols are not what the Gentiles suppose or claim they are. The uniqueness of the Epistle of Jeremiah lies not in the types of arguments presented, many of which have parallels elsewhere, but in the persistence with which the author pursues his point by means of repetition and rhetorical devices which make that point in a variety of ways.

The author's message is explicit in a refrainlike formula that punctuates and concludes each of the ten sections. The wording varies slightly from place to place, but the point is always the same.[50] Typical is v. 23:

> Thence you will know that they are not gods.
> Therefore do not fear them.

Four distinct elements occur in this refrain: (1) The initial word, "thence,"[51] indicates that the content of the refrain is an inference made on the basis of the paragraph it is bringing to a conclusion. (2) Each occurrence of the refrain contains a word denoting knowledge; the readers are to learn something from what they have read. (3) What they learn is that the alleged gods of the Gentiles are in fact not gods.[52] (4) Consequently ("therefore") the readers need not fear these false gods (vv. 16, 23, 29, 65, 69). Thus the theme in vv. 4–5 is repeated.[53]

The author's claim that idols are not gods is negative in form and antithetical in function. He rejects the religious claims of the Gentiles, refutes their beliefs, implies that their religious practices are inappropriate, and in general argues that reality contradicts appearance. He does this by means of a number of specific arguments and rhetorical and grammatical devices that are explicitly or implicitly antithetical.

The most persistent idiom in this work is the use of the negative. The claim that idols "are not gods" is a conclusion drawn from a multitude of observations about the things that idols do not and, more strongly, "cannot" (vv. 8, 19, 34, 35) do. Idols do not and cannot do all the things that gods do. They cannot set up or depose kings, bestow wealth, enforce the keeping of oaths, rescue from death, deliver the weak from the strong, give sight to the blind, deliver a person in distress, show mercy to the widow and treat the orphan kindly (vv. 34–38), send rain (v. 53), administer justice and act beneficently (v. 64), curse or bless kings, show heavenly portents, shine like the sun and give light like the moon (vv. 66–67). In a parallel argument that remains implicit the author recounts without comment practices in the idol cult or by its priests which he considers inappropriate. Thus from a Jewish point of view the touching of sacrifices by women in a state of ritual impurity, the service of women at cultic meals, and cultic prostitution (vv. 29, 30, 43) speak for themselves. Equally devastating are the hypocrisy and cynicism of the priests who steal gold and silver and robes from the idols and sell for profit the sacrifices offered to them (vv. 10, 28, 33).

Carrying his argument one step further the author points out that these false gods cannot even do the things that humans do: speak, see, and breathe (vv. 8, 19, 25). Put in the strongest way possible, they cannot even help themselves (vv. 12–14, 18, 24, 27, 55). This last point is also implied by describing how the idols are the object of a number of human actions: they are decked out with crowns and robes (vv. 9–12), carried in procession (v. 26), hidden in time of war or calamity (v. 48). But most fundamentally they are fabricated by human beings (vv. 8, 45–51). They are nothing more than what they have been made by the human beings who revere them as gods. The fabrication process itself is a parable of their falseness: gold and silver on the outside but wood underneath; they are not what they appear or are claimed to be (vv. 50, 44).

The ironic use of simile provides the author with yet another means of mocking the false gods. He likens them to all manner of things that are useless and altogether inappropriate as images of the deity: a broken dish (v. 17), an imprisoned criminal (v. 18), a scarecrow that guards nothing, a thornbush on which birds light, a discarded corpse (vv. 70–71). Thus lifeless, disintegrating (vv. 12, 20, 72), and useless, they are not to be feared. They will perish in disgrace, and the reader will do well to dissociate himself from them and hence avoid this disgrace (vv. 72–73).

Although our author's purpose is argumentative the progression of the book shows little development in the argument. Similar arguments, techniques, and implications recur from section to section. The author's technique is to overpower the reader by repetition and reinforcement.

The date of the work cannot be determined with any certainty. A clear reference to the Epistle of Jeremiah in 2 Maccabees 2:2 indicates a date before 100 B.C.E.[54] Reference to an exilic period of up to seven generations (v. 3) may indicate a date no later than 317 B.C.E.[55] The author's evident familiarity with aspects of Babylonian religion[56] may indicate composition in Mesopotamia, although an author so informed could have written the book anyplace where idolatry presented a threat.[57] Although the epistle is extant only in Greek (including a fragment from the Qumran caves)[58] it may well have been translated from Hebrew.[59] This would suggest that the intended audience was Jewish, as seems to be indicated by vv. 29–30, 43, which assume that the audience shares the Jewish presuppositions of the author's critique of Babylonian religion. In the Greek Bible and some oriental versions dependent on it the book is placed either between Lamentations and Ezekiel, as a separate book, or more often as a last chapter in the book of Baruch (see below, pp. 109–14).

NOTES

1. See below, p. 90.
2. Elias J. Bickerman, *Four Strange Books of the Bible,* 92; J. J. Collins, "The Court Tales in Daniel and the Development of Apocalyptic," *JBL* 94 (1975) 229.
3. On the ancient legendary figure of Daniel see S. B. Frost, "Daniel," *IDB* 1:761.
4. See below, n. 14.
5. There are historical problems with this sequence. Babylon fell not to the Medes under Darius but to Cyrus, the king of the Medo-Persian Empire. Darius was a later Persian king; see below, n. 13.
6. Chapter 1 may be largely the editor's own composition. The story is shorter and more sketchy than chaps. 2–6.
7. See Bickerman, *Four Strange Books,* 61–71.
8. Hesiod, a Greek author of the eighth century B.C.E., spoke of succeeding ages of gold, silver, bronze, and iron (*Works and Days* 109–201).
9. John J. Collins, *The Apocalyptic Vision of the Book of Daniel,* 43–44.
10. The events described fit the reign of Nabonidus rather than that of Nebuchadnezzar. Among the Dead Sea Scrolls is the Prayer of Nabonidus, a version of the present story with Nabonidus as the central figure. It is doubtless descended from a form of the story earlier than that preserved in Dan 4. For a translation see Vermes, *Scrolls,* 229. For a translation and brief comments see Cross, *Library,* 167–68.

11. For another connection with chap. 4 cf. 5:4 with the Prayer of Nabonidus. Just as Dan 4 has changed Nabonidus to Nebuchadnezzar so chap. 5 has changed Belshazzar's father from Nabonidus to Nebuchadnezzar—a common process of associating a story about a less familiar figure with a better-known figure. At an earlier stage the cycle might have included stories about Nebuchadnezzar (chaps. 1[?], 2, 3), Nabonidus (chap. 4), and Belshazzar (chap. 5); see Cross, *Library*, 167–68.

12. For a vivid musical interpretation of the dramatic potential of this story cf. William Walton's *Belshazzar's Feast*.

13. Evidently this is Darius I, king of Persia, who reigned after Cyrus (522–486). See H. H. Rowley, *Darius the Mede* (Cardiff: University of Wales, 1935).

14. For the *Story of Ahikar* see R. H. Charles, *APOT* 2:715ff. For the many formal similarities in these stories see Nickelsburg, *Resurrection*, 48–58. See also W. Lee Humphreys, "A Life-Style for Diaspora," 211–23.

15. The nature of their wisdom varies. Joseph predicts the future by interpreting dreams. Ahikar is a composer of proverbs, and his quick thinking spares his own life and saves his nation. Mordecai is notable for his cleverness in the midst of palace intrigues.

16. On the provenance of these tales see Collins, *Apocalyptic Vision*, 54–59.

17. Carey A. Moore, *Daniel, Esther, and Jeremiah: The Additions*, 90, n. 23.

18. Daniel's name, which denotes God as judge, is also appropriate to the youth's function in the story.

19. Cf. v. 12//Gen 39:10; v. 23//39:9; v. 26//39:14–15; v. 39//39:18.

20. The wordplay involves the respective words for the trees and for cutting. B. Metzger reproduces the effect in English with this paraphrase: "under a *clove* tree . . . the angel will *cleave* you;" "under a *yew* tree . . . the angel will *hew* you asunder" (*Oxford Annotated Apocrypha, Expanded Edition* [New York: Oxford University, 1977], ad loc.). For arguments supporting a Semitic original see Moore, *Daniel*, 81–84.

21. Moore (*Daniel*, 121–25) argues that the two parts of the story may originally have been separate.

22. The term "living God" (Bel, vv. 5, 6, 24, 25) occurs several times in Dan 4–6, as do certain cultic terms. However, only chap. 3 and 5:4 make specific reference to idolatry.

23. Cf. Isa 44:9–20; Wis 13–14; Ep Jer; *Apoc. Abr.* 1–8.

24. There are a number of legendary expansions in Bel and the Dragon that heighten the miracle as it is described in Dan 6. See Nickelsburg, "Stories," 40. Moreover, the incident with Habakkuk is an unnecessary intrusion into the action.

25. The versification used here follows that of standard translations of the Apocrypha. Editions of the Greek Daniel begin versification with v. 24 (i.e., English v. 1 becomes v. 24, etc.).

26. Cf. Dan 9:7; Bar 1:15; 2:6. Cf. also, e.g., *Ps. Sol.* 2:16–18 and 8:30–40 for the same idea in the context of covenant theology.

27. Cf. Bar 2:29 for an explicit citation of Deut 28:62.

28. Cf. 1 Macc 4:30–34; 2 Macc 3:15–24; 3 Macc 2; and Esth 14–15, an addition to the Greek translation of Esther, placed after 4:17 in the canonical book with the same effect.

29. Reference to the lack of a prophet could have been made at *any* time that the author believed there was no prophet.

30. Verse 25 has been taken over from v. 22 in the original, which has dropped out of some manuscripts of the Greek. Perhaps the author of the addition displaced it for the above-mentioned reason.

31. The original story does not actually describe the deliverance but only the king's discovery of the miracle. In order to insert the prayer before that discovery the author of the addition must mention the deliverance here.

32. Pfeiffer, *History*, 448; Gerhard von Rad, "Hiob 38 und die altägyptische Weisheit," in *Gesammelte Studien zum Alten Testament* (Munich: Kaiser, 1958) 264–65.

33. Moore, *Daniel*, 44–49.

34. We know little about the reasons for the inclusion or insertion of hymnic material in biblical narratives or the functions of this material. For other examples cf., e.g., Exod 15; 1 Sam 2; Luke 1:46–55, 68–79.

35. Tobit is the Greek form of the original Semitic name, *Tobi* ("my good"). Tobias, his son, represents *Tobiyah* ("Yahweh is my good").

36. The sequence of events is reminiscent of the court tales discussed in the previous section.

37. There is a wordplay in the names of Tobit's relatives: Azariah = "Yahweh has helped"; Ananiah = "Yahweh has had mercy"; Shemaiah = "Yahweh has heard." All hint at the salvation yet to be revealed through Raphael.

38. Both books begin with descriptions of the hero's piety, move on to a lengthy treatment of his suffering, and end with a description of his restoration to health.

39. Frank Zimmermann (*The Book of Tobit*, 24–27) argues that chaps. 13 and 14 date after 70 C.E. However, both chapters are found in several pre-Christian Hebrew and Aramaic manuscripts of Tobit among the Dead Sea Scrolls.

40. Psalm 89:32–34; *Ps. Sol.* 7:8–10; 10:1–4; 18:4–7; Wis 12:22.

41. The material relating to Raphael is structured after the typical biblical form describing an angelic appearance. Not infrequently these biblical passages construe the angel as God's presence. That Tobit is, in a sense, an extended angelophany was pointed out to me by Professor Norman R. Petersen. Other elements in my discussion also reflect his insights.

42. See 3:11; 4:19; 11:1, 14, 16–17; 12:6.

43. See Zimmermann, *Tobit*, 15–21. Places suggested include the Eastern Dispersion, Egypt, Antioch in Syria, and Judah. J. T. Milik ("La Patrie de Tobie," *RB* 73 [1966] 523–30) suggests that Tobit is a Samaritan writing touched up to make it orthodox in Judean circles.

44. J. Lebram ("Die Weltreiche in der jüdischen Apokalyptik," *ZAW* 76 [1964] 328–31) suggests a date soon after Alexander's conquest of the Persian Empire and argues that the scheme of events in 14:4–7 has been altered by a later editor.

45. See Milik, "Patrie," 522, n. 3.

46. See W. M. W. Roth, "For Life, He Appeals to Death (Wis 13:18)," *CBQ* 37 (1975) 21–47, who discusses Isa 40:18–41:7; 44:9–20; 46:5–8; Jer 10:3–8; Hab 2:18–19; Ps 115:4–8; 135:15–18; Wis 13:10–19; 15:7–13; the Epistle of Jeremiah; Bel and the Dragon; *Jub.* 12:2–5; 20:8–9.

47. Cf. vv. 67–70 with Jer 10:2–5. For details see Moore (*Daniel*, 357–58), who also notes the influence of Isa 44 and 46; Ps 115 and 135; Deut 4:27–28 (ibid., 319–23).

48. For yet another pseudepigraphic Jeremianic letter see the discussion of the *Paraleipomena of Jeremiah*, below, pp. 313–16.

49. I interpret vv. 6–7 to be referring to a common topic. For the idea cf. Wis 1:6–10. The Greek verb *ekzētein* frequently has connotations of judgment and refers to searching out for the purpose of requiting. Cf. *1 Enoch* 104:7–8.

50. The formulas occur in vv. 16, 23, 29, 40, 44, 49, 52, 56, 64, 65, 69, 72.

51. Greek, *hothen*, in vv. 14, 22, 63; "from these things," v. 28; cf. v. 71; "(how), therefore," vv. 39, 44, 49, 51, 56, 64, 68.

52. Cf. Deut 32:17.

53. This motif is drawn from Jer 10:5.

54. See J. A. Goldstein, *1 Maccabees*, AB 41 (Garden City, N.Y.: Doubleday, 1976) 36.

55. Subtracting seven generations of forty years from 597 B.C.E., the year of the first deportation; see Moore, *Daniel*, 334–35.

56. On the details see Weigand Naumann, "Untersuchungen über den apokryphen Jeremiasbrief," 3–31.

57. Cf. *1 Enoch* 99:7 and 104:9, in a Palestinian document.

58. See M. Baillet, DJDJ 3:143.

59. Moore, *Daniel*, 326–27.

BIBLIOGRAPHY

DANIEL

TRANSLATION: The Bible and the Apocrypha.

TEXT: For a critical edition of the Greek text, including the Additions, see Joseph **Ziegler**, *Susanna, Daniel, Bel et Draco*, Septuaginta, Vetus Testamentum Graecum 16:2 (Göttingen: Vandenhoeck & Ruprecht, 1954).

LITERATURE: Commentaries on Daniel include: James A. **Montgomery**, *A Critical and Exegetical Commentary on the Book of Daniel*, International Critical Commentary (Edinburgh: Clark, 1927); R. H. **Charles**, *A Critical and Exegetical Commentary on the Book of Daniel* (Oxford: Clarendon, 1929); André **Lacocque**, *The Book of Daniel* (Atlanta: Knox, 1979). On the stories in Dan 1–6 see: Elias J. **Bickerman**, *Four Strange Books of the Bible* (New York: Schocken, 1967) 61–100; **Nickelsburg**, *Resurrection*, 49–58; W. Lee **Humphreys**, "A Life-Style for Diaspora: A Study of the Tales of Esther and Daniel," *JBL* 92 (1973) 211–23; John J. **Collins**, *The Apocalyptic Vision of the Book of Daniel*, HSM 16 (Missoula: Scholars Press, 1977) 27–65. For a very helpful commentary on the Additions to Daniel see Carey A. **Moore**, *Daniel, Esther, and Jeremiah: The Additions*, AB 44 (Garden City, N.Y.: Doubleday, 1977).

TOBIT

TRANSLATION: The Apocrypha.

TEXTS AND OTHER TRANSLATIONS: Alan E. **Brooke**, Norman **McLean**, and Henry St. J. **Thackeray**, *The Old Testament in Greek* 3:1 (Cambridge: University Press, 1940) 35–144, critical edition of the two Greek texts and the Old

Latin version. D. C. **Simpson,** *APOT* 1:174–241, introduction, translation, detailed textual apparatus. Frank **Zimmermann,** *The Book of Tobit,* JAL (New York: Harper, 1958), introduction, the Greek texts, annotated English translation.

LITERATURE: **Pfeiffer,** *History,* 258–84, copious introductory material. For additional details and documentation, see **Nickelsburg,** "Stories," 40.

THE EPISTLE OF JEREMIAH

TRANSLATION: The Apocrypha.

TEXT: Joseph **Ziegler,** *Jeremias, Baruch, Threni, Epistula Ieremiae,* Septuaginta, Vetus Testamentum Graecum 15 (Göttingen: Vandenhoeck & Ruprecht, 1957) 494–504, critical edition of the Greek text.

LITERATURE: Weigand **Naumann,** "Untersuchungen über den apokryphen Jeremiasbrief," BZAW 25 (Giessen: Töpelmann, 1913) 1–53. For further bibliography and comments on details see Carey Moore, *Daniel,* above under Daniel.

2

Palestine in the Wake of Alexander the Great

THE OVERLORDS OF PALESTINE

For more than one hundred years the Persian Empire founded by Cyrus the Great held sway over the lands around the eastern Mediterranean. Only the Greeks, and the Scythians to the north of them, successfully withstood attempts at Persian domination. Nonetheless, the vast empire that stretched from the borders of India in the east to Egypt and Thrace in the west was difficult to hold together. The reign of Artaxerxes I (during the time of Ezra and Nehemiah) saw the beginning of a century-long series of revolts.

The mortal threat arose in the little backwoods kingdom of Macedonia. Its king, Philip II (359–336 B.C.E.), maneuvering with equal expertise on the battlefield and in the political arena, succeeded in making himself master of almost all of Greece, which was now spent from the agonies of the Peloponnesian War. Philip's conquest of Thrace set the stage for a massive confrontation with Persia. When he was assassinated at the age of forty-six, the task fell to his twenty-year-old son, Alexander III ("the Great").

Once he had consolidated his power the young general moved with incredible speed and efficiency. In four years the fragile Persian Empire crumbled before the relentless drive of Alexander's military machine. In 334 he crossed the Hellespont and defeated the Persian army at the River Granicus near the site of ancient Troy. There was no other sizable Persian force in the whole of Asia Minor. In a year Alexander swept across the peninsula and stood facing the armies of Darius II at the Cilician Gates near Issus (333). The Persian army was routed, and the king fled for his life, leaving his family and possessions behind. Alexander marched south along the coast, accepting the surrender of one Phoenician seaport after the other. Only the island of Tyre resisted, its inhabitants feeling se-

43

cure in their position a quarter of a mile off the coast. Alexander's army constructed a causeway from the mainland to the island. After seven months of hard labor and bitter siege the city fell and its walls were leveled. Alexander continued south into Palestine. Gaza capitulated after a siege of two months, and for its resistance it too was razed (332). Egypt welcomed Alexander as successor to the Pharaohs and acclaimed him son of the god Amon. He then started north again toward Syria (330). A revolt in Samaria was swiftly punished, and the city was converted into a Greek *polis* manned by a Macedonian garrison.

With Asia Minor, Syria-Palestine, and Egypt now firmly in his control Alexander turned eastward toward the heartland of the empire. He engaged the army of Darius at Gaugamela just east of the Tigris River. Again the Persian army was badly defeated, and the king fled. Alexander turned to other conquests: Babylon, Susa, Persepolis the Persian capital, and Ecbatana. From Ecbatana he pursued the fugitive Darius, but the king was murdered by his own troops (330).

Alexander was now sole ruler of the Persian Empire. His ambitions carried him on through the eastern reaches of his empire to the Indus River. He would have gone farther, but his troops rebelled at the prospect and he was forced to return west (326). He spent his last year in Babylon consolidating his gains and administering his empire. The end came swiftly. He died in 323 at the age of thirty-three.

The young Alexander left no eligible heir to his empire. Immediately after his death his generals appointed Perdiccas, one of their number, to be regent over the whole empire. He in turn appointed his colleagues to be satraps over the various provinces. The orderly arrangement was short-lived, however. In 321 Perdiccas was assassinated by his own commanders, and chaos broke out as the generals and satraps maneuvered for control. These wars of the Diadochi ("successors") lasted for forty years.

The province of Coele-Syria (southern Syria and Palestine) was a frequent bone of contention because it was located along the principal trade routes by land and sea and comprised a major military highway between Egypt and the countries to the north and east. In a period of twenty-one years (323–302) it changed hands seven times and was frequently the site of military campaigns. Ptolemy, the satrap of Egypt, invaded Coele-Syria in 320. He drove out its rightful governor, Laomedon, and annexed it to Egypt. Meanwhile Antigonus, who was satrap of parts of Asia Minor, began to annex other parts of the empire as he sought to make himself sole successor to Alexander. Ptolemy, Seleucus (whom Antigonus had expelled from Babylon), and other satraps formed an alliance against Antigonus, demanding that he accept Ptolemy's sovereignty over Coele-Syria. Antigonus responded in 315 by invading the country and bringing it under his control. Ptolemy countered in 312, defeating Antigonus's son Demetrius while his father was engaged elsewhere. Antigonus returned, Ptolemy fled, and control over Coele-Syria reverted to Antigonus. In 302 the Macedonian generals once more made common cause against Antigonus. Ptolemy swept through Palestine. At Sidon he heard a rumor that Antigonus had defeated his allies, and he retreated swiftly to Egypt. The rumor was false. The decisive battle took place at Ipsus in central Asia Minor. Antigonus was slain in battle, his army was defeated, and his territory was divided.

The precise details of this settlement are disputed by historians. They were also disputed by the principals, Ptolemy and Seleucus, both of whom claimed the right to rule Coele-Syria. For the present time, however, Ptolemy's armies were in the province, and he and his successors continued to rule there until the beginning of the second century. Thus the result of Ipsus was the following division of the empire: Lysimachus in western Asia Minor; Ptolemy in Egypt and Coele-Syria; Seleucus in northern Syria and Babylon. In 281 Seleucus defeated Lysimachus and annexed Asia Minor to his kingdom. Seleucus and Ptolemy were now the sole successors of Alexander, and their heirs would rule two rival kingdoms.

Ptolemaic Palestine remained peaceful for almost a hundred years. In 219 the old feud between the two dynasties flared up again as the Seleucid king Antiochus III ("the Great") sought control over Palestine. A series of battles ensued. Ptolemy IV defeated him at Raphia in 217. When Ptolemy died in 204 and was succeeded by his five-year-old son, Antiochus once more set out to take Coele-Syria. The final battle was fought in 198 at the Panion near the sources of the Jordan River. Antiochus was victorious, and Palestine passed into the hands of the Seleucid house, where it would remain until the successful conclusion of the Jewish wars of independence later in the century.

EARLY HELLENIZATION IN PALESTINE

Alexander was a Greek steeped in Greek culture and schooled under Aristotle. As he marched eastward intent upon military conquest and political domination he brought his culture with him, and his practices and policies helped to institutionalize it. Alexandria was the first of some thirty cities he established as centers of Greek culture, religion, and language. He encouraged his soldiers to marry foreign wives.

Alexander's successors shared his enthusiasm for the Greek way of life. Some thirty cities were founded in Palestine by order of the Macedonian kings. They were located in three areas, which excepted the territory of Judah: the Mediterranean coast; Samaria and Galilee; and Trans-Jordan, where they formed the nucleus of what would later be the Decapolis (or league of "ten cities"). These cities adopted the political structure of the Greek *polis* ("city"). They had an official enrollment of Greek "citizens." Some people assumed Greek names. Greek educational institutions were established. Temples, theaters, and other fine buildings were constructed.

It is a matter of debate to what extent and in what ways Palestinian Judaism was Hellenized before the momentous events of 175 B.C.E., of which we shall speak in the next chapter. In any event Judah did not remain isolated from its environment, and we shall note evidences of Hellenistic influence in the writings we discuss in the present chapter.

LITERATURE ATTRIBUTED TO ENOCH

Enoch walked with God; and he was not, for God took him (Gen 5:24).

The two halves of this cryptic passage suggest *in nuce* the two principal elements of a sizable amount of Jewish revelatory literature that is attached to the name of this ancient patriarch: (1) Enoch was righteous in an unrighteous age. (2) Therefore God saw fit to remove him from this earth in order to transmit to him esoteric revelation about the nature of the universe and about the end-time; he wrote down this revelation so that it could be transmitted to the righteous who would live in the last days. The portrayal of Enoch in this literature reflects an interesting blend of motifs that are at home in Jewish theology and elements that appear to have been drawn from Babylonian Flood traditions.[1]

A considerable number and variety of these pseudo-Enochic traditions, dating from various times in the three centuries B.C.E., have been collected in a writing that has come to be known as *1 Enoch*. Most of these traditions were composed in Aramaic. The collection was translated into Greek and from Greek into Ge'ez, the language of ancient Ethiopia, in which version alone the entire collection is preserved. Fragments of eleven Aramaic manuscripts of various sections of *1 Enoch* have been identified among the Dead Sea Scrolls.[2] We shall discuss the individual sections in their likely historical settings.[3]

1 ENOCH 72–82

These chapters constitute a major treatise on cosmic and astronomical phenomena. Originally a more extensive form of this treatise existed as an independent work. Fragmentary copies of the Aramaic text of this longer version have been found among the Dead Sea Scrolls, always on manuscripts separate from those containing other parts of *1 Enoch.* Paleographical analysis of these fragments indicates a date at least well back into the third century B.C.E. It is one of the most ancient sections of *1 Enoch.*[4]

Enoch was guided through the heavens by the archangel Uriel ("light of God") and saw the celestial luminaries and the gates through which they appear and disappear, the gates of the winds, and the four quarters of the earth. As he led Enoch on this tour Uriel explained the laws by which these heavenly phenomena operate. Enoch now writes an account of all this and transmits the information to his son, Methuselah.

With monotonous repetition and calculations and predictions ad infinitum this treatise demonstrates the uniformity and order of God's creation as it is evidenced in the movements of the luminaries and the blowing of the winds. The universe is very much alive, with thousands of angels in charge of its many facets and functions.

Enoch's heaven is a great hemispherical vault stretched over the flat disk of the earth and set upon its outer edge. At the point where the firmament and the earth meet are twelve gates through which the sun and the moon rise and set as they move toward and away from perpendicular during their respective annual and monthly cycles. Enoch's descriptions of the movement and phases of the moon (chap. 73) are close enough to empirical reality to have been based on actual observation. The description of the sun's movement (chap. 72), however, does not coincide with empirical reality but seems to have been based on an a priori scheme that demonstrated mathematical uniformity in the heavens.[5] In his description of the twelve winds (chap. 76) the author similarly abandons empirical reality in favor of a sophisticated mathematical or literary symmetry that once more demonstrates uniformity in God's universe.

Crucial to this treatise is a solar calendar of 364 days, twelve months of thirty days plus four intercalated days. The same calendar is advocated in the *Book of Jubilees* (see below, Chapter 3), which invests it with special religious status and strongly polemicizes against the "Gentile" lunar calendar. The major parts of *1 Enoch* 72–82 lack such a polemical element, although 80:2–8 and 82:4–6 indicate that this material was employed for such a purpose at some point in the document's literary history. Both the Enochic astronomical treatise and the *Book of Jubilees* have been found in multiple copies among the Dead Sea Scrolls of Qumran together with other writings that presuppose the use of this calendar.[6] Behind all this appears to have been a bitter calendrical dispute with the Jewish religious establishment. The heart of the Enochic treatise was doubtless the theoretical undergirding used in the dispute. Both *1 Enoch* 72–82 and *Jubilees* antedate the formation of the community at Qumran.[7] The calendrical dispute was evidently an old one, and it came to be one of several basic issues that were a point of contention between the Qumranites and the Jerusalem establishment.

1 ENOCH 1–36

These chapters are a collection of traditions that have accreted over a period of time. We shall treat the component sections in the order of their appearance in *1 Enoch*. Our earliest Aramaic manuscript evidence indicates that chaps. 1–11 were already a literary unit in the first half of the second century B.C.E.[8] As we shall see, chaps. 1–5 are the introduction to a larger number of chapters—either 6–19 or 6–36. Evidence in *1 Enoch* 85–90 indicates that *1 Enoch* 1–36 was known before the death of Judas Maccabeus in 160 B.C.E.[9] Hence we are justified in treating these chapters as a product of the period before 175 B.C.E.

Outline

A. Introduction	chaps.	1–5
B. The rebellion of the angels		6–11
C. Enoch's vision of heaven		12–16
D. Enoch's journey to the West		17–19
E. Additional journey traditions		
1. List of accompanying angels		20
2. Journey back from the West		21–27
3. Journey to the East		28–33
4. Journeys to the four corners of the earth		34–36

1 Enoch 1–5

Presently these chapters constitute the introduction to the whole of *1 Enoch*. Similarities between 1:1–3 and 19:3, the subscript of an early Enochic collection, may indicate that chaps. 1–5 originally introduced that work. On the other hand the emphasis on the great judgment in chaps. 1–5 and other points of similarity with chaps. 20–36 suggest that chaps. 1–5 may have been composed as an introduction to chaps. 6–36.[10]

The opening verses (1:1–2) are a paraphrase of Deuteronomy 33:1 (the Blessing of Moses) and Numbers 24:3–4 (Balaam's Oracle). Thus the author sets himself in the line of the prophets and cites certain heavenly visions and auditions as the authority for his revelation. The passages 1:4–9 + 5:4–9 are a lengthy oracle in late prophetic style announcing the theme of the book: an imminent judgment in which God will vindicate the righteous and punish the wicked.[11] The first half of the oracle (1:4–9) is reminiscent of such biblical theophanic texts as Deuteronomy 33, Micah 1, and Zechariah 14:5. The latter half (5:4–9) draws to some extent on the imagery and language of Isaiah 65 with its contrast between the long life and blessing awaiting the righteous and the curses that will befall the wicked. The prose passage in the middle of the oracle (2:1–5:3), written in the style of wisdom literature,[12] contrasts nature's obedience with human rebellion. Sinful humans are culpable because they do not obey the moral order which God has created in the cosmos.

1 Enoch 6–11

This story about the rebellion of the angels ("the watchers") and their judgment is the nucleus and fountainhead of the traditions in chaps. 1–36 and is presumed throughout. With the possible exception of chaps. 72–82 it is the earliest tradition in *1 Enoch*. Unlike the other sections of *1 Enoch*, chaps. 6–11 contain no references to Enoch himself or any indications that they were composed in his name.

Outline

A. The Proposal (Gen 6:1–2a)	6:1–8
B. The Deed (Gen 6:2b, 4b)	7:1abc
[Teaching	7:1de]

C. The Results   (Gen 6:4cd, 4a)   7:2–5
   1. Birth of the giants   7:2
   2. Ensuing desolation   7:3–5
D. The Plea   7:6–8:4
   1. of the earth (Gen 4:10)   7:6
   [2. What ʿAsael taught   8:1]
   [3. Its results   8:1–2]
   [4. What the other angels taught   8:3]
   5. of man   8:4
E. The Angelic Response (Gen 6:5)   9:1–8
   1. They hear   9:1–3
   2. They intercede   9:4–11
     [a. ʿAsael   9:6]
     [b. Shemiḥazah and mysteries   9:8c]
F. God's Response   (Gen 6:13)   10–11
   1. Sariel sent to Noah   10:1–3
   [2. Raphael sent to ʿAsael   10:4–8]
   [3. Gabriel sent against giants   10:9–10]
   4. Michael sent
     a. against Shemiḥazah   10:11–14
     b. against the giants   10:15
     c. to cleanse the earth   10:16, 20
   5. Description of the end-time   10:17–19, 21–11:2

Literary analysis indicates that the passages bracketed in the outline are secondary additions to a story about the rebellion and punishment of the angelic chieftain, Shemiḥazah, his subordinates, and their progeny, the giants.[13] The original story was an elaboration of Genesis 6:1–4. It divides into three parts, each with certain significant departures from the biblical text:[14]

I. *The origins of a devastated world* (A–C): The intercourse between the sons of God and the daughters of men (Gen 6:1–2, 4) is here depicted as an act of conscious and deliberate angelic rebellion against God. The giants are described as a race of powerful and bellicose half-breeds who devour the fruits of the earth, slaughter humankind and the animal kingdom, and then turn on one another. Thus the human race and "all flesh" are not the perpetrators of great evil, which God will punish (Gen 6:5–7, 11–13), but the victims of that evil, which has been committed by the giants.

II. *The turning point: a plea for help* (D–E): Here the archangels, and not God (Gen 6:5), behold the state of the earth. The author places on their lips a long, eloquent, and impassioned plea in behalf of humankind.

III. *The divine resolution of the situation* (F): The divine Judge issues his orders to the archangels. Sariel instructs Noah about the ark. Michael is commissioned to bind the rebel watchers until their final punishment on the day of judgment and to destroy the giants. The passage then flows into a commission to obliterate all evil and to cleanse the earth. It concludes with a description of a renewed earth, in which elements from Genesis 9 have been modified, intensified, and augmented with mythic material that is appropriate to a description of the end-time: fabulous fertility and life span, the permanent absence of all evil of every sort, the conversion of the Gentiles—in short the final and full actualization of God's sovereignty on earth.

In addition to being biblical interpretation this story is myth. Conditions in the author's world are the result of events in the unseen, heavenly realm. Moreover, the end-time will be characterized by a quality that is beyond human ken and experience.

The author's thought is also typological. The events of the last days (the author's own time) are mirrored in the events of primordial times. At the time of the Flood, God judged a wicked earth and its inhabitants and started things anew. Once again the world has gone askew, but judgment is imminent and a new age will begin. Within the framework of this typological scheme the author's variations from the biblical text may be read as reflections of his own purposes and of the events and circumstances of his own time. His enemies are a breed of mighty warriors whose bloody deeds threaten the very existence of creation—or so it seems to him. Since the archangels are intercessors between humanity and God their prayer relays the prayer of the author's constituency. It reflects a crisis in the faith of his people, who ponder over the contradiction between God's complete foreknowledge and his inactivity in the midst of the present disaster. The author places his answer in the mouth of God himself. He has given his orders. The judgment is at hand.

Our author is making a statement about the nature of evil in his own time and about its obliteration. This evil is more than the wicked deeds of violent men. Behind the mighty of the earth stand demonic powers. Given the supernatural origins of this evil, only God himself and his angelic agents can annihilate it. And they will do so. Therefore the audience can find comfort and take heart. Thus, in its viewpoint and function this story foreshadows the apocalyptic literature of the second century to which we shall turn in the next chapter.

Because the story of Shemiḥazah is ostensibly about primordial times, attempts to determine the concrete historical setting of its composition will always fall short of absolute certainty.[15] Given this qualification, a possible setting appears to be the Diadochan wars. Alexander's conquests had begun a period of war and bloodshed. The large number of the Diadochi, the repeated campaigns in Palestine, and the multiplicity of wars and assassinations provide a suitable context for the descriptions of the battles of the giants—their devastation of the earth and humanity and their destruction of one another. Within this context the myth of supernatural procreation might be read as a parody of the claims of divine procreation attached to certain of the Diadochi.[16] The author would be saying, Yes, the "giants'" parentage is supernatural but their fathers are demons and rebels against heaven.

At some point the Shemiḥazah story was expanded either by ad hoc elaboration or by the addition of a second tradition about rebel angels.[17] The angelic chieftain is now 'Asael,[18] and the rebellion involves the revelation of heavenly secrets. In large part these secrets relate to the arts of metallurgy and mining, and the result is the creation of weapons of war.[19] The motifs reflect the influence of Greek myths about Prometheus or perhaps other Near Eastern myths about similar figures.[20] In subsequent developing tradition the angelic figure of 'Asael comes to be identified with Azazel in Leviticus 16.[21]

1 Enoch 12–16[22]

This section reinforces the message of chaps. 6–11. It does not retell the story of the watchers' revolt, but it does refer to it. Like chaps. 6–11 it also anticipates the coming judgment of the watchers. This announcement comes from the mouth of Enoch, "the scribe of righteousness," who is the central figure in these chapters.

Enoch is the recipient and transmitter of revelation about the nature and implications of the angelic revolt. He first receives this revelation from an angel. When he informs the watchers of their coming judgment, they ask Enoch to intercede for them. In response to this prayer he sees a vision of heaven that reinforces the first revelation. As he relates this to the watchers (chaps. 14–16), he describes in great detail his ascent to heaven and his vision of the divine throne room. This description has a specific function within the narrative. Because the watchers have come from heaven they know what it is like. By telling them of his experience of heaven Enoch leaves no doubt in their minds that the message he brings comes straight from the divine throne room. This fictional setting in the story is quite likely the real setting for this piece of literature. The author presents an interpretation of chaps. 6–11 and offers it to his audience as a piece of divine revelation. The descriptions of his ascent and of the throne room are his documentation.

These chapters mention only briefly the angelic revelation of secrets. They focus instead on the watchers' sinful intercourse with women. The act involved the unnatural mixture of heavenly and earthly, spirit and flesh (12:4; 15:3–7). It was a violation of the divine order of creation. As such it was bound to fail and to result in disaster. The union of angels and women could produce only half-breeds and bastards. And the deed could not be easily undone. When the giants died their spirits were set loose in the world as evil spirits (15:8–12). The author interprets chaps. 6–11 as a description of the incarnation of evil into the world, but he does so with his own nuance. The giants were an ancient race whose evil spirits—the progeny and incarnation of the watchers' rebellious spirits— now infest a troubled world.

The narrative of Enoch's call to preach to the rebel angels has been shaped according to the form of biblical prophetic commissionings. The author is especially beholden to Ezekiel 1–2 and to the account of that prophet's tour of the eschatological temple in Ezekiel 40–48. Making use of these materials he depicts Enoch's ascent to heaven and his progress through the courts of the heavenly temple right up to its holy of holies, where the deity is enthroned. His use of the prophetic commissioning form suggests that he saw himself in the line of the prophets. At the same time these chapters mark an important transitional point at which the tradition about Ezekiel's throne vision is moving in the direction of later Jewish mysticism. His description of the heavenly temple is shot through with paradox. The temple is constructed of hailstones, ice, and snow but is surrounded by fire. When Enoch enters it he is as hot as fire and as cold as ice. The throne room that stands at the heart of the ice temple is a raging inferno. The transcendence of the deity, which is presumed and depicted throughout, foreshadows the viewpoint of later mysticism.

The oracles against the watchers describe them as priests of the heav-

enly temple who have forsaken their stations and defiled their purity
(15:3–4; cf. 12:4). The language is reminiscent of polemics against the
Jerusalem priesthood.[23] Taken in conjunction with elements in chaps.
12–13 that parallel the story of Ezra,[24] they may indicate that the author
looked upon the Jerusalem priesthood as in some sense defiled. The
events in these chapters are set in upper Galilee near Mount Hermon. The
multiple references to this area, and their accuracy, suggest that this tradition emanated from this geographical region, which had a long history
as sacred territory.[25]

1 Enoch 17–19

Angelic guides lead Enoch on a cosmic tour. With the exception of
18:1–5 (a topically arranged section about the seer's visit to the winds
and about their functions) the direction of his journey is toward the west.
It culminates beyond the mountain throne of God in the northwest with
a vision of the watchers' places of punishment. In its pattern the present
section presumes chaps. 12–16; like them it relates a journey to the throne
of God which climaxes in a word of judgment against the rebellious
watchers. Here, however, the narrative has been shaped after the model
of the Greek *nekyia*, which recounted a journey to the place of the dead
and a vision of their punishments.[26] The author has employed that form
with his own nuances as a means of reinforcing the message of the book
as a whole, namely, the judgment and punishment of the watchers. The
rapid listing of the places in the cosmos through which Enoch passes
again provides the reader with a kind of documentation of the fact that
Enoch has made the trip all the way out there. The places he lists indicate that he was somewhat familiar with popular Greek geography.[27]

The author's subscript in 19:3 concludes a work whose central theme
is the coming judgment (chaps. 6–19 or 1–19). The primary focus
throughout is on the angelic, supernatural level—on the rebel angels, the
giants, and the demons, who are the cause of the present evil, and on
the divine figures and functionaries who will execute judgment on them.

1 Enoch 20–36

A second set of traditions about Enoch's cosmic journeys have been
gathered into these chapters. Chapter 20 serves as a preface, introducing
the cast of angels who serve as Enoch's guides. Thereafter a stereotyped

vision form is employed: arrival, vision, question, angelic interpretation, blessing (I came to . . . I saw . . . I asked the angel . . . he said. . . . Then I blessed the Lord).

In chaps. 21–27 Enoch retraces his journey from the far northwest eastward to Jerusalem, the center of the earth. The point of departure and direction of the journey indicates that this journey narrative presumes the existence of chaps. 17–19. Doublets of the traditions in those chapters are here interpolated with eschatological elements and are interwoven with descriptions of places of special eschatological significance. Chapter 21 describes the places of punishment already described in 18:10–19:2.[28] In chap. 22 Enoch arrives at the place of the dead, whose spirits are compartmentalized according to type until the day of judgment. The righteous receive a foretaste of their coming bliss. The wicked are already suffering. In chaps. 24–25 the seer is once again at the mountain throne of God. The description of 18:6–9 has been augmented by reference to God's final visitation of the earth, mention of the Tree of Life, and a description of the blessings that will accrue to the righteous. The description of Jerusalem in chaps. 26–27 has a similar emphasis.

Chapters 28–32:2 break with the typical vision form mentioned above. Paralleling 17:1–5 they rapidly recount landmarks that document the seer's journey along the eastern spice routes, which culminates in his arrival at Paradise (again the vision form in 32:3–6) and beyond it at the ends of the earth (33:1). In 33:2–4 Enoch refers to the astronomical treatise (chaps. 72–82). Chapters 34–36 summarize his vision of the winds (chap. 76). The book closes with an expanded form of the blessing that concludes most of the visions in chaps. 21–33.

THE WISDOM OF JESUS THE SON OF SIRACH
(OR ECCLESIASTICUS)

Joshua ben ("the son of") Eleazar ben Sira[29] was a professional scribe or sage who studied and taught in Jerusalem during the first quarter of the second century B.C.E. He collected the fruits of his labors in a volume which he published in his own name (50:27)—a fact that makes it unique in our literature. The title of the book given above, "The Wisdom of Jesus the Son of Sirach," which includes the Grecized form of his names, is derived from manuscripts of a Greek translation of the work made by ben Sira's grandson. In genre and contents the book can generally be compared to the book of Proverbs, although it is about twice as long as its canonical counterpart. For fifty-one chapters ben Sira expounds his views on right and wrong conduct and their consequences.

Author

Ben Sira offers us a few glimpses of himself in his professional activities. In 38:24–39:11 he contrasts the labor of the farmer and the tradesmen with that of the scribe. Each had to "set his heart" on his particular task (38:26–28, 30; 39:5). Thus the scribe (38:24) devoted himself full-time to a study of "the law of the Most High . . . the wisdom of all the ancients . . . and prophecies." He was a scholar of what would later emerge as Israel's Scriptures and what in part was already recognized as such (Torah and Prophets). Moreover, his study quite possibly included not only the wisdom traditions of Israel but also the wisdom lore of other parts of the ancient Near East (cf. 39:4 and 39:1, *"all* the ancients"). As a sage he served as counselor to rulers (39:4; cf. 38:33). His experience was not limited to his homeland; he traveled abroad, where he "tested the good and evil among men" (39:4; cf. 34:9–12 [Gk. 31:9–13]). The scribe was not only a scholar but also a teacher (39:8; cf. 24:33; 51:23). To judge from ben Sira's warning about association with the unscrupulous rich and powerful, his instructions on etiquette at banquets, and his frequent advice on riches, lending, and almsgiving, his students must have included in good part the youth of the Jerusalem aristocracy.[30]

Literary Aspects

Prefixed to the Wisdom of Jesus the Son of Sirach is a translator's prologue. The body of the book divides into two major sections which begin with analogous poems about Wisdom (chaps. 1–2 and 24). The book climaxes with a doxology of the Creator (42:15–43:33) and a recitation of Israel's history in the form of an extensive song of praise to the heroes of the past (chaps. 44–50). Ben Sira concludes his work in the first-person singular: an author's subscript and a blessing on the reader (50:27–29);[31] a psalm of thanksgiving for deliverance from death (51:1–12); and a traditional poem about the seeking of Wisdom (51:13–22),[32] which topically relates back to chap. 1 and links with 51:23–30, the author's final exhortation that the reader join with him in the pursuit of Wisdom.[33]

A selective analysis of chaps. 1–23 provides entrée to the literary forms and techniques employed by ben Sira and offers a basis on which the reader may analyze the literary aspects of chaps. 24–51. Chapters 1–2 are the first of a number of sections on the personified figure of Wisdom. Chapters 2:1–4:10 are addressed to the sage's pupil(s) under the familiar title "child" or "children" (2:1; 3:1, 17; 4:1). Continuing the theme of "the fear of God" in 1:11ff., chap. 2 exhorts the reader to the patient pursuit of Wisdom. In 3:1–16 ben Sira discusses from a variety of perspectives the honoring of one's parents. The verses below are typical of this reflection and of the distich (a proverb of two parallel lines) which constitutes the basic building block of this work (as it does of the book of Proverbs).

> He who honors his father atones for sins,
>> and like one who lays up treasure is he who glorifies his mother. (3:3–4)
> He who honors his father will be gladdened by his own children,
>> and in the day of his prayer he will be heard. (3:5)
> Honor your father in deed and word,
>> that a blessing from him may come upon you. (3:8)
> For the blessing of a father strengthens the houses of his children,
>> but the curse of a mother uproots their foundations. (3:9)

Here, as often, the idea of action and consequence is expressed, whether in the two halves of a line (vv. 3–4, 9), in the succession of lines (v. 8), or in both (v. 5). Typical of ben Sira is the combination of related proverbs with an identical formula ("He who honors/glorifies his father," vv. 3, 5, 6) and the linking of proverbs by word association or catchword ("blessing," vv. 8–9). The result is a more polished literary product than is found in many analogous collections in Proverbs (cf., e.g., Prov. 12: 13–23 on speech). In 3:17–31 ben Sira develops the theme of humility and pride, which may have been placed here because the reference to almsgiving in 3:30 links with 4:1–10 and its exhortations to help the poor and needy. To be a father to the orphans is to be like a son of the Most High (4:10), a thought that links with another section on Wisdom (4:11–19) who "exalts her sons" (4:11).

The proper and improper use of speech is the topic of 4:23–6:1. An apparently unrelated section on wealth (5:1–8) has been attached quite possibly because of the introductory formula "Do not *say*" in 5:3–6. A discussion of friendship (6:5–17) follows the section on speech, perhaps due to word association—the reference to "voice" and "tongue" in 6:5. Common introductory formulas are again evident (6:8–10, 14–16), indicating a conscious literary style. Another poem on Wisdom follows (6: 19–31), with some related injunctions attached to it (6:32–37).

The negative imperative is a formal device that holds together 7:1–16, although topical subsections on public office (vv. 4–7), escaping God's judgment (vv. 8–9), and speech (vv. 11–14) are in evidence. The use of the negative imperative in 7:18–20 may have been the linking device at the beginning of a major section on human relations and associations (7:18–9:18); friends and family (7:18–28); the priesthood (7:29–31, linked to the previous by the common idea of gift in v. 28 and vv. 29–31); the poor and troubled (7:32–36); the rich and powerful (8:1–2); boors (8:3–4); the aged (8:6–9); sinners and the insolent (8:10–11); those stronger than oneself (8:12–14, perhaps originally connected with 8:1–2); other undesirables (8:15–19); women (9:1–9); others desirable and undesirable (9:10–16). A section on magistrates and rulers (10:1–11:9), interpolated with a subsection on honor and riches (10:19–11:1), leads to a lengthy discussion of poverty and wealth, rich and poor (11:10–14:19), which again indicates subcollections and subtopics. Another poem on Wisdom follows (14:20–15:10).

In 15:11–18:14 ben Sira switches from his practical, deed-oriented discussion to theological speculation. His topic, however, is related. He discusses responsibility for one's deeds, the certainty of divine knowledge and retribution, creation, covenant and Torah, and the possibility of repentance of one's sinful deeds.

Returning to the realm of the practical and specific ben Sira discusses caution in speech and other matters (18:19–19:17, introduced by several other sayings on speech [18:15–18]). Four sayings beginning with "Question!" comprise a subunit (19:13–17). A brief section on wisdom and folly is connected by word association (19:30) with another lengthy discussion of proper and improper speech (chap. 20). Sin and the sinner constitute the topic of 21:1–10. Given the essential identity of sin and folly in the wisdom tradition, we have a natural transition to 21:11–22:18, where "fool" is the primary catchword in a wide variety of observations. Ben Sira uses a similar device in 41:17–42:8, a catalog of things of which one should be ashamed or not ashamed. Likewise, in 40:18–26 he combines diverse ideas by a common formula (x and y are good, but z is better).

The catchword "heart" connects 22:18 with 22:19, which begins a section on speech (22:19–23:15) that includes a prayer (22:27–23:6) with a brief mention of that subject (22:27). The first major section of the book concludes with a discussion of sexual sins (23:16–27). Perhaps the adulterous woman is intended as a foil or counterpart to Lady Wisdom, who is celebrated in 24:1ff. and at the end of part two (51:13–22).[34]

Our analysis of chaps. 1–23 has laid out the major literary forms and devices employed by ben Sira: short two-line proverbs, some of them with similar formulas, assembled in topical collections; the use of word association and common topics and formulas to link these collections to others; the interweaving of sections on concrete topics and examples with poems about Wisdom, prayers and hymns, and extended theological discussion.

Practical Advice

Ben Sira includes under the category of wisdom instruction a spectrum of interests and concerns ranging from practical to speculative, from secular to religious and theological. He can speak of such down-to-earth matters as table etiquette (31:12–32:13 [Gk. 34:12–35:9]), caution in one's dealings with others (18:15–19:17), and wise and unwise associations (12:8–13:20). In treating these topics ben Sira speaks as a man of experience, accumulating examples as he looks at the topic from a wide variety of viewpoints. Wisdom about life is not simple, and proper action requires the discernment that comes from experience. As a man of experience ben Sira knows that a mistake or *faux pas* in these matters can have the gravest consequences. These consequences are generally seen to be natural and inevitable and are seldom defined as divine retribution, as they are when he is speaking of breaches of God's law.

Wisdom and Torah

It is in ben Sira's identification of Wisdom and Torah that we find the heart and dynamic of his thought. The practical sides of his advice notwithstanding, he is concerned for the most part with one's conduct vis-à-vis the Torah and with the consequences of that conduct. Although the book of Proverbs identifies the fear of God as the beginning of wisdom, and the author of Psalm 119 extols at great length the joy of the Torah, the Wisdom of Jesus the Son of Sirach is the earliest datable work in our literature that discusses the relationship of Wisdom and Torah in detail and in theory.

In chap. 24 ben Sira sets forth the heart of his speculation about

Wisdom and Torah. This lengthy passage is a counterpart to Proverbs 8 and also bears striking resemblance to Hellenistic texts about the goddess Isis.[35] The main part of the chapter is a hymn in which Wisdom praises herself (vv. 1–22). Here Wisdom is personified and depicted as a female, the first of God's creatures (24:3; cf. 1:4; Prov 8:22). Proceeding from God's mouth (24:3) she participated in the creative process[36] whether as his creative word (Gen 1:3, etc.), as his breath construed as the life-giving mist that covered the barren primordial earth (24:3; cf. Gen 2:4–6), or as his endowment on his created beings (24:6; cf. 1:9). After Wisdom had pierced the heights of the ether and plumbed the depths of the abyss (24:4–6), God commanded this denizen of his angelic council (24:2) to pitch her tent and find her resting place in Israel, where she would minister to him in his Temple (24:8–11). Thus the universal endowment of humankind became the Creator's unique gift to his chosen people. Employing the language of simile, Wisdom now describes how she took root and grew in Israel like a pleasant tree (24:12–18), and she concludes by inviting her hearers to partake of her life-giving fruit, which satisfies any hunger and quenches all thirst (24:19–22).

Ben Sira interprets Wisdom's hymn:

> All this is the book of the covenant of the Most High God,
> the law which Moses commanded us
> as an inheritance for the congregations of Jacob. (24:23)

Employing a new simile the sage likens Torah to the Jordan River and to the life-giving streams that surrounded paradise. As such it gushes forth Wisdom into a boundless ocean and fathomless and inexhaustible abyss (24:25–29).

There is a further stage in the mediation of Wisdom. The sage, in this case ben Sira, is a channel that conveys the life-giving waters of Torah's Wisdom into another sea—his collective teaching, to be found in his book (24:30–34). In another simile, like Wisdom he is an enlightener of Israel (24:32; cf. v. 27). Through prayerful, inspired study of Torah, wisdom, and prophecy (39:1–8) the sage or scribe becomes a secondary but evidently necessary channel of God's Wisdom. The place of prophecy has been taken by the scribe's study and interpretation of the ancient writings, especially the Torah. This produces a deposit of teaching which ben Sira considers to be authoritative, to judge from his claim to prophecy (24:33) and perhaps his use of prophetic forms.[37]

Ben Sira presents a kind of drama of salvation—salvation not in the sense of deliverance from something but as the bestowal of goodness, blessing, and life. His theological starting point is the biblical (especially the Deuteronomic) view of covenant and Torah. Through the covenant, God bestowed on Israel their status as his chosen people. In the same covenant he set before them his commandments. The alternative possibilities of obedience and disobedience of these commandments would lead like two roads to blessing and life or to curse and death.[38] One could not short-circuit the process that led from the grace of covenantal election to the fullness of covenantal blessing and life. Responsible obedience to the commandments of Torah was an integral and necessary part of the covenant. In this sense Torah was a gift that brought the possibility of life.

The focus of ben Sira's covenantal theology is governed first by the fact that he is a teacher of ethics. For this reason, though he takes for granted Israel's covenantal status as God's chosen people (24:12; 46:1), he rarely speaks of the covenant except in the context of Torah.[39] From this same perspective his recitation of Israel's history—a rarity in Israelite wisdom literature—focuses on the right deeds, piety, and obedience of individual Israelites of renown. The catalog provides, in part, a multiplicity of examples of the life and attitudes ben Sira seeks to inculcate throughout the book.[40]

Ben Sira's covenantal theology is also marked by a kind of mythicizing which superimposes an ahistorical and heavenly dimension onto the historical phenomenon of Torah. The chronological starting point for his drama of salvation is not Mount Sinai or even the Exodus. In the beginning was Wisdom. This personified entity is functionally an agent or power. She first brought life to the world. At a particular point in history she was sent to earth and embodied in Torah, where she offers the dynamic for obedience and hence the possibility for life. Thus ben Sira's myth of Wisdom is the story of how God's freely given, innervating, vivifying goodness has been made present in Torah. It is the story of grace told from the perspective of eternity.

In chap. 24 and in his other poems about Wisdom (chaps. 1–2; 4:11–19; 6:18–31; 14:20–15:10; 51:13–30) ben Sira describes several aspects of the Wisdom that resides in Torah. Through Torah, Wisdom enlightens and instructs, revealing the will of God which leads to life if it is obeyed. Wisdom is also a means toward obedience. She is preacher and proclaimer (24:19–22; 51:23–30 through the mouth of the teacher) and helper (4:11). However, ben Sira is under no illusion that the way of obedience is easy. It requires steadfastness, perseverance, and endurance (2:1–18). Wisdom has her own tortuous discipline, her fetter, yoke, and collar (4:17; 6:18–31; 51:26). Nonetheless, those who pursue her she will feed and exalt and bless with gladness and goodness and the life and blessing that God offers through the covenant (4:18; 6:28–31; 15:1–6).[41] The theme of blessing through discipline we have already met in the story of Tobit.[42]

The myth of Wisdom reappears in the book of Baruch with explicit reference to the Deuteronomic covenant.[43] Early Christianity also employs the Wisdom myth, substituting Jesus for Torah as the unique historical embodiment of Wisdom.[44]

Ethical and Religious Teaching

As a teacher of Torah, ben Sira is concerned more with ethical matters than ritual matters. In 3:1–16 and 7:27–28 he expounds the commandment to honor one's parents. Another section that provides a context for the prayer of Jesus speaks of the reciprocity of forgiveness (28:1–7; cf. Matt 6:12). Repeatedly ben Sira turns to the topic of wealth, discussing its ethical implications. He contrasts generosity and stinginess (14:3–8); enjoins almsgiving and other acts of kindness to the poor and needy (4:4–6; 7:32–36; 29:9–13); recommends lending, with all its problems (29:1–7, 14–20); and warns against fraud and ill-gotten riches (4:1–3; 5:8; 21:8). Wealth in itself is not wrong, but ben Sira is not sanguine about the possibility of the rich remaining honest and God-pleasing in their dealings with others (26:29–27:2; 31:1–11). Ben Sira's attitude toward sexual matters is based on the biblical viewpoint. Adultery and incest are wrong (23:16–18). Other sexual relationships without benefit of marriage are not condemned per se, but they are to be avoided from a pragmatic point of view (9:1–9, where his advice applies also to adultery). Ben Sira's attitude toward women is ambivalent.[45] There are good and bad wives. Nonetheless, his viewpoint is strongly male-oriented and chauvinistic in places.[46]

Although ben Sira concentrates on ethical issues he does not ignore the cult. He holds the priesthood in high regard. In his catalog of heroes he devotes twice as much space to Aaron as he does to Moses (45:6–22; cf. vv. 1–5), and he concludes with a lengthy section in praise of the high priest Simon. In a passage that expands on the biblical commandment to love God (Deut 6:5) he commands his readers to honor the priests and to give them their due (7:29–31). The cult is God's means of repairing violations of the covenant (45:16), and participation in the cult is encouraged (35:4–11 [Gk. 32:6–13]). Nonetheless, in true prophetic style ben Sira warns against contradictions between cult and life, specifically the offering of sacrifices from ill-gotten riches and possessions. On the other hand obedience and deeds of charity function like cultic acts and provide "atonement" (34:18–35:3, 12–20 [Gk. 31:21–32:5, 14–26]; 3:3, 30). Ben Sira includes three prayers in his wisdom collection (22:27–23:6; 36:1–17 [Gk. 33:1–13; 36:16–22]; 51:1–12).

Retribution and Theodicy

Divine retribution in the form of blessing and curse was essential to the covenant, as we have seen. The idea is built into the very structure of many of ben Sira's proverbs, which describe the consequences of one's conduct. Where such conduct involves obedience or disobedience of Torah the consequences are understood as divine retribution.

> Lay up your treasure according to the commandments of the Most High,
>   and it will profit you more than gold.
> Store up almsgiving in your treasury,
>   and it will rescue you from all affliction. (29:11–12)

Ben Sira did not of course expect perfection, and he speaks of the means of atonement and of forgiveness (2:11; 28:2). Nonetheless, God's mercy is not to be presumed upon, as if he would continue to forgive a multitude of sins heaped one on the other (5:4–7).[47] On a number of occasions ben Sira speaks about retribution in polemical fashion.[48] He argues against the idea that God does not see sin or is not concerned with punishing it (15:19–20; 16:17–23; 17:20; 23:18–20). His programmatic treatment of the subject is in 15:11–18:14. The passage appears to be arguing on a theoretical and intellectual level against certain fixed points of view: the kind of determinism that excludes free will (15:11–20), and the theory that there can be no retribution in the universe (16:17).[49] While this possibility cannot be excluded[50] it should be noted that ben Sira's argument moves in a practical direction. He discusses creation (16:26–17:6), God's covenant with Israel (17:7–17), and God's charge that they obey his commandments and heed his warning of retribution (17:14–23). He then moves into an exhortation to repent (17:24–29) and concludes with a passage in praise of God's uniqueness, especially God's patience and compassion (17:30–18:14). Ben Sira appears to be less interested in arguing for free will and retribution than in preaching and in exhorting his audience to *act* responsibly within the covenant. The same practical direction in his argument is evident in 5:7 and 23:21.

A doctrine of creation is central to ben Sira's understanding of covenantal responsibility and retribution. God created man with the free will that places in his hands the choice to obey or disobey (15:14–17). Deuteronomy 30:15–19 is put in the context of creation. Humanity's created endowments are the presupposition for covenant obedience also in 17:1–13. In 39:16–35 the goodness of creation (Gen 1:31) is related to the manner in which the Creator uses his creation for blessing and curse on those who obey and disobey him. God's knowledge of human actions, which is the presupposition for his judgment, is an aspect of his creative power (42:18–21). He knows that which he has created. But in the final analysis theology gives way to doxology. His creative deeds are described in order that he might be praised (39:16–35; 42:15–43:33).

Date, Setting, Language, and History

The Wisdom of Jesus the Son of Sirach was written between 198 and 175 B.C.E. The high date is set by the death of the high priest Simon ("the Just"), the last of ben Sira's men of renown (50:1–21), who is described as a figure of the past.[51] The low date is the beginning of the Hellenistic reform under Antiochus IV (see Chapter 3). Had ben Sira written after that time his deep concern for Torah would scarcely have permitted him to bypass sure and certain references to those events.

It is something of a commonplace in scholarship that ben Sira wrote partly in reaction against the increasing inroads of Hellenism among the Jews.[52] However, the evidence is not all that clear. While it is *possible* to construe many of ben Sira's statements as polemics against Hellenizing tendencies, they are general enough to have had other intended applications.[53] Indeed, this book is striking for its lack of specific, pointed, and explicit polemics against Hellenism.[54] On the other hand ben Sira's thought is sometimes couched in language that was at home in Hellenistic philosophy, specifically in Stoicism.[55]

Ben Sira wrote in Hebrew. His grandson translated the book into Greek in Egypt near the end of the second century.[56] Fragments of two manuscripts of the Hebrew original have been found at Qumran and in the ruins of the Herodian fortress at Masada.[57] Large parts of the remainder of the Hebrew text have been recovered from five fragmentary medieval manuscripts.[58] The work was widely circulated and held in high regard by the Jews, and it was still referred to after the decision not to include it in the Hebrew Bible.[59] In the early Latin church the book was known as Ecclesiasticus, "belonging to the church," that is, the deuterocanonical book par excellence.[60]

NOTES

1. See P. Grelot, "La légende d'Hénoch dans les apocryphes et dans le Bible," 5–26.
2. Milik, *Books of Enoch*, 6.
3. In this chapter we shall discuss chaps. 72–82 and 1–36. For chaps. 83–90 see below, Chapter 3; for chaps. 91–105 see below, Chapter 4, where the collection as a whole is also discussed. For chaps. 37–71 see below, Chapter 6.
4. Ancient Hebrew and Aramaic documents can be dated quite closely on the basis of the handwriting. For a brief summary see Cross, *Library*, 117–19. For a detailed analysis see idem, "The Development of the Jewish Scripts," in *The Bible and the Ancient Near East*, ed. G. E. Wright (Garden City, N.Y.: Doubleday, 1961) 133–202. On the dating of chaps. 72–82 see Milik, *Books of Enoch*, 7–8.
5. For certain points in this discussion I am indebted to my student Jay Cassel and my colleague Robert Mutel.
6. J. T. Milik, *Ten Years of Discovery in the Wilderness of Judaea*, SBT 26 (London: SCM, 1959) 107–18; and idem, *Books of Enoch*, 7–22, 273–97.
7. On the date of *Jubilees* see below, pp. 78–79. On the Qumran community see below, pp. 122–23.
8. See Milik, *Books of Enoch*, 6.
9. See below, pp. 91, 93–94.
10. The author of chaps. 20–36 has reused the traditions in chaps. 17–19, with eschatological additions that have parallels in chaps. 1–5. Cf. in particular 25:3–6 and 27:2.
11. On the relationship of 1:1–2 to the Blessing of Moses and the Balaam oracles see Michael E. Stone, "Lists of Revealed Things in the Apocalyptic Literature," in *Magnalia Dei*, Fs. G. Ernest Wright, ed. F. M. Cross et al. (Garden City, N.Y.: Doubleday, 1976), n. 1. On the form of the oracle in chaps. 1–5 see Paul D. Hanson, *The Dawn of Apocalyptic* (Philadelphia: Fortress, 1975).
12. Cf. Sir 16:26–28; 43:1–12; *Ps. Sol.* 18:11–14; *T. Napht.* 3.
13. For the details of this analysis see George W. E. Nickelsburg, "Apocalyptic and Myth in 1 Enoch 6–11," 384–86; and idem, "Reflections upon Reflections . . . ," SBLASP (1978) 1:311–12.
14. Nickelsburg, "Apocalyptic and Myth," 386–89.
15. See ibid., 389–91; J. J. Collins, "Methodological Issues in the Study of 1 Enoch . . . ," SBLASP (1978) 1:320–21; Nickelsburg, "Reflections," 313–14.

16. Nickelsburg, "Apocalyptic and Myth," 396–97, nn. 61–62.

17. For the alternative possibilities, see Paul D. Hanson, "Rebellion in Heaven, Azazel, and Euhemeristic Heroes in 1 Enoch 6–11," 220–27; and Nickelsburg, "Apocalyptic and Myth," 397–404.

18. In 6:8 he is the tenth of Shemiḥazah's lieutenants, while in 10:8 he is the angel most responsible for the rebellion, as is hinted by his prominence in 8:1–3; see Devorah Dimant, "1 Enoch 6–11: A Methodological Perspective," 323–24.

19. The revelation of other secrets is attributed to Shemiḥazah and his angels in 8:3.

20. For the alternatives see Nickelsburg, "Apocalyptic and Myth," 399–404; and Hanson, "Rebellion," 227–31.

21. For some of the complexities of tracing the development of this tradition in *1 Enoch* see Hanson, "Rebellion," 220–26; and Nickelsburg, "Apocalyptic and Myth," 401–4.

22. This section is based on my article "Enoch, Levi, and Peter."

23. Cf. *Ps. Sol.* 8:13; CD 5:6–7.

24. Cf. Ezra 9. Ezra the scribe and priest comes to Jerusalem, where he finds that some of the Jews, including priests, have married foreign women and thus defiled the holy race and of course the priesthood. He prays in their behalf (cf. Ezra 9:6 with *1 Enoch* 13:5). He orders the marriages dissolved. In 1 Enoch 12–16 the damage is irreparable and the angelic priests are under irrevocable judgment.

25. Cf. Judg 17–18; 1 Kgs 12:26–31; Amos 8:14; *T. Levi* 2–7; Matt 16:13–19; Jos. *Ant.* 15.363–64; *J.W.* 1:404–6.

26. E.g., Homer, *Od.* 11 (see esp. ll. 576–600); Plato, *Rep.* 10.614–21 and *Phaedo* 113D–114C; Plutarch, *Mor.* 563–68.

27. Influence from Babylonian geography is argued by P. Grelot, "La géographie mythique d'Hénoch et ses sources orientales," *RB* 65 (1969) 33–69. However, much of Grelot's argument is built on a comparison with the Babylonian epic about Gilgamesh's search for immortality and ignores the closer analogy of the Greek *nekyia*. Similarly the fiery river, Pyriphlegethon (cf. 17:5), is known in Greek but not in Babylonian sources. See also T. Francis Glasson, *Greek Influence in Jewish Eschatology*, 8–11.

28. The original order of these verses appears to have been 18:6–11, 19:1–2, 18:12–16, and 19:3. The text as it now stands has two visions in a row (18:10–11 and 12–13), the first having no interpretation, the second having two (18:14–16 and 19:1–2).

29. The form of his name differs in the Greek and Hebrew texts of 50:27. See G. H. Box and W. O. E. Oesterley, *APOT* 1:511–12.

30. Contra Tcherikover (*Hellenistic Civilization*, 146–47), who cites 8:1–2 and 13:2, 7, 15–23. These passages contrast rich and poor and warn against association with the mighty but do not explicitly address the poor.

31. Cf. Dan 12:12; Rev 22:7.

32. J. A. Sanders (DJDJ 4:79–85) has published an earlier Hebrew version of the poem, which was included in a manuscript of the canonical Psalter explicitly ascribed to David.

33. Cf. 6:23–31.

34. For the contrast between the personified Wisdom and the wicked woman cf. Prov 1:20–2:19; cf. also 4Q184 (J. Allegro, DJDJ 5:82–84, and the review

by J. Strugnell in *RevQ* 7 [1970] 263–68); cf. also the two women in Rev 12 and 17–18.

35. H. Conzelmann, "Die Mutter der Weisheit," in *Zeit und Geschichte*, Fs. R. Bultmann, ed. E. Dinkler (Tübingen: Mohr, 1964) 225–34; Martin Hengel, *Judaism and Hellenism*, 1:157–59.

36. Cf. Prov 8:30.

37. See Hengel, *Judaism*, 1:134–35; and W. Baumgartner, "Die literarischen Gattungen in der Weisheit des Jesus Sirach," ZAW 34 (1914) 161–98.

38. On the Jewish development of this two-ways theology see Nickelsburg, *Resurrection*, 156–65.

39. Cf. 17:12; 24:23; 28:7; 39:8; 41:19; 42:2; 44:18, 20, 22; 45:5. In 45: 7, 15, 17, 24 he speaks of the priestly covenant, and in 45:25 and 47:11 of the Davidic covenant.

40. For a similar function of such a catalog cf. 1 Macc 2:49–64 and Heb 11:1–12:13.

41. The materials in chaps. 2, 4, and 6 have a similar structure: one seeks Wisdom, who provides blessings after and through difficulty.

42. See above, pp. 32–33.

43. See below, pp. 110–12. For ben Sira's reference to Deuteronomy see below, p. 64.

44. Cf. John 1:1–18; Phil 2:5–11; Col 1:15–20; Heb 1:1–3.

45. His sections on women include 7:19–26; 9:1–9; 22:3–5; 25:16–26:18; 42:12–14; see H. McKeating, "Jesus ben Sira's Attitude to Women," *ExpTim* 85 (1973) 85–87.

46. See esp. 22:3; 25:19, 24; 42:14.

47. Cf. *Ps. Sol.* 3, on which see below, p. 210.

48. James L. Crenshaw, "The Problem of Theodicy in Sirach," 48–55.

49. For this section as an attack on Epicureanism see Hengel, *Judaism*, 1: 141, tentatively; and G. Maier, *Mensch und freier Wille*, WUNT 12 (Tübingen: Mohr, 1971) 88–90.

50. See Nickelsburg, *Resurrection*, 164, n. 121, for a comparison of the Qumran Rule of the Community (1QS 3:13–4:26) with Sir 15:11ff. The latter might be considered a critique of something like the former.

51. Box and Oesterley, *APOT* 291–94.

52. See Tcherikover, *Hellenistic Civilization*, 143–45; and in great detail, Hengel, *Judaism*, 1:131–53.

53. E.g., on 15:11–18:14 see above, p. 63; on 41:8–9 see below, n. 54. Similarly, 3:21–24 might be a warning against apocalyptic speculation (contra Hengel, *Judaism*, 1:139).

54. We might find one such reference in 41:8–9; so Tcherikover, *Hellenistic Civilization*, 145; Hengel, *Judaism*, 1:151. It is interesting, however, that the expression "forsake the covenant/law" refers in Dan 11:30, *Jub.* 23:16, and 1 Macc 1:15 and 2:21 to the radical apostasy of the Hellenistic reform of 175 and after, a time considered too late by both Tcherikover (*Hellenistic Civilization*, 143) and Hengel (*Judaism*, 1:131).

55. For details see Hengel, *Judaism*, 1:146–50. More radical Hellenistic influence on ben Sira is proposed by Th. Middendorp, *Die Stellung Jesus ben Siras zwischen Judentum und Hellenismus*, 7–34.

56. See the discussion regarding lines 14–15 of the prologue in Box and Oesterley, *APOT* 1:293–94.

57. For the Qumran fragments see M. Baillet, *DJDJ* 3:75–77. For the Masada fragments see Yigael Yadin, *The Ben Sira Scroll from Masada*; and J. Strugnell, "Notes and Queries on 'The Ben Sira Scroll from Masada,'" *Eretz-Israel* 9 (1969) 109–19.

58. On the history of the Hebrew text see Alexander A. di Lella, *The Hebrew Text of Sirach;* Yadin, *Scroll,* 5–11; and Strugnell, "Notes," 119.

59. On the references to ben Sira in rabbinic literature see Box and Oesterley, *APOT* 1:297–98.

60. Ibid., 270–71, and on its use in the early church, ibid., 298–303.

BIBLIOGRAPHY

HELLENISM

W. W. **Tarn** and G. T. **Griffith**, *Hellenistic Civilization*, 3d ed. (London: Arnold, 1952), a wide-ranging account of the period from 323 to 31 B.C.E. **Tcherikover**, *Hellenistic Civilization*, 1–151, political, economic, and social history of Palestine from Alexander to Antiochus IV. Martin **Hengel**, *Judaism and Hellenism*, 2 vols. (E.T.; Philadelphia: Fortress, 1974), indispensable treatment of the encounter of Judaism and Hellenism in Palestine. T. Francis **Glasson**, *Greek Influence in Jewish Eschatology* (London: SPCK, 1961).

1 ENOCH

TRANSLATION: Michael A. **Knibb**, *The Ethiopic Book of Enoch: A New Edition in the Light of the Aramaic Dead Sea Fragments* (Oxford, Clarendon, 1978).

TEXTS AND OTHER TRANSLATIONS: Ibid., critical edition of the Ethiopic text, textual notes with detailed reference to the Greek texts and the Aramaic fragments. Matthew **Black**, *Apocalypsis Henochi Graece*, PVTG 3 (Leiden: Brill, 1970), text of the extant Greek manuscripts. **Milik**, *Books of Enoch*, the text of the Qumran fragments with prolific reconstruction and detailed notes on textual and other matters, historical introduction, a wealth of material; but see the reviews in *CBQ* 40 (1978) 411–19 and *JTS* 29 (1978) 517–30. R. H. **Charles**, *APOT* 2:163–281; Ephraim **Isaac**, *PsOT*.

LITERATURE: R. H. **Charles**, *The Book of Enoch* (Oxford: Clarendon, 1912), introduction, translation, and (useful, though often outdated) commentary. P. **Grelot**, "La légende d'Hénoch dans les apocryphes et dans la Bible," *RevScRel* 46 (1958) 5–26, 181–210, basic study of the figure of Enoch, its background and its development in Jewish literature. James C. **VanderKam**, "Enoch Traditions in Jubilees and Other Second Century Sources," SBLASP (1978) 1:229–51. Michael E. **Stone**, "The Book of Enoch and Judaism in the Third Century B.C.E.," *CBQ* 40 (1978) 479–92. On *1 Enoch* 1–5 and 72–82 see Eckhard **Rau**, "Kosmologie, Eschatologie und die Lehrautorität Henochs" (Diss. Hamburg, 1974). On *1 Enoch* 6–11 see Paul D. **Hanson**, "Rebellion in Heaven, Azazel, and Euhemeristic Heroes in 1 Enoch 6–11," *JBL* 96 (1977) 195–233; George W. E. **Nickelsburg**, "Apocalyptic and Myth in 1 Enoch 6–11," *JBL* 96 (1977) 383–405; and Devorah **Dimant**, "1 Enoch 6–11: A Methodological Perspective,"

SBLASP (1978) 1:323–39. On *1 Enoch* 12–16, see George W. E. Nickelsburg, "Enoch, Levi, and Peter: Recipients of Revelation in Upper Galilee," *JBL* 100 (1981), 575–60.

THE WISDOM OF JESUS THE SON OF SIRACH

TRANSLATION: The Apocrypha.

TEXTS AND OTHER TRANSLATIONS: Joseph **Ziegler**, *Sapientia Iesu Filii Sirach*, Septuaginta, Vetus Testamentum Graecum 12:2 (Göttingen: Vandenhoeck & Ruprecht, 1965), critical edition of the Greek text. Francesco **Vattioni**, *Ecclesiastico* (Napoli: Istituto Orientale di Napoli, 1968), Greek, Latin, Syriac, and Hebrew texts. Yigael **Yadin**, *The Ben Sira Scroll from Masada* (Jerusalem: Israel Exploration Society, 1965). G. H. **Box** and W. O. E. **Oesterley**, *APOT* 1:268–517, introduction, annotated translation with detailed textual apparatus.

LITERATURE: Alexander A. **di Lella**, *The Hebrew Text of Sirach: A Text-Critical and Historical Study* (The Hague: Mouton, 1966). Th. **Middendorp**, *Die Stellung Jesu ben Siras zwischen Judentum und Hellenismus* (Leiden: Brill, 1973). James L. **Crenshaw**, "The Problem of Theodicy in Sirach: On Human Bondage," *JBL* 94 (1975) 47–64.

3

Reform—Repression—Revolt

Antiochus III extended many benefits to the Jews after his victory over the Ptolemies in 198 B.C.E. Among these was the right to live "according to their ancestral laws." The Torah was officially recognized as the constitution of the state, and the authority to govern was delegated to the high priest in Jerusalem.

The afterglow of Antiochus's victory was short-lived. The military might of Rome loomed on the horizon. In 190 the army of Scipio Africanus dealt Antiochus a crushing blow in Asia Minor, at the battle of Magnesia, and the Seleucid emperor was forced to pay heavy indemnities. Three years later he was killed and was succeeded by his son, Seleucus IV. The financial burdens imposed by Rome weighed upon him. This was probably the cause of the unsuccessful attempt of his agent Heliodorus to confiscate money deposited in the treasury of the Jerusalem Temple (2 Macc 3; Dan 11:20). Seleucus was succeeded in 175 by his brother, Antiochus IV ("Epiphanes"), who had been a hostage in Rome since 189. Events in Palestine took a turn for the worse.

Shortly after he ascended the Seleucid throne, Antiochus issued a decree offering the status of Antiochene citizen to inhabitants of his empire who were ready to take up the Greek way of life.

Those Jews who thought it was to their advantage to accept Antiochus's invitation and to enter into a closer association with Greeks found their champion in a priest named Jason (a Greek substitute for the name Joshua), the brother of Onias III, the reigning high priest. Jason appeared before Antiochus and offered him a large sum of money for the privilege of establishing a community of Antiochenes in Jerusalem. Antiochus accepted Jason's proposal and appointed him high priest in place of his brother. Jason returned home to draw up a list of citizens and to establish the typical Greek educational institutions, the *gymnasion* and the *ephebeion*, which were to feed the roll of citizens. Those who opted for the new Hellenistic way of life set aside at least significant aspects of the Torah. The athletic games of the *gymnasion* were a big attraction in which even some of the priests participated. Some Jews, evidently ashamed of their circumcision (considered a barbarism by the Greeks), resorted to surgical means to remove the sign of the covenant.

Three years later Jason was beaten at his own game when his envoy to Antiochus, Menelaus, offered the king a sizable amount of revenue and obtained the office of high priest. Jason fled across the Jordan River to the land of Ammon. Menelaus was unable to meet the heavy payments he had promised Antiochus. When the king was away from his capital, Menelaus bribed Antiochus's minister Andronicus with gold vessels taken from the Temple. When this action was decried by Onias (the former high priest), Menelaus convinced Andronicus to entice Onias out of his place of asylum and murder him. Antiochus learned of the treacherous affair and had Andronicus executed, but Menelaus escaped any blame and continued his imperious ways. About this time sources begin to indicate considerable Jewish opposition to Menelaus's policies and practices. A bloody clash took place between these Jews and the soldiers of Lysimachus, Menelaus's brother, who had plundered the Temple vessels. Lysimachus himself was killed. The Jews accused Menelaus before the king, but the high priest was acquitted when he successfully bribed one of Antiochus's counselors.

In 170/69 Antiochus mounted a military expedition against Egypt and overran most of the country. When the rumor came back to Asia that Antiochus was dead, Jason rallied his supporters, crossed the Jordan, and attacked Jerusalem. Pious Jews in the city seized the opportunity to take up arms against both Menelaus and Jason.[1] Antiochus returned rapidly from Egypt, stormed the city, slaughtered much of the population, sold some into slavery, and plundered the Temple. He confirmed Menelaus as high priest and left a certain Philip the Phrygian to keep order in the city. Two years later (early in 167), evidently in response to more unrest among the pious Jews, Antiochus dispatched his lieutenant Apollonius, who fell upon the city on a Sabbath and repeated the terrible massacre of two years previous. Apollonius fortified the "Akra," the citadel near the Temple, and manned it with a garrison of troops who would continue to trouble the Jerusalemites for twenty-six years.

Antiochus had had his fill of uprisings, and so he struck at the heart of the matter. Religion according to the Torah had been responsible for the rebellions, and so religion in that form was proscribed by royal edict. Circumcision and the celebration of festivals, including the Sabbath, were forbidden. All copies of the Torah were to be burned. A polytheistic cult was instituted in the Jerusalem Temple, and Jews were forced to eat unclean swine's flesh. Opposition to the edict was punishable by death. On the fifteenth day of Chislev (December) 167 the "desolating sacrilege," an idolatrous structure, was erected upon the sacrificial altar in Jerusalem. Thus the Temple in Jerusalem was defiled, and throughout Judea the king's officers were enforcing violation of the Torah. Sides had to be chosen. Many forsook the covenant in order to save their lives, but many pious Jews took their stand and chose to die rather than transgress the laws of their fathers. Others fled to the wilderness and hid out in caves; and not a few died, refusing to defend themselves on the Sabbath.

The Hasmonean family now appeared on the scene: a priest named Mattathias and his sons John, Simon, Judas, Eleazar, and Jonathan. They quickly brought direction and much-needed leadership to the dispersed bands of the pious, striking out against both apostasizing Jews and government troops. When the old patriarch died the leadership passed on to his son, Judas. Nicknamed Maccabeus (perhaps "Mallethead"), this brilliant general possessed all the advantages of a warrior employing guerrilla tactics in his home territory to defend a cause for which he was willing to die. He took on Antiochus's finest commanders and picked troops, and in a series of lightning strokes his little army put to flight the hordes of the foreign invader. In three years the Temple mount was retaken, and in December 164 the sanctuary was purified, its lights rekindled, and the orthodox cult reestablished.

A RESPONSE IN APOCALYPTIC LITERATURE

Out of the turbulence and violence of the years 169–64 there appeared a series of writings which exhorted pious, Torah-abiding Jews to stand fast in the face of persecution, confident of swift divine judgment against their enemies. Each of these writings claimed to be a revelation written by an ancient prophet or sage: Moses, Daniel, Enoch.

THE BOOK OF JUBILEES

The longest of these writings, the *Book of Jubilees*, is an extensive elaboration of Genesis 1–Exodus 12, put forward as a secret revelation which the angels of God's presence transmitted to Moses on Mount Sinai.[2]

With a few exceptions it follows the order of the Bible itself; however, the author treats the *wording* of the biblical text in a variety of ways. Often he reproduces the text verbatim. Occasionally he deletes what he does not find useful. Most typically, however, he recasts the narrative or makes additions to it in keeping with his interests and purposes.

Our author is especially interested in *halakhah* (from the Hebrew "to walk"), a "way" of life spelled out in teachings, ordinances, and practices derived from the interpretation of biblical laws. He employs a number of techniques to incorporate this legal material into the biblical narratives.

Running throughout the book is a chronological framework that presupposes and advocates the use of a solar calendar. Events in biblical history and the establishment of religious festivals are dated according to this calendar, which has the force of law because it is rooted in the created structure of the universe. This structure is the subject of the astronomical part of *1 Enoch* (see above, pp. 47–48), to which *Jubilees* 4:17 makes reference.

Typical expansions of the biblical narratives depict the patriarchs observing the Torah. Noah offered a proper sacrifice (7:3–5). Levi discharged the office of priest (32:4–9). Major holy days were observed by the patriarchs: First Fruits by Noah, Abraham, Isaac, Jacob, and Ishmael (6:18; 15:1–2; 22:1–5); Tabernacles by Abraham (16:20–31); the Day of Atonement by Jacob (34:12–20). Special prescriptions are given for Passover, the jubilee year, and the Sabbath (chaps. 49–50). Again our author's calendrical interests are evident.

On occasion the author exhorts his readers through admonitions which he places in the mouth of a patriarch. On his deathbed Abraham delivers three exhortations to his sons and grandsons, warning them against fornication, intermarriage with the Canaanites, idolatry, the consuming of blood, and other cultic abominations (chaps. 20–22).

Perhaps the most interesting of our author's additions are a number of brief halakhic commentaries that often begin with the expression "For this reason it is written (or "ordained") in the heavenly tablets that. . . ." In these commentaries the author utilizes some element in the biblical narrative as the basis for his exposition of a point of law. God's clothing of Adam and Eve shows that nakedness is prohibited (3:31). Various events relating to the Flood and its abatement demonstrate that feasts are to be observed according to the solar calendar (6:17–22). The vengeance of Simeon and Levi on Shechem and their refusal to allow him to marry Dinah show that marriage to a foreign spouse is categorically prohibited (30:7–23). The stories about Reuben and Bilhah and Judah and Tamar illustrate the forbidden sin of incest (33:10–20; 41:23–27).

For this author Torah is eternal and immutable, recorded on the heavenly tablets. His alleged source of authority is angelic revelation. An angel of the presence dictated these *halakhoth* to Moses. In the case of the solar calendar, details of the celestial structures on which it is based were revealed to Enoch by the angel Uriel (4:17; cf. *1 Enoch* 72:1). Alongside these claims to direct revelation the author also provides an exegetical base for his laws. Specific laws derive from some item or detail in the biblical text that he is transmitting (and interpreting through revision!).

The nonhalakhic revisions of the biblical text vary in their content and function. Some implicitly exhort the reader to proper behavior. Others "predict" or explain the origin of situations in the author's own time. Still others make a theological point. Some of these revisions were composed by the author. He derived others from oral or written tradition.

We have already noted formal exhortations placed in the mouths of the ancients. In other cases moral admonitions are implied by narrative additions and commentaries on them. Most notable in this respect are the stories about Abraham, who is depicted as a model of a variety of virtues. He is a paragon of wisdom and insight. As such he sees through the folly of idolatry, teaches the Chaldeans the science of agriculture, learns of the futility of astrological forecasting, and studies "the books of his fathers" (11:5–12:27). Moreover, his zeal leads him to burn the local idolatrous temple (12:12).[3]

The stories of the sacrifice of Isaac and the purchase of the Cave of Machpelah are expanded to depict Abraham as a model of faithfulness and patient endurance under trial. The biblical story of the sacrifice states simply that "God tested Abraham" (Gen 22:1). His celebrated *faith* is mentioned not in Genesis 22 but in Genesis 15:6, with reference to his belief in God's promise of a son. Taking the biblical motif of testing as his point of departure, the narrator transforms the biblical story (which is repeated almost verbatim) into a full-blown courtroom scene. He prefaces it with a confrontation between the angel(s) of the presence and the satanic accuser, "the prince of *mastēmā*," which is reminiscent of Job 1–2 (*Jub.* 17:15–16), and he concludes the story with the defeat of the accuser (18:9–12). The incident was but one example (though probably the example par excellence) of Abraham's lifetime of faithfulness to God and patient endurance (17:17–18). The author appears to have drawn on a tradition about the ten trials of Abraham, of which he names the bargaining over the Cave of Machpelah as the tenth (19:1–9).[4] In short the author takes characteristics the Bible attributes to Abraham in one situation and applies them to his behavior in a number of circumstances.[5]

Some of the author's additions to the biblical narrative allude to events in his own time. Chapters 35–38 are a lengthy expansion on the list of Edomite kings in Genesis 36:31–39 (*Jub.* 38:15–24). The passage reflects contemporary Jewish-Idumean hostility and explains its origin, stressing Jewish superiority. The point is made in a lengthy narrative describing relationships between Jacob and Esau that culminate in a war in which Jacob slays Esau. The author alludes to other contemporary events by means of predictions that are included in some of his commentaries (e.g., 6:34).

Frequently the biblical text is expanded to make a theological point. The author interpolates traditions from *1 Enoch* 6–16 into the story of the Flood and its aftermath in order to explain the causes of the Flood (chaps. 5 and 7) and, more important, the origin of that demonic world which is presupposed throughout the book.[6] These evil spirits have come forth from the giants who were born to the fallen angels and the daughters of men. Far from being exterminated by the Flood, these spirits seduce the children of Noah into committing the same sins that led to the extermination of the giants (7:20–33). References to the judgment in *1 Enoch* 10 are drawn into the narrative in *Jubilees* 5:10–16 and are expanded. Other eschatological additions occur from place to place.

The longest of the eschatological additions in the *Book of Jubilees* is 23:16–32. In form it is a historical apocalypse, that is, a "revelation" of events that lie in the future of the alleged author. It shares a common outline with several other texts to which we shall turn later in this chapter. It begins with a prediction of events that are described in increasing detail and lead up to the present crisis. The crisis is resolved in a judgment that involves direct divine or angelic intervention and that ushers in a new age in which the earth or the whole cosmos is restored permanently to the state which the Creator had intended.

In context *Jubilees* 23:16–32 is a commentary on Genesis 25:7, "These are the days of the years of Abraham's life, a hundred and seventy-five years" (cf. *Jub.* 23:8). Abraham's life was much shorter than those of the prediluvian patriarchs, but after him human life would become increasingly shorter, due to sin. When repentance takes place human life will be restored to its former longevity. Verses 11–15 describe in stereotyped terms the terrible woes that will come in post-Abrahamic times. From v. 16 on we are in the midst of a description of the times of Antiochus. The apocalypse may be schematized as follows:

1.	Sin	vv. 16–21
2.	Punishment	vv. 22–25
3.	Turning point	v. 26
4.	Salvation	vv. 27–31

Part 1 describes a deep schism between Jews who "forsake the covenant" (v. 16; cf. v. 19) and their compatriots who take up arms to bring them back to "the path of righteousness" (vv. 16, 19, 20). Although much blood is shed, the apostates continue in their sinful ways and even "defile the holy of holies with their uncleanness and the corruption of their pollution" (v. 21; *APOT* 2). The description fits admirably the events in Jerusalem before Antiochus's decree of 167: the apostasy of the Hellenizers; the strife in Jerusalem at the time of Jason's attempted coup; the continued presence of Menelaus, the corrupt and bloody high priest.

According to part 2, God punishes this generation (v. 22), sending against them the merciless "sinners of the Gentiles" (vv. 22–23). These verses are in accord with the bloody reprisals of Antiochus and Apollonius in 169 and 167. Almost all the other sources from this time make specific reference to the person of Antiochus and to various of the details of his decree. The lack of any such specificity in the present passage argues strongly for a date no later than early 167. Verse 25 continues the theme of premature old age that runs throughout the passage.

The crucial event in the action occurs in v. 26 (part 3). If apostasy is responsible for God's punishment the return of God's favor requires repentance—a return to the "path of righteousness." This is precipitated by a study of the laws.

As the author moves to the events of salvation (part 4) his language breaks the bonds of human experience, and history gives way to myth. Life will return to its prediluvian longevity (v. 27; cf. v. 9). It will be characterized by peace, blessing, healing, and the absence of Satan and evil. The passage reflects Third Isaiah's descriptions of life on the renewed earth and in the new Jerusalem (Isa 65:17–25). It supersedes that prophet's vision with a promise that death itself will be conquered. The bones of the righteous will rest in the earth, but their spirits will experience the joy of heaven (v. 31—probably an interpretation of Isa 66:14).

Parts 1 and 2 of the passage are marked by a tension. On the one hand there is a clear distinction between the apostates and the pious Jews who attempt to bring them back to the way of righteousness. On the other hand the suffering of Israel as a whole is due to its sins. There is a deep sense of corporate guilt, which recurs in other documents dealing with this period of time. In any event it is not clear who the children are that will return to the path of righteousness (v. 26). Does the author expect that some of the apostates will repent when the power of the oppressor has reached its full fury, or is he speaking of the righteous who share the guilt of Israel but will turn the tide by their increased righteousness?[7]

The explicit reference to Moses in v. 32 and the command to write down these words are striking. They are reminiscent of Deuteronomy 31:19 and the broader context of Deuteronomy 28–32, where the pattern of sin-punishment-(repentance)-salvation is spelled out. This same pattern, with unmistakable verbal echoes of Deuteronomy 28ff., occurs in *Jubilees* 1 and in the *Testament of Moses* (see below, pp. 80–81).

The dating of the *Book of Jubilees* can be determined in two stages.[8] Several factors indicate ca. 175 and 100 B.C.E. as the outer limits. The *terminus post quem* is provided by passages reflecting matters that were at issue in the Hellenistic reform. Prohibitions of nudity and uncircumcision à la Gentiles (3:31; 15:34) are cases in point.[9] Explicit citation of the *Book of Jubilees* in the Qumran Damascus Document (CD 16:3–4) indicates a lower limit ca. 100–75 B.C.E. Paleographical evidence from Qumran manuscripts of *Jubilees* suggests a date closer to 100 B.C.E. Within this time span, two dates are possible.

A high date would be 168 B.C.E., contemporaneous with the composition of the apocalypse in chap. 23. The author's many prohibitions of contact with and imitations of the Gentiles would well suit a document stemming from this period. Among the practices interdicted are nudity and uncircumcision (3:31; 15:33–34); observance of "the feasts of the Gentiles," i.e., the lunar calendar (6:35); intermarriage (20:4; 22:20; 25:1;

27:10; 30:1–15); idolatry (20:7–9; 22:16–18); and consuming blood (6:12–14; 7:30; 21:6). In the context of such a date the *Book of Jubilees* would be that corpus of laws referred to in 23:26. Israel's study of these laws and obedient return to them will catalyze the return of fortune and the inception of the end-time described in vv. 27–31.

A second proposed date of composition would be between 161 and 152–140 b.c.e.[10] Supposed references to the Maccabean wars (34:2–4; 37–38) would provide the *terminus post quem*. The *terminus ad quem* would be the rise of the Hasmonean high priesthood and the establishment of the Qumran community (see below, pp. 122–23), both of which stand in tension with the book's high appraisal of the priesthood and the Jerusalem cult. Three difficulties attach to this dating. First, we cannot be certain that 34:2–4 and chaps. 37–38 refer to the Maccabean wars.[11] Second, if one accepts the dating one must minimize the import of the many anti-Gentile polemics, reading them as post factum reflections of the enormity of the deeds that brought on the disaster of the 160s[12] or as otherwise undocumented evidence of continued Hellenization and Jew-Gentile contact.[13] Third, if the book was written later and the earlier apocalypse in chap. 23 incorporated into it, we might expect the latter to be updated with some reference to the person of Antiochus IV, his pollution of the Temple, and his edict.

Connections between the *Book of Jubilees* and the Qumran community are especially close. The Damascus Document cites it as authoritative (CD 16:3–4). Twelve fragmentary Hebrew manuscripts of *Jubilees* have been found at Qumran. The religious ideas, theology, and laws in *Jubilees* closely parallel and are often identical with those in writings unique to Qumran.[14] Either of the early dates suggested above precludes its actual composition at Qumran, and there are some differences between *Jubilees* and the Qumran texts. The *Book of Jubilees* issued from an unnamed sect related to those responsible for the composition of Daniel 10–12, *1 Enoch* 72–82, 85–90, and 93:1–10 + 91:12–17.[15] The historical relationships between these sects and the Qumran sect are now obscure, but the latter fell heir to their literature.

Jubilees was composed in Hebrew, then translated into Greek and from Greek into Ethiopic, in which language alone it is extant in its entirety.[16] The book is still printed in editions of the Ethiopic Bible.

Like the Wisdom of Jesus the Son of Sirach, the *Book of Jubilees* reflects the increasing significance of Scripture and the importance of its interpretation. The centrality of *halakhah* is symptomatic of the growing concern to expound the Torah—God's revelation of his will for his covenantal people—in a way that spoke relevantly to their needs and situations. However, the stress on *halakhah* should not overshadow the expositor's other tasks: to instruct, encourage, and admonish. These twin features of the biblical interpretation in *Jubilees* would continue to characterize Judaism in the centuries to come. Their later counterparts are the so-called halakhic and haggadic exegesis of the rabbis. In this exegesis, as in the Qumran commentaries (see below, pp. 126–32), the mixture of scriptural quotation and paraphrase used in *Jubilees* has been replaced by the format of quotation and commentary—evidence of the continually growing authority of Scripture.

THE TESTAMENT OF MOSES

The *Testament of Moses* (commonly known as the *Assumption of Moses*)[17] is in its present form a product of the first decades of the Common Era (see below, p. 213). However, analysis of the text indicates that the references to the Hasmonean princes and to Herod and his sons (chaps. 6–7) are secondary to the original form of the work, which was written in the time of Antiochus Epiphanes.[18]

The *Testament of Moses* retells the events described in Deuteronomy 31–34. The two writings have the following elements in common:

1. The announcement of Moses' death	Deut 31:1, 14	*T. Mos.* 1:15
2. The commissioning of Joshua	Deut 31:7, 14, 23	*T. Mos.* 1:7–11
3. Commands to preserve the book	Deut 31:19, 25–26	*T. Mos.* 1:16–18
4. Extensive revelation of the history of Israel	Deut 32 (also 28–30)	*T. Mos.* 2–9
5. The blessing of Moses	Deut 33	Cf. *T. Mos.* 10
(6. Moses' death and burial	Deut 34	presumably in the lost conclusion of *T. Mos.*)

By beginning his revision of Deuteronomy where he does (and presumably ending it with the end of Deuteronomy)[19] the author structures his book as a testament—a writing containing the alleged last words of a famous figure of the past (see below, pp. 231–48).

Integral to the author's conception of his work is his rewriting of Deuteronomy 31:24–26 in the *Testament of Moses* 1:16–18. Moses is transmitting to Joshua secret prophecies that are to be stored in earthen

vessels until it is time to reveal them in the days before "the consummation of the end of days." In 12:4 he again refers to the "end of the age."
Our author's belief that he is living in the last times has led him to re-
write the prophecies of Deuteronomy in a striking way. He employs a
double cycle of the Deuteronomic scheme that we detected in *Jubilees* 23
(*T. Mos.* 2–4 and 5–10).

	Testament of Moses		*Deuteronomy*	
1. Sin	2	5:1–6:1	28:15	32:15–18
2. Punishment	3:1–4	8	28:16–68	32:19–27
3. Turning point	3:5–4:4	9	30:2	32:28–34
4. Salvation	4:5–9	10	30:3–10	32:35–43

However, he has fleshed out that scheme with clearly identifiable events
in the nation's history: In the second cycle of the scheme (chaps. 5–9),
he describes the events of his own time in great and explicit detail. His
reasoning is as follows: I am living in the end-times; therefore what
Moses the prophet wrote refers to the present. He then proceeds to re-
write Deuteronomy as if Moses himself were describing the specific
events.

In the first cycle, the author establishes the validity of the Deuteronomic scheme by reciting earlier history. Judah sinned (2:7–9). God punished them at the hand of Nebuchadnezzar (3:1–3). The people recalled
the words of Moses in his song (3:10–14). An unnamed intercessor
pleaded their case (4:1–4). The Lord had compassion and returned them
to their land. However, the scheme did not come to complete fulfillment,
and life in restored Judah still left much to be desired (4:8).

The cycle has repeated itself in the events contemporary to the author.
The Hellenizers and their opponents are divided with respect to the
truth (5:2), as was the case in *Jubilees* 23:16–20. Special mention is made
of the deeds of the priests who defile the sanctuary (5:3; cf. *Jub.* 23:21).
Chapters 6 and 7 are late, at least in their present form.[20] The persecution
of Antiochus, described in unmistakable detail in chap. 8, is God's punishment ("visitation," 8:1) of the sins of the nation. The very end of 8:5
appears to contain a reference to the notorious "desolating sacrilege"
erected above the altar. Like the return to the laws in *Jubilees* 23:26,
chap. 9 functions as the turning point in the scheme. The mysterious
Taxo gathers his sons about him and echoes the sentiment that both 1
and 2 Maccabees later attribute to the pious Jews during the persecution,

"Let us die rather than transgress the commands of the Lord of Lords, the God of our fathers" (9:6; *APOT* 2). They die with an appeal that God avenge their blood (9:7). Taxo's words echo Deuteronomy 32:43. The repetition of the theme in 10:2 indicates that God will hear their prayer. Their innocent deaths and their cry for vengeance will trigger the wrath of God and move the drama into its final act, described in chap. 10.

Here, as in *Jubilees* 23:27–31, history gives way to myth. Unlike the corresponding part of the first cycle of the scheme, salvation is here final and surpasses human experience. As in *Jubilees* 23:27–31, the end-time reverts to ancient times. The author draws on the language of Deuteronomy 33 and describes God's final epiphany in terms of his ancient appearance on Sinai. God's victory will be complete. His reign will be evident throughout all his creation (10:1). Satan, the power of evil and the opponent of God, will be annihilated (cf. *Jub.* 23:29). The Gentiles —the persecutors of his people—will be punished, and their idols will be obliterated. And then the incredible—Israel will be exalted to the stars (10:9). The boundary between the mortal and the immortal will be transcended. Heaven will become the dwelling place of God's people while earth will be converted into the place of punishment for their enemies. The passage ends with an aggregation of themes similar to *Jubilees* 23:30–31: exaltation to heaven, punishment of the enemies, thanksgiving to God.

Our author writes some time after the beginning of Antiochus's persecution. The last datable event is the construction of the desolating sacrilege (December 167). Judas Maccabeus is not yet on the horizon. At least he is not mentioned. Instead, our author expects deliverance in the form of direct divine intervention. The event precipitating the judgment is the innocent death of the pious. The author may have witnessed such, or he may be writing to encourage such deaths. Perhaps both. In any event he trusts in the faithfulness of God's ancient word through Moses. God will speedily answer the cry of the righteous.

We do not know to what group our author belonged. Although there are many similarities in form and content with *Jubilees* 23 there are significant differences. No mention is made of the righteous taking up arms against their Jewish compatriots (cf. *Jub.* 23:20), nor is there any militant ideology.[21] A consuming interest in Temple matters, lacking in *Jubilees* 23, runs through the *Testament of Moses*. It raises some interesting though probably unanswerable questions. Was the author a priest? What then do we make of his statement about the substandard nature of postexilic sacrifices (4:8)? Is this simply a reflection of the common view that Zerubbabel's Temple was far inferior to the Solomonic edifice? Or are these sour grapes from a member of some group of disenfranchised priests?[22]

The *Testament of Moses* was composed either in Hebrew or in Aramaic[23] and then translated into Greek. It is extant in only one incomplete, corrupt, and partly illegible manuscript of a Latin translation of the Greek version.

DANIEL 7–12

The second half of the book of Daniel contains a series of visions that Daniel allegedly saw during the reigns of Belshazzar, Darius, and Cyrus. In reality the visions date from the time of Antiochus's persecution of the Jews, and they reflect various events in that persecution. Through the use of mythic symbolism they depict the persecution as rebellion against heaven and announce an act of divine judgment that will quash the rebellion and usher in an era of salvation.[24]

Daniel 7

A. The Vision			vv. 1–14
1. The first three beasts appear		vv. 1–6	
2. The fourth beast		vv. 7–11	
a. The beast appears	v. 7		
b. The eleventh horn	v. 8		
c. The heavenly court	vv. 9–10		
d. The judgment of the beast	v. 11		
3. The other beasts neutralized		v. 12	
4. Exaltation of one like a son of man		vv. 13–14	
B. The Interpretation			vv. 15–27
1. of the four beasts		vv. 15–18	
2. of the fourth beast, the eleventh horn, and the judgment		vv. 19–26	
3. of the exaltation		v. 27	

The action in the vision takes place on two levels. The beasts appear, act, and are destroyed on earth (1, 2abd, 3). The court is a heavenly one, and it is there that the one like a son of man is exalted (2c, 4).

Continuing the tradition in Daniel 2 (see above, pp. 20–21) the beasts represent four kingdoms, the last of these being the Macedonian. The imagery of the beasts arising from the sea is reminiscent of ancient Near Eastern myths that depict the ancient chaos monster of the sea and his combat with and ultimate defeat by the high god. Here all four beasts are powerful and fearful predators, emphasizing the military might that reaches its climax in Macedon. The iron teeth of the fourth beast suggest the army's weaponry and correspond to the iron feet of the statue in chap. 2. The ten horns plus one represent Macedonian kings, the last of these being Antiochus IV.

The vision focuses on the fourth beast, and especially the eleventh horn, on their confrontation with heaven, and on their judgment and destruction. After a description of the warlike deeds of this ferocious beast and the boastful words of the little horn the action moves to the heavenly court (vv. 9–10) where God, described as an old man, is seated on his throne in the midst of his angelic entourage. The judgment passed in heaven has immediate consequences on the earthly level. The fourth beast is destroyed. The Macedonian kingdom (and hence its king, Antiochus) is annihilated (v. 11). Reference to the other three beasts is perfunctory (v. 12).

Again the scene moves back to heaven for the final act of the drama:

> And behold with the clouds of heaven there came one like a son of man,
>   and he came to the Ancient of Days,
>   and he was presented before him. (v. 13)

The Semitic expression "son of man" means simply a human being. A humanlike figure is brought before the divine throne. However, the author does not say that the figure *is* a man. In 8:15 a similar expression describes the angel Gabriel (cf. 10:18; 9:21), and in the present context of a heavenly scene it is most likely that the author is describing an angel being presented before God. His humanlike appearance is mentioned perhaps in contrast to the beasts. Verse 14 indicates the reason for the presentation:

> And to him was given dominion and glory and kingdom,
>   that all peoples, nations, and languages should serve him;
> his dominion is an everlasting dominion, which shall not pass away;
>   and his kingdom one that shall not be destroyed.

The angel is invested with authority that has its repercussions on the earthly level: all human kingdoms will be subservient to this authority.

Daniel himself has been caught up into the vision and seeks an interpretation from a member of the heavenly court (vv. 15–16).[25] The initial interpretation is brief (vv. 17–18). The four beasts are four kingdoms,[26] and the investiture means that the holy ones of the Most High will receive the kingdom and possess it forever. The term "holy one" or "saint," as it is often translated, is a typical name for angels; as we shall see, however, there are broader implications.

Daniel inquires further about the fourth beast and the eleventh horn, about whose actions we now hear more (vv. 19–22). The interpreting angel responds (vv. 23–27). The mouth of the little horn (Antiochus) has uttered blasphemy against the Most High (v. 25). His persecution of the Jews involves the "wearing out" of the holy ones of the Most High (v. 25), that is, war against their angelic patrons. Verse 25 goes on to allude to his proscription of the Torah and of the observance of religious festivals. The author expects that in three and a half years the persecution will end and Antiochus will be destroyed (vv. 25–26).

The apocalyptist views reality on two separate but related levels. Events on earth have their counterparts in heaven and vice versa. When Antiochus persecutes the Jews he is wearing out their heavenly angelic patrons. By the same token the actions of the heavenly court have repercussions on earth. When judgment is passed in heaven the earthly king and his kingdom fall. Furthermore, when dominion is given *in heaven* to the chief angelic patron of Israel *the people* of the holy ones of the Most High are given dominion over all the kingdoms *under heaven* (v. 27). Israel will be preeminent among the nations of the earth. In and through his people God's everlasting and indestructible reign (kingdom) will be present and operative and will succeed the kingdoms of this world (cf. Dan 2:44; 4:3, 34; 6:26). With this promise the author concludes his drama, which has moved from rebellion to judgment and from persecution to deliverance and exaltation. It will serve as the fountainhead of later Jewish and Christian traditions (see below, pp. 217, 222, 292).

Daniel 8

This chapter also divides into vision (vv. 1–14) and interpretation (vv. 15–26). The animal imagery symbolizes the military might of the kingdoms in question. The charging ram is the Medo-Persian kingdom, and the he-goat is the Macedonian kingdom. Alexander's lightning conquest of the Persian empire is depicted by the goat's moving across the face of the earth without touching ground (v. 5; cf. Isa 41:3 of Cyrus). Alexander dies; the great horn of the he-goat is broken (v. 8). He is succeeded by four other kingdoms, represented by four little horns. As in chap. 7, the action focuses on the one little horn, which represents Antiochus (vv. 9–12, 23–25). Antiochus's chief sin according to this chapter was his desolation of the Temple, his abolition of the burnt offering in the Temple (vv. 12–13). This moratorium of the two daily sacrifices would continue for 1,150 days (2,300 mornings and evenings, v. 14), a little more than three years. As in chap. 7, this prediction was made before the actual restoration of sacrifice in 165—just three years after its cessation. Like chap. 7, vv. 11–12 and 24–25 depict Antiochus's actions as a challenge against heaven, an attack against the angelic host.[27] The imagery is reminiscent of Isaiah 14:12–14. There the arrogance of the king of Babylon is described in terms of the ancient Canaanite myth about Athtar, the god who attempts to sit on El's throne but must descend to earth. Although Antiochus magnifies himself he will be cut down. By no human hand, that is, by God himself, he will be broken (cf. Dan 2:34).

Daniel 9

In v. 2 "Daniel" ponders the meaning of Jeremiah's prophecy that Jerusalem would remain desolate for seventy years (Jer 25:11–12; 29:10). In reality, a writer in Antiochan times is speaking about the king's desolation of the Temple. Daniel's prayer for enlightenment is answered by the appearance of Gabriel, who interprets the meaning of the seventy years (vv. 21–27). It refers to seventy weeks of years, that is, 490 years. The precise meaning of this chronology is obscure.[28] The author breaks it down into three periods. The first of these ends in 538 with the appearance of an anointed one, either Zerubbabel or Joshua the high priest. The second period ends when an anointed one is cut off—evidently a reference to the removal or death of Onias III. The last week of years is the time of Antiochus's actions regarding Jerusalem. For a half week (three and a half years), the sacrifice would cease in Jerusalem. This chronology approximates that in chaps. 7 and 8.

Verses 4–19 are a long prayer calling for the restoration of Jerusalem and the return of the Dispersion. The Deuteronomic pattern is presumed. The nation's present condition is a curse for their violation of the Law of Moses (v. 11). Their prayer reflects the repentance required for salvation and restoration. Clearly the prayer is part of a tradition that is also witnessed to in Baruch 1:15–2:35.[29] In its present context it fits the typical literary pattern: prayer, epiphany.[30] Many scholars have argued that the prayer is a later interpolation that has been made to fit the context by the addition of v. 20, which duplicates v. 21,[31] expanding it to fit the contents of the prayer.

Daniel 10–12

These chapters constitute the most detailed revelation in the second part of Daniel.

A. Introduction			10:1–11:2a
B. The Revelation			11:2b–12:3
1. Historical Events		11:2b–39	
a. Persia	11:2b		
b. Alexander	11:3		
c. Breakup of the kingdom	11:4		
d. Wars between Syria and Egypt	11:5–9		
e. Antiochus III	11:10–19		
f. Seleucus IV	11:20		
g. Antiochus IV	11:21–39		
2. The Time of the End		11:40–12:3	
a. Events on earth	11:40–45		
b. Judgment, resurrection, eternal life	12:1–3		
C. Conclusion			12:4–13

In its broadest outlines this section employs the structure typical of biblical epiphanies and commissioning scenes:[32] (1) circumstantial introduction, 10:2–4; (2) appearance of the revealer figure, 10:5–7; (3) reaction, 10:7b–10; (4) response and reassurance, 10:11–12; (3') reaction, 10:15–17; (4') reassurance, 10:18–19; (5) message or commission, 11:2b–12:3; (6) conclusion, 12:4–13. In two significant aspects, however, these chapters differ from prophetic commissionings. First, the message given to the seer is not a brief oracle but a long prediction of events to come. Second, the seer is not to proclaim this message but to write it down and seal the book until "the time of the end," when the events described will come to pass (12:4). At that time the wise will read it and understand that it refers to their own time (12:9–10). The idea is paralleled in the *Testament of Moses* (see above, pp. 80–81). The author is conscious of living at the time of the end, and he writes the book for his community. If one breaks the pseudepigraphic code, the command to seal the book until its publication at the end-time is really a command for the author to proclaim his revelation to his contemporaries. In this sense, the present text functions like a prophetic commissioning.

The primary content of the revelation is a recitation of selected events in the history of the Macedonian kingdom, particularly the dealings of the Ptolemies and the Seleucids with each other and with the Jews. This historical and earthly level has a corresponding heavenly and mythical level, on which there is a multitude of patron angels for the nations of the earth. War between the kings and the nations involves on the heavenly level a battle between their angelic princes. As Daniel is receiving the revelation during the reign of Cyrus, Michael the patron angel of Israel is battling with the "prince of Persia" (10:13). When the latter is defeated Persia will fall (10:20). Then a battle will ensue with the prince of Greece (10:20). His fall will coincide with the death of Antiochus.[33]

Although the revelation is set in the time of Cyrus the author moves quickly to the rise of the Macedonian Empire and beyond it, to the conflicts between the Ptolemies and the Seleucids, the kings of the south and the kings of the north.[34] He details the campaigns of Antiochus III at Raphia (11:11–12) and the Panion (11:15) and his defeat by the Romans at Magnesia (11:18). Although Antiochus III had done many good things for the Jews, for this author he was another example of royal arrogance (vv. 16, 18). Antiochus's son Seleucus is mentioned in a single verse with reference to the incident of Heliodorus (11:20; cf. 2 Macc 3). The narrative then moves on to Antiochus IV, whose reign is portrayed as unmitigatedly evil.

Verses 30–35 describe Antiochus's relationship with the Jews. He makes common cause with the Hellenizers, "who forsake the covenant" (v. 30). Then he desecrates the Temple, halts the sacrifice, and constructs the idolatrous "desolating sacrilege" (v. 31). Verses 32–35 refer to his persecution of the Jewish people. Special mention is accorded "the wise," who "make many understand." These are the teachers who help the people stand fast in the persecution. Some of their number are put to death. The author of Daniel was doubtless one of these "wise," and his book was likely intended to help in the process of teaching and exhorting the people.[35]

In 11:36–39 the author employs biblical language to describe Antiochus's arrogant defiance of God as he storms heaven.[36] Verse 40 opens a new section. We have arrived at the "time of the end." Again the author draws heavily on biblical passages, believing that the prophets had foretold how things would be at the time of the end.[37]

In 11:40–12:3 the author moves from the historical back to the angelic and mythical realm. It is time for Michael to confront the heavenly prince of Greece. The patron angel of Israel takes his stand for the final battle.[38]

Michael is both the warrior chieftain of the heavenly armies and God's appointed agent in the judgment. The final battle has the character of judgment. It will be a time of unprecedented trouble. Michael will strike down the demonic power behind Antiochus and his kingdom.

The judgment will also separate between the righteous and wicked of Israel, that is, the Hellenizers and the pious Jews. Only those whose names are written in the book of the living will be saved.

The judgment will extend also to the dead:

> Many of those who sleep in the land of dust will awake,
>   some to everlasting life, some to everlasting contempt. (12:2)

Here the author deals with the problem of the righteous who were unjustly put to death because they chose to obey the Torah. God will right the injustice of their deaths by raising them to a new life. Similarly, the apostates who have died will be raised in order to be punished.

In chap. 11 the author mentioned the "wise" who made many to understand. Their special role during the persecution will entitle them to special glory at the end-time.

> And those who are wise will shine like the brightness of the firmament,
>   and those who bring many to righteousness, like the stars forever and ever.
>   (12:3)

Although the author uses the language of simile, he may be implying an exaltation to heaven. As in the *Testament of Moses* 10:9 the barrier between the heavenly and the earthly breaks down, and man is brought into the place of God himself. Our author draws on the language of Isaiah 52:13 and 53:11, identifying the righteous teachers of his time with the suffering Servant of the Lord, whom God would exalt. The tradition on which he was drawing will recur in other writings that have their roots in this time.[39]

In his concluding section the author speaks of the period of time until the end. As in chaps. 7, 8, and 9, there will be three to three and a half years between the cessation of sacrifice and the end (12:7, 11). Verse 12 appears to be a later recalculation of this time.

There are a number of similarities among Daniel 10–12 and *Jubilees* 23:16ff. and the *Testament of Moses*. All three have a similar outline, as we noted above (recitation of historical events, judgment, new age). All three await the destruction of death. The *Book of Jubilees* and the *Testament of Moses* speak of the end of Satan. The same idea is implied in the mention of Michael, whose angelic opponent, the epitome of anti-God, is the equivalent of Satan.[40] Like *Jubilees* and the *Testament of Moses* Daniel notes the distinction between the righteous Jews and the Hellenizers, who forsake the covenant. However, the pattern of sin-punishment-repentance is missing in Daniel 11. Antiochus's action against the righteous is not construed as punishment for sin.

The visions in Daniel 7–12 were composed at some time between Antiochus's desecration of the Temple (December 167) and Judas's recapture of the Temple mount in 164. In 11:34 the author perhaps makes passing and not very complimentary reference to the battles of Judas. Judgment will come not by human hand but by direct divine intervention, and it will come quickly. Each of the visions posits a period of three to three and a half years.

THE COMPOSITION OF DANIEL 1–12

Sometime during the persecution of Antiochus the four visions in Daniel 7–12 were collected and attached to the collection of stories in chaps. 1–6. The appropriateness of the stories is evident. Chapters 1, 3, and 6 describe faith and piety under pressure. The three youths and Daniel are examples of the persecuted righteous. Nebuchadnezzar in chap. 3 could readily be understood as a king like Antiochus. The willingness of the young men to go to their death with no expectation of deliverance (3:18) would have been especially appropriate during Antiochus's persecution. The two sections of Daniel are also connected through their portrait of Daniel. In the stories Daniel is depicted as a wise man who was able to predict the future through the interpretation of dreams. In chaps. 7–12 Daniel is himself the recipient of visions about the future. Not only do these visions predict the future, they also bring the readers up to current events and thus assure them that they stand at the brink of the judgment, when God will destroy the oppressor and initiate the new age with all its blessings. The book is itself part of the exhortatory task of the wise.

1 ENOCH 83–90

First Enoch 83–90 contains two "dream visions" about future events that Enoch saw when he was a young man. In the first of these he foresaw the Flood (chaps. 83–84). The narrative in chap. 83 parallels stories about Noah in *1 Enoch* 65 and 106–7,[41] and the prayer in chap. 84 is probably dependent on the angelic prayer in *1 Enoch* 9 (see above, p. 50).

In his second dream vision (chaps. 85–90) Enoch saw the history of the world played out in allegorical form. Human beings are depicted as animals,[42] the sinful angels are fallen stars, and the seven archangels are human beings.[43]

The apocalypse begins with a resumé of Genesis 2–5 (85:3–10). All the dramatis personae are depicted as cattle, either bulls or heifers. For his account of the events described in Genesis 6:1–4 (chaps. 86–88) the author has drawn heavily on *1 Enoch* 6–11 (see above, pp. 49–51). The first star to fall is 'Asael (86:1–3; 88:1; cf. *1 Enoch* 10:4). Other stars descend from heaven, become bulls, and mate with the heifers (i.e., women), thus producing camels, elephants, and asses (i.e., the giants, 86:3–6).[44] The tendency to make 'Asael the chief of the rebel angels is clearly at work here, and Shemihazah is not at all distinguished from his companions.[45] The four archangels, Sariel, Gabriel, Michael, and Raphael, have the same functions here as in *1 Enoch* 6–11. The three other angels who escort Enoch to heaven (or paradise) have their counterparts in Uriel, Remiel, and Raguel, who are part of Enoch's angelic entourage in his journey through the heavenly world in *1 Enoch* 17–19, 20–36, and 81:5.[46]

Although our author is aware of the typology between primordial history and the end-time employed in *1 Enoch* 6–11, and although he himself implies it, he nevertheless maintains a clear distinction between the two periods. The fall of the angels, the birth of the giants, the binding of the angels, the destruction of the giants, and the Flood are events of past history. Thus he provides a detailed account of the Flood (89:1–9; cf. Gen 6:13–9:29), whereas in *1 Enoch* 6–11 the Flood is mainly a type of the coming judgment, which is described in detail. On the other hand our author has moved humanity's cry to heaven (8:4), the angelic intercession (9:1–11), and the description of a renewed earth (10:7–11:2) from the narrative about Noachic times to his description of the last times (89:76; 90:3, 12–14, 20–38).

With the death of Noah the menagerie begins to diversify, signifying a developing differentiation between the patriarchs of Israel and the Gentiles. From the red and black bulls, who represent Ham and Japheth, there arise many species of animals and fowl, all of them unclean by Jewish standards and many of them predators. From the line of Shem, a white bull, come Abraham and Isaac, also white bulls. Thereafter cattle become an extinct species, and we enter a second period in world history, marked by the creation of Israel. To Isaac are born a black wild boar—

a derogatory representation of Esau, the patriarch of the hated Edomites —and a white sheep, Jacob, the patriarch of the twelve tribes of Israel (89:10–12).

The image of Israel as sheep is of course a common biblical metaphor,[47] but the author employs it consistently with two biblical nuances that are fundamental to his interpretation of Israelite history. First, the sheep are often blinded and go astray; that is, that nation is guilty of unbelief and apostasy (89:32–33, 41, 51–54, 74; 90:8).[48] The author's second nuance is that the sheep of Israel are frequently the helpless victims of the wild beasts that represent the Gentiles, often as divine punishment for their apostasy (89:13–21, 42, 55–57; 90:2–4, 11–13, 16).[49]

Israel's mounting apostasy leads to a new period in the nation's history, which begins with either the Assyrian conquest or Babylonian conquest (89:59ff.). The Lord of the sheep summons seventy angelic shepherds who will pasture the sheep until the end-time. The conception is a conflation of several biblical ideas:[50] the guardian angels of the (seventy) nations;[51] the term "shepherd" used to describe the leaders of God's sheep;[52] the idea that these shepherds are derelict in their duty and will be called to task;[53] the interpretation of Jeremiah's prediction of seventy years to refer to seventy periods of time.[54] For our author the shepherds are angelic patrons or overseers, each "on duty" for a particular period of time (89:64; 90:5). Over against these angels stands another angel, who records their misdeeds and pleads Israel's case before God (89:61–64, 68–71, 76–77; 90:14, 17, 20, 22). He is the equivalent of Michael in Daniel 12:1 and the angel in the *Testament of Moses* 10:2 and is probably to be identified with Michael (90:22).

Like *Jubilees* 23, the *Testament of Moses*, and Daniel 7–12 this apocalypse focuses in considerable detail on events during the Seleucid rule. This is a time of unmitigated violence. The sheep are picked clean to the bone (90:2–4). It is also a time of awakening. The younger generation (the pious Jews) open their eyes and appeal to the older ones (the Hellenizers) to return from their wickedness, but to no avail (90:6–8; cf. *Jub.* 23:16–20). The violence continues in the death of Onias III (90:8) and Antiochus's and Apollonius's attacks against Jerusalem (90:9–11). The text is difficult to decipher at this point. Verses 13–15 closely parallel vv. 16–18. We have either duplicate versions of the same block of text[55] or an updating of the original text of the apocalypse.[56] In any event, in the present form of the apocalypse the action centers around the ram with a great horn, namely, Judas Maccabeus. Verses 13–14 very likely reflect the tradition about a heavenly apparition at the battle of Beth Zur recounted in 2 Maccabees 11:6–12.[57]

The historical section of the apocalypse concludes with a theophany (90:18). God appears in order to judge (v. 20).[58] A threefold judgment is executed against the rebel angels (v. 24; cf. 10:7, 12), the disobedient shepherds (v. 25), and the apostate Jews (vv. 26–27; cf. 10:14). These last are cast into the fire of the Valley of Hinnom in full sight of Jerusalem.[59]

With the judgment complete, a new and final era begins. God removes the old Jerusalem and sets up a new one (90:28–29). All the Gentiles come to pay homage to the Jews (v. 30; cf. Dan 7:14, 27). The dispersed people of God return, and perhaps the dead are raised (90:33).[60] The sword given to the sheep is sealed up, for an era of peace has begun (90:34). However, the real sign of the new age is the birth of a white bull and the transformation of all the beasts and birds into white bulls or cattle (vv. 37–38). The first white bull may be the Messiah,[61] although he has no active function here. More important is the imagery. The end-time is a reversion to the primordial time of creation. Like Adam this white bull is the first of many. The distinction between Jew and Gentile is obliterated (cf. *1 Enoch* 10:21). Therewith ends the strife between the sheep and the beasts and birds of prey. Israel's victimization at the hands of the Gentiles has ceased.

The outline of *1 Enoch* 85–90 parallels *Jubilees* 23, the *Testament of Moses,* and Daniel 10–12, though with its own nuances. This historical survey from creation to end-time is much more extensive.[62] A pattern of sin and punishment appears in the sections about Israel. The author's use of allegory is reminiscent of Daniel 7–8 but is far more detailed. In a way that is similar to Daniel 7–12 the author describes reality on two levels: the earthly realm of history and the heavenly sphere of angelic activity. It is from the latter that effective prayer for deliverance comes.

Although the author writes (or the apocalypse is revised) during the campaigns of Judas Maccabeus, that is, between 164 (Beth Zur) and 160 (Judas's death), no mention is made of Antiochus's decrees and his pollution of the Temple. This surprising omission may be due to the nature of the author's imagery[63] or to his tendency to concentrate on the clashes between Israel and the Gentiles. On the other hand it may be related to the author's stated opinion on the Second Temple. From the time of its rebuilding, all the bread on the altar was polluted and not pure (89:73). Taken at face value this statement mitigates the effect of Antiochus's deed. The Second Temple was polluted from its construction. This radical attitude is reminiscent of a similar statement in the *Testament of Moses* 4:8.[64]

In his celebration of the militant resistance of Judas Maccabeus this author differs from the passive resistance espoused by the authors of the *Testament of Moses* and Daniel.[65]

SUMMARY

We have discussed in this chapter a series of writings from the period of Antiochus IV which purport to be revelations received in various ways[66] and transmitted by ancient prophets and sages. While the phenomenon of pseudonymity may suggest that in the Antiochan period prophecy in one's own name was not credible among many, the fact remains that behind these pseudonyms lies the authors' conviction that they had a revealed message to transmit. We know little enough about the sources and psychology of this self-consciousness. It is noteworthy, however, that often it is connected with an interpretation of Scripture. The author of the *Book of Jubilees* rewrites Genesis and Exodus. The *Testament of Moses* is a detailed contemporizing explication of the last chapters of Deuteronomy. In chap. 9 Daniel ponders over Jeremiah's seventy years until an angel reveals its "true" meaning. The author of Daniel 10–12 clothes his references to contemporary events in the language of biblical prophecy. Thus the belief that one lived in the last times was bound up at least in part with the conviction that these times were predicted and described in ancient prophecy.

In *Jubilees* 23, the *Testament of Moses*, Daniel (especially chaps. 10–12), and *1 Enoch* 85–90 the message of the imminent end is embodied in the form of historical apocalypses, which bring one in increasing detail up to the present moment. By describing events that lie behind him the real author seeks credibility for his message about the imminent future. By ascribing the whole to a sage of the remote past he builds into his apocalypse a determinism that views both the past and the future which he forecasts as irrevocable.[67] The extensive linear sweep of these historical surveys is complemented by a vertical cross section of the universe that sees a cosmic reality operative simultaneously in heaven and earth. The heavenly and earthly levels come together in the end-time, when God or his agents touch history with finality. Either (righteous) humanity is assumed to heaven, or the earth is transformed into the realm where God's intent and sovereignty are finally and fully realized.

In their claim to revelation and their conviction that God will soon act in superlative fashion to right the wrongs of an unjust world, these authors express an apocalyptic eschatology that is reminiscent of Third Isaiah. In their use of pseudonymity and their dependence on Scripture (including Third Isaiah), their long deterministic historical surveys, the prominence of their two-storied view of reality, and their extension of God's future judgment and deliverance to include the dead, they have transcended the apocalyptic eschatology of Third Isaiah in qualitative and significant fashion.

Not all revelatory literature from this period took the form of historical apocalypses. In *1 Enoch* 12–36 the message of an imminent judgment was carried in a commissioning scene based on Ezekiel 1–2 and in reports of a series of cosmic journeys.[68]

NOTES

1. I use the term "pious" to refer to those Jews who oppose their compatriots' Hellenizing ways. They are usually called *Ḥasidim* in the scholarly literature. This Hebrew term, which may be roughly translated "loyalists" (i.e., those loyal to the Torah), is used of a "group of mighty warriors" who made common cause with Mattathias (1 Macc 2:42). However, on the difficulties of using this term broadly and indiscriminately see J. Collins, *The Apocalyptic Vision of the Book of Daniel,* HSM 16 (Missoula: Scholars Press, 1977) 201–5.

2. See 1:27, 29; 2:1; cf. also 18:9–11; 30:17–21; chap. 48.

3. For similar stories, see *T. Job* 1–5 and *Apoc. Abr.* 1–2. On these books see below, pp. 241–42, 294–95.

4. The author refers to ten trials but does not mention all ten (cf. 17:17–18). For a later, rabbinic reference to the traditions see *m. Abot* 5:4.

5. The motif of Abraham's faithfulness in connection with the sacrifice becomes traditional. Cf. Sir 44:20 (which is older than *Jubilees*); 1 Macc 2:52; Jdt 8:24–27; Heb 11:17; Jas 2:21–23.

6. Cf., e.g., chaps. 10; 11; 17:16; 48:2–19.

7. On the children chiding the parents cf. *1 Enoch* 90:6. On this section of *1 Enoch* see below, pp. 91–94.

8. For a more detailed discussion of the dating see James C. VanderKam, *Textual and Historical Studies in the Book of Jubilees,* 207–85; and Nickelsburg, "Bible," 101–3.

9. Cf. 1 Macc 1:15; 2 Macc 4:12–14; Jos. *Ant.* 12.241 (12.5.1).

10. See the detailed discussion by VanderKam, *Textual and Historical Studies,* 207–85.

11. See my review of VanderKam in *JAOS* 100 (1980) 84.

12. Suggested to me by VanderKam.

13. One could harmonize the two dates by positing two stages of composition, as does Gene L. Davenport (*The Eschatology of the Book of Jubilees*, 10–18); however, see Nickelsburg, "Bible," 102.

14. For these similarities, as well as for differences, see VanderKam, *Textual and Historical Studies*, 258–82.

15. Nickelsburg, "Bible," 103; Collins, *Apocalyptic Vision*, 205–10.

16. On these texts and versions, as well as on the Latin version, of which a sizable part has been preserved, see VanderKam, *Textual and Historical Studies*, 1–18.

17. On the identification of this work see R. H. Charles, *The Assumption of Moses*, xlv–l.

18. See the papers of J. Collins, G. Nickelsburg, and J. Goldstein in George W. E. Nickelsburg, ed., *Studies on the Testament of Moses*, 15–52.

19. The one extant manuscript of the *Testament of Moses* is missing its last page or pages, and we must surmise how it ended. It is curious that the announcement of Moses' death in chap. 1 must wait nine chapters for Joshua's response (11:1). Perhaps an old narrative expansion of Deut 30–34 has been reworked with the material about the history of Israel; cf. Günther Reese, "Die Geschichte Israels in der Auffassung des frühen Judentums," 89–93.

20. For an ingenious attempt to see behind chap. 6 an earlier description of the attacks of Antiochus and Apollonius see J. Goldstein, "The Testament of Moses: Its Content, Its Origin, and Its Attestation in Josephus," in *Studies on the Testament of Moses*, 44–47.

21. Collins, *Apocalyptic Vision*, 198–201.

22. Cf. the discussion of *1 Enoch* 12–16 above, pp. 53–54; and the discussion of *1 Enoch* 83–90 below, pp. 93–94.

23. Charles, *Assumption*, xxxvi–xlv; D. H. Wallace, "The Semitic Origin of the Assumption of Moses," *TZ* 11 (1955) 321–28.

24. For an important discussion of myth and symbol in Dan 7–12 see Collins, *Apocalyptic Vision*, 95–152. On this issue and in other specific matters I am indebted to this work.

25. For a more elaborate use of this pattern of vision and interpretation see the discussion of *1 Enoch* 20–36 above, pp. 54–55.

26. The Aramaic of 7:17 reads "four kings." By changing one easily confused letter we get "four kingdoms," which is the reading of the Greek and Latin translations. This is supported by the Aramaic and the versions of 7:23, which explain the fourth beast as a "fourth kingdom."

27. Collins, *Apocalyptic Vision*, 106–8. On the background of this idea in Isa 14 see Nickelsburg, *Resurrection*, 14–15, 69–70.

28. R. H. Charles, *A Critical and Exegetical Commentary on the Book of Daniel* (Oxford: Clarendon, 1929) 242–52.

29. C. A. Moore, *Daniel, Esther, and Jeremiah: The Additions*, AB 44 (Garden City, N.Y.: Doubleday, 1977) 291–93. Cf. also the Qumran prayer called "The Words of the Heavenly Lights," Vermes, *Scrolls*, 202–5.

30. Cf., e.g., *1 Enoch* 12–16; *3 Bar* 1; Tob 3; Luke 3:21–22; 9:29; cf. also above, Chapter 1, n. 28, and the unquestionable instance of an interpolated

prayer.

31. Charles, *Daniel*, 226–27; Collins, *Apocalyptic Vision*, 185–87.

32. See B. Hubbard, *The Matthean Redaction of a Primitive Apostolic Commissioning*, SBLDS 19 (Missoula: Scholars Press, 1974) 25–67. The revelations in the New Testament book of Revelation are framed by the same structure in chaps. 1 and 22:6–19.

33. This portrayal of two corresponding levels of reality here and in chaps. 7–8 has precursors in ancient Israelite literature; cf. Judg 5:19–20.

34. R. Clifford, "History and Myth in Daniel 10–12," *BA* 220–21 (1975–76) 23–25.

35. Collins, *Apocalyptic Vision*, 212–14.

36. Clifford, "History and Myth," 25.

37. Ibid.

38. On this and other matters relating to the interpretation of 12:1–3 see Nickelsburg, *Resurrection*, 11–27.

39. See below, pp. 178–79, 219–20.

40. Nickelsburg, *Resurrection*, 11–15.

41. See the discussion in Nickelsburg, "Bible," 93–95.

42. Noah and Moses are transformed (temporarily?) into human beings evidently so that they can carry out tasks inappropriate to animals, namely, building the ark and tabernacle (note the use of the passive in 89:50 with respect to the temple). Cf. also 86:3, where the stars become bulls in order to mate with heifers.

43. Cf. Dan 8:15 and 7:13, where one like a son of man is perhaps contrasted with the beasts.

44. For reference to three kinds of giants cf. Sycellus's text of *1 Enoch* 7:2–3, which is supported by *Jub.* 7:22.

45. On this tendency in *1 Enoch* see Milik, *Books of Enoch*, 43.

46. *First Enoch* 20 mentions these three angels in addition to the other four. In chaps. 21–36 the seven escort the seer through the universe, and in 81:5 either the seven or the three (the texts differ) return him to earth.

47. Cf., e.g., Ps 74:1; 79:13; 95:7; Isa 53:6; Jer 50:6; Ezek 34; Zech 13:7.

48. On blindness cf. Isa 56:10; 59:9–10; on straying cf. Ps 119:176; Isa 53:6; Jer 50:6.

49. See esp. Ezek 34 and its juxtaposition of scattered sheep, wild beasts, and derelict shepherds.

50. R. H. Charles, *APOT* 2:255; M. Hengel, *Judaism and Hellenism* (E.T.; Philadelphia: Fortress, 1974) 1:187–88.

51. Deut 32:8; Sir 17:17; *Jub.* 15:31; Dan 10:13, 20.

52. Isa 56:11; Ezek 34; Zech 13:7.

53. Ibid.

54. Jer 25:11–12; 29:10, as interpreted in Dan 9:2, 24–27.

55. Charles, *APOT* 2:258.

56. See the detailed discussion ʰy Jonathan A. Goldstein, *1 Maccabees*, 41, esp. n. 12.

57. Ibid.; Milik, *Books of Enoch*, 44.

58. Cf. also *1 Enoch* 1 and *T. Mos.* 10:3–7.

59. The idea is also implied in Dan 12:2; Nickelsburg, *Resurrection*, 19–23.

60. The term "destroyed" is ambiguous, but it may refer to the dead.
61. Charles, *APOT* 2:260.
62. For a (very sketchy) apocalypse with almost the same scope cf. the Apocalypse of Weeks, *1 Enoch* 93:1–10 + 91:11–17, on which see below, p. 146.
63. See above, n. 42. By analogy with 89:1, 9, 36, 38 the construction of the desolating sacrilege would require that the birds representing the Seleucids be transformed into men.
64. See Goldstein, "Testament of Moses" 48–50.
65. Collins, *Apocalyptic Vision*, 194–210.
66. In the *Book of Jubilees* Moses is the recipient of angelic revelation. In *1 Enoch* 85–90 Enoch receives a dream vision which is not interpreted. In Dan 7–12 there is an angelic mediator or interpreter. In the *Testament of Moses* there is no indication of the source of the prophet's message.
67. See Collins, *Apocalyptic Vision*, 80, 87–88. Connected to this determinism is a sense of order implied in the periodizing of history, for example, in the Animal Apocalypse.
68. For an entrée into the problems of defining revelatory literature see J. Collins, "Apocalypse: Toward the Morphology of a Genre," *Semeia* 14 (1979) 1–20.

BIBLIOGRAPHY

HISTORY

Schürer, *History,* 1:137–63. Elias J. **Bickerman,** *The God of the Maccabees,* SJLA 32 (Leiden: Brill, 1979). **Tcherikover,** *Hellenistic Civilization,* 117–203, more detailed account with emphasis on social and economic factors. Martin **Hengel,** *Judaism and Hellenism* (E.T.; Philadelphia: Fortress, 1974) 1:175–218, 255–314. Jonathan A. **Goldstein,** *1 Maccabees,* AB 41 (Garden City, N.Y.: Doubleday, 1976) 104–73, detailed reconstruction of the civic and political policies of Antiochus IV.

THE BOOK OF JUBILEES

TRANSLATION: Orval S. **Wintermute,** *PsOT.*

TEXT AND OTHER TRANSLATIONS: R. H. **Charles,** *The Ethiopic Version of the Hebrew Book of Jubilees,* Anecdota Oxoniensia (Oxford: Clarendon, 1895), critical edition of the Ethiopic text and the Greek, Syriac, and Latin fragments. Idem, *APOT* 2:1–82.

LITERATURE: R. H. **Charles,** *The Book of Jubilees* (Oxford: Clarendon, 1902), introduction, translation, brief commentary. M. **Testuz,** *Les idées religieuses du Livre des Jubilés* (Geneva: Druz, 1960), introduction to the thought of the book. Gene L. **Davenport,** *The Eschatology of the Book of Jubilees,* SPB 20 (Leiden: Brill, 1971). James C. **VanderKam,** *Textual and Historical Studies in the Book of Jubilees,* HSM 14 (Missoula: Scholars Press, 1977), comparison of all published Qumran Hebrew fragments with the Ethiopic manuscripts, discussion of the biblical text employed in *Jubilees,* detailed investigation of the book's date and relationship to the Qumran community. For other bibliography see **Nickelsburg,** "Bible," 152–53.

THE TESTAMENT OF MOSES

TRANSLATION: John **Priest,** *PsOT*.

TEXT AND OTHER TRANSLATIONS: R. H. **Charles,** *The Assumption of Moses* (London: Black, 1897), Latin text, introduction, translation, brief commentary. Idem, *APOT* 2:407–24.

LITERATURE: George W. E. **Nickelsburg,** ed., *Studies on the Testament of Moses,* SBLSCS 4 (Cambridge: Society of Biblical Literature, 1973), papers on the date, provenance, form, and function. On the figure of Taxo see: Charles C. **Torrey,** " 'Taxo' in the Assumption of Moses," *JBL* 62 (1943) 1–7; H. H. **Rowley,** "The Figure of 'Taxo' in the Assumption of Moses," *JBL* 64 (1945) 141–43; Charles C. **Torrey,** " 'Taxo' Once More," *JBL* 64 (1945) 395–97; Sigmund **Mowinckel,** "The Hebrew Equivalent of Taxo in Ass. Mos. ix," in *Congress Volume, Copenhagen 1953,* VTSup 1 (Leiden: Brill, 1953) 88–96; Jacob **Licht,** "Taxo, or the Apocalyptic Doctrine of Vengeance," *JJS* 12 (1961) 95–103; **Nickelsburg,** *Resurrection,* 97–102.

DANIEL

See bibliography for Chapter 1.

1 ENOCH 85–90

TEXTS AND TRANSLATIONS: See bibliography for Chapter 2.

LITERATURE: Günther **Reese,** "Die Geschichte Israels in der Auffassung des frühen Judentums" (Diss. Heidelberg, 1967) 21–68.

4

The Hasmoneans and Their Opponents

FROM JUDAS TO ALEXANDRA[1]

The victories of Judas and the restoration of the Jerusalem cult created new problems for the Jewish people. Perhaps troubled by these evidences of power, the neighboring peoples began to make war on the Jews who lived outside the borders of Judea. Judas and his brothers led a series of sorties against the Idumeans to the south, the Ammonites in Trans-Jordan, and other Gentiles in Galilee and Gilead, and they brought the Jews from these latter two areas back to Judea, where they were resettled safe from Gentile oppression.

Antiochus IV died late in 164 and was succeeded by his young son Antiochus V and his regent Lysias. At the outset of his reign, the new king issued a proclamation that officially rescinded the decrees of Antiochus IV. Jewish religious freedom was now *de jure*.

In 161 Demetrius I, son of Seleucus IV, seized the throne in Antioch, and Antiochus V and Lysias were executed by the army. Demetrius confirmed as high priest a certain Alcimus (Heb. "Yakim"). He replaced Menelaus, whom Lysias had deposed. Alcimus reflects the complexity of the political and religious situation in Judea at this time. He was supported at first by members of the Jewish community who opposed Judas. These were not Hellenizers, however, because Alcimus's credentials satisfied the Ḥasidim, that group of pious Jews who had made common cause with the Hasmoneans against the Hellenizers. After having received the support of the Ḥasidim, Alcimus turned on them and had sixty of them slaughtered in one day. As high priest, Alcimus found an opponent in Judas. When he appealed to the king, Demetrius sent the general Nicanor, who threatened to destroy the Temple if Judas was not turned over to him. In the battle that followed, Nicanor was killed. His head and right hand, "which he had stretched out against the Temple," were cut off and hung up as trophies in Jerusalem.

Judas sought to consolidate his position through an alliance with Rome. Demetrius sent his general Bacchides against Judas at the head of a huge army. Most of Judas's troops deserted him, but he rejected the counsel to retreat. In the bitter battle that ensued, the remnant of the Jewish army was crushed and Judas Maccabeus fell.

The followers of Judas chose his brother Jonathan as their leader, and for seventeen years he maneuvered successfully through a series of Syrian kings and pretenders, developing and consolidating military and political power. In the year 160 Alcimus the high priest ordered the wall of the inner court of the Temple demolished. His death shortly there-after was viewed by some of the Jews as punishment for tearing down this "work of the prophets" (1 Macc 9:54–56). Whether Alcimus had an immediate successor is uncertain, because our sources say little about events in Judea during the next seven years.

Evidently Jonathan had become a force to be reckoned with. In the year 152 Demetrius had to defend his throne against Alexander Balas, a pretender who claimed to be the son of Antiochus IV. Both Demetrius and Alexander sought the help of Jonathan, who sided with Alexander when he appointed Jonathan high priest. A year or two later Jonathan was named civil and military governor of the province of Judea.

In 145 Alexander was deposed by Demetrius II, the son of Demetrius I, whom Alexander had ousted. Although Jonathan had supported Alexander in this rivalry, he was able to win the favor of Demetrius II and to extract concessions from him.

Conflict over the throne of Syria flared up again when Trypho, a general of Alexander, set up Alexander's son Antiochus as a rival of De-metrius. Eventually Jonathan went over to the side of Trypho, who defeated Demetrius. Evidently fearful of Jonathan's growing power, Trypho captured him by treachery and had him murdered. Simon buried his brother in the family tomb in their native city of Modein and assumed the reins of leadership. The year was 143/42.

Events in Syria took yet another turn when Trypho ascended the throne after having Antiochus killed. This time Simon sided with De-metrius, who pardoned past offenses against the crown, legitimized forti-fications, and granted tax exemption. Judea was now politically inde-pendent. "The yoke of the Gentiles was removed from Israel" (1 Macc

13:41). The following year (June 141) Simon succeeded in ending the Gentiles' twenty-seven-year occupation of the citadel in Jerusalem. The next year the people formally acclaimed him high priest, military commander, and ethnarch of the Jews, and it was decreed that he and his family should be high priests *in perpetuum*—at least until God should send a prophet to declare otherwise (1 Macc 14:41). Thus the high-priestly and princely dynasty of the Hasmoneans was founded. For a few years the country was at peace.

When Demetrius II was captured by the Parthians in 139 his brother Antiochus VII took up the struggle against Trypho, and the latter was killed in battle. At first Antiochus confirmed for Simon all the favors granted by past monarchs. Later he revoked these concessions, but he was not able to enforce his will. His army was defeated by Simon's.

Simon's reign would not end on this high point. In 135 he and his sons Mattathias and Judas were feted at a banquet in the fortress of Dok near Jericho. When all three were drunk they were assassinated by Ptolemy, the commander of the fortress and Simon's son-in-law. Some forty years after' Mattathias's revolt the last of the Hasmonean sons had died a violent death.

Simon was succeeded by his surviving son, John Hyrcanus. During the first year of his reign Antiochus VII once again invaded Judea. Besieged in Jerusalem, Hyrcanus sued for peace. The price was high: the demolition of fortifications, heavy tribute, hostages. Hyrcanus had lost the political freedom his father had gained.

Hyrcanus's setback was only temporary. When Antiochus VII was killed he was succeeded by Demetrius II, who returned from captivity. The time was ripe for new conquests. First Hyrcanus struck across the Jordan and took the city of Medeba, then he marched north. Some time earlier the Samaritans had broken religiously with Jerusalem and had built their own temple atop Mount Gerizim near Shechem. John captured the city, razed the temple, and subdued the people. Then he moved south, where he conquered Idumea and forced the Idumeans to submit to circumcision and to accept the Torah. Later he again marched north and captured the important fortified city of Samaria. All this was possible because of the rapidly waning power of the Seleucid Empire during the reigns of Demetrius II and Antiochus VIII and IX.

It is in Josephus's account of Hyrcanus's reign that we first hear of the activities of the religious parties of the Pharisees and the Sadducees.

Previously the Hasmoneans had been favorably disposed to the Pharisees. However, a falling out between Hyrcanus and the Pharisees led to the rise in power of the Sadducees, a group made up largely of priestly aristocrats who traced their descent back to the high priest Zadok.

The thirty-year reign of John Hyrcanus witnessed the expansion of Judea's territorial limits and the growth of its political independence beyond anything that had been known since the Babylonian Exile.

The longest of the Hasmonean reigns was followed by the shortest. Hyrcanus's son Aristobulus ruled for only one year. Defying his father's will, he seized the secular power that had been delegated to his mother, and he cast his brothers and his mother into prison, where his mother died. He assumed the title "king." When Aristobulus died in 103 his widow, Salome Alexandra, released the brothers and bestowed on the eldest, Alexander Janneus (Heb. "Jonathan"), the high priesthood and her hand in marriage.

Alexander's twenty-seven-year reign was marked by frequent wars and many conquests. Extending his control north into Galilee, east into Trans-Jordan, and west along most of the Philistine coast, he governed an Israelite state larger than anything since Solomon. Like his brother, he took the title "king." His reign, however, was badly marred by acts of incredible cruelty and consequent internal strife. On one occasion, when he was executing the high-priestly office on the Feast of Tabernacles, the crowd pelted him with the citrons that they were carrying for ritual purposes. He responded by slaughtering six thousand of the people. Another time, after many Jews had deserted him in a battle against Demetrius III, he crucified eight hundred of his opponents in Jerusalem while, it is said, he caroused with his mistresses and forced the crucified to watch the slaughter of their own wives and children. The antipathy between the Pharisees and the Hasmonean house was exacerbated during this period. After a three-year illness that resulted from overdrinking, Alexander died in 76 B.C.E.

Alexander's widow, Salome Alexandra, ascended the throne and appointed their son Hyrcanus II high priest. Her reign was in general peaceful and prosperous. Reversing the policy of Hyrcanus I and Alexander, she effected rapprochement with the Pharisees. However, when she died in 67 B.C.E. the scene was set for a confrontation between her sons Hyrcanus II and Aristobulus II, which resulted in Judea's annexation into the Roman Empire and the end of its short-lived independence.

JUDITH

For your power depends not upon numbers,
    nor your might upon men of strength.
For you are God of the lowly,
    helper of the oppressed,
    upholder of the weak,
    protector of the forlorn,
    savior of those without help. (Jdt 9:11)

With these words Judith summarizes the central assertion of the book named after her. The plot of the story manifests the truth of this assertion and depicts the characters in diverse reactions to it.

Chapters 1–7 describe the developing crisis facing Israel. Nebuchadnezzar, the epitome of irresistible military might, breaches the impregnable defenses of his enemy to the east, "Arphaxad," and dispatches Holofernes, his general, against the nations that have refused him aid. Holofernes sweeps across Mesopotamia and down into Syria and Palestine (2:21–3:10). The Israelites prepare to resist and seek divine help through prayer and rituals of humiliation (chap. 4). Achior the Ammonite explains to Holofernes why they dare to resist (5:5–21). From their history one can see that their strength is not in their armies but in their God. When they are faithful to him they are invincible. When they sin they go down in defeat. In the present situation, if there is no transgression in the nation they had best be left alone, lest the Assyrian army be put to shame before the whole world (5:21). Holofernes retorts in a mock oracle that acclaims Nebuchadnezzar as the only God, the lord of the whole earth, whose command to destroy his enemies will not be in vain (6:2–4). The fundamental tension in the story is now explicit. Who is God? Yahweh or Nebuchadnezzar?[2] When Holofernes's army appears in full array at the city of Bethulia, the people's courage melts (chap. 7). They conclude that God has sold them into the hand of the foreigner, and the exhortations of Uzziah their ruler are futile.

Judith's appearance serves as a turning point in the narrative. Her address to the rulers and her prayer are crucial in several ways (chaps. 8–9). They depict Judith as a person of great faith and as a wise and eloquent spokeswoman of that faith. Through them she presents a formal exposition of the view of God which the book as a whole dramatizes. Her censure of the people expresses the author's criticism of a lack of faith in this God. Judith's prayer wins the help of God.

Judith's wisdom has its practical side, and her faith becomes operative in deed. A clever and resourceful assassin, she allows no detail to escape her preparations (10:1–5). Once she is inside the Assyrian camp, deceit is her *modus operandi* (10:6–12:20). Her great beauty disarms the sentries and the rest of the army, leaving them wide-eyed with wonder and hence blind to her treacherous intent. Playing up to Holofernes's arrogant pretensions, Judith addresses him as if he were the king himself (11:8, 19). Her conversation is a string of lies, half-truths, and double entendres.[3] Dazzled by Judith's beauty Holofernes "loses his head before it has been cut off."[4] His desire to possess Judith provides her with the opportunity she has been awaiting, and she parries his proposition with ambiguous answers (12:14, 18). Tossing caution to the winds Holofernes drinks himself into a stupor. The time for ambiguities has ceased. Judith beheads the drunken general with his own sword and tumbles his body onto the floor. His humiliation "at the hand of a woman" is complete (13:1–10).

The various themes in the story now resolve themselves. Judith returns to the city, proclaiming that God is still with his people, showing mercy to them and destroying their enemies (13:11, 14). The Assyrian camp is the scene of chaos and terror. Bagoas, Holofernes's eunuch, laments their defeat and disgrace, describing the fallen Holofernes as if he were a toppled statue that had lost its head (14:18; cf. Dan 2:34–35). It is evident who alone is God. The God of Israel has fulfilled Achior's warning (5:21; cf. 14:18b). He has vindicated the faith of Uzziah (7:30; 13:14) and especially Judith (8:15–17; 9:11) and has shown the people's despair to have been groundless (7:24–28). He has met Holofernes's challenge (6:3). Nebuchadnezzar's pride has been turned to disgrace, and his attempt to be "lord of the whole earth" (2:5; 6:4) has been foiled by the hand of a woman (9:10; 13:15; 16:6). His army is routed, and we hear no more of him in the book (16:25). Judith's song is a reprise of the central assertion in the book: the God of Israel is the champion of the weak and the oppressed; he destroys the power of the mighty and humbles the pride of the arrogant (16:1–17).

The book of Judith is patently fiction, abounding in anachronisms and historical inaccuracies.[5] Nebuchadnezzar is introduced as king of the Assyrians (1:1), who makes war on Israel *after* their return from the Exile (5:18–19; 4:3). The story combines features of a number of biblical stories,[6] and Judith is a personification of several Israelite heroines: Miriam (Exod 15:20–21), Deborah and Jael (Judg 4–5), the woman of

Thebez (Judg 9:53–54), and the woman of Abel-beth-maacah (2 Sam 20:14–22).

By conflating biblical characters and events the author presents a condensation of Israelite history that has a parabolic quality.[7] It demonstrates how the God of Israel has acted—and continues to act—in history, and it provides models for proper and improper human actions and reactions vis-à-vis this God. The God of Judith is the deliverer of his people, yet he remains sovereign and *not obligated* to act in their behalf (8:15–17). In moments of evident defeat he tests the faith of his people (8:25–27). The citizens of Bethulia and Judith exemplify respectively those who fail the test and those who pass it. Judith's activism is noteworthy. She does not passively await direct divine intervention. Her appeal to the activism of "my father Simeon" is reminiscent of 1 Maccabees 2:24–26, which cites Phineas as a paradigm for Mattathias's activist zeal, and of the laudatory descriptions of Levi's participation in the slaughter at Shechem in the *Testament of Levi* 2–6 and *Jubilees* 30. The book of Judith evinces considerable interest in halakhic matters, depicting Judith and the people faithfully adhering to the commands of God as they were doubtless construed in the author's own time and community.[8]

Judith's speech, at the heart of the book, suggests that the work had a didactic and exhortatory function. In its literary context this formal exposition of the ways of God and exhortation to act accordingly are addressed to the rulers of Bethulia. As the speech is *read*, however, the reader is addressed. At one point in her song Judith speaks like the mother of her people (16:5).[9] As such she also addresses the reader.

The didactic character of the book suggests connections with the wisdom tradition. In the broad outlines of its plot and in certain particulars Judith parallels some of the narrative wisdom literature that we have discussed in Chapter 1. Judith is "wise" (8:29; 11:8, 20–21). The story is reminiscent of Daniel 3. Through his functionary, Holofernes, Nebuchadnezzar challenges the power of Israel's God to deliver his people from the king's hand (6:3; cf. Dan 3:15). As the spokeswoman of that God, Judith maintains that God has the power to save and will do so if he so chooses (8:15–17; cf. Dan 3:17–18). Trusting in him she makes herself the test case. In the end Bagoas must admit that Nebuchadnezzar has been defeated in the contest (14:18; cf. Dan 3:28). In several respects Judith is also reminiscent of Tobit. Each protagonist is depicted as a genuine Israelite (Tob 1:1; Jdt 8:1) whose piety is exemplary and

beyond the call of duty. Like Tobit, the Israelites in Judith are brought
from expressions of despair to the praise of the God who has delivered
them. Both books end with a hymn and reference to the death of the
protagonist.

The book of Judith is especially striking for its feminism. In creating
a protagonist the author has chosen a woman, who calls to mind the
Israelite heroines of the past—Judith, "the Jewess."[10] As the narrative
unfolds, Judith is consistently depicted as superior to the men with whom
she is associated: Uzziah and the elders; the Assyrian army and their
general. Bagoas must admit that "one Hebrew woman has brought disgrace on the house of Nebuchadnezzar" (14:18). At the end of the story
she gains the plaudits of Uzziah, Achior, and Joakim the high priest.
Although some passages seem to be saying that God's power is operative
through the weakest of human agents, that is, a woman (9:10; 14:18;
16:6–7), Judith is no weakling. Her courage, her trust in God, and her
wisdom—all lacking in her male counterparts—save the day for Israel.
Her use of deceit and specifically of her sexuality may seem offensive
and chauvinistic. For the author it is the opposite. Judith wisely chooses
the weapon in her arsenal that is appropriate to her enemy's weakness.
She plays his game, knowing that he will lose. In so doing she makes
fools out of a whole army of men and humiliates their general.

Because the book of Judith is fiction, attempts to date it are always
tenuous, depending as they do upon the identification of the events in
the book with other events in real history. These events are usually
sought in the late Persian period or in the wars of Judas Maccabeus.

Several considerations indicate undeniable influence from the Persian
period.[11] Holofernes and Bagoas have the same names as one of the
generals of Artaxerxes III and his eunuch. Events in the story are paralleled in Artaxerxes's campaign against Phoenicia, Syria, and Egypt in
353 B.C.E.[12] and in the Satraps' Revolt during the reign of Artaxerxes II,
which spread across the western part of the Persian Empire. Many items
in Judith reflect the socio-historical situation during the Persian period.[13]

At the same time the story of Judith has striking similarities to the time
of Judas Maccabeus.[14] Nebuchadnezzar may be understood as a figure
for Antiochus IV.[15] The predominance of Holofernes tallies well with the
presence of a number of Syrian generals in Palestine during the Maccabean uprising. The defeat of a vastly superior invading army parallels
Judas's defeat of the Syrians. Especially noteworthy are the similarities

between this story and Judas's defeat of Nicanor.[16] Although Judith is set shortly after the Return from Exile (4:3) the book speaks not of the rebuilding of the Temple but of the consecration of the vessels, the altar, and the Temple after their profanation. The similarity to Judas's consecration of the Temple is noteworthy (1 Macc 4:36–51). Furthermore, Nicanor's subsequent threat against the Temple, his defeat and decapitation, and the public display of his head in Jerusalem all find remarkable counterparts in the story of Judith (cf. 1 Macc 7:33–50).

If we accept a date in Hasmonean times we can explain two of the patently unhistorical features of the book. The designation of Nebuchadnezzar (= Antiochus) as an Assyrian would correspond to the identification of the Assyria of biblical prophecy with Syria in some of the biblical interpretation of this period.[17] A deliberate allusion to events in the Maccabean wars would explain why the author has described a *post*-exilic threat against the Temple (5:12; 9:8) by a general of the *pre*exilic king. Nicanor's defeat was significant enough to be commemorated in an annual celebration (1 Macc 7:48–49; 2 Macc 15:36).

Neither the connections with the Persian period nor the similarities to the Maccabean wars can be easily dismissed as coincidence. Perhaps we can best solve the problem of dating by suggesting that a tale which originated in the Persian period has been rewritten in Hasmonean times. In its present form the book celebrates God's victories over the Syrians, perhaps using Judith as a personification of Judea. The setting in Bethulia may indicate, however, that the story was originally composed in Samaria near Dothan.[18] It is generally agreed that the Greek form of the book is a translation from a Hebrew archetype.[19]

Long after it was excluded from the canon of the Hebrew Bible the story of Judith continued as a living part of Jewish haggadic tradition.[20] It has also been the inspiration for a great deal of sculpture, painting, and dramatic music.[21]

BARUCH

This is the first of several works attributed to Baruch, the secretary of Jeremiah.[22] The book divides into four sections that are probably of diverse origins: narrative introduction (1:1–14), prayer (1:15–3:8), Wisdom poem (3:9–4:4), and Zion poem (4:5–5:9). These sections are bound together by the common theme of Exile and Return, which is often expressed in biblical idiom.

The introduction describes the alleged purpose of the book and circumstances of its origin. In the fifth year after the destruction of Jerusalem (i.e., in 582 B.C.E.), Baruch assembled the Jewish leaders in Babylon for a formal hearing of the book.[23] Then after rituals of repentance (1:5) they contributed money to be sent to Jerusalem together with the Temple vessels that Nebuchadnezzar had taken as booty (1:6–9). The high priest was to offer sacrifice, pray for Nebuchadnezzar and his son Belshazzar, and intercede for the exiles (1:10–13). Proper sacrifice could be offered only at the Temple site, and the prayer that follows was to accompany the sacrifice and also be prayed "on the days of the feasts and at appointed seasons."

The prayer is comprised of a corporate confession of sins and a petition that God will withdraw his wrath and return the exiles to their homeland.[24] Its logic follows the scheme of Deuteronomy 28–32, and the language of both Deuteronomy and Jeremiah has heavily influenced its wording.[25] Verbal parallels to Daniel 9:4–19 indicate a very close relationship also to that prayer.[26]

The inhabitants of Jerusalem are first to confess their own sins (1:15–2:5).[27] The people are to acknowledge God's righteousness, confess their rebellion against covenant and the prophetic word, and admit that they are now suffering the curses of the covenant, which Moses predicted in Deuteronomy. The repetition of the confession (1:17–18, 21) and the admission that this sin has continued to the present (1:19–20)—both missing in Daniel 9[28]—underscore the sense of guilt that pervades the prayer. Also lacking in Daniel 9 is a counterpart to 2:3–5, which reflects Deuteronomy 28:53, 13.

In a second, parallel confession the people in Jerusalem are to speak in the name of the exiles (2:6–10). Again the sense of guilt is expressed by a double confession (2:8, 10) and by the admission that the people have not turned away from their evil thoughts (2:8, missing in Dan 9:8).

The petitionary section of the prayer (2:11–18) begins with the formulaic "And now. . . ." Here, as throughout the prayer (and the introduction), God is addressed by his proper name, YHWH (translated "Lord"), and the covenantal relationship is indicated by the title "God of Israel" (cf. 3:1, 4; and "our God," passim) and by reference to the Exodus (cf. 1:20). The petition itself is preceded by yet another confession of sin (2:12). The exiles pray that God's wrath will turn from them (2:13), that he will deliver his people and grant them favor with their captors

(2:14), and that he will look down and consider his people (2:16–17). The language of Exodus 3:7–8, 20–21 is reflected throughout this passage, for the author, like Second Isaiah, construes return from Exile as a second Exodus (see above, pp. 11–12). Each of the three parts of the petition differs from its Danielic counterpart by referring to the situation in Exile rather than to the desolation of the Temple (cf. Dan 9:16–18).

In his penultimate word in 9:18 Daniel contrasts the people's lack of righteousness with God's mercy, to which he appeals as the grounds for God's action. Baruch 2:19 contrasts the fathers' lack of righteousness with God's mercy and employs this thought as a transition to yet another confession of sin (2:20–26). (At this point this prayer continues at length beyond Daniel 9.) The people fell under God's wrath because they did not obey the prophetic warning to submit to the king of Babylon (cf. Jer 27:11–12). The motif is reminiscent of Baruch's admonition in 1:11–12.[29] The pattern of sin and the fulfillment of predicted punishment (2:20–24) parallels 1:20–2:1.

In 2:27–35 the prayer returns to Deuteronomy for a word of hope.[30] Although God predicted punishment for sin, he promised that when the people repented in the land of their Exile he would return them to their land, increase their numbers, and make an everlasting covenant with them. In 3:1–8 the people do precisely what God had said they would do (cf. 2:31–33 and 3:7–8). The prayer breaks off without an explicit request for return, but the implications are clear.

Chapters 3:9–4:4 contain a Wisdom poem in the tradition of Sirach 24 (see above, pp. 59–61). Its poetic (as opposed to prose) form, its concentration on Torah as Wisdom, its dependence on the language of Job, and its use of "God" rather than "Lord" differ from the previous section. These differences notwithstanding, it has been made an integral part of Baruch.

The poem is connected to the previous section by 3:9–13.[31] Israel is "dead" in the land of their enemies (3:10–11; cf. 3:4)[32] because they have forsaken the fountain of wisdom (3:12; cf. Jer 2:13), that is, the Torah, the commandments of *life* (3:9).

The specific topic of the poem is the finding of Wisdom, and it is beholden to Job 28:12–28. The opening strophe admonishes the readers to learn where there is Wisdom and strength and life (3:14). The next three strophes enumerate those who have *not* found Wisdom: the rulers of the Gentiles (3:15–19), others among the wise of the earth (3:20–23), the giants of old (3:24–28).[33] By contrast God alone found the way to Wisdom (3:29–37), and he has given it to Israel alone among human beings (3:36). The last strophe (4:1–4) makes explicit the identification of Wisdom and Torah hinted at in the wording of 3:29–30 (cf. Deut 30: 11–13). Like Sirach 24, this poem asserts that Wisdom is embodied in Torah and promises life to those who "hold her fast."[34] It threatens death to those who forsake her, which explains why Israel is now "dead" in the land of their captivity. The author appeals to the people to repent (4:2) and find life, which here implies return, and he ends with a blessing on the people (4:4; cf. Deut 33:29) who know God's will.

Although this poem paraphrases Job 28 its explicit nationalism is foreign to its archetype (cf. 3:36–37 with Job 28:23–28), while it parallels Sirach 24 and fits well with the rest of Baruch. Explicit references to Israel (3:9, 24, 36; 4:2, 4) and "our God" (3:35) are complemented by the identification of Wisdom with Torah and the consequent distinction between Israel and the Gentiles.

The personification of Wisdom in Baruch 3:8–4:4 is less clear than it is in Sirach 24. This poem is *about* her rather than *by* her. She is the object of a search rather than the one who searches the universe. Only in 4:1 is she the subject of a verb of action.

Having appealed for that obedience that can change Israel's fortunes the author begins his last major section, issuing the first of several exhortations to "take courage." God's punishment is not final (4:6; cf. 2 Macc 6:12). This section is again stamped with the language of Deuteronomy,[35] but the controlling metaphor is Second Isaiah's image of Mother Zion and her children.

Before the author turns to his hope of the future he again rehearses the past. Israel's plight is due to her sin (4:6–20). This rebellion against God brought bereavement to their widowed mother, who describes to her neighbors how she had nurtured her children with joy but sent them into exile in sorrow (4:9–20). Now addressing her children in a pair of strophes that also begin with "take courage" (4:21–26, 27–29), she appeals to them to offer that prayer for deliverance that stands at the beginning of the book. The individual units of these strophes are generally marked by a contrast between past calamity and future salvation: the mother sent her sons out in sorrow, but God will return them in joy; captivity will turn to salvation; the enemy himself will be destroyed; calamity will be turned to joy.

In view of this prospect the author addresses four strophes to Jerusalem herself, each beginning with an imperative to act out a stage of the unfolding drama of salvation. Like her sons she is to "take courage" (4:30–35) in view of the coming reversal that will inflict on the enemy the ills that Israel suffered (cf. 4:33 with 4:11).[36] Then Israel is to look to the east for the return of her sons (4:26–37).[37] She is to replace her mourning clothes (cf. 4:20) with glorious robes (5:1–4).[38] Then she is to ascend to the height to view the return of her children, led in procession by their God (5:5–9).[39]

With the prospect of Return the author has solved the dilemma with which the book began. Prayer has been answered. Exile and Dispersion have ended. Sorrow has turned to joy.

Baruch is a prime example of a book whose time of composition is difficult to date.[40] There are no unambiguous historical allusions. The theme of Dispersion and Return fits any period after 587 B.C.E. Attempts to date the book by comparing 1:15–3:8 with Daniel 9 and chap. 5 with *Psalms of Solomon* 11 fall short of certainty. The nature of the interrelationships is uncertain, as are the dates of the other documents in question.[41]

The style of the Greek in Baruch appears to provide a *terminus ad quem* in 116 B.C.E. There are indications that at least the first part of Baruch and the Hebrew of Jeremiah were translated by the same person and that the translation of the whole prophetic corpus was known to ben Sira's grandson, who translated the Wisdom of Jesus the Son of Sirach before 116 B.C.E.[42]

The fictional date in 1:2 may provide a clue to the date of composition.[43] If Nebuchadnezzar is a stand-in for Antiochus IV the book is possibly to be dated to 164 B.C.E., five years after Antiochus's sack of Jerusalem and after Judas's purification of the Temple. The high priest Jehoiakim would be none other than Alcimus. The book would be an appeal both to accept the authority of Antiochus V, the son of Antiochus IV (i.e., Belshazzar, son of Nebuchadnezzar; cf. 1:11–13 and the emphasis in 2:21–23), and to seek that obedience to the Torah that would facilitate the return of the Dispersion and God's own judgment of the Macedonian kingdom. Dating the book in this time would explain the fictional setting and would also fit well with the strong consciousness of sin, guilt, and punishment that pervades chaps. 1–3. On the other hand, if one is inclined to play down the importance of the fictional setting and

to emphasize the discrepancies between the narrative and the circumstances of 164, then a date higher in the second century, or perhaps
earlier, may seem more plausible.[44]

1 MACCABEES[45]

First Maccabees recounts the history of Israel from the Hellenistic
reform to the death of Simon the Hasmonean. Different from the pseudonymous apocalypses that we have discussed in the last chapter and the
fictional book of Judith, 1 Maccabees is straightforward historical narrative. Together with 2 Maccabees it constitutes our main source material
for the history of Israel in the mid-second century B.C.E. Being a historian rather than a chronicler, this author *interprets* the events he recounts. His purpose is to defend the legitimacy of the Hasmonean high-
priestly dynasty by showing how the family of Mattathias delivered the
Jews from the persecution, reimposed the rule of the Torah, and brought
the nation to an era of peace and political independence.

Chapter 1 depicts the developing crisis in Israel: the Hellenization of
Jerusalem (vv. 11–15), the attacks against Jerusalem by Antiochus and
Apollonius (vv. 16–28 and 29–40), and the interdiction of the Jewish
religion and the persecution of those who disobey (vv. 41–61). Because
the Hasmoneans are to be the heroes of the piece, the author does not
indicate that Antiochus's decrees are the result of pious Jewish opposition
to the Hellenizers.[46] He mentions Jewish resistance to the royal government only at the very end of chap. 1, when he is ready to introduce
Mattathias and his sons as the ones who will turn away the "very great
wrath" that has befallen Israel (vv. 62–64).[47]

Chapter 2 is pivotal to the action of the book and the author's purpose.
Mattathias is introduced as the father of John, Simon, Judas, Eleazar,
and Jonathan (vv. 2–5), whose heroics and accomplishments are the
subject of chaps. 3–16. In the present chapter, however, Mattathias is the
main character, and his words and deeds predominate throughout. In
vv. 7–14 he is the spokesman of Israel's grief over its ill fortunes. In answer to the command to apostasize he rejects the officer's bribe and
gives expression to the pious Jewish determination to adhere to the covenant (vv. 15–22; cf. 1:63; contrast 1:15, 52). However, Mattathias's ideology is not pacifist; his zealous resistance is militant. He is likened to the
priest Phineas, who stayed God's wrath against Israel and thus won for
himself an eternal priestly covenant (vv. 23–26; cf. Num 25:6–12).

Thereby the author implies that Mattathias's action has stayed God's wrath against Israel's apostasy, and he recounts the deed that was foundational for the high-priestly credentials of the Hasmonean house.[48]

Only after Mattathias has issued his rallying cry to those who are zealous for the law and who support the covenant (vv. 27–28) do we hear of other Jews who flee to the wilderness (vv. 29–38). The deaths of many of them in wilderness caves and their cries for heavenly vindication (vv. 32–38) are reminiscent of the story of Taxo and his sons in the *Testament of Moses* 9 (see above, pp. 81–82). Thereafter Mattathias is depicted as the leader of a sizable resistance movement against the Syrian crown and its Jewish adherents (vv. 39–48).

In his testament at the end of the chapter (2:49–68) Mattathias duly transfers authority to his sons (vv. 65–66). At the same time, he expresses his militant ideology, indicating that divine vengeance is enacted through human agents (vv. 50, 66–68). In listing the heroes of faith, whose obedience brought them glory (vv. 51–60), he both exhorts his sons and promises them deliverance and divine blessing, and he suggests that they will hold authority as rulers.[49] In the predictive style typical of testaments Mattathias foretells the punishment of Antiochus and the failure of his oppressive measures (vv. 61–63).

The chapter as a whole is remarkable for its many parallels, both to the story of Taxo and to the story of the seven brothers and their mother in 2 Maccabees 7.[50] All three stories relate in their own way an event that turns the course of history in this particular situation. First Maccabees 2 is unique and remarkable both for its militant ideology and for the special status that it grants to a historically identifiable person—the patriarch Mattathias.

The succession announced by Mattathias becomes fact when his son Judas "arises in his place" (Gk. *anti,* 3:1) as the leader of his brothers and of his father's followers (3:2). The author then devotes 40 percent of his history to an account of the exploits of Judas. This section is framed by a poem in praise of Judas as a warrior par excellence (3:3–9) and by this epilogue:

> Now the rest of the acts of Judas, and his wars and the brave deeds that he did, and his greatness, have not been recorded, for they were very many (9:22).[51]

These passages notwithstanding, our author does not simply sing the praises of a great hero. Judas's victories are possible only through divine help. He enters battle with prayer (3:46; 4:30–33; 5:33; 7:40–42) and celebrates victory by praising God (4:24, 33, 55). His exhortations to his army remind them of other times in the past when God supported his people against overwhelming odds (4:8–9, 30; 7:41). "It is not on the size of the army that victory in battle depends, but strength comes from heaven" (3:18–19). Some of the descriptions of Judas's wars make clear that he was following the ancient practices of holy warfare.[52] Our author believes that through Judas "the savior of Israel" (9:21) God "the savior of Israel" (4:30) delivered his people.

When Judas dies in battle "the lawless" rise to power in Israel (9:23–27). Judas's friends approach Jonathan and ask him to fight in their behalf (9:28–31), and so he takes the leadership and arises "in the place of [Gk. *anti*] Judas his brother." The succession continues. Like his brother, Jonathan is a mighty warrior who also understands that his victory comes only through the help of heaven (9:43–46; 11:71; 12:15). Our author depicts Jonathan functioning as a ruler, like the judges of old (9:73),[53] and the sword ceases in Israel during this time. Although "lawless men" try to discredit him, he is vindicated in the eyes of the monarchs, Alexander and Demetrius (10:61; 11:21–27), and the land is quiet (11:38, 52). Of special importance for our author is Jonathan's appointment as high priest, and he notes the date on which he was invested with the robes of office (10:21). In contrast to Jonathan, Alcimus the priest is consistently depicted as a scoundrel who finally reaps the just rewards of his wicked deeds (7:9–25; 9:54–56).

When Jonathan is captured, Simon assembles "the people" and delivers a stirring speech that is both a summary of the glorious achievements of the Hasmonean house and an exhortation that the people accept his leadership (13:3–6). The people respond by acclaiming him their leader "in the place of" (*anti*) Judas and Jonathan (13:8–9). Thus the succession passes to Simon. Some three years later this popular acclamation is fully legitimized by "the great assembly of the priests and the rulers of the nation and the elders of the country." In keeping with his purpose the author preserves the full text of this decree, which rehearses the great deeds of the Hasmonean house and of Simon in particular (14:27–45). Thus he draws attention to the event toward which, in his opinion, the whole history of the period has been moving: the establishment of the Hasmonean house as the legitimate seat of the Jewish high priesthood and as the ruling dynasty in Israel. The author is quick to point out that the honors heaped on Simon were well deserved, and he lists the Hasmonean prince's accomplishments in considerable detail (13:33–53). Not least among these was the ushering in of a time of peace, which is described in a poetic passage that may well date from the reign of Simon (14:4–15). It is virtually a pastiche of biblical allusions, and it suggests that some of Simon's contemporaries believed that to all intents and purposes the messianic age had arrived. At the very least the poem attributes to Simon's era some of the glories of the Davidic and Solomonic age and the fulfillment of some of the hopes awaited in the golden age of the future. In context the poem, with its description of peace, stands in striking contrast to the description of Judas's warlike deeds in 3:3–9. Perhaps the author wished to frame the body of his work with two passages that would dramatize the progress made during these thirty years.

Although this history of the Hasmoneans reaches its climax with the reign of Simon, there remains a final act of succession. Simon appoints his two sons, John and Judas, to fight for their nation in the place of him (*anti*) and his brother (16:1–3). There follows the story of the treacherous assassination of Simon and his sons, Judas and Mattathias (16:11–17), and the mantle of leadership falls on John Hyrcanus. His deeds are only alluded to (16:23–24), partly because they have already been recorded but also because the author has accomplished his purpose. He has recorded the history of the founding, the succession, and the establishment of the Hasmonean house, and he has documented its legitimacy by royal decree, popular acclaim, and the attestation of the God who has worked his purposes through the Hasmonean family and its early heroes. He has told the story of "the family of those men through whom deliverance was given to Israel" (5:62). Thereby he has proclaimed the gospel according to the Hasmoneans.

The reference to the chronicles of John Hyrcanus's high priesthood (16:23–24) suggests that 1 Maccabees was written after his death.[54] The favorable references to the Romans in chap. 8; 12:1–4; 14:24, 40; and 15:15–24 give no hint that Rome would later be the invader and overlord of Israel. Thus a date between 104 and 63 B.C.E. is indicated. First Maccabees was very likely composed during the reign of Alexander Janneus as propaganda against opponents of the Hasmoneans—including the Pharisees and the Essenes (see below, pp. 122–23). The book was composed in Hebrew.[55]

2 MACCABEES

Second Maccabees is a condensation of a five-volume history of Israel during the years 180–161 B.C.E., composed by one Jason of Cyrene. In his prologue the anonymous epitomizer describes Jason's work in a way that tallies well with the emphases and scope of 2 Maccabees (2:19–23).[56] For that reason and because the epitomizer claims no originality in his work we shall treat 2 Maccabees as a unified whole, without attempting to distinguish between Jason's work and the epitomizer's abridgment.

Second Maccabees is generally characterized as "pathetic" history, in which the author "strove to entertain his reader by playing strongly upon the emotions [Gk. *pathos*], with vivid portrayals of atrocities and heroism and divine manifestations and with copious use of sensational language and rhetoric, especially when presenting the feelings of the characters."[57]

Second Maccabees supplements 1 Maccabees by providing our only detailed account of the situation just before and during the Hellenizing of Jerusalem (chaps. 3–5). On the other hand the history ends when Judas has defeated Nicanor and secured the city (chaps. 14–15 // 1 Macc 7). We can outline the book as follows:

A. Two prefixed letters	1:1–9; 1:10–2:18
B. The epitomizer's prologue	2:19–32
C. The history	3–15
1. *Blessing*: Jerusalem during the priesthood of Onias	3:1–40
2. *Sin*: Hellenization of Jerusalem under Jason and Menelaus	4:1–5:10
3. *Punishment*: Antiochus's reprisals	5:11–6:17
4. *Turning point*: Deaths of the martyrs and prayers of the people	6:18–8:4
5. *Judgment and salvation*: The victories of Judas	8:5–15:36
D. The epitomizer's epilogue	15:37–39

As can be seen in C.1–5 of the outline, the author employs the same Deuteronomic scheme that governs the apocalyptic recitation of these events in *Jubilees* 23:16ff. and the *Testament of Moses* 5, 8–10 (see above, pp. 77, 81). This scheme of sin and divine retribution is also the context of the author's frequent moralizing comments (3:1; 4:16–17, 26, 38, 42; 5:10, 19–20; 6:12–16; 15:32–33). Essential to his account are the status and fate of the Temple.

The peace and prosperity of Jerusalem and the Gentiles' high regard for the Temple during the days of Onias III are attributed to the fact that the "laws were very well observed because of the piety of the high priest" (3:1–3). The angelic attack against Heliodorus demonstrates how God protects the Temple as long as his people are obedient (3:39; cf. 5:18). It is the first of a number of "manifestations" (*epiphaneia*) that illustrate divine intervention in the affairs of Israel. As told it draws the reader into an emotional involvement in the incident and the characters' various responses to it.

In his extensive account of Hellenization in Jerusalem the author stresses that Israel or its leaders have forsaken the covenant and violated the laws (4:7, 11–15, 25, 34, 39, 50; 5:6). Herein lies the reason for the disaster that subsequently befalls the nation. Antiochus is the agent of God's judgment (5:17–18), and because the Temple has been a principal site of the Hellenizers' sin (4:14, 32, 42) judgment falls swiftly on the house of the Lord (5:15–20; 6:2–5). In 6:12–17 the author pauses to remind his readers that Israel is still God's people, subject to his discipline but never to utter destruction. He will yet have mercy.[58]

The account of the martyrs' deaths in 6:18–7:42 is both the climax of the account of Antiochus's cruelty (again told in typical "pathetic" fashion) and the turning point in the historical drama. The paradox evident in *Jubilees* 23 and the *Testament of Moses* (see above, pp. 78, 81–82) is again present. The persecution is punishment for Israel's sins (7:18); nonetheless, these martyrs are put to death precisely because they refuse to capitulate to sin (6:27, 30; 7:2, 9, 11, 23, 37). This obedience to the Torah and these innocent deaths, together with the prayer of Judas and companions (8:2–4), are instrumental in reversing Israel's dire circumstances. The brothers and their mother believe and confess that God will again have mercy on his people. As evidence they refer to what "Moses declared in his song" (7:6), quoting Deuteronomy 32:36, which describes God's salvation in the final part of the historical scheme. The last brother appeals to God that with these deaths God would show mercy and bring his wrath to an end (7:37–38). This is also the thrust of the prayer in 8:2–4.

A comparison with the *Testament of Moses* 9 and 1 Maccabees 2 indicates that we have here yet another version of the same story.[59] Each instance recounts the event which the respective author interprets as the catalyst that turns God's wrath from Israel and brings release from the persecution. Each is a story about parent and sons who are ready to die rather than transgress the Torah. The *Testament of Moses,* written in the heat of persecution, anticipates an apocalyptic denouement in which God will avenge the innocent blood of his servants, notably Taxo and his sons. The Deuteronomic scheme of the *Testament of Moses* turns on this author's interpretation of Deuteronomy 32:43 (9:7; 10:2). For the pro-Hasmonean author of 1 Maccabees, Mattathias's zealous deed stays God's wrath (cf. Num 25:8, 11). The Maccabean victories are an answer to the dying patriarch's appeal to execute judgment on the Syrians (2:66–68; cf. Deut 32:43). The version of the story in 2 Maccabees 7 takes cognizance of the fact that it was Judas Maccabeus who turned back the Syrian armies and brought deliverance to Israel. However, although Taxo's prediction has not been fulfilled as stated, our author nevertheless espouses in part the ideology of the *Testament of Moses.* The innocent deaths of the martyrs and their appeal for vengeance before and after death (7:37; 8:3) contribute to turn God's wrath to mercy (8:5) and facilitate the Maccabean victories that are recounted through the rest of the book.

Thus the final act of the historical drama unfolds. True to the brothers' predictions (7:17, 19, 31, 35–37), Antiochus is struck down by divine judgment and is forced to confess the only God (chap. 9). The Temple is regained, purified, and rededicated (10:1–8). Nicanor's final onslaught against it is foiled (chaps. 14–15), and the people sing praises to him "who has kept his place undefiled" (15:34). The story has come full circle. Divine blessing has returned to Israel, and the sanctuary is once more secure.

Not only does our author depict God's judgment on the sins of Israel and the arrogance of Antiochus, but he also treats the theological problem of the unjust deaths of the martyrs. God will undo these violent and unjust deaths by raising the dead to life.[60] This theme of judgment is carried in the speeches of three of the brothers and their mother (7:9, 11, 14, 23). The brothers are tried and condemned for violating the king's command. Their civil disobedience is synonymous with their obedience to the divine law. At the resurrection their disobedience of the king's law will be vindicated in the divine court because they have obeyed the law of the "king of the world" (7:9). Theirs will be a bodily resurrection (7:10–11)—an appropriate remedy for their bodily tortures. God will heal what Antiochus has hurt; he will bring to life those whom

Antiochus has killed.[61] What God created he will recreate—in spite of the king's attempt to destroy it (7:22–23, 28–29; cf. 14:37–46).[62] The treatment of resurrection in this story has its roots in the theology of Second Isaiah. The theme of suffering and vindication draws on a traditional interpretation of Isaiah 52–53. Antiochus's arrogance and punishment, depicted in chap. 9 in terms of Isaiah 14 (cf. above, pp. 86, 88), were also drawn from that tradition (see below, pp. 178–79). The mother represents Second Isaiah's Mother Zion, who awaits the return of her dispersed sons (7:17–29; cf. Isa 49:14–23; 54:1ff.; 60:4–9), and her language reflects the interpretation of Second Isaiah in Baruch 4:17–29 (see above, pp. 112–13). The description of resurrection as new creation has its roots in Second Isaiah's theology of creation and redemption (Isa 43:1–2, 6–7; 44:1–2; 46:3–4). Thus the prophet's announcement of Return from Exile is here reinterpreted as deliverance and vindication in spite of death.

The scope of our author's history may offer a clue to his purpose. Mattathias is never mentioned, and the story of the brothers and their mother is his version of 1 Maccabees 2 and its functional equivalent. When the exploits of Judas are mentioned, the central figures are never "Judas and his brothers," as in the early chapters of 1 Maccabees, but instead the more vague "Judas (or Maccabeus) and those with him." Jonathan is mentioned only once (8:22). Simon is referred to on two other occasions, both times in a bad light (10:20; 14:15–18). For 2 Maccabees, *the* Hasmonean hero is Judas (15:30). The narrative ends before his death, and we never hear of the accomplishments of Jonathan and Simon. In view of the author's intense interest in Temple and priesthood, and his emphasis on Judas as the deliverer of the Temple, his silence about Jonathan and Simon may well indicate that he was opposed to the Hasmonean high priesthood.[63] His version of the story then might be setting straight what he considered to be the distortions of the account related in 1 Maccabees.[64] If such is the case the reign of Alexander Janneus would be a likely time of composition.[65]

Second Maccabees and its source, the history of Jason, were composed in Greek. Two letters addressed to Jews in Egypt have been prefixed to 2 Maccabees. Their exhortation to celebrate the Feast of Dedication and the second letter's emphasis on God's accreditation of the Second Temple may be covert polemics against the Jewish temple that Onias IV built in Leontopolis in Egypt.[66]

THE QUMRAN SCROLLS

Progress in the study of ancient history is sometimes due as much to accidental discovery as to painstaking scholarship. In the spring of 1947 two teenage Bedouin shepherds were searching for a straying goat on the steep cliff face that overlooks the northwest corner of the Dead Sea about a half kilometer from some ruins known as Khirbet Qumran. One of the youths, Mohammed-edh-dhib ("the wolf"), tossed a stone into a hole—one of thousands that pockmark these limestone cliffs. With an accuracy that defies aim the stone shattered one of several ceramic jars that were embedded in the floor of the cave below. Thus were found the first of the celebrated "Dead Sea Scrolls."[67] Subsequently eleven caves yielded nine scrolls substantially preserved and large and small fragments of hundreds of others. The discovery of these scrolls led to the exploration of other caves and the discovery of more documents.[68] The process of decipherment, interpretation, and publication still goes on thirty-three years later.

The Qumran manuscripts include our earliest fragments of all books of the Hebrew Bible except Esther and copies of some of the Apocrypha and Pseudepigrapha, notably Tobit, the Wisdom of Jesus the Son of Sirach, *Jubilees,* parts of *1 Enoch,* and some documents related to the *Testaments of the Twelve Patriarchs.* In addition there are a large number of hitherto unknown works, many of which are products of the community that had its headquarters at Qumran from the mid-second century B.C.E. to the late first century C.E.[69]

While scholars continue to debate many points of interpretation, and new historical hypotheses appear from time to time, there is a general consensus on certain major points. The Scrolls were the property of members of the Essene sect, one of four "philosophies" or religious groups mentioned by Josephus.[70] The name "Essene" is thought by some to represent *ḥasēn,* an Aramaic equivalent of *Ḥasîdîm* ("the pious" or "loyal ones"), although the precise historical connections between the Essenes and the *Ḥasidim* mentioned in 1 Maccabees is uncertain.[71] The name, however, does correspond to a sectarian self-consciousness that is evident in many of the Scrolls. These people saw themselves as true and loyal Israelites, to the exclusion of all others.

Khirbet Qumran was the community center for at least one group of these Essenes, who retreated to the desert, fleeing what they considered to be the pollution of Jerusalem and awaiting the coming of God and the dawn of a new age. Their archenemies were the Hasmoneans, personified in "the Wicked Priest," who is probably to be identified with either Jonathan or Simon.[72] The founder and early leader of the sect was a high priest known in the Scrolls as the Teacher of Righteousness (i.e., either "the righteous teacher" or "the one who teaches righteousness").

Thus we have the physical setting, some of the literature, and some glimpses of the history of an apocalyptic sect that flourished during the period that is of concern to us. We should emphasize that what we have are only glimpses. The texts are often ambiguous, and their interpretation is much debated. Moreover, although the chief opponents were the Hasmonean princes and other groups or persons who broke with the sect, there are good reasons to believe that some of the issues at stake among the Essenes go back to older, more long-standing debates in Judaism, to which the *Book of Jubilees* and parts of *1 Enoch* may be witnesses.[73] The discovery and study of the Scrolls have shown us that the parties and sects in Judaism were more in number and greater in diversity than the account of Flavius Josephus would lead us to believe.

In the section that follows we shall sample the Scrolls for some of the beliefs, practices, and experiences of this group.[74]

THE DAMASCUS DOCUMENT (CD)

This work first came to the attention of modern scholars at the end of the last century, when two fragmented copies of it were discovered in the storeroom of a Cairo synagogue. Its Essene character, though often proposed, was not demonstrated until fragments of seven copies of the work were found among the Qumran Scrolls.[75] The writing, as attested by published fragments, is comprised of two clearly defined parts: (1) *admonitions* based on history and (2) *commandments* for the life of the Community.

Central to the document as a whole is a sharp distinction between the in-group and the outsiders. The Community understands itself to be the true people of God, bound together by a new covenant and having the correct understanding of the Torah. As such they keep themselves separate from the rest of the Jewish people, particularly the priestly establishment (i.e., the Hasmonean high priests), who have profaned the Temple. The end of the age is at hand, and the full fury of Satan is loose in the land, as witnessed by the wickedness of their opponents.

Both halves of the work are heavily dependent on the Scriptures. In the first half, prophetic oracles are interpreted as predictions of events relating to the life of the Community. The second half presents the Community's special interpretation of the Torah. Paleographical analysis suggests a date between 100 and 75 B.C.E. for the composition of the whole.[76]

The Admonitions

This part is evidently a composite of several earlier documents that originated in circles very closely connected to Qumran.[77] The Cairo fragments begin with a general historical introduction (1:1–2:1) that sketches the origins of the Community early in the second century B.C.E.[78] The imagery is reminiscent of the Apocalypse of Weeks in *1 Enoch* 93:1–11, and the idea of an awakening has parallels in *Jubilees* 23 and *1 Enoch* 90:6. The group finds a leader in the Teacher of Righteousness, who will appear elsewhere in the Qumran literature. This teacher guides his followers on the right path and stands in opposition to "the Scoffer," who is depicted as a false leader and deceiver of Israel. The language of Isaiah 30:8–21 stands behind this section at a number of points.[79]

There follows a *theological* prologue to the writing (2:2–13), with elements that parallel the two-ways teaching found in the Qumran Rule of the Community (see below, pp. 135–36). God's foreknowledge and predestination are asserted. He has chosen his own to be a remnant in the land and has shown them the truth, but the wicked he has led astray. In spite of this deterministic action by God each group will receive the reward or punishment of their actions.

The first major section of the Admonitions (2:14–6:2) begins with the admonition to "hear," as did the introductory sections.[80] The writer speaks of "the works of God" in history. Again we see two groups: (1) the wicked who were punished (the "watchers" of heaven, the children of Noah, the children of Jacob) and (2) the occasional righteous (Abraham, Isaac, and Jacob), who "were recorded as friends of God and party to the covenant forever." The author is particularly concerned with the latter-day manifestation of these righteous few, "the remnant" (3:12ff.). When the majority in Israel strays this group remains faithful. To them has been revealed the proper interpretation of the Torah, not the least the correct calendar. They have dug a well to the waters of the Torah (Num 21:18) and will live forever, whereas the outsiders will "not live" (Deut 30:15). This remnant, which is to be identified with the Community, has been built as "a sure house in Israel" (cf. 1 Sam 2:35). Others may still join them, but the end of the age is near, and soon the wall of that house will be complete and outsiders will be excluded.

During this last time Belial (Satan) is set loose in Israel (4:12–5:15). A mark of his presence is the commonly accepted interpretation of the Torah which has the appearance of "righteousness." By not following the Community's stricter interpretation the Jerusalem priests have committed fornication and defiled the Temple. Moreover, they blaspheme the laws of the covenant when they reject this stricter interpretation. The section concludes with the warning that anyone who goes near such persons will be punished, as God punished Israel in the past (5:15–6:2).

A brief exegetical section now follows (6:2–11). Numbers 21:18 is interpreted to refer to the Community. The "well" is the Torah. The "stave" appears to be an earlier leader in the history of the Community who expounds the proper interpretation of the Torah and is succeeded by the Teacher of Righteousness, whose appearance marks the end of days.[81]

The next major section begins with a kind of memorandum, calling the Community's attention to their responsibility to live according to their particular understanding of the Torah (6:11–7:4).[82] The basic content of this section is found in the Holiness Code in Leviticus 17–26; however, the repeated qualification "according to" indicates that the author has in mind a specific interpretation of the requirements of the Torah. The section concludes with a promise and a threat. Those who walk in these commandments will live for thousands of generations. Those who despise them will be punished (7:4–6:9).

Another exegetical interlude interprets prophecies of Isaiah and Amos as referring to events in the Community's life (7:10–8:2). It contains one of many references to a sojourn in Damascus (hence the title of the document). Whether such a time of voluntary exile was actually spent in Damascus or whether "Damascus" is a symbol for another place is a point of scholarly debate.[83]

There follows a bitter censure against "the princes of Judah" (8:3–13), the ruling priestly aristocracy,[84] who are accused of violating the Torah and cooperating with the Gentiles. Such action can result only in divine retribution.

The final section of the Admonitions envisions three or four groups that have belonged to the Community. The first group have left the Community, and their names are to be erased from its register (Ms.

B 1:32–2:1).[85] According to this section the final segment of the last times spans between the death of the Teacher of Righteousness and the coming of the Messiah, who combines the functions of high priest and civil ruler.[86] The second group have remained in the Community but do not follow its laws. They will be lost (B 2:1–8).[87] The third group are similar to the first, and the passage may be a doublet of the first (B 2:8–13). The final group are the faithful, who adhere to the Covenant and engage in mutual admonition and help (B 2:17–22). Their names are inscribed in God's book. This final section of the Admonitions concludes with a promise. When God's eschatological glory is manifest in Israel the faithful of the Community will experience great joy. These faithful are those who have adhered to the correct interpretation of the covenantal laws as expounded by the Teacher of Righteousness and have confessed their sins when they have strayed.

The Commandments

The second half of the Damascus Document spells out the Community's specific interpretation of the Torah.[88] We have here a counterpart to the halakhic interpretation of the written Torah which we saw in the *Book of Jubilees* and which will become an essential feature of rabbinic Judaism. Among the subjects included are juridical matters, purification, Sabbath regulations, and charity. Column 9 contains repeated concern about relationships within the community and proper procedures regarding the rebuke and accusation of the brother. The end of col. 15 excludes certain physically and mentally "imperfect" people from the Community because of the presence of angels in the assembly. Column 16:2–4 cites the *Book of Jubilees* as the authority for establishing chronology.

QUMRAN BIBLICAL INTERPRETATION

. . . And God told Habakkuk to write down that which would happen to the final generation, but He did not make known to him when time would come to an end. . . . God made known [to the Teacher of Righteousness] all the mysteries of the words of His servants the Prophets (Comm. on Hab 2:1–2; Vermes).[89]

Here in a nutshell is the basis for Qumran interpretation of the Bible.[90] The prophets (Moses included) wrote about the events that would take place at the end-time. The group at Qumran believed that they were living during that crucial time. Thus the prophetic texts contained cryptic references ("mysteries") to contemporary events. God had given the Teacher of Righteousness special insight to interpret these mysteries.

The Teacher was not the first to employ such a method of interpretation. We have already seen various forms of it in a number of second-century texts. The author of the *Testament of Moses* rewrites Moses' prophecy so that it makes explicit reference to contemporary events. In *Jubilees* 23, Daniel 10–12, and *1 Enoch* 85–90 phrases from the prophets and allusions to these books are employed to describe contemporary events and to flesh out descriptions of the imminent *eschaton*. The author of Daniel 9 reinterprets Jeremiah's seventy years as seventy weeks of years that reach their culmination in the author's own time.

The commentaries from Qumran are a peculiar embodiment of this type of interpretation. They comment verse by verse on lengthy blocks of text: parts of Isaiah, Hosea, Micah, Nahum, Habakkuk, Zephaniah, and the Psalter. Typically a passage is quoted and then followed by the interpretation, which is formally introduced with the words "Its interpretation concerns" (*pishrô 'al*) or "the interpretation of the passage is" (*pēsher haddābhār*). The Hebrew *pēsher* ("interpretation") is the same word employed in the stories about Joseph and Daniel where the seer offers a divinely revealed interpretation of a mysterious dream or message. Here it refers to the unraveling of the mysteries hidden in Scripture.[91]

In keeping with this viewpoint the content of the interpretations is generally limited to the identification of events and persons mentioned in the Bible with contemporary events and persons and to some explication of how the biblical text is being fulfilled in detail in the present time. The commentaries appear to have been written during the second half of the first century B.C.E. and are extant in only one copy each—perhaps in some cases the autograph (original copy). They are evidently a compilation of the sect's interpretive traditions, reaching back to the Teacher himself and covering events from a century of the sect's history—from the Teacher's conflict with the Wicked Priest to the Roman occupation of Palestine.

The commentaries are the earliest examples of a literary genre that became popular in rabbinic circles in the second century C.E. and later. Certain similarities are evident: the technique of commenting on lengthy blocks of Scripture; the format of quotation and interpretation (although the rabbis did not use the same formal introduction to the interpretation); and the quotation of parallel passages from Scripture. The differences, however, are just as significant and help us to understand the peculiar nature of the Qumran commentaries. The rabbinic commentaries concentrate on the Torah and the Writings. The exposition is of two types: halakhic (how the laws are to be applied in specific circumstances) and haggadic (largely homiletical comments). The commentaries compile the opinions of many rabbis, who are mentioned by name. In the Qumran commentaries the interpretations are anonymous and reflect community interpretation. They deal mainly with the prophetic writings, but even in the Psalms commentary the interpretations are limited to the type discussed above. We should not be far off the mark in describing the commentaries as an eschatological key or index to the Scriptures.

THE HABAKKUK COMMENTARY (1QpHab)

This is the best preserved of the Qumran commentaries. Its twelve columns contain comments on the whole of Habakkuk 1–2. For the most part these comments relate to two series of events: (1) circumstances relating to the Teacher of Righteousness and his conflict with the Wicked Priest and "the Man of Lies" and (2) the appearance of the Roman army in Palestine.

The commentary on Habakkuk 1:7–17 deals almost entirely with the Romans, who appear under the name "Kittim." It describes how the irresistible Roman military machine grinds out its victories with merciless ferocity. The descriptions have the marks of fresh memory, and the document was probably written only a decade after the fact.[92]

The second set of historical allusions concerns the earliest history of the sect and provides tantalizing but vague information about the Teacher of Righteousness and his opponent, the Wicked Priest. The Teacher was an inspired interpreter of the prophetic Scriptures (Comm. on 1:5 and 2:1–2). In this role he met with two divergent reactions. On the one hand a community of the faithful gathered around him:

"But the righteous shall live by his faith" (2:4). Its interpretation concerns all who observe the Torah in the House of Judah, whom God will deliver from the House of Judgment because of their toils and their faith in the Teacher of Righteousness.

The faithful are the true doers of the Torah (cf. Comm. on 1:12–13), presumably as it was expounded by the Teacher, and this piety is described in terms of "faith in" or "faithfulness to" the Teacher. Their way of life causes toil or suffering for the group, as it does for the master. Elsewhere in the commentary the group is known as "the elect," a term with strong exclusivistic and sectarian connotations (Comm. on 1:12–13; 2:8, 12–13).[93] The community of the pious have their counterparts: the unfaithful, who reject the covenant and the Torah and do not heed the revelation received by the Teacher (Comm. on 1:5; cf. 1:4).

Rejection of the Teacher is epitomized in the (Wicked) Priest,[94] who is the main subject of the commentary on 2:5–17. The list of charges against him is considerable. He is a rebel against God and he amasses great wealth (Comm. on 2:5–6) and uses this to complete his building projects (Comm. on 2:9–11). He persecutes the Teacher and his community (Comm. on 2:8b, 15, 17). His indulgence in abominable and unclean things defiles the Temple (Comm. on 2:5–6, 17). Noteworthy in these passages is the repeated stress on the punishment or judgment (variously described) meted out to the Wicked Priest.

Scholarly opinion is divided on the interpretation of these passages as it relates to the identity of the Wicked Priest. The two most frequently mentioned candidates for the dishonor are the first Hasmonean high priests, Jonathan and Simon.[95] The comment on 2:16 fits Simon's drunken demise.[96] The evident references to a lingering death in the Comm. on 2:7–8a, 8b are of little help because we have no certain information on the precise manner of either Jonathan's or Simon's death. The comment on 2:5–6 has been applied to both Jonathan and Simon:

> Its interpretation concerns the Wicked Priest, who was called by the name of truth when he first took office, but when he ruled in Israel his heart was lifted up and he forsook God and betrayed the statutes for the sake of wealth.

The writer might be contrasting Jonathan's early days as a military hero with his later reign as high priest.[97] On the other hand the passage is reminiscent of the Jewish decree that named Simon and his sons high priests *in perpetuum*. According to 1 Maccabees 14:32, 35 Simon was made ruler and high priest in virtue of his faithfulness.[98]

Several passages in the commentary speak of the "Man of Lies" and the "Dripper of Lies" (i.e., "False Oracle"; cf. Mic 2:11; Comm. on 1:5, 13; 2:12–13). These terms seem to refer to another opponent of the sect, who was construed as a false teacher.[99]

A COMMENTARY ON PSALMS (4QpPs^a)

Parts of four columns of this commentary have been preserved. They contain comments primarily on Psalm 37 and, immediately after it, on Psalm 45.[100] The commentary on Psalm 37 makes evident reference to the

Teacher of Righteousness and his opponent, the Wicked Priest (Comm. on vv. 23, 32). Both passages are broken by lacunae in the manuscript. The latter passage appears to refer to the Wicked Priest's attempt on the Teacher's life. If we may judge from the biblical passage being interpreted the attempt was unsuccessful, for God "will not abandon" his righteous one. The Wicked Priest, however, is given over into the hands of violent Gentiles. This suggests the death of Jonathan rather than that of Simon, but the meaning is uncertain.[101] The Man of Lies is mentioned at least once in a passage closely parallel to the description of the False Oracle in the Habakkuk Commentary.

> Its [interpretation] concerns the Man of Lies, who has led many astray with words of falsehood, for they chose worthless things and did not listen to the Mediator of Knowledge (Comm. on v. 7; J. Allegro, DJDJ 5).

The Mediator of Knowledge is presumably the Teacher, and the passage combines elements from the Comm. on Habakkuk 1:5 and 2:12–13. The Man of Lies stands in opposition to the Teacher and gathers his own following, who disregard the words of the Teacher. The expression "lead many astray" is a technical term for the activity of false teachers, which we shall meet again in the Commentary on Nahum.[102] The term par excellence for the Teacher's community is "the elect" (Comm. on vv. 9, 20, 34), and a sense of community is evident in the repeated use of the term "congregation" ("congregation of his elect," "congregation of the poor," etc.). The community is defined as "those who observe the Torah" (2:14, 22), "those who turn back to the Torah, who do not refuse to turn from their evil" (2:2–3; Comm. on vv. 8–9). Running through the commentary is the prediction of punishment for the wicked and also reward for the righteous, often triggered by the psalmic refrain that the righteous "will possess the land." The commentary on vv. 21–22 promises that they will possess the high mountain of Israel, that is, Mount Zion and the sanctuary, a promise of considerable significance to a group who separated themselves from the Temple because they considered it to be defiled. The commentary anticipates the time when all this will be changed.

THE NAHUM COMMENTARY (4QpNah)

The events described in col. 1 took place during the reign of Alexander Janneus,[103] when on two occasions Alexander slaughtered large numbers of his enemies (see above, p. 104). While Josephus nowhere says so, it is generally assumed that these enemies of Alexander were Pharisees, who are known to have been bitter opponents of the king.

The Lion of Wrath is Alexander, who wreaks vengeance on his enemies by "hanging them alive" (i.e., crucifying them). The title the commentary applies to these enemies is "the Seekers-after-Smooth-Things" (*dôrshê hahalaqôth*). The Hebrew *dārash* is a technical term for the kind of "seeking" that goes on in biblical interpretation, and hence the phrase can be translated "the Facile Interpreters."[104] It is not surprising that the Essenes should so describe the Pharisees. Essene interpretation of the Law was often stricter than that of the Pharisees. We very likely have a wordplay between the Hebrew *halakhoth* ("legal prescriptions") and *halaqoth*. That is, Pharisaic legal interpretations (*halakhoth*) are really facile bypasses (*halaqoth*) of the strict intent of the Torah. Thus the use of the term stresses what we have already seen in the commentaries, namely, that the Qumran group considered themselves to be the genuine observers of the Torah. The Facile Interpreters are mentioned five times in the extant fragments of the Nahum Commentary. "They conduct themselves [Heb. *halakh*, perhaps a wordplay] in lies and falsehood" (2:2; Comm. on 3:1ab). They "lead many astray by their false teaching, their lying tongue, and their deceitful lips" (2:8; Comm. on 3:4; cf. 3:3, 6–8; Comm. on 3:6–7a, 7b).[105] The indictment of this group, who are at odds with the Qumran Community, could hardly be stronger, and their punishment is repeatedly mentioned. They received their just deserts from Alexander, whose title seems to imply that he was the instrument of God's wrath; and their influence will come to an end.[106]

A COMMENTARY ON ISAIAH (4QpIsa^c)

Fragments of five commentaries on Isaiah have been recovered.[107] The third commentary contains comments on Isaiah 30–31. It mentions the "congregation of those who seek smooth things, which is in Jerusalem."[108] It is almost certain that the expression "the Facile Interpreters" (see the previous section) is derived ultimately from this portion of Scripture, specifically Isaiah 30:10:

> . . . who say to the seers, "See not"; and to the prophets, "Prophesy not to us what is right; speak to us *smooth things*, prophesy illusions, leave the way, turn aside from the path."[109]

That this portion of Scripture would have been especially meaningful to the Community is understandable in light of the passage that follows shortly thereafter:

> And though the Lord give you the bread of adversity and the water of affliction, yet your Teacher will not hide himself anymore, but your eyes shall see your Teacher. And your ears shall hear a word behind you, saying, "This is the way, walk in it." (Isa 30:20–21)

OTHER EXEGETICAL WRITINGS

Two Qumran documents interpret Scripture not by commenting on a running block of text but by combining (and commenting on) several texts. The so-called Florilegium[110] begins with comments on 2 Samuel 7:10–14. The "house" is interpreted to mean the Community. The reference to David's son is interpreted in the light of Jeremiah 23:5 and Amos 9:11. The Davidic Messiah will appear at the end of time together with the "Interpreter of the Torah." The end of col. 1 quotes the royal psalm, Psalm 2, which figures in later Christian speculation on Jesus' messianic status. The so-called Testimonia[111] quotes three passages that are evidently intended to be scriptural references to three eschatological figures awaited by the Community: the prophet like Moses, the royal Messiah, and the priestly Messiah.[112] The document then quotes the hitherto unknown "Psalms of Joshua." The passage makes reference to an "Accursed Man" and his two sons. The reference may well be to Simon and his sons, whose deaths at Jericho fulfilled the ancient curse of Joshua cited in the text.[113] The passage could support the identification of Simon with the Wicked Priest if we posit the identification of the Wicked Priest with the Accursed Man.

THE RULE OF THE COMMUNITY (1QS)

The present form of this document was compiled between 100 and 75 B.C.E.[114] It is an expansion and collection of earlier writings, which have been compiled as a handbook for the life of the Qumran Community. We can with some probability dissect the stages of the document's development.[115]

A Program for Community

The nucleus of the work, 8:1–16 and 9:3–10:8, sets forth the program for the establishment of a minuscule community.[116] Very possibly it is the product of the Teacher of Righteousness himself. The Community is to be formed of twelve laymen (representing the twelve tribes of Israel) and three priests. They will be a remnant dedicated to righteous conduct, which will effect expiation in the land (8:3–10). For two years (8:10–12) they will live in the land, nevertheless keeping themselves, their possessions, and their understanding of the Torah separate from "the men of perversity." During this time they will prepare the way to go out into the wilderness (9:19–20), where they will constitute the nucleus of a larger group dedicated to the same strict observance of the Torah (8:12–16). *This* group as a whole will serve an expiatory function (9:3–5). In the light of statements in the Scrolls about the defilement of the Temple, this cultic language suggests that the Community and its pious conduct are understood to be a substitute for the Jerusalem cult. The Community will continue to live in the wilderness until the appearance of the eschatological figures: the Prophet, and the Anointed Ones of Aaron and Israel (9:10–11). The leader of the group is called a "man of understanding." The Hebrew term (*máskil*) occurs in Daniel 12:3 with reference to the righteous teachers during the persecution of Antiochus (see above p. 89). Rules for *máskil*'s conduct during the first two years are spelled out in 9:12–26. These are followed by a hymn, presumably placed on his lips, about the divine decree which governs the movement of the heavenly bodies (10:1–8). This concern is of central importance for the group, which holds the "orthodox" calendar to be heterodox.

Into the midst of this basic document have been interpolated two later sets of rules, which provide for the discipline of backsliding members of the Community (8:16b–19; 8:20–9:2).

The Rule

Columns 5–7 are an expanded Rule for life in the Community. Its detailed prescriptions for the admission of new members (6:13–23) and for the conduct of a fairly large assembly (6:8b–13) and its detailed penal code (6:24–7:25) reflect an established group with considerable experience in the communal life.

The opening section establishes the authority for the Community, namely, the Zadokite priests and the majority of the lay people of the Community (5:1–7). There follows a discussion of the meaning and implications of joining the Community (5:8–20). Explicit in these lines is a sectarianism of the strictest order. To join the Community is to "enter into the covenant of God" (5:8). In this view the outsider, although he is an Israelite by birth, stands outside the covenantal relationship. To enter the covenant is "to be converted to the Mosaic Torah," which one is to obey "with all one's heart and soul, (abiding by) everything of it that is revealed to the sons of Zadok" (5:8–9). Thus obedience to the covenant requires that one obey the Torah, following the "revealed" *halakhoth* which are set down by the Zadokite priests of the Community. In short, a covenantal relationship with the God of Israel can exist only within this Community and as one abides by its unique understanding of the Torah. The implication is simple. Those who enter the Community must break all relationships with outsiders, who are "perverse men who walk in the way of wickedness" (5:10–11). These latter stand outside the covenant (5:11), and enmity against them is so strong that one must not reveal the Community's *halakhoth* to them, presumably lest they be saved.

Within the Community itself there is a strict ranking of the members according to their "understanding" and their "perfection" of conduct. Each year the members are examined, and a document giving their names and ranking is drawn up (5:20b–24). Community means mutual concern, which reflects itself in reproof that is spoken out of "faithfulness, humility, and loving kindness." Grudges may not be harbored, nor is one to be denounced publicly unless the process has first been carried out privately before witnesses (5:25–6:1). Provisions are made for smaller groups of ten persons (6:2–8). In each group there is to be a priest who presides over the common meal, and the study of the Torah is to go on perpetually.

Parliamentary procedure for the conduct of the assembly is simple (6:8–13). Seating and the order of speaking are determined by one's rank. No one may interrupt another. Only the "chairman" can speak without the consent of the majority (6:8–13).

Detailed rules for entrance into the Community are given (6:13–22). One must be a natural-born Israelite. The novitiate is two years in length. After one year of instruction in the Community's *halakhoth,* one is admitted to the purificatory baths. After a second year if the person is voted in by the majority he becomes a full-fledged member and is granted the privilege of full table fellowship.[117] Most of the offenses listed in the lengthy penal code may be described as "violations of community" (6:24–7:25), actions carried out without respect for or in defiance of other members of the Community or of the Community as a whole. The list culminates in rules dealing with apostasy.

A Book for Study

The Rule proper has been prefixed and appended with diverse materials. Column 1:1–15 serves as an introduction to the whole document. It sets forth the goals and ideals of the Community: obedience to the commandments of God, love to the members of the Community (the sons of light), and hatred toward the outsiders (the sons of darkness). When the initiates enter the Community, they are to bring with them their "understanding and their powers, and their possessions."

The introduction is followed by (part of) the liturgy employed on the occasion of initiation (1:16–2:18). It has much in common with the biblical covenant forms, which suggests that initiation took place on the occasion of an annual covenant-renewal ceremony.[118] The liturgy begins with a recitation of the mighty acts of God and, in contrast to these, the wicked deeds of Israel (1:18–23). Grace has been met by rebellion. The initiates confess their participation in these sinful acts (1:24–26) but affirm their faith in his eternal mercy (2:1). Reminiscent of the ancient covenant ceremony described in Joshua 24, the choruses of the priests and the Levites respond with the pronouncement of blessings and curses (2:1b–9). The blessing, which is an expansion of the Aaronic benediction (2:2b–4; cf. Num 6:24–26),[119] invokes God's mercy on the new members of the covenantal Community. The curses, which are aimed at the outsiders, include a reversal of the Aaronic benediction (2:8–9). Then priests and Levites join in a curse upon anyone whose commitment is not sincere or wholehearted (2:11–17). The initiates respond to each of the choruses with the words "Amen, Amen!" Thus they are at one with the sentiments of the Community.

This liturgy is followed by a brief rubric on the mode of convocation at the annual ceremony (2:19–24). Rank is of the essence. The next section picks up the theme of 2:11ff. Outward ceremony is of no avail unless there be inward conversion (2:25b–3:12). Similar themes occur in the two halves of the passage, in negative and then positive forms.

The covenantal form recurs somewhat differently in the Teaching of the Two Ways: (1) the acts of God in creation (3:15b–4:1); (2) the ways of the righteous and the wicked (4:2–6a, 9–11); (3) the rewards and punishments that accrue to them (4:6b–8, 11b–14). This section is permeated by a powerful cosmic dualism between two angels or spirits that function as the guides on the two ways of life. So powerful is the influence of these two angels in the lives of the two types of people that the deeds listed are viewed as the deeds of the two angels. A strong sense of predestination or determinism is evident in the passage (3:15b–16). Nevertheless, human beings are still responsible for their deeds and receive their reward or punishment accordingly. Unlike the temporal blessings and curses of the older covenantal forms (e.g., Deut 28) the present section specifies final and eternal rewards and punishments, which are closely paralleled in the eschatological sections of apocalyptic writings.[120]

The original form of the two-ways section appears to have ended with 4:14, if we may judge from the table of contents in 3:13–15. Two additional sections describe the present battle between the two spirits and contrast it with God's resolution of that situation in the *eschaton* (4:15–18a/18b–23a; 4:23b–25a/25b–26). The terminology in 4:18–21 implies that the purification and cleansing and washing that were part of the Qumran ritual life were tentative and partial at best. Only at the *eschaton* will God cleanse humanity completely of their wicked and perverse deeds. Then all evil will be annihilated and "man" will revert to his original glory. The passage is reminiscent of motifs in the description of the *eschaton* in *1 Enoch* 10:16–22. According to 4:23b–25a the battle of the two spirits takes place in the human heart. The terms "wisdom" and "folly" suggest a strong element of human responsibility.

Appended to the end of the Rule is a lengthy hymn in the style of certain of the compositions in the Qumran Hymn Scroll (see below, pp. 138–39). It contrasts humanity's frailty and sinfulness with God's salvatory activity and concludes the document on a doxological note.

Certain tendencies are evident in the additions to the Rule. There is a stress on the possibility of less than wholehearted and thoroughgoing participation in the life-style of the covenantal Community (2:25a–3:11, 2:11a–17, and possibly 5:13–15, which looks like an interpolation).[121] The additions to the two-ways section remind the reader of the ambiguity and precarious nature of the human predicament. The liturgy calls the reader back to his origins, God's merciful acceptance of him into the covenant. The final hymn also stresses this moment of salvation, particularly if, as some suppose, it was used in the initiation ritual.[122] The introduction serves a similar function: Here, dear reader, is the obligation you assumed when you entered the Community. The addition of these materials suggests that the document was not intended simply as a reference tool for leaders, a handy compilation of rules. It could have had a broader function—to remind the reader, whatever his status in the Community, of the broader context of the rules. The necessity for such a reminder suggests some flagging in the zeal of the Community, some abating of the fire of first love and enthusiasm—a phenomenon neither unexpected nor uncommon in a group of this sort.

THE HYMN SCROLL (1QH)

Hymns of thanksgiving comprise the contents of this lengthy Scroll. In the columns yet intact, we can count at least twenty-five separate compositions, each of which begins (where the beginning is preserved) with an expression of thanksgiving or praise: "I give thanks to you, O Lord (or God)"; "Blessed are you, O Lord." The hymns are of two different types.

Hymns of the Teacher

Included in this group are at least seven hymns: 2:1–19, 2:31–39, 4:5–5:4, 5:5–19, 5:20–7:5, 7:6–25, and 8:4–40. The speaker and principal figure in this group is a teacher or revealer of saving knowledge who is persecuted by his enemies but delivered by God. The author of these compositions may well have been the Teacher of Righteousness himself.[123]

The Hymn Scroll 2:1–19

The first-person singular dominates the hymn: "I have been . . . to . . ."; "You have made me . . . to. . . ." By use of these forms the speaker describes his opposite and contrasting relationships to the righteous and the wicked.

> to the elect of righteousness you have made me a banner,
> and a discerning interpreter of wonderful mysteries.
>   (2:13; Vermes, adapted)

The author's followers are "the elect of righteousness," the true people of God. He has been an eschatological rallying point for them (cf. Isa 11:12; 49:22; 62:10). He is the interpreter of the marvelous mysteries which God is now revealing in and concerning the end-time.

> I have been a snare to those who rebel,
> but healing to those of them who repent. (2:8–9; Vermes)

He is a touchstone. To the repentant he brings divine healing (i.e., salvation), but in the wicked he creates an adverse effect and is a cause for sin (cf. 2:8). The speaker's opponents are not just the wicked in general but a group of opposing teachers: "deceivers," "interpreters of error," and the familiar "Facile Interpreters." The opposition instigated by Belial leads to persecution (2:17). The speaker sees himself at the center of a battle between heaven and hell. The revelation he mediates brings salvation to the Community of the elect, his followers. It triggers satanic reaction through his opponents, who counter his teaching and seek to annihilate its source—and do so to their own damnation. The purpose of the hymn is to thank God for deliverance.

The Hymn Scroll 2:31–37

The speaker's teaching activity may be inferred from the description of his opponents: "the congregation of those who interpret smooth things," "interpreters of falsehood." His special function is described as "your service" (2:33, 36). Because he has served the Lord his opponents have plotted to kill him (2:32–34). Unlike the previous hymn, the speaker is here in every case the *object* of a verb. His enemies seek to destroy him. God has "delivered," "redeemed," and "helped" him. This is the occasion for thanksgiving.

The Hymn Scroll 4:5–5:4

The speaker gives thanks to the Lord for enlightenment, for divinely given insight into the true nature of the covenant (4:5–6a). It is with respect to this understanding of Torah that his enemies take issue with him. In two sections he mentions their erring interpretations and then expresses the threat of divine judgment (4:6b–12a/12b–13a; 13b–18a/18b–21a). The lying interpreters and false seers seek to lead astray the Community of the righteous by opposing the speaker's interpretation, which God has engraved in his heart (i.e., revealed to him). They hope to make the group sin with respect to the observance of their sectarian holy day (cf. Comm. on Hab 2:15). Persecution here seems to take the form of banishment, and the speaker uses language from Isaiah 53:3 to describe his rejection by his opponents (4:8). Moreover, at the time of judgment he will take part in their destruction (4:21–22; cf. below, pp. 177–79, on Wis 5). His thought moves on to his relationship to his followers (4:23–29a). The enlightenment he has received he has mediated to them. He is God's instrument for revelation. But that treasure is contained in an earthen vessel (4:29b–33a). In a passage typical of the hymns, he contrasts the power, righteousness, and holiness of God with his own humanity. The thought of it leads him to shudder as he meditates upon his sin. Do the onslaughts of the enemy mean that God has forsaken him because of that sin? Surely not. With God there is forgiveness and mercy, and therefore he can take courage, confident that God's judgment will be the final word (4:33–5:4). The hymn as a whole provides a remarkable insight into the public and private sides of the speaker as he deals with "fighting without and fear within."

The Hymn Scroll 5:20–7:5

If in the hymn we have just discussed the speaker had voiced his earlier doubts about being "abandoned," here and in 5:5, he gives thanks precisely because he has not been abandoned. When he has given thanks to God for his presence (5:20–22) he moves into a lengthy description of his predicament (5:22b–6:3). Even members of his group have forsaken him, heeding the words of his opponents. The passage is filled with biblical clichés, and hence it is impossible to discover the "historical facts" of his persecution. The heaping up of descriptive phrases functions to portray his situation in the darkest colors possible. All this contrasts with the affirmation of God's salvation and deliverance that follows (6:4–19). In the midst of the tumult he has the vision of God's final triumph and his vindication of those who belong to the Community. Again he repeats the cycle of thought (6:22–34). He is like a sailor tossed on the chaotic waves and brought to the very gates of Death itself. But again there is deliverance. Within his Community, the true city of God, he finds refuge as in a fortress. He depicts it as if it were the heavenly Jerusalem itself— impregnable to the invasion of the enemy. He anticipates the imminent time of judgment, when its gates will open and its members will sally forth in the final battle. Meanwhile the turmoil goes on (7:1–5).

The Hymn Scroll 7:6–24

This hymn contains many of the motifs we have already seen. God is to be thanked for the strength he has given the speaker to face the troubles connected with his office (7:6–8a). Here he applies the metaphor of the fortress to himself to describe the security which God affords him or others through him. As true teacher he will be God's criterion in the judgment (7:10–12). People will be saved or damned in accord with how they have responded to his teaching. Again he reflects on his own humanity and on the grace of God (7:13–19). He likens his relationship to the Community as that of father—or nurse—to child (7:19b–22a). He concludes with reference to the judgment and the time when he will be exalted in glory. The passage is reminiscent of Daniel 12:3 and its reference to the glorification of the persecuted righteous teachers.

These hymns comprise a consistent body of literature. The speaker is the recipient of divine truths that he passes on to his Community, which is construed as the true people of God gathered around the correct understanding of the Torah. In his activities the teacher is challenged and persecuted by opponents who are counterteachers. At times they are successful in eroding his support. Nevertheless he is confident of God's support and saving activity, and he looks forward to the resolution of the situation in the coming judgment, when he will be exalted and his enemies will be condemned for their opposition to him.

Hymns of the Community

A second group of hymns speak of the sectarian's place in the Community.[124] Lacking are references to the teacher and his relationship to the Community and his persecution at the hands of his enemies.

The Hymn Scroll 3:19–23

In the introductory section the speaker praises the Lord, who has rescued him from the pit of Sheol (3:19–20b). He then explicates the nature of his redemption (3:20b–23b). He has been created anew from the "dust" of his humanity, cleansed from sin, and brought into fellowship with the angels. He has been delivered from the wiles of Belial, the snares of hell, and the furious judgment of the Almighty (3:26–36). The imagery is strongly eschatological in tone. "Eternal inheritance" and "lot" are terms which contemporary Jewish writings apply to eschatological salvation, and it is in descriptions of this salvation that the righteous are depicted in the presence of the angels (see esp. Wis 5:5, below, pp. 177). Thus the blessings of the *eschaton* are already a reality for this author. Upon his entrance into the Community, he passed from the sphere of death into the realm of life, and he describes this graphically as ascension from Sheol to the "eternal height" (i.e., heaven). The Community, as the true people of God, is the arena of salvation. The final section (3:28b–35) describes either the speaker's plight before his entrance into the Community or more likely his status in the world, which is still the realm of wickedness. In such a case the passage introduces a tension between the "now" and the "not yet." The full consummation of salvation belongs to the future.

The Hymn Scroll 11:3–14

The speaker gives thanks because God has made him—a mere human being ("dust," "creature of clay")—the recipient of divine revelation and enabled him to sing his Creator's praise (11:3–5a). The emphasis upon the receipt of revelation is repeated in 11:9–10. God has cleansed man from sin, and therefore certain consequences follow (11:10b–14). He is now holy to the Lord, and he stands in the company of the holy ones, that is, the Community of the eschatological elect. Moreover, God has taken man, alienated from him ("the perverse spirit") and prone to death ("dust," "mortal worm"), and given him access to the divine mysteries and to the company of the immortals, the angels. As in the previous hymn, entrance into the Community is an eschatological event, and it is depicted in language traditionally used of the *eschaton*: resurrection from the dead.

From the point of view of these hymns the Community is the arena of salvation. Outside is the realm of death. To enter the Community is "to pass from death to life." It is construed as an event of eschatological salvation. Entrance involves access to divine mysteries and knowledge. Presumably these involve insights into God's purposes and activities in the present time, as well as the proper interpretation of the Torah. This latter point is evident from the Rule, which forbids the members of the Community to pass on the Community's interpretation to outsiders (1QS 5:15–16). That this kind of knowledge is crucial for salvation is a natural (sectarian) inference from the Jewish understanding of Torah. Within the compass of the covenant, God gives certain laws and commandments. The obedient receive the blessings ("life"), the disobedient are cursed ("death"). It follows that one can "live" only if he has a correct perception of the requirements of the covenant. The Qumran group narrows the scope of Torah to mean Torah-as-we-perceive-it, that is, as it has been divinely revealed through the Teacher. The shape of the covenant is now recast in narrow sectarian and eschatological terms. True Israel is equated with the sect, the Torah with the sect's interpretation of it, and blessing and curse with eternal life and eternal destruction. For this Community, election is the presupposition for membership in the covenantal Community. Hence they call themselves the elect. However, such election is not their birthright as natural-born Jews. It is due to an eternal decree of God that divides through the midst of Israel itself. The hymns state their sectarianism in another way. Not only is Israel outside their Community damned, but the situation is even more radical. Humanity *qua* humanity, "dust," "ashes," "clay," and "flesh," is alienated from God and doomed to destruction. Only by an act of divine salvation—variously construed as re-creation, revelation, justification, and renewal—are such human beings enabled to stand in the presence of God (see, in addition to the hymns discussed, 1QH 13:10–20, 15:21–22, 18:9–29, and 1QS 11:2–22). The hymns continually emphasize that this salvation belongs to the members of the Community and celebrate the process by which one obtains this salvation. It is quite likely that the hymns were used in the initiation ceremonies, thus providing an opportunity for the initiate to give thanks for his newfound salvation.[125]

THE MARTYRDOM OF ISAIAH

The *Martyrdom of Isaiah* is a Jewish legend that forms the nucleus of a Christian work, the *Ascension of Isaiah*.[126] The Jewish legend probably included the following verses from the *Ascension of Isaiah*: 1:1–2a, 1:7–3:12, and 5:1–14.[127] We shall treat it here because of certain similarities to the Qumran Scrolls.

Three years before his death Hezekiah summons his son Manasseh and transmits certain commands to him (1:1–2, 7). Isaiah predicts that Manasseh will set aside these commands, that he will become an instrument of Beliar, and that he will put Isaiah to death. Hezekiah's protests are to no avail; Isaiah's martyrdom is determined and must come to pass (1:7–12).

When Manasseh succeeds his father, the prophecy begins to be fulfilled (2:1–6). Jerusalem becomes a center of apostasy, lawlessness, the occult arts, and fornication, and the righteous are persecuted (2:4–6). Isaiah withdraws into the Judean wilderness, where he is joined by a group of faithful prophets who nourish themselves on wild herbs (2:7–11).

The false prophet Bechir-ra[128] (a descendant of Zedekiah ben Chena-'anah, the opponent of Michaiah ben Imlah [2:12–16; cf. 1 Kgs 22:1–36]) discovers the hiding place of Isaiah and his friends and brings a threefold accusation before Manasseh. The prophets predict the fall of Jerusalem and Judah and the captivity of king and people (3:6–7). Isaiah contradicts Moses by claiming to have seen God (Isa 6:1ff.; cf. Exod 33:20). He calls Jerusalem "Sodom" and the princes "the people of Gomorrah."

Because Beliar dwells in the hearts of Manasseh and his court, the king seizes Isaiah and has him sawn asunder (4:11–5:14). As Isaiah is being tortured, Bechir-ra, acting as the mouthpiece of Satan, attempts to get the prophet to recant. With the aid of the Holy Spirit, Isaiah refuses, curses Bechir-ra and the demonic powers he represents, and dies.

The biblical bases for our story are 2 Kings 20:16–21:18 and 2 Chronicles 32:32–33:20,[129] the accounts of the last years of Hezekiah and the reign of Manasseh. Detailed similarities are, however, very few in number—mainly the enumeration of Manasseh's sins. For the most part the author has created his own story.

The quasi-testamentary scene in chap. 1 has a twofold function. Isaiah's predictions introduce the scenario that follows. Hezekiah's commands are mentioned because Manasseh will disobey them. This contrast between pious father and wicked son, mentioned three times in 2:1–3, is explicit at only one point in each of the biblical accounts (2 Kgs 21:3; 2 Chr 33:3).

Isaiah's withdrawal to the wilderness is especially significant because it is not *required* for the action of the story. The author could have had Isaiah apprehended in Jerusalem, following the model of the biblical accounts about Jeremiah. Similarly there is no dramatic necessity for the presence of a group of prophets in Isaiah's company. Indeed, they become a problem for the author, who must explain why they were not martyred along with Isaiah (5:13).

In contrast to Isaiah and his companions are the false prophet Bechir-ra and his entourage. They are at least as important as Manasseh in our author's view. The tracing of Bechir-ra's ancestry to Zedekiah ben Chena-'anah reminds the reader of a similar situation in Israelite history. Michaiah opposed Zedekiah and his bevy of false prophets in the presence of wicked Ahab. At issue was true prophecy versus false prophecy. Michaiah claimed to have had a vision of God upon his throne. Zedekiah was possessed by a lying spirit. Michaiah, because of his opposition to both king and false prophet, was punished.

The Bible nowhere mentions Isaiah's death, much less his martyrdom at the hand of Manasseh. Chapter 5 is reminiscent of martyr stories from the time of Antiochus Epiphanes, specifically those in 2 Maccabees 6 and 7. Nonetheless, the *Ascension of Isaiah* 5 has its own unique contours. The opponent of Isaiah is not the king but Bechir-ra the false prophet.

Moreover, there is a more basic polarity and struggle in the narrative between Satan, who dwells in Manasseh and supports Bechir-ra, and the Holy Spirit, who sustains Isaiah in his moment of trial. Human personages are in reality the agents and instruments of supernatural powers, whether Satan or the Holy Spirit.

Any hypothesis about the date and provenance of this writing must account for these many points which define its peculiar character and constitute deviations from the biblical accounts. This story is not a natural outgrowth from or expansion of the biblical accounts of Manasseh's reign. Only 2 Kings 2:5 mentions a persecution, and there is no biblical evidence that Isaiah outlived Hezekiah. Our author chose Manasseh's reign as a setting for Isaiah's martyrdom evidently because it paralleled the situation he wished to reflect in his pseudepigraphic account. He lived in what he considered to be a time of great wickedness in Jerusalem, when the temple cult had been turned into the worship of Satan.

Two times suggest themselves as a setting for this story. The first is Antiochus's pollution of the temple and his persecution of the Jews. The description of the retreat of Isaiah and his friends to the wilderness is reminiscent of accounts about Mattathias and Judas and his friends (1 Macc 2:6, 27ff.; 2 Macc 5:27). We have already noted parallels to 2 Maccabees 6–7. The difficulty with this hypothesis resides in the figure of Manasseh. The archvillain ought to be not an Israelite king—or false prophet—but a foreign oppressor. We should expect a story about Nebuchadnezzar.

A second, more tenable setting would be in the orbit of the Qumran Community.[130] The angelic dualism that permeates the writing is characteristic of Qumran writing.[131] Especially close is the conception of two spirits resident in humanity and warring against one another.[132] The Qumranites' disenchantment with the Jerusalem cult and its Wicked Priest could easily lead to the writing of a story about Manasseh and his Satan worship.[133] A retreat into the wilderness to escape the wickedness of the Jerusalem establishment is central to the Qumranic self-understanding.[134] The cast of characters fits well with those mentioned in the Scrolls.

Isaiah and his friends	The Teacher of Righteousness and his Community
Manasseh	The Wicked Priest[135]
Bechir-ra	The False Oracle

The Teacher's claims to have special insights into the meaning of the

Scriptures could well be the basis for the charge reflected in *Ascension of Isaiah* 3:8–9,[136] and the emphasis on the polarity of true and false prophecy is consonant with such texts as the *pēsherim* on Nahum and the Psalms.[137] The calling of Jerusalem and its princes "Sodom" and "the people of Gomorrah" is reminiscent of Qumranic typological exegesis.

The similarities are extremely close. At the very least we must attribute the writing to a sect with a dualistic theology that withdraws into the wilderness in order to escape what it considers to be a satanic cult in Jerusalem. Our closest analogy is the Qumran Community, but this does not exclude the possibility of some other similar group within the general orbit of Qumranic theology and self-understanding.[138]

The function of the story is less clear. While we cannot demonstrate that the story implies the martyrdom of a saintly leader (the Teacher of Righteousness if one accepts a Qumranic identification), it does imply persecution of some sort. The story about Isaiah provides an example of how the present woes of the group were foreshadowed in sacred history. It exhorts the readers to stand fast, for in their battle with Satan—even if it be to the death—they will be sustained by the power of the Holy Spirit. At a later time the writer of the Epistle to the Hebrews would incorporate this legend into his recitation of sacred history as he exhorted his readers to faith in the midst of (possible) persecution (Heb 10:32–12:13). There, however, Jesus is cited as the final paradigm of faith and faithfulness (12:1–2).

1 ENOCH 92–105

Writing in the name of Enoch this author has composed an "epistle"[139] ostensibly addressed to Enoch's children but in fact directed to the author's own contemporaries, "the future generations that will practice righteousness and peace" (92:1; cf. 1:1–2; 37:2). On the basis of his revealed knowledge of the heavenly realm he assures his readers that God's imminent judgment will bring vindication and eternal blessing to the righteous and swift punishment to their powerful oppressors. Thus, although the times are troubled he can exhort the righteous to faith, steadfastness, and joy.

After the usual superscription that mentions author and addressees (92:1), an initial comforting exhortation typical of these chapters (92:2), and a brief scenario of the coming salvation (92:3–5), the author has Enoch recite the Apocalypse of Weeks (93:1–10 + 91:11–17)[140] on the basis of a threefold appeal to revelation (through a heavenly vision, the interpreting words of the angels, and the contents of the heavenly tablets, 93:2). The ancient sage summarizes world history from his time to the *eschaton,* employing a scheme of ten periods of very uneven length called "weeks." The historical survey focuses on "the elect of eternity" and "the plant of righteousness" (93:2). Initially this means Israel sprung from Abraham (93:5). Running through the apocalypse from its beginning is the countermotif of wickedness, often construed as violence, deceit, and apostasy (93:4, 8, 9; 91:11 [Aram.]).[141] These are met by God's judgment in the Deluge and the Exile, although the occasional righteous person is delivered (Noah and Elijah, 93:4, 8). History climaxes in the seventh week, the author's own time. The plant of righteousness has been pruned to an elect remnant. These comprise the author's Community, which is endowed with revealed, sevenfold (complete) wisdom, that is, the contents of the author's message and perhaps the rest of the Enochic corpus. They will function as "witnesses of righteousness" and will be instrumental in uprooting the counterstructure of deceit (93:10 Aram.). In the eighth week they will execute judgment against their oppressors. A second judgment will destroy all the grossly wicked, and the rest of humanity will be converted to righteousness (91:14; cf. 10:21). With the *earth* thus purged of evil, God will judge the rebel angels and renew the *heavens* and its luminaries (91:15–17).

The apocalypse is followed by a prose section that meditates on the uniqueness of the revelation granted Enoch. A comparison of 93:11 with Deuteronomy 5:26 suggests that an idea originally referring to Israel as a whole has been here applied to a sect, the private possessors of special knowledge.

A few verses of two-ways instruction (94:1–5; see above, pp. 135–36) serve as a bridge to the main section of the epistle, which spells out (by condemnation) the way of wickedness as followed by "the sinners" and encourages "the righteous" to steadfastness in the hope of vindication.

This central part of the epistle is comprised almost entirely of three literary forms well known from the biblical tradition, especially from the prophets.[142] All three carry the theme of the coming judgment. The Woe (a distich in its simplest form) juxtaposes in its two major components the paradox of historical injustice and belief in divine judgment. The first part describes the sinners' misdeeds, and the second part announces the coming judgment which is the cause for the lament, "Woe," which introduces the form.

> Woe to you who repay your neighbor with evil;
>> for you will be repaid according to your deeds. (95:5)

Collectively the indictments in these Woes provide something of a description of the author's world. The charges are of two types. The first are religious, strictly speaking. The sinners are accused of idolatry (99:7) and of consuming blood (98:11), of blasphemy (94:9; 96:7) and cursing (95:4). Others among them disregard and pervert Torah as the righteous ("the wise") understand Torah (99:2; 98:9; 99:14), and as false teachers they lead many astray (98:15).[143] Most often, however, the misdeeds attributed to the sinners are social in nature. The rich and powerful sinners abuse the righteous poor. They build sumptuous houses at the expense of others (94:6–7; 99:13), banquet in luxury while the poor are made to suffer (96:5–6), hoard wealth and food (97:8–9), parade about in fine clothes and jewelry (98:1–3), and perjure themselves (95:6). In the judgment the security they have sought in their riches will be suddenly undermined.[144]

The Exhortations embody the same paradox as the Woes. In their first line they call the righteous to courage, faith, and hope in view of the sinners' coming judgment described in the second line:

> Fear not the sinners, O righteous;
>> for the Lord will again deliver them into your hands,
>> so that you may execute judgment on them as you wish. (95:3)

The participation of the righteous in the judgment is reminiscent of the description of the eighth week in 91:12, and the phraseology reflects holy-war contexts in Numbers 21:34, Deuteronomy 3:2, and Joshua 8:1. A second kind of Exhortation exhorts courage in the face of present calamity (first part) on the basis of a promise of vindication and eternal life for the righteous (second part):

> Be of good courage, for you were formerly worn out through afflictions
>> and tribulations;
>> but now you will shine as the luminaries of heaven. (104:2)[145]

The introductory words of these Exhortations, as well as the frequent conclusions of the Woes, "You will have no peace," are reminiscent of the language of Second Isaiah.

Descriptions of the judgment or events leading up to it comprise the third major form in these chapters. Generally introduced by the adverbial expressions "then" or "in those days," they call to mind parallel passages in the prophetic books.

The author's use of forms familiar from the prophets suggests that he is presenting his message as revelation. The impression is strengthened by his use of formulas that elsewhere introduce revelations and especially forecasts of the future: "Know!" "Be it known!" "I say to you," "I show you." Stronger yet is the oath formula "I swear to you." References to happenings in the heavenly realm also presume Enoch's claim to revelation (97:6; 98:6–8).[146]

The main section of the epistle reaches its climax in 102:4–104:8, which takes the form of a dispute about the existence or nonexistence of retribution, that is, the judgment which has been the epistle's main subject.[147] In each of the four parts of this dispute the author addresses a particular group, quotes certain words about or by them, and then refutes these words with an appeal to revelation. The first part is an expanded Exhortation addressed to the righteous dead (102:4–103:4). In spite of the claims of the sinners, the sad lot of the righteous in life, their grievous death, and their lamentable existence in Sheol do not belie divine justice. Enoch reveals a mystery he has read on the "heavenly tablets." The spirits of the righteous will come to life, and they will receive all the good things that they missed in life and that (according to the next part) the sinners had enjoyed in theirs. The second part is an expanded Woe addressed to the dead sinners (103:5–8). It asserts the converse of the first part. The sinners, prosperous and happy in life and honored in their death, face an intensified and eternal form of the miseries that the righteous had experienced in their lives.

In the third and fourth parts of the dispute (103:9–104:6; 104:7–8) the author refutes words the living righteous and sinners speak about themselves. The righteous complain that they are experiencing the covenantal curses described in Deuteronomy 28 (103:9–15).[148] Again citing his knowledge of the heavenly realm the author assures them that their frustrated cries for vindication have been heard in heaven, that their oppressors will be judged, and that they themselves have a blessed heavenly existence awaiting them (104:1–6). To the wicked who claim that their sins are not seen he makes reference to the angelic record of their deeds, which will seal their doom on the day of judgment (104:7–8).

The epistle closes with explicit reference to the transmission of Enoch's teaching. In the end-time his books will be given to the righteous (cf. 93:10) and will be a source of wisdom, faith, and joy (104:11–13), and they will serve as a testimony to the children of earth (105:1–2). With this reference to the future generation, the paths of righteousness, and the peace that belongs to the righteous the author returns to the themes of his superscription (92:1).

The epistle of Enoch is similar to other apocalyptic writings in the kind of situation it presumes, the message it conveys, and the purpose for which it was written. The author exhorts his readers to steadfastness on the basis of a revealed message about an imminent judgment that will remove oppression and adjudicate injustice. This work shares with the apocalypses we have treated the claim that it is an ancient writing intended for latter-day readers. It differs from them in form. Although it contains a brief, sketchy apocalypse, as a whole it is not an ordered account of events to come.

Certain aspects of the epistle of Enoch are reminiscent of the Qumran literature. The Apocalypse of Weeks with its movement toward the formation of the elect community of the end-time is similar to col. 1 of the Damascus Document (see above, p. 124).[149] Reference to false teachers and halakhic disputes also have parallels in the Scrolls. However, the author of the epistle does not specify the exact nature of these disputes. It is safest to suggest that this writing, or parts of it, may have emanated from a group related to Qumran. The broader context of the Enochic literature, with its emphasis on the solar calendar and possible allusions to irregularities in the Jerusalem priesthood (see above, pp. 53–54, 93–94), may indicate yet a closer relationship.

Scholars have tended to date these chapters to the late Hasmonean period and to detect in them polemical references to the excesses of Alexander Janneus or perhaps John Hyrcanus.[150] The suggestion is plausible, but it should be adopted with caution. Although the tension between rich and poor appears to be much sharper here than in the Wisdom of Jesus the Son of Sirach,[151] the two writings have very different settings. Ben Sira addresses the rich, admonishing them to use their wealth responsibly. Whether a group of the poor living in ben Sira's time could have perceived the actions of the wealthy as "Enoch" does and might have cursed the rich among themselves as he does is a question that we cannot answer on the basis of present evidence. Hence the date of these chapters remains in question. One piece of external evidence may indicate an earlier date for these chapters. Writing around the year 169 B.C.E.[152] the author of *Jubilees* recounts the written works of Enoch (*Jub.* 4:17–19). Prominent in this list is reference to Enoch's testimony and testifying. This language is most closely paralleled in *1 Enoch* 81:5–82:2; 91:3; 104:11–13; 105:1. If the latter two passages were part of the original epistle, and the former two part of the redactional framework that connected the epistle to the first chapters of *1 Enoch*, then the epistle might well have been written early in the second century B.C.E.[153]

STAGES IN THE LITERARY DEVELOPMENT OF 1 ENOCH

The growth of *1 Enoch* constitutes a literary puzzle. From the Qumran evidence we can be almost certain that neither the Parables (chaps. 37–71) nor the astronomical book (chaps. 72–80)[154] were written on the same Qumran manuscripts as chaps. 1–36 and 92–105. On the other hand chaps. 1–36 and 92–105 have many things in common. The oracle in chaps. 1–5 and the Apocalypse of Weeks have similar introductory formulas (1:1–3; 93:1–3) and share uniquely the idea of the elect (and) righteous. Chapters 12–16 (+ 17–36) provide the heavenly ascent presumed in 92–105. Enoch's concern with the heavenly realm in 92–105 relates especially to the intercessory activities of the angels and heaven's knowledge of human activity (cf. chaps. 9–10; 14–15). The author of the epistle encourages human prayer as a means of triggering angelic intercession and divine action (cf. chaps. 8–10). As the verbs in the Exhortations indicate, he considers the real danger of his readers to be capitulation to fear, hopelessness, and disbelief in God's justice (cf. chap. 9; see above, p. 51). Chapter 101 bears a striking resemblance to 2–5:4. The antideterministic passage in 98:4–5 would help counterbalance a tendency to avoid human responsibility on the grounds that sin is the fault of heaven (cf. chaps. 6–11, 12–16).

At an early stage in the literary history of *1 Enoch*, chaps. 1–36 and 92–105 may have formed the major parts of an Enochic testament, with chaps. 81–82 and 91 serving as a narrative bridge between the two parts. The following elements in these chapters suggest the outline of such a testament: Enoch ascends to heaven and visits the cosmos, learning the secrets of both. These journeys culminate in his meeting with Uriel (chap. 33) and his viewing of the heavenly tablets (81:1; cf. 80:1 and the reference to Uriel). After he has blessed God (81:3; cf. the similar blessings in chaps. 22–36) the angels return him to earth with the command that he instruct and testify to his sons. He writes his books and delivers them to Methuselah (82:1–3). Chapter 91 provides the testamentary setting for Enoch's final instructions to his children, which climaxes in the epistle. Enoch's account of his two dream visions, transmitted to Methuselah (chaps. 83–90), may have been part of this testament or may have been a later addition. It is noteworthy that in the second dream vision (chaps. 85–90) his ascent to heaven, his vision of all the deeds of humanity, his account of angelic scribes and their intercession, and his return to earth all duplicate important elements in chaps. 6–16 + 81 + 92–105.[155] The hypothetical testament that we are suggesting may have been modeled on Deuteronomy 31–33. The first part of the opening oracle (1:1–9) echoes the introduction to Moses' final blessing in Deuteronomy 33:1–2. Chapters 81:5–82:2 + 91 parallel parts of Deuteronomy 31. The prose and poetic predictions in 91:5–10 and the Apocalypse of Weeks have counterparts in Deuteronomy 31:16–18 + 32:1ff.[156]

However one construes the details of this development, the account of Noah's birth (chaps. 106–7) was added to chap. 105. As in chaps. 6–11, the Deluge is a type of the coming judgment and the collection ends with the promise of this salvation. At some later time chaps. 72–80 were inserted by attraction to 33:2–4, and then chaps. 37–71 were inserted between these two. Chapter 108 was appended to form the book as we know it.

NOTES

1. Our major Jewish primary sources for this period are 2 Macc 8–15 (Judas), 1 Macc 5–16 (Judas, Jonathan, and Simon), Jos. *J.W.* 1.54–119 (2.3–5.4), and *Ant.* 12.327–13.432 (12.8.1–13.16.6 [Hyrcanus through Alexandra]).

2. Cf., e.g., Jdt 6:2 and Isa 45:5.

3. E.g., 11:5, 11–15, 16; 12:4. On irony in Judith see Luis Alonso-Schöckel, "Narrative Structures in the Book of Judith," 8–11.

4. The wordplay is that of Paul Winter ("Judith, Book of," 1024) and is worthy of our author's irony.

5. Pfeiffer, *History*, 292–95.

6. A.-M. Dubarle, *Judith*, 1:137–56.

7. The term "parabolic" is drawn from the exposition of Judith by Ernst Haag (*Studien zum Buch Judith*), who sees the book as a freely composed parabolic presentation of the forces inherent in and behind the empirical history of Israel.

8. For examples of specific references to halakhic matters see 8:2–7; 9:1; 10:5; 11:13; 12:2, 5–8; 16:18, 24. For a discussion of the particulars see Y. M. Grintz, *Sefer Yehudith*, 47–51.

9. Cf. also 2 Macc 7 (below, p. 121), where the mother of the seven brothers speaks in the idiom of Second Isaiah's Zion figure.

10. Judith also recalls certain Israelite heroes. Cf. her prayer in 13:7 with that of Samson in Judg 16:28; cf. also 13:6–8 and 1 Sam 17:51, where David beheads Goliath with his own sword. The author clearly parallels Judith's action with that of the patriarch Simeon; cf. 9:2–3//9:8–10. If one accepts a Hasmonean date (see below) the name "Judith" naturally suggests a comparison with Judas Maccabeus.

11. Dubarle, *Judith*, 1:131–32.

12. Pfeiffer, *History*, 294.

13. Grintz, *Sefer Yehudith*, 15–55.

14. Pfeiffer, *History*, 294–95; O. Eissfeldt, *The Old Testament* (E.T.; New York: Harper, 1965) 586; Solomon Zeitlin, *The Book of Judith*, 26–31.

15. In Dan 3 the final redactor of Daniel certainly intends Nebuchadnezzar to be a figure for Antiochus.

16. See Zeitlin, *Judith*, 28–30.

17. See H. L. Ginsberg, "The Oldest Interpretation of the Suffering Servant," *VT* 3 (1953) 400–401.

18. On the location of a Simeonite settlement in this area see Grintz, *Sefer Yehudith*, 33; summarized in idem, "Judith, Book of," col. 452.

19. See F. Zimmermann, "Aids for the Recovery of the Hebrew Original of Judith," *JBL* 57 (1938) 67–74; Grintz, *Sefer Yehudith*, 56–63.

20. See Dubarle, *Judith*, 1:80–110.

21. See the notes by "Ed" and B. Bayer, "Judith, Book of," *EncJud* 10: 460–61.

22. For the other works see below, pp. 218–87, 299–303, 313–16. On the figure of Baruch, cf. Jer 32, 36, 43, and 45.

23. For this meaning of "to read in one's hearing" see H. Orlinsky, "The Septuagint as Holy Writ . . . ," *HUCA* 46 (1975) 94–96.

24. Carey A. Moore (*Daniel, Esther, and Jeremiah: The Additions*, 291) suggests that 2:5–3:8 may originally have been three independent prayers; his divisions are unconvincing, however. "And now . . ." (2:11) would hardly begin a prayer. 2:31–35 and 3:6–8 are logically related (see above) and represent similar clusters of motifs that are hardly coincidental.

25. See, e.g., the notes in O. C. Whitehouse, *APOT* 1:583ff., and in the *Oxford Annotated Apocrypha* (New York: Oxford University, 1977).

26. See Carey A. Moore, "Toward the Dating of the Book of Baruch," 312–17; and idem, *Daniel*, 291–93. The prayer may well be a traditional piece. For another prayer in the same style see "The Words of the Heavenly Lights," in Vermes, *Scrolls*, 202–5. However one solves the problem of the relationship between the composition of 1:1–15 and 1:16–3:8, it is clear that many stylistic elements bind them together.

27. See 1:15 and 2:1–2 and note the contrast between "we" in Jerusalem and "they" in dispersion in 2:3–5.

28. Noted by J. Goldstein in the work cited below in n. 43.

29. Cf. 1:12 and Jer 27:12.

30. Cf. Deut 30:1–5 but also 1 Kgs 8:47; cf. also Tob 13:7.

31. The passage may be redactional; the reference to the dead refers to 3:4. However, the direct address to Israel and the appellative "God" (rather than Lord) are at home in the poem.

32. Cf. Ezek 37 for the exposition of this idea.

33. On the giants see above, pp. 49–52.

34. Cf. esp. 3:37–4:2 with Sir 24:8–11, 24.

35. Cf. 4:7–8 with Deut 32:17–18 and 4:25 with Deut 33:29 (LXX).

36. Cf. Deut 30:7, and for the image of the enemy personified as a woman with children, cf. Isa 47:1–9.

37. Cf. Isa 49:14–23; 54:1–13; 60:4–9.

38. Cf. Isa 52:1–2.

39. On the relationship of chap. 5 to *Ps. Sol.* 11 see Moore, *Daniel*, 314–16.

40. See Pfeiffer, *History*, 415–16.

41. Moore's arguments (*Daniel*, 314–16) on the relationship of chap. 5 to *Ps. Sol.* 11 are problematic. If one grants that chap. 5 is dependent on *Ps. Sol.* 11 it is highly unlikely that 4:36–37 just happened to be close enough to *Ps. Sol.* 11 to draw other material from that psalm into chap. 5; nor, in view of *Ps. Sol.* 11:8, is Bar 5:1–3 simply a reversal of 4:20.

42. Emanuel Tov, *The Septuagint Translation of Jeremiah and Baruch*, 111–33, 165.

43. For this dating, see Jonathan Goldstein, "The Apocryphal Book of Baruch," Jubilee Volume of the American Academy for Jewish Research: Proceedings, vols. 46–47 (1979–80) 179–99.

44. Moore (*Daniel*, 260) suggests the early part of the second century B.C.E.; however, his arguments are at least partly met by Goldstein. We may mention a couple of elements that fit the time of the Exile but not 164. In the fifth year, Nebuchadnezzar was alive but Antiochus IV was not. Unlike 582, the principal problem in 164 was not captivity.

45. This section and the following section are based on my article "1 and 2 Maccabees—Same Story, Different Meaning," *CTM* 42 (1971) 515–26.

46. On this opposition see Tcherikover, *Hellenistic Civilization*, 188–92; and Jonathan A. Goldstein, *1 Maccabees*, 212–13.

47. Verses 43, 52–53 allude to this opposition.

48. At other times in Israelite history zealous deeds grant priestly credentials; in addition to Num 25, cf. Exod 32:25–29 and *Jub.* 30:17–19.

49. For the propriety of these examples see Goldstein, *1 Maccabees*, 6–7, 240–41. For similar catalogs, see above, Chapter 2, n. 40.

50. Nickelsburg, *Resurrection*, 97–102.

51. The form of this epilogue is typically biblical; cf. e.g., 1 Kgs 22:39, and below, 16:23–24. However, the negative "have not been recorded" is best paralleled in John 20:30; 21:25.

52. Note the preparations in 3:47–49; the dismissal of those not fit (3:56); and the practice of slaughtering all males, taking spoils, and total annihilation of the city in 5:28, 35, 51; cf. L. E. Toombs, "War, Ideas of," *IDB* 4:797–98.

53. Goldstein, *1 Maccabees*, 395.

54. On the date of composition see ibid., 63.

55. Ibid., 14–16.

56. Only chaps. 14–15, set in the reign of Demetrius I, seem to move beyond the scope of 2:19–22, which mentions Antiochus IV and Antiochus V.

57. See Goldstein, *1 Maccabees*, 34, and the references listed in n. 70.

58. For the same idea cf. above, pp. 32–33 (Tobit), and below, pp. 210–12 (*Pss. Sol.*).

59. Nickelsburg, *Resurrection*, 97–102.

60. Ibid., 102–9.

61. For other instances of the author's view of strictly appropriate retribution cf. 4:26, 38, 42; 5:10.

62. For another resurrection passage cf. 12:39–45.

63. For other instances of evident anti-Hasmonean sentiment see Goldstein, *1 Maccabees*, 78–80.

64. Ibid., 85–89.

65. Ibid., 84–85.

66. Ibid., 34–36.

67. See the account by L. Harding in DJD 1:5–7.

68. On the documents from the Second Revolt discovered in the Judean desert see below, p. 312. On the discovery of papyri from the late Persian period, see F. M. Cross, "The Papyri and Their Historical Implications," in *Discoveries in the Wâdi-ed-Dâliyeh*, AASOR 41 (1974) 17–29.

69. For an overview of the contents of the Qumran library, see Cross, *Library*, 30–47. On the results of the Qumran finds on the study of the biblical text itself see F. M. Cross and S. Talmon, eds., *Qumran and the History of the Biblical Text* (Cambridge: Harvard University, 1975).

70. See the discussion by Cross, *Library*, 70–106, and the references to Josephus and Philo cited by him on p. 71, n. 30.

71. The Greek equivalent of this word *(hosioi)* occurs frequently in the *Psalms of Solomon*, but the term may be used there in a generic sense rather than of a party.

72. See the discussion by Jerome Murphy-O'Connor, "The Judean Desert," in *Early Judaism and Its Modern Interpreters*, ed. R. A. Kraft and George W. E. Nickelsburg (Philadelphia: Fortress, 1986) 139–40.

73. See above, pp. 54, 78.

74. I have not treated two major sectarian scrolls; see Y. Yadin, *The Scroll of the War of the Sons of Light against the Sons of Darkness* (London: Oxford University, 1962); Y. Yadin, *The Temple Scroll* (see Preface to this edition).

75. For the original publication of the Cairo manuscripts see S. Schechter, *Documents of Jewish Sectaries* (1910), reprinted with a prolegomenon by J. A. Fitzmyer (New York: KTAV, 1970). For an early translation and commentary see R. H. Charles, *APOT* 2:785–834. The Cairo manuscripts provide the fullest text, but they are themselves fragmentary. Other parts of the document have been filled in from Qumran fragments. For a handy reconstruction based on unpublished fragments see Joseph A. Fitzmyer, *The Dead Sea Scrolls: Major Publications and Tools for Study*, 90–92. Treatments of various aspects of the document are found in Cross, *Library*, see index; and in J. T. Milik, *Ten Years of Discoveries in the Wilderness of Judaea*, see index. For other articles and bibliography see below, nn. 80, 82, 84, 87.

76. Cross, *Library*, 81–82.

77. J. Murphy-O'Connor, articles cited below in nn. 80, 82, 84, 87.

78. On the 390 years see Cross, *Library*, 132–33. On the unpublished Qumran fragments that probably preceded col. 1 see Fitzmyer, *Scrolls*, 90.

79. See below, pp. 131–32.

80. For a discussion of this section see J. Murphy-O'Connor, "An Early Essene Missionary Document?" *RB* 77 (1970) 201–29.

81. On the options of interpreting this passage see Cross, *Library*, 226–30. Some have suggested that the Hebrew word translated "staff" is behind the name Taxo in *T. Mos.* 9, ibid., 228, n. 73.

82. On this section see J. Murphy-O'Connor, "A Literary Analysis of Damascus Document VI,2-VIII,3," *RB* 78 (1971) 210–32.

83. For bibliography see Vermes, *Scrolls*, 159–60.

84. On this section see J. Murphy-O'Connor, "The Critique of the Princes of Judah," *RB* 79 (1972) 200–216.

85. At this point the two Cairo manuscripts overlap briefly.

86. The title "Messiah of Aaron and Israel" suggests a conflation of the two anointed leaders mentioned in Zechariah; see K. G. Kuhn, "The Two Messiahs of Aaron and Israel," in *The Scrolls and the New Testament*, ed. K. Stendahl (New York: Harper, 1957) 54–64. The Qumran Rule of the Community speaks of the messiahs of Aaron and Israel (9:9–11). If the manuscripts are correct the two figures have here merged into one.

87. On this section see J. Murphy-O'Connor, "A Literary Analysis of Damascus Document XIX,33–XX,34," *RB* 79 (1972) 554–64.

88. Parts of this section are missing; see Fitzmyer, *Scrolls*, 90–92. For a study of Qumran halakhah see L. Schiffman, *The Halakhah at Qumran*, SJLA 16 (Leiden: Brill, 1975).

89. Passages from the commentaries are cited by Scripture passage rather than by column and line.

90. See also Comm. on Hab 1:5. For a discussion see Cross, *Library*, 111–13, and the literature cited by him.

91. On the commentaries and Qumran interpretation see Maurya P. P. Horgan, *Pesharim: Qumran Interpretations of Biblical Books*, CBQMS 8 (Washington, D.C.: Catholic Biblical Association of America, 1979).

92. For this date, see Cross, *Library*, 120, n. 20.

93. The term has its roots in Third Isaiah, where it denotes righteous as opposed to unrighteous Israel. It is a favorite term in the Scrolls, and we meet it elsewhere, notably in parts of *1 Enoch*.

94. Certain passages refer only to "the Priest who [does something wrong]." The qualifying relative clause is an explication of the concept "wicked," which term is then usually not mentioned.

95. See above, n. 72, for references.

96. Cross, *Library*, 143–47.

97. So Milik, *Ten Years*, 65–66; and Cross, *Library*, 142.

98. See George W. E. Nickelsburg, "Simon—A Priest with a Reputation for Faithfulness," *BASOR* 223 (1976) 67–68.

99. See G. Jeremias, *Der Lehrer der Gerechtigkeit*, SUNT 2 (Göttingen: Vandenhoeck & Ruprecht, 1963) 36–126. B. E. Thiering ("Once More the Wicked Priest," *JBL* 97 [1978] 191–205) makes an unconvincing case for the identification of the Wicked Priest and the Man of Lies.

100. For publication see J. Allegro, DJD 5:42–50. See the important review and corrections of Allegro's work by J. Strugnell, "Notes en marge du volume V . . . ," *RQ* 7 (1970) 163–276, and the bibliography compiled by J. Fitzmyer in *CBQ* 31 (1969) 59–71.

101. Cross, *Library*, 147, n. 78.

102. Cf. also *1 Enoch* 98:15 (Gk.); Mark 13:6.

103. See Cross, *Library*, 124–27, and the literature cited by Y. Yadin, "Pesher Nahum Reconsidered," *IEJ* 21 (1971) 1, n. 2. For publication see DJD 5:37–42 and Strugnell's review cited above in n. 100.

104. So Cross, *Library*, 123, n. 25.

105. The Facile Interpreters are not mentioned by name in Comm. on 3:4, but a comparison with the other passages indicates that they are meant.

106. In a new interpretation on the basis of new evidence, Yadin ("Pesher Nahum") argues that the commentary is condoning the action of Alexander.

107. See Allegro, DJD 5:11–30.

108. Ibid., 24–25.

109. Cf. CD 1:18, which quotes this section of Isaiah, substituting the word *dārash* in the quotation of 30:10.

110. For a translation see Vermes, *Scrolls*, 245–47.

111. For a translation see ibid., 247–49.

112. Cf. The Rule of the Community, 1QS 9:11.

113. See the discussion of Cross, *Library*, 147–52, who enters into lengthy dialogue with Milik. Strugnell ("Notes en marge," 229) points out in this passage a quotation of Gen 49:5, which refers to Levi and Simeon (!) as "instruments of violence."

114. Cross, *Library*, 119.

115. This likely development, which I have followed in my discussion, has been worked out by J. Murphy-O'Connor, "La genèse littéraire de la Regle de la Communauté," *RB* 76 (1969) 528–49. For an alternative see C. H. Hunzinger, "Beobachtungen zur Erwicklung der Disziplinarordnung der Gemeinde von Qumran, in *Qumran-Probleme*, ed. H. Bardtke (Berlin: Akademie, 1963) 231–45.

116. That this section is a kind of "manifesto" is accepted by many scholars; see A. R. C. Leaney, *The Rule of Qumran and Its Meaning* (Philadelphia: Westminster, 1966) 211.

117. See the discussion in ibid., 191–95.

118. See K. Baltzer, *The Covenant Formulary* (E.T.; Philadelphia: Fortress, 1971) 167–69.

119. For a similar expansion in oracular form see *1 Enoch* 1:8. See also the blessings in the second appendix to the Rule, Vermes, *Scrolls*, 206–9.

120. See, e.g., *Jub.* 23:27–31. For a discussion of the eschatological dimensions of the Teaching of the Two Ways see Nickelsburg, *Resurrection*, 156–65, where reference is also made to other Jewish and Christian two-ways documents.

121. Murphy-O'Connor, "La genèse," 546. The plurals in this section are at odds with the singular forms before and after it.

122. Ibid., 544–45.

123. On these hymns and their authorship see Jeremias, *Lehrer*, 168–267.

124. On these hymns see H.-W. Kuhn, *Enderwartung und gegenwärtiges Heil*, SUNT 4 (Göttingen: Vandenhoeck & Ruprecht, 1966). For the broader

context of the kind of realized eschatology spelled out here see Nickelsburg, *Resurrection*, 144–69.

125. See Kuhn, *Enderwartung*, 29–33.

126. In Heb 11:37 the author alludes to the incident as to a familiar incident in the sequence of Jewish sacred history. Elements from the legend occur in Jewish literature: *b. Yebam.* 49a and *b. Sanh.* 103b; *y. Sanh.* 10:2 and *Vit. Isa.* 1.

127. So Charles, *APOT* 2:156–57.

128. For this name ("the elect one of evil") see David Flusser, "The Apocryphal Book of Ascensio Isaiae and the Dead Sea Sect," 35. The form does occur in some places in some manuscripts.

129. *Asc. Isa.* 2:6 suggests dependence only on the book of Kings; cf., however, *Asc. Isa.* 3:6 and 2 Chr 33:11.

130. Flusser, "Book," 30–37. The idea is developed in more detail by Marc Philonenko, "Le Martyre d'Ésaïe et l'histoire de la secte de Qoumrân," 1–10. See also A. Caquot, "Bref Commentaire du Martyre d'Isaïe," 93.

131. Cf. esp. 1QS 3:13–4:26 and the documents in J. T. Milik, "Milkî-ṣedeq et Milkî-reša'," *JJS* 23 (1972) 126–44. The closest parallel to the satanic name "Melchi-ra'" (*Asc. Isa.* 1:8) is Milkî-reša', and Isaiah's curse of Bechir-ra (5:9) closely parallels the curses in 4Q280 2:2 and 4Q287 4:4ff.; see Milik, ibid., 127, 130–31.

132. Cf. 1QS 3:13–4:26.

133. Cf. CD 4:12–18. Attribution of Satan worship to Manasseh may reflect the view that connects pagan deities with Satan and demons (*Jos. As.* 12:9–10; 1 Cor 10:19–21).

134. 1QS 8:12–16.

135. The civil functions of the Hasmonean princes facilitate a comparison with Manasseh.

136. So Flusser, "Book," 41–43. See 1QpHab 7:1–5.

137. 4QpNah; 4Q171 1:12–19.

138. The New Testament accounts about John the Baptist indicate that there were other apocalyptic prophets who retreated to the wilderness.

139. For the word *epistolē* see 100:6. See also Milik, *Books of Enoch*, 51–52.

140. One section of the Apocalypse (91:11–17) has been misplaced in the Ethiopic version. The original order, attested by the Aramaic, is 91:1–10, 18–19; 92; 93:1–10; 91:11–17; 93:11–14; 94; see Milik, *Books of Enoch*, 260–70.

141. The Aramaic text in question is 4QEn^g. References can be found in Milik, *Books of Enoch*, 260–70, ad loc.

142. See Nickelsburg, "Message," 310–15.

143. See Nickelsburg, "Texts," 107.

144. See Nickelsburg, "Riches."

145. See Nickelsburg, "Texts," 129.

146. See Nickelsburg, "Message," 315–18.

147. Ibid., 318–22.

148. Nickelsburg, *Resurrection*, 119.

149. Cf. also 1QS 8:4–7.

150. See, e.g., Charles, *Enoch*, 222; Tcherikover, *Hellenistic Civilization*, 258–59, 492; Nickelsburg, *Resurrection*, 113.

151. Tcherikover, *Hellenistic Civilization*, 258–59, 492.

152. See above, pp. 78–79.

153. For some other parallels between the redactional framework and the epistle, cf. 81:1//103:2. 81:4//102:4–5; 103:3; 104:5, 7. 82:4//99:10. 91: 3–4, 18–19//94:1–5.

154. There is no manuscript evidence that chaps. 81–82 belonged to the Qumran version of the astronomical book. See below, n. 156.

155. In addition to the parallels noted below see above regarding 93:11 and 95:3; see above, n. 148; and cf. 104:2 and Deut 28:12.

156. Milik (*Books of Enoch*, 13–14) thinks that 81:5ff. is subsequent to chaps. 85–90. The question is open.

BIBLIOGRAPHY

HISTORY

Schürer, *History*, 1:164–232.

JUDITH

TRANSLATION: The Apocrypha.

TEXT: Robert **Hanhart**, *Judith*, Septuaginta, Vetus Testamentum Graecum 8:4 (Göttingen: Vandenhoeck & Ruprecht, 1978), critical edition of the Greek text.

LITERATURE: Y. M. **Grintz**, *Sefer Yehudith* (Jerusalem: Bialik Institute, 1957 [Hebrew with English summary]), introduction, commentary, and retroversion into Hebrew. Idem, "Judith, Book of," *EncJud* 10:451–61, summary of Grintz's arguments, editorial addenda on Judith in the arts. Paul **Winter**, "Judith, Book of," *IDB* 2:1023–26. Ernst **Haag**, *Studien zum Buch Judith*, Trierer Theologische Studien 16 (Trier: Paulinus, 1963). A.-M. **Dubarle**, *Judith*, 2 vols., AnBib 24 (Rome: Biblical Institute, 1966), studies the Greek and Latin texts in relation to the Hebrew, traces the story through the midrashim and early Christian writers, presents texts and translations of the hypothetical Hebrew and of the midrashim. Morton S. **Enslin** and Solomon **Zeitlin**, *The Book of Judith*, JAL (Leiden: Brill, 1972), introduction, Greek text and annotated translation, good bibliography. Luis **Alonso-Schöckel**, "Narrative Structures in the Book of Judith," *The Center for Hermeneutical Studies in Hellenistic and Modern Culture*, Colloquy 11 (Berkeley: Graduate Theological Union, 1975) 1–20.

BARUCH

TRANSLATION: The Apocrypha.

TEXTS: Joseph **Ziegler**, *Ieremias, Baruch, Threni, Epistula Ieremiae*, Septuaginta, Vetus Testamentum Graecum 15 (Göttingen: Vandenhoeck & Ruprecht, 1957) 450–67, critical edition of the Greek text. Emanuel **Tov**, *The Book of Baruch also Called 1 Baruch*, SBLTT 8 (Missoula: Scholars Press, 1975), Greek text and translation; for 1:1–3:8, a retroversion into Hebrew with linguistic parallels from the Bible. J. J. **Kneucker**, *Das Buch Baruch* (Leipzig: Brockhaus, 1879), still an excellent commentary.

LITERATURE: Emanuel **Tov**, *The Septuagint Translation of Jeremiah and Baruch*, HSM 8 (Missoula: Scholars Press, 1976). Carey A. **Moore**, "Toward the Dating of the Book of Baruch," *CBQ* 36 (1974) 312–20. Idem, *Daniel, Esther, and Jeremiah: The Additions*, AB 44 (Garden City, N.Y.: Doubleday, 1977), introduction and commentary.

1 AND 2 MACCABEES

TRANSLATION: The Apocrypha.

TEXT: Werner **Kappler** and Robert **Hanhart**, *Maccabaeorum liber I, Maccabaeorum liber II*, Septuaginta, Vetus Testamentum Graecum 9:1–2 (Göttingen: Vandenhoeck & Ruprecht, 1967 [2d ed.], 1959), critical edition of the Greek text.

LITERATURE: For commentaries see F.-M. **Abel**, *Les livres des Maccabées*, EBib (Paris: Gabalda, 1949); F.-M. **Abel** and J. **Starcky**, *Les Livres des Maccabées*, EBib (Paris: Le Cerf, 1961); Jonathan A. **Goldstein**, *1 Maccabees*, AB 41 (Garden City, N.Y.: Doubleday, 1976); idem, *2 Maccabees*, AB 41a (Garden City, N.Y.: Doubleday, 1983).

THE QUMRAN SCROLLS

TRANSLATION: **Vermes**, *Scrolls.*

TEXTS: Eduard **Lohse**, *Die Texte aus Qumran*, 2d ed. (Munich: Kösel, 1971), vocalized Hebrew text with facing German translation.

LITERATURE: The secondary literature is massive. For three good introductions see J. T. **Milik**, *Ten Years of Discoveries in the Wilderness of Judaea*, SBT 26 (London: SCM, 1959); **Cross**, *Library*; Geza **Vermes**, *The Dead Sea Scrolls* (Cleveland: Collins, 1978). For an entrée to further bibliography see Joseph A. **Fitzmyer**, *The Dead Sea Scrolls: Major Publications and Tools for Study*, SBLSBS 8 (Missoula: Scholars Press, 1975).

THE MARTYRDOM OF ISAIAH

TRANSLATION: Michael A. **Knibb**, *PsOT* (the whole *Ascension*).

TEXTS AND OTHER TRANSLATIONS: R. H. **Charles**, *The Ascension of Isaiah* (London: Black, 1900), extensive introduction, annotated translation, critical edition of Ethiopic version with a synoptic presentation of the Greek, Latin, and Slavonic (in Latin translation) versions. Idem, *APOT* 2:155–62 (only the *Martyrdom*).

LITERATURE: David **Flusser**, "The Apocryphal Book of Ascensio Isaiae and the Dead Sea Sect," *IEJ* 3 (1953) 30–47. Marc **Philonenko**, "Le Martyre d'Ésaïe et l'histoire de la secte de Qoumrân," *Cahiers de la Revue d'histoire et de philosophie religieuses* 41 (1967) 1–10. A. **Caquot**, "Bref commentaire du 'Martyre d'Isaïe,'" *Sem* 23 (1973) 65–93. Michael E. **Stone**, "Isaiah, Martyrdom of," *Enc Jud* 9:71.

1 ENOCH 92–105

For relevant bibliography also pertaining to the whole of *1 Enoch* see the bibliography for Chapter 2.

TEXT: Campbell **Bonner,** *The Last Chapters of Enoch in Greek* (London: Chatto & Windus, 1937), introduction and annotated text of the Greek papyrus of *1 Enoch* 97:6–107.

LITERATURE: George W. E. **Nickelsburg,** Jr., "Enoch 97–104: A Study of the Greek and Ethiopic Texts," in *Armenian and Biblical Studies,* ed. Michael E. Stone, Sion Suppl. 1 (Jerusalem: St. James, 1976) 90–156. Idem, "The Apocalyptic Message of 1 Enoch 92–105," *CBQ* 39 (1977) 309–28. Idem, "Riches, the Rich, and God's Judgment in 1 Enoch 92–105 and the Gospel According to Luke," *NTS* 25 (1979) 324–44.

5

Israel in Egypt

As early as the Babylonian Exile, Egypt was the location of Jewish settlements. The written products of Egyptian Jewry comprise a large corpus of literary and nonliterary documents that run the gamut from everyday correspondence and business records to highly polished philosophical treatises. From the island of Elephantine we have the correspondence of a Jewish military colony in the fifth century B.C.E. but also Aramaic fragments of the *Story of Ahikar,* a court tale of Mesopotamian origin that migrated through Jewish and, later, Christian circles.[1] Sizable collections of papyri from Ptolemaic to Byzantine times have been uncovered in Oxyrhynchus and in other locations.[2] The Greek translation of the Bible, the Septuagint, is itself a literary product of third- to second-century Egyptian Judaism that reflects interpretive traditions and cultural conditions in the land of its origin.[3] The bulky works of Philo of Alexandria not only are a tribute to the fertile mind of this Jewish philosopher of the first century C.E. but also testify to how Jews participated in the intellectual climate of the great center of Hellenistic learning and ferment.[4] Other theological works of possible Egyptian origin which we shall treat in subsequent chapters include the *Testament of Abraham,* the *Testament of Job, Joseph and Aseneth,* and *3 Baruch.*

In the present chapter we shall discuss six texts written between ca. 140 B.C.E. and 70 C.E. We treat them as a group because it is virtually certain that they were written in or for Egypt and because, with the exception of *2 Enoch,* they share an explicit concern with life in the Dispersion. How ought one to relate or respond to one's Gentile neighbors and the culture that they represent? The answers vary. *Aristeas* recommends rapprochement. Book 3 of the *Sibylline Oracles* exhorts the Gentiles to worship the one true God. Wisdom of Solomon may be making a similar appeal to righteous conduct. At the same time, this book and 3 Maccabees are wary of the abuse of power by Gentile rulers and their rich friends, and these writers appear to be smarting from the experience. Opposition to pagan idolatry and sexual promiscuity is a common motif even in the writings that have a relatively positive view toward the Gentiles. On these issues there can be no compromise.

Their setting in the Dispersion notwithstanding, these authors reveal various concerns and connections with Palestinian Judaism. In different ways Temple and cult are a topic of discussion, sometimes peripherally. Wisdom of Solomon knows apocalyptic traditions at home in Palestine, and *2 Enoch* is a massive rewriting of what appears to have been a penultimate form of *1 Enoch*.

Because we are dealing with a long time-span and in view of the many complexities involved in reconstructing the history of Egyptian Judaism during this period, we shall make only brief historical observations as these relate to the individual books. The reader may consult the bibliography for detailed discussions.

THE SIBYLLINE ORACLES, BOOK 3

"Sibyl" is a term that the ancients used to designate a woman who in a state of ecstasy uttered generally gloomy oracles about future events.[5] Our earliest sources speak of only one sibyl, who was believed to have lived in Erythrae in Ionia. Over the centuries, however, pagans, Jews, and Christians generated a massive oracular literature—most of it now lost—which was ascribed to some thirty or forty different sibyls. Our present collection of *Sibylline Oracles* was compiled no earlier than 500 C.E. and is comprised of twelve books.[6] As an example of the genre, we shall discuss book 3, which was composed in Egypt in the second century B.C.E.

The *Sibyllines* were composed in Greek hexameters and generally lack the parallelism typical of Semitic poetry. They are particularly noteworthy for their explicit references to political events in named places. These often function as signifiers of the time of the end. The oracles are also marked by a syncretistic use of pagan mythologies and conversely by powerful polemics against pagan idolatry and immorality. Frequent references to the uniqueness, eternity, and omnipotence of the God of the Jews dominate the compositions.

Lines 1–96 of book 3 are widely considered to be of an origin different

from that of the rest of the book.[7] Lines 1–45 constitute a general introduction that proclaims the creative power and activity of God and indicts idolatry and immorality. The section is prefaced by an ecstatic
prophetic formula that recurs several times in the book:

> Nay, why did my heart again flutter,
>   and why is my soul, lashed with a spur from within,
>   compelled to announce my message to all? (ll. 4–6; Lanchester, *APOT* 2)

The introduction is followed by three oracles that describe events of the
end-time (46–62, 63–74, 75–96). The first and last of these oracles date
from the time of Cleopatra (ca. 30 B.C.E.).[8] In the first oracle the author
alludes to the second Roman triumvirate (52) and announces that the
kingdom of God will appear when Rome has conquered Egypt. The third
oracle anticipates the dissolution of the universe during the reign of
Cleopatra, the widow, who is here depicted as a personification of Isis,
the universal queen (77). The second oracle is probably contemporary
with book 5 and reflects the late first-century C.E. legend of the return of
Nero as a wonder-working, prophetic personification of Beliar (Satan).[9]

The succession of kingdoms and their fates is the subject matter of ll.
97–349. In the first major part of this section, the author uses the story of
Babel (97–107; Gen 11) as preface to a summary of the Greek myths of
the Titans (110–58), which provide a paradigm for the succession of the
kingdoms listed in ll. 158–61.[10] A second list of kingdoms begins with
"the house of Solomon" and continues through Greece and Rome to the
"seventh reign," when a king of Greek origin will rule over Egypt (162–
93). Then Israel will be great again, and the nations will be punished
(194–210). There follows a survey of Israel's history from Abraham to
the building of the Second Temple (211–94), including an impressive
eulogy to the Jewish people (218–47), which acts as a foil to the anti-
Gentile indictments that occur throughout the book. The section ends
with a series of Woes against the nations (295–349). Lines 316–18 allude
to the struggle between Ptolemy VI Philometor and Ptolemy VIII Euergetes (169–145 B.C.E.) and thus identify the aforementioned "seventh
reign" with that of either Philometor or Euergetes.

Lines 350–489 contain three oracles of diverse origin. Lines 350–80 date
from the time of Cleopatra. A strong anti-Macedonian bias is evident in
ll. 381–400. An oracle that originally made reference to Alexander the

Great (388–91) has evidently been updated on the basis of Daniel 7 to make reference to Antiochus IV (396–400). The predominance of references to Asia in ll. 401–88 suggests that this oracle is an adaptation of material originally attributed to the Erythraean sibyl. An allusion to the Roman civil war (464–69) indicates a date after 88 B.C.E.

After the typical prophetic formula (489–91) the Woes that began in 303 are continued (492–519). A lengthy indictment of the Greeks (520–71) leads to an even longer description of the end-time (573–808). First the Jews are eulogized for their observance of Law and cult, and this piety is here explicitly contrasted with the idolatry and immorality of the Gentiles (573–600). God's punishment will follow (601–15) during the time of the seventh king (608), and then God will bring blessing and fertility to the human race (616–23). The wise reader is exhorted to repent and turn to the worship of the only God (624–31) lest he suffer God's wrath (632–51). God will send a king "from the sun" as executor of his judgment (652–55). The people of the mighty God will grow wealthy, and when the kings of the nations assault Jerusalem and its Temple, God will turn the elements against them (657–701). Then the sons of the great God will dwell securely around his Temple, and the nations will come confessing their sins and acknowledging him as God (702–31).[11] All this is a warning that Greece should repent (732–40; cf. 520–72). The author again envisions the fecundity of the end-time (741–60), and reference to God's wrath leads to a warning to shun immorality (761–66). When God ushers in his everlasting kingdom all the nations will bring him tribute, and the world will revert to paradisiacal peace (767–95). After a description of the signs of the end (796–808) the book closes with prophetic formulas and an ascription of the work to the sibyl of Erythrae (809–29).

Several factors suggest that book 3 was composed during the reign of Ptolemy VI Philometor around the middle of the second century B.C.E. As we have seen, the author connects the end-time with the reign of the seventh king (193, 318, 608). Furthermore, he speaks of a savior king whom God will send "from the sun" (652–56). This terminology appears to refer to an Egyptian king, and the analogy of l. 286 (God will send Cyrus) supports the idea that this author looks to the Ptolemaic line for a deliverer. The best setting for such a messianic expectation is the reign of Philometor, whose friendship for the Jews is recorded elsewhere.[12]

Book 3 shows a remarkable openness to the Gentiles and may well have been written to be read by them. It employs Greek literary forms and draws on motifs from Greek mythology. More important, its attacks on Gentile idolatry and immorality are balanced by exhortations that the Gentiles repent of these evils in order to escape divine judgment and obtain the blessings of the one true God. These demands notwithstanding, the author does not call for the wholesale surrender of the Hellenistic way of life, and, as we have seen, his messianic hope reflects an eirenic attitude toward the ruling house of Egypt. From this cross-cultural stance the author envisions the time when Jews and Gentiles may be joined in the worship of the one God, the universal Creator.[13]

ARISTEAS TO PHILOCRATES

In the whole of our literature this writing presents the most positive estimate of the Greeks and Greek culture and of the possibility for peaceful and productive coexistence between Jews and Greeks. The author has taken the name of Aristeas, who is alleged to be an influential courtier of Ptolemy II Philadelphus (283–247 B.C.E.). The book is a fictional account of the circumstances surrounding the Greek translation of the Torah, and it was purportedly written for the edification of Aristeas's brother Philocrates, whose interest in religious matters is duly noted in the prologue to the work (1–8).

The first major section of the book recounts the events surrounding Ptolemy's request for a translation of the Law (9–82). Narrative is interwoven with lengthy quotations of appropriate official documents. The request originates with Demetrius of Phalerum, who is alleged to have been in charge of the king's library in Alexandria (9–11).[14] When Ptolemy agrees to the project, Aristeas seizes this opportunity to convince the king that he should free all the Jewish slaves in his realm (12–20). The narrative in this section exemplifies the view of God to be propounded later. He answers prayer and rules the hearts of his creatures and guides their actions. Aristeas documents the king's accession to his request by quoting the decree of emancipation (21–25), which may be a reworked version of a genuine decree of Ptolemy II calling for the registration of slaves in Egypt.[15] After the release of the slaves (26–27) Ptolemy requests from Demetrius an official memorandum regarding the translation, which is of course quoted (28–32). The Jewish Law is recommended as "most philosophical" (cf. 4 Macc 1:1; see below, pp. 223–24) and "flawless" thanks to its divine origin, and the alleged opinion of the Greek historian Hecateus of Abdera is mustered in support of this viewpoint. Ptolemy orders gifts prepared for the Jerusalem Temple (33–34). Aristeas reproduces in full Ptolemy's letter to Eleazar the high priest, requesting the translation (35–40) and Eleazar's letter, acceding to the request and listing the names of the seventy-two men who will be sent to Alexandria as translators (41–51). The section closes with a lengthy and detailed description of the gifts sent to Jerusalem (51–82). Such descriptions were a well-known literary genre in the ancient world.[16] The description of the table of shewbread quotes the Septuagint version of the biblical descriptions of this furnishing (Exod 23:23–30; 37:10–15).[17]

The second major section is set in Judea (83–171). Aristeas first describes the Temple and its cult and the city (83–106). Twice he mentions his emotional responses to Eleazar's high-priestly apparel and ministrations (96, 99; cf. Sir 50:1–21). His idealized description of the country is marked by utopian elements that characterize travelogues in classical and Hellenistic literature (107–20).[18] After these extensive digressions Aristeas returns to his main topic, the translation (120–29). He praises the qualifications of the men chosen to be translators: their proficiency in both Jewish and Greek literature and their ability to carry on learned conversations about the Law. Aristeas then records Eleazar's lengthy speech on the Law (130–71). The first part stresses the justice of the code and of the omniscient God who gave it and enforces it (130–33). This one God, the Creator, is contrasted with the idols and idolatry of the Egyptians (134–38). In the heart of his speech Eleazar employs the allegorical method to explain and defend the rationality of the Jewish food laws in terms that would be understandable to his Greek audience and in large part compatible with their own views. Carnivorous animals are not to be eaten because they "oppress the rest and procure their food with injustice" (144–49; Hadas). As we shall see, tyranny and justice are the ultimate vice and virtue in this author's theory of kingship. The parted hoof of kosher animals symbolizes the Jews' discrimination in their deeds and their being set apart from other people, especially those guilty of promiscuous sexual unions (150–52). The chewing of the cud of kosher animals is symbolic of the pious remembrance of God (153–60). Then, employing a bit of folk physiology, Eleazar makes the weasel symbolic of the sinful practice of gossip and informing (165–67). The section as a whole foreshadows the massive use of allegory that will characterize the biblical exposition of Philo of Alexandria.

The longest and major section of the writing recounts Ptolemy's reception of the Jewish translators and the table talk during the banqueting that preceded the beginning of the translation work (172–300). The king is so anxious to meet the sages that they are given immediate and unprecedented access to Ptolemy, who pays homage to them and the divine Law (172–80). Thereupon they are feted at a daily banquet seven days in a row. Authors in antiquity often made such banquets the setting for wise and witty talk and for learned answers to the weighty questions posed by kings.[19] Here at each of the seven banquets the king addresses questions to ten or eleven of the seventy-two translators and compliments each on his prompt and sagacious response. The topic of conversation is the theory and practice of kingship. The seventy-two answers provide many variations on a few basic themes. Each answer climaxes with a reference to "God" or "divine" activity. God is the Creator, the "giver" of all good things, who inspires the human heart and rules, governs, and guides kings and kingdoms. His help and guidance are readily accessible to those who pray for them, and the good and wise king imitates God's characteristics and virtues. Chief among these are justice, munificence, gentleness, mercy, and patience. Arrogance, cruelty, and tyranny are to be avoided. There is little that is peculiarly Jewish in these answers. Most of their contents and themes, including the references to God and the imitation of God, are paralleled in pagan Hellenistic treatises on kingship.[20] It is all the more remarkable then that Ptolemy praises the sages for exceeding the philosophers in their wisdom and particularly in making God their starting point (235). Aristeas concludes his account of the banquets by commenting on the "incredible" instantaneous wisdom of these sages and affirming several times the veracity of the account (295–300).

Aristeas's account of the translation work itself is very brief (301–8). Translation results are compared and harmonized. Coincidentally and possibly providentially the work is completed in seventy-two days. Thereafter the translation is ratified by the Jewish community, whose rulers anathematize any revisions, additions, transpositions, or excisions (308–11). Then the entire translation is read to Ptolemy, who expresses his admiration for Moses' intellect. Several incidents that stress the divine origin of the Law and explain why it cannot be copied or quoted by

Gentile authors are recounted (312–16). After promising that the books will be cared for with great reverence, the king sends the translators home with great praise and lavish gifts (317–21). The book concludes with an epilogue addressed to Philocrates.

It is universally agreed that this work was written by a Jew rather than by an Egyptian courtier named Aristeas. Archaizing statements and historical anachronisms indicate that it was composed not during the reign of Ptolemy Philadelphus but at some later time.[21] Scholars do not agree on the actual date of composition, but linguistic and other considerations may well point to the last third of the second century B.C.E., perhaps during the reign of Ptolemy VIII Euergetes.[22] Its milieu appears to have been Alexandria.

The author's message and general purpose are evident in his remarkable portrait of Gentiles and Jews and their interaction. Differences between Jews and Gentiles are reduced to a minimum. Among pagan practices only idolatry and sexual immorality are singled out for serious criticism. While the Law is binding on Jews, Eleazar emphasizes that the Law's intent is compatible with the finest in Gentile ethics and wisdom. By the same token the author employs a variety of genres and motifs common to the Hellenistic literary world in general.[23] Particularly noteworthy is the manner in which things Jewish (Temple, cult, land, Jewish wisdom, and of course the Law) are repeatedly the objects of Gentile admiration and amazement, expressed by Ptolemy and his courtiers, including Aristeas himself, whose alleged authorship of the book is surely tied to this function. Consonant with these reactions is the manner in which the one God, by definition the Creator and the God of Israel, effectively moves the heart of the king and catalyzes his action. Ptolemy's decree of emancipation comes in response to Aristeas's prayer. Moreover, the obvious should not be forgotten: it is at the suggestion of the Gentile courtier Demetrius and by request of his king that the Law is translated into a Greek version that is ratified as definitive in the Jewish community of Alexandria. The wisdom of the Jewish sages provides the theoretical undergirding for the view of God as universal sovereign and guide and mover of Gentile kings. In this portrait we see the assertion and probably the plea that Greeks can be right and good and beneficent and that the influence and acts of God make it possible for Jews to coexist and interact with them to the mutual benefit of both.[24]

Of the variegated contents of this book, it was the story of the translation that most attracted Jewish and Christian authors, who progressively embellished it into a highly miraculous account.[25]

3 MACCABEES

Persecution, oppression, and miraculous deliverance are the stuff of this piece of "pathetic history" (see above, p. 118). Elaborate and often bombastic Greek is the language of its composition. In contrast to the eirenic and inclusive approach of *Aristeas*, the point of view of this work is narrowly Jewish and strongly anti-Gentile. Ptolemaic Palestine and Egypt provide the settings for its two separate parts, which are held together loosely by a common theme and plot.

Chapters 1–2, the first part, are themselves comprised of two separate episodes. The original beginning of the book appears to have been lost,[26] and the story begins abruptly in the middle of a narrative that leads quickly to a brief but vivid account of the battle at Raphia in 217 B.C.E. between Ptolemy IV Philopator and Antiochus III ("the Great"). The accuracy of some of the details in 1:1–7 indicates dependence on a reliable historical source.[27] Dositheus's loyalty to the crown and his later apostasy from Judaism (1:3) are motifs that foreshadow later developments in the book (3:3; 2:31–33).

Royal arrogance and divine judgment are the leitmotifs in the story of Ptolemy's visit to Jerusalem (1:8–2:24), and we shall meet them again in the second part of the book. When Ptolemy expresses his intention to enter the holy of holies he provokes a mass demonstration, which the author describes at length in typical pathetic style for the purpose of building suspense (1:8–29). When Ptolemy is refused entrance to the holy of holies, curiosity gives way to arrogance (1:25–26). In his prayer for deliverance Simon the high priest repeatedly addresses God as (sole) King and Ruler and invokes his judgment on Ptolemy's arrogance, citing similar incidents in the past as paradigms for intervention in the present (2:1–20). He confesses the nation's sins, which have caused the subjugation to the Gentiles and led to the present disaster, and he beseeches God to vindicate his glory by protecting the place dedicated to his name. The divine scourge rescues the Temple from defilement but reinforces the king's arrogance (2:21–24; contrast 2 Macc 3:9–39 and the related story of Heliodorus, who learns his lesson).

Intent upon revenge, Ptolemy returns to Egypt and orders a census of the Alexandrian Jews for the purpose of reducing them to the status of slaves (2:25–30). They may escape this burden and disgrace by being initiated into the mysteries of Dionysus.[28] Some Jews accept the offer, thereby cutting themselves off from their compatriots. The literary function of this scene is to highlight the king's arrogance and to emphasize the courage of the majority of Jews, who refuse to abandon their traditional religion for a cult incompatible with it.

For the second part of his book (chaps. 3–7) the author has reworked a legend originally set in the reign of Ptolemy VIII Euergetes (145–117 B.C.E.),[29] identified its main character with the villain of chaps. 1–2, intertwined motifs from those chapters, and introduced yet others, shaping the whole as a story of the persecution, vindication, and exaltation of the righteous (see above, pp. 22–26).[30] The thrust of the narrative is clear, but the conflation of sources and traditions leads to more than a little confusion and contradiction.[31]

The legend behind these chapters is sketched by Josephus (*Ag. Ap.* 2:53–56). When Ptolemy VIII sought to exterminate the Jews of Alexandria by turning drunk elephants against them in the hippodrome the animals turned on Ptolemy's friends, killing a large number of them. Upon seeing an apparition, and with the encouragement of his concubine, the king repented of his deed. The Jews in their turn celebrated the event with an annual festival.

Ptolemy's intent to kill the Jews is tied in 3:1 to their refusal to apostasize (2:32–33) but is extended to include all the Jews of Egypt. Alongside this intent is a conspiracy by certain other people (3:2–7), an element typical of the story of the persecuted righteous. The Jews' loyalty to the king is contrasted with accusations of treason that grow out of their peculiar cultic and legal observances. The loyalty and innocence of the Jews is attested by certain "Greeks" and friends and neighbors, who, however, are unable to help them (3:8–10). Ptolemy's decree of extermination stresses their unique way of life, indicts them as traitors, and cites as evidence the incidents in 1:8–2:24 and 2:27–33.

The narrative that follows is characterized by motifs and literary devices already familiar to us from 3 Maccabees. The section as a whole reveals a number of contradictions. The people are brought from all over Egypt (4:1), yet they can fit into the confines of the hippodrome (4:11). Although they are marked for death they are still subject to registration

(4:14–21). As in the first part, the author narrates pathetic history (4:4–10; 5:25, 48–51). Three times, Hermon the keeper of the elephants tries to carry out his orders (5:1–22, 23–35; 5:36–6:21). This repetition serves to build up the suspense, to underscore the king's arrogance, and to stress God's sovereign power and response to prayer (5:12–13, 25, 27, 30, 35). These motifs are brought to a head in chaps. 6–7. Eleazar's prayer—which parallels Simon's—cites previous examples of deliverance from Gentiles (in Jonah's case, from the depths of Sheol), contrasts Israel and their Gentile oppressors, and implores judgment and deliverance (6:2–15). The climax of the work is typical of the stories of the persecuted righteous. The enemy soldiers are killed (6:16–21). The Jews are vindicated of the accusations against them and are set free (6:24–29). In this scene and the decree that follows (7:1–9), the king publicly acclaims the God he had opposed. The Jews are granted authority to execute the apostates (7:10–15). Feasts of celebration are held, and the book ends on a note of jubilation and doxology.

Third Maccabees accentuates the differences between Jews and Gentiles and thus stands in marked contrast to *Aristeas,* a book with which it otherwise shares many literary and other features. Whereas *Aristeas* asserts that the best in Greek culture has much in common with Judaism and that Jews and Gentiles can coexist peacefully, 3 Maccabees recounts how exclusivistic attitudes about the sanctity of the Temple, the worship of the one God, and the observance of God's Law have been the object of Gentile derision and the cause of political and social oppression and persecution. In contrast to Pseudo-Aristeas's glowing portrait of Ptolemy II as a model ruler and a patron of the Jews, the present author depicts Ptolemy IV—the main character of this work—as the epitome of the cruel, insolent, and unreasoning tyrant who instigates serious troubles for the Jews and is brought to their side only through direct, repeated intervention by God. According to 3 Maccabees, Jerusalem suffers under Gentile subjugation and Egypt is a place of exile where the Jews live as strangers in a strange land (6:3, 10)[32] even if they sometimes find friends and neighbors who admire and help them. The references to apostasy may indicate that the author perceives this as a real danger among his readers. In any event, he celebrates the courage of those who stand fast and promises them deliverance and vindication—elements essential to the literary genre of chaps. 3–7.

Two different kinds of considerations suggest two different dates for

3 Maccabees. According to one viewpoint the Greek word for census (*laographia*) indicates a date between 20 and 15 B.C.E.[33] This interpretation finds the closest analogy to our narrative in the seventh year of Augustus's reign (24/23 B.C.E.), when a census was taken in Egypt for the purpose of imposing a poll tax that discriminated between the citizens of the Greek cities and the people of the land, who were effectively reduced to a degraded and enslaved status. A second possible date for 3 Maccabees is derived from literary considerations. According to this interpretation a comparison of parallels in 3 Maccabees and the Greek additions to Esther indicates the priority of 3 Maccabees,[34] which must then be dated before 77 B.C.E., the *terminus ad quem* for the translation of Esther (see below, p. 173). It is possible that these conflicting indications of different dates reflect different stages in the literary history of 3 Maccabees, which is patently a conflation of traditions or sources.

Third Maccabees is related to a number of other Jewish writings. The differences notwithstanding, its style and language, the content of Ptolemy's second decree, and its division into scenes in Jerusalem and Alexandria resemble similar features in *Aristeas*.[35] Its historical style is akin to that of 2 Maccabees, and the stories in 3 Maccabees 2 and 2 Maccabees 3 are obviously variants of the same tradition.[36] With respect to its genre 3 Maccabees is most closely related to the tales of persecution and exaltation in Daniel 1–6 (see above, pp. 22–24) and Esther. Moreover, specific details in the plots of 3 Maccabees and the canonical book of Esther are essentially the same. Jews are cited for their peculiar laws and accused of disobeying royal law. Their death is decreed, but they are rescued and celebrate the occasion with a special feast. Even closer to 3 Maccabees is the Greek translation and expansion of Esther, in which the two royal decrees and the prayers of Mordecai and Esther reveal verbatim parallels with their counterparts in 3 Maccabees (see below, pp. 174–75). Finally, as a story of the persecuted and vindicated righteous, 3 Maccabees has important formal similarities with Wisdom 2, 4–5 as well as a number of verbal parallels (see below, pp. 176–79).[37]

ADDITIONS TO THE BOOK OF ESTHER

The Greek translation of Esther includes six passages not found in the Hebrew, canonical version of the book. When Saint Jerome revised the Old Latin version of the Bible, he removed all but the last of them and appended them as a collection at the end of the canonical book. From this position they received the chapter and verse numbers found in modern editions. Here is the order of the Greek translation:

Sections from Hebrew	The Additions
	A. 11:2–12:6, introduction, Mordecai's dream, transition
1:1–3:13	
	B. 13:1–7, Artaxerxes's decree of extermination
3:14–4:17	
	C. 13:8–14:19, Mordecai's, Esther's prayers
5:1–2 (omitted)	D. 15:1–16, Esther before the king
5:3–8:12	
	E. 16:1–24, Artaxerxes's decree
8:13–10:3	
	F. 10:1–11:1, interpretation of dream, conclusion, colophon

The purpose of these additions[38] was to add an explicitly religious dimension to the original form of the book (which never mentions God), to enhance its dramatic appeal, and to add a note of authenticity.[39] Alongside the additions certain passages in the Hebrew have been changed, usually for purposes of harmonization. Sections B and E appear to have been composed in Greek, while the others may translate additions already made to the Hebrew text.[40] The colophon, or "publisher's postscript," attributes the translation to "Lysimachus, the son of Ptolemy, one of the residents of Jerusalem" and indicates that it was brought to Egypt during the fourth year of the reign of Ptolemy and Cleopatra, that is, in 77 B.C.E. (11:1).[41]

Additions A and F

The book is framed by Mordecai's dream and its interpretation. The battle of the dragons (Mordecai and Haman), the phenomena in heaven and earth, and the Gentiles' preparation for war against the Jews add a cosmic dimension to the tale. In the midst of this tumult appears Esther, the tiny spring become a river, God's appointed deliverer sent in answer to the people's prayer. Chapter 12 expands on 2:21–23, which is altered at that place in the Greek translation to indicate that Mordecai's promotion was the cause of the conspiracy against the king (cf. Dan 6:3–4).

Addition B

The "copy" of Artaxerxes's decree adds a note of authenticity to the narrative.[42] The charges against the Jews (13:3–5) elaborate on 3:8, stressing the Jews' peculiarity and alleged disobedience by adding the motifs of hostility and strangeness. This hostility and other wording unique to 13:4–7 are paralleled in 3 Maccabees 3:7, 24–26.[43]

Addition C

The prayers of Mordecai and Esther add an important religious dimension that is not explicit in the Hebrew book. The deliverance of the Jews comes in response to prayer. Mordecai's prayer is roughly paralleled by the prayers of Simon and Eleazar in 3 Maccabees 2 and 6 (cf. 13:9; 3 Macc 2:2). Mordecai's "remembrance" of all the works of the Lord may indicate the priority of 3 Maccabees, where God's deeds are enumerated. In chap. 14 Esther's acts of self-abasement constitute a foil for her self-adornment in chap. 15. Her prayer climaxes in a petition that God use her speech as an instrument of deliverance (14:13–14; cf. Jdt 9). Verses 15–18 answer questions about the propriety and problems of Esther's Jewish-Gentile marriage. The attack on the Temple which Esther antici-pates (14:9) is not mentioned earlier in the book. This would seem to indicate the priority of 3 Maccabees, where the king attempts to enter the Temple and then contemplates its destruction (chaps. 1–2; 5:42–43; cf. also Esth 14:8, 10; 2 Macc 4:16).

Addition D

This expansion and replacement of 5:1–2 adds a strong dramatic and emotive element to the story. Esther's audience with the king is depicted with language at home in biblical epiphanies. Verses 2 and 8 interpret the king's response to Esther as an answer to her prayer, made the more dramatic and miraculous by the king's sudden change of disposition.

Addition E

This decree adds a note of authenticity. More important, it resolves tensions created in the first part of the story. God has judged the arrogant enemy who accused his people (16:2–6). Thereby he vindicates their innocence, which is acclaimed by the king (16:15–16), who also publicly acclaims the universal sovereignty of this God (16:21). These elements are all typical of the stories of the persecuted righteous (see above, pp. 22–26). Moreover, verbatim parallels indicate a close relationship between 16:3–6, 10–16 and 3 Maccabees 6:23–28, 7:2, 3:18, and 5:20.

In the Hebrew book of Esther the tale of the persecuted and exalted courtier (Mordecai) is the nucleus of a story about the persecution and rescue of the Jewish people.[44] The additions in the Greek version embellish and reinforce the genre, focusing on the fate of "the righteous nation." If our interpretation is correct these additions were made on the analogy of 3 Maccabees. The occasion for the revision may have been to introduce the celebration of the feast of Purim in the place of the festival that commemorated the Jews' deliverance from death in the hippodrome.[45]

THE WISDOM OF SOLOMON

The Wisdom of Solomon is an exhortation to pursue Wisdom and thereby to live the righteous life that issues in immortality. In order to accomplish his purpose the author employs the popular Hellenistic genre of the protreptic, a treatise that made "an appeal to follow a meaningful philosophy as a way of life."[46] Working with this literary form and its typical rhetorical devices and modes of expression and structuring his material with consummate artistry,[47] the sage combines the wisdom and apocalyptic traditions of Israel, synthesizing them with an eclectic use of Greek philosophy and religious thought.[48] In assuming the identity of King Solomon he specifies wisdom as his chief topic, roots that wisdom in the religious tradition of Israel, and claims authority for his address to the kings and rulers of the earth (1:1; 6:1–11). The Wisdom of Solomon is divided into three closely related and interlocking parts: the "book of eschatology" (1:1–6:11), the "book of wisdom" (6:12–9:18), and the "book of history" (chaps. 10–19).

God's judgment of the righteous and the ungodly is the subject of 1:1–6:11. This "book of eschatology" is framed by a pair of exhortations addressed to rulers, kings, and judges (1:1–15; 6:1–11). The initial exhortation introduces the major subjects of the work—wisdom, righteousness and sin, immortality and death—and indicates their interrelationship. Wisdom is God's Spirit. This cosmic force which fills the world and holds all things together (v. 7) is also a divine gift that dwells within individuals (vv. 2–5; cf. 7:27). She is God's self-manifestation to those who seek him in uprightness (v. 1) and the means by which pious souls become friends of God and prophets (7:27). Wisdom also has a juridical function as witness against the ungodly (vv. 6–11). Verses 12–15 contrast the consequences of sin and righteousness: death and immortality. Death is not the termination of biological life, nor is immortality something that is awaited beyond the grave. Death and immortality are states in which the ungodly and the righteous participate here and now and which continue unbroken in spite of biological death.

As the primary vehicle of his thesis the author tells a two-part story (1:16–2:20; 4:16–5:13) that is narrated primarily in two matched speeches (2:1–20; 5:4–13). In the first of these "the ungodly" make a series of assertions; in the second they retract some of the assertions, while they recognize that others have come true. The basic claim of the ungodly is that death means extinction (2:1–5). Because there is only this life, one should enjoy it (2:6–11), even when this means the oppression and persecution of others (2:10–20). In vv. 10–20 and especially vv. 12–20 the author takes up the typical elements of the story of the persecution and exaltation of the righteous one: the conspiracy and its cause, the condemnation, the construal of death as an ordeal (see above, pp. 22–26).[49] The hero of this story is an unnamed righteous man who preaches against the sins of the ungodly and legitimates his actions by claiming to be God's son or servant and under special divine protection. In condemning him to death the ungodly propose to test his claims. When God does not rescue him from death they will have proven that the righteous one is not God's son and that there is no divine retribution. Because their argument is based on the premise that death is extinction, this rescue and retribution must occur in this life. The author has the ungodly narrate the story (as they expect it to happen) in order to have them present as forcefully as possible the false viewpoint he will later have them retract.

The author now offers his own refutation (2:21–3:9). God created man in his own image and destined him for incorruption. Therefore the righteous only *seem* to die. In reality they pass to the fullness of immortality; their souls are in the hands of God and rest in his peace. The ungodly, in their blindness and folly, fail to perceive the hidden purposes of God. What they offer as proof of their claim—the shameful "death" of the righteous one—is God's means of testing the righteous one and is the moment of his rescue. This rescue and the vindication and exaltation of the righteous one, as well as the punishment of the ungodly (3:7–11), will be narrated in the second part of the story.

Before he returns to the story of the *persecuted* righteous one, however, the author generalizes his discussion of right and wrong perspectives on judgment by declaring invalid certain classical examples of this-worldly reward and punishment (3:12–4:15). The undefiled barren woman "will have fruit" in the judgment. The righteous eunuch will have his place in the temple of the Lord. Conversely the children of adulterous unions will suffer, and they will witness against their parents in the judgment. The author begins to return to his story. Premature death is no sign of divine punishment (4:7–9), as is evident from the case of Enoch, the righteous one par excellence (4:10–15).

Verses 16–17 provide a transition between the example of Enoch and the story of the persecuted righteous one, and a brief reference to the death of the ungodly in vv. 18–19 leads to the second part of the story (4:20–5:13). As in the stories typical of the genre, it describes the exaltation and vindication of the persecuted righteous one and the punishment of the persecutors. In its form and nuances it provides a detailed reversal of the first part. When the ungodly come to the judgment, they meet the righteous one whom they persecuted and mocked. Exalted in the heavenly court he confronts them as judge. In astonishment they finally see. He was rescued. With their premises shattered they quake in fear, anticipating the dreadful consequences of their false logic—the reality of the divine retribution they had previously denied. In repentance they utter a second speech that corresponds to the first. Assertions previously made with confidence must now be retracted. They who thought that the righteous one's life was madness were themselves the fools. In their view his dishonorable "death" disproved his claim to be God's son and under his protection. Now they must acknowledge that he stands among the angels, the sons of God, par excellence. Moreover, they confess that they were guilty of sin, and thus they vindicate his indictment of them. In all these things they were wrong, but in one way they were right. They face the extinction they anticipated. This is so because they themselves summoned death (1:16), and now it claims them. Their nihilistic belief led to sinful actions, and these are punished by the annihilation they had posited in the first place. On the other hand the righteous will live forever (5:15–16). Theirs is the gift of immortality in which they had believed. Thus God will be the protector of those who trust in him to be their protector, and he will wreak vengeance on their foes, even the kings of the earth (5:15–23).

The "book of eschatology" ends with a second exhortation to the kings and judges (6:1–11). In view of God's judgment, mentioned in 1:6–12 and vividly portrayed in chap. 5, they should learn wisdom and avoid the iniquity of the ungodly.

Perhaps the most striking feature in these chapters is the repeated contrast between right and wrong perception. Right knowledge, which is the medium of salvation, is the recognition that things are not as they appear to be. The righteous one, who typifies the righteous in general, has insight into God's secret world and hidden purposes. Because he trusts in God's deliverance—all appearances to the contrary—and lives in consonance with that trust he is rewarded and vindicated. The ungodly are empiricists who view life and the world at face value. Because they act in accordance with this misperception of reality, they reap the consequences. In contrasting these two viewpoints the author is not engaging in an academic debate about life after death. His very *practical* purpose is evident in the exhortations that frame the book. He appeals to his readers to live righteously and pursue wisdom so that they may receive the crown of everlasting life. To accomplish his purpose he does not present rational arguments in favor of immortality. He *asserts* the validity of the paradoxical belief in God's hidden world and secret ways, and he appeals to his audience to espouse that belief.

These chapters have many close associations with apocalyptic literature.[50] The ultimate reality of the heavenly world is an important constituent of such texts as Daniel 7–12, *1 Enoch* 37–71 and 92–105, and *2 Baruch* 51. The emphasis on one's knowledge of God's hidden purposes (*mystēria*, 2:22) is paralleled in Daniel 1–6 and in Qumranic biblical interpretation (see below, pp. 126–27). The structure and content of the argument in 2:1–4:9 may be compared to *1 Enoch* 102:6–103:15,[51] and the exaltation language in 3:7–8 is reminiscent of Daniel 12:3 and 7:27 as well as *1 Enoch* 104:2 and *2 Baruch* 51:10.

Of special interest is the scene of exaltation and vindication in 4:20–5:14. Here the author has reused an apocalyptic tradition that dates back at least to the persecution by Antiochus Epiphanes.[52] This tradition employed the structure of the last Servant poem of Second Isaiah (52:13–53:12), as the following comparison indicates:

Second Isaiah	*Wisdom of Solomon*
A. Exaltation of Servant (52:13)	Mention of exalted righteous man (5:1a)
B. Parenthetical comment on Servant's former state (52:14)	Righteous man's former state (5:1bc)
C. Reaction of nations and kings (52:15)	Reaction of persecutors (5:2)
D. Their confession (53:1–6)	Their confession (5:3–8)

Conflated with the scene of the Servant's exaltation was material from Isaiah 14, a lament over the king of Babylon, the anti-God figure who stormed heaven and was hurled down to Sheol. In this conflated tradition the prophetlike figure of the Servant (Isa 50:4–5) was interpreted to refer to the persecuted righteous teachers in the time of Antiochus (cf. Dan 12:3). The kings and nations, more or less neutral bystanders in Isaiah 52–53, were identified with the anti-God figure in Isaiah 14 and were interpreted to refer to the royal persecutor of the righteous. According to the tradition, after their death the persecuted righteous teachers would be exalted and would judge their persecutors. In the Wisdom of Solomon, the Servant figure is identified with the wise protagonists in the stories of persecution and vindication. The scene of exaltation and vindication is preceded by a scene that contains most of the elements of the stories of persecution and exaltation (2:12–20). In order to match the lengthy speech in chap. 5 and to fulfill the author's purpose of assertion and refutation this scene is narrated in the form of a speech. The description of the righteous one in chap. 2 has also been influenced by the language of Isaiah 52–53.[53] This heavy influence of Isaianic language is also evident in 3:13–4:15, where the author's examples reflect Isaiah 54:1, 56:3–5, and 57:1–4.

In 6:12–9:18 the author focuses on the figure of personified Wisdom, alternating references to Solomon's quest for Wisdom with descriptions of her characteristics and gifts. Wisdom was introduced in 1:6–11. The last appeal in the exhortation in 6:1–11 was to learn wisdom (6:9). Verses

12–16 are related to the poems in the Wisdom of Jesus the Son of Sirach that describe the seeking and acquiring of Wisdom (see above, pp. 56–59). The *sorites,* or logical chain, in vv. 17–20 may reflect 1 Kings 3:11–13. After a final exhortation to the kings (6:21; cf. 6:9) the author introduces the subject matter to follow (vv. 22–25).

In chaps. 7–9 the author assumes the identity of King Solomon and recounts his quest for Wisdom (1 Kgs 3:5–15). Like all humans, Solomon was born mortal (7:1–6), in need of the immortality that Wisdom could grant (8:13). Therefore he prayed for her and received all good things (vv. 7–14), including friendship with God (v. 14; cf. v. 27). Solomon will now describe her for the reader (vv. 15–16). From her he learned the structure of the cosmos (vv. 17–22). This catalog has points of contact with lists of secret things in apocalyptic literature, and it hints at the later development of a Solomonic literature that recounts his magical and demonological knowledge and his control of nature.[54]

Solomon now stresses those characteristics of Wisdom that enable her to permeate all creation (7:22b–8:1). He begins with a list of twenty-one attributes (vv. 22b–23) and discusses her mobility and purity, which is related to her divine nature (vv. 24–26). As in chap. 1 she is both the orderer of the cosmos (8:1) and God's gift to individuals. In all things she is God's life-giving, renewing agent.

Solomon describes his quest for Wisdom as the courting of a bride (8:2–18; cf. Sir 51:13–22, on which see above, p. 59). A digression in 8:3–8 again praises the characteristics and gifts of Wisdom, among them the four cardinal virtues celebrated by Platonic and Stoic philosophy (v. 7; cf. 4 Macc 1:3–4). In vv. 10–16 Solomon anticipates the many benefits he will receive from his association with Wisdom, and he returns to the account of his search for her (vv. 17–21). Verses 19–20 presume a view of the preexistence of the soul akin to that of Platonic philosophy. Verse 21 stresses Wisdom's character as God's gift and leads to Solomon's prayer for that gift (chap. 9).

This carefully structured didactic prayer is governed by the belief that Wisdom is the agent of God's works and the divine gift without which no human can please God.[55] The doxology typically mentions God as Creator (9:1–3) but identifies his word and Wisdom as the instruments of creation. Solomon then prays for Wisdom (v. 4), without whom he cannot properly rule and fulfill God's command to build the Temple (vv. 5–8).

He notes that Wisdom was God's companion at creation (cf. v. 1) and that she is "with" him now and knows what is pleasing to him (v. 9). He asks that God send her (cf. v. 4) to be "with" *him* and teach him what is pleasing to God (vv. 10–12). Verses 13–17 stress the plight of mortals apart from the gift of Wisdom and God's Spirit (cf. vv. 5–6). Verse 18 provides a ground for Solomon's prayer: in the past Wisdom has taught what is pleasing to God. The verse also forms a transition to the third major part of this work, which begins with an account of Wisdom's works in history.

The "book of wisdom" is related to the "book of eschatology" in two important respects. First, Solomon's quest for Wisdom is paradigmatic of the search for Wisdom which the author recommends to his readers. Because Solomon was a king, his words have special relevance for the kings and rulers the author addresses. Second, the author's description of Wisdom clarifies why the quest for Wisdom is important and even necessary for salvation. Through his search for Wisdom, Solomon the mortal hopes to gain that immortality which is the gift of God. The indwelling presence of Wisdom, moreover, makes the eschatological gift of immortality a reality in the present life of the righteous.[56]

The figure of Wisdom in these chapters has characteristics in common with both Jewish wisdom speculation and Greek thought. Wisdom's presence at creation and her function as God's instrument are paralleled in Proverbs 8 and Sirach 24. Although Wisdom is not here identified with Torah, as she is in Sirach and Baruch, she is closely connected with righteousness and is the means to immortality (cf. Sir 24:19–24; Bar 4:1, where Wisdom grants life to the righteous). At the same time, the descriptions of Wisdom in these chapters employ language most likely drawn from the praises of Isis.[57] Other characteristics of Wisdom, notably her permeation of the cosmos and her ordering of all things, are beholden to Stoic conceptions.[58]

God's acts of judgment in history are the subject matter of chaps. 10–19. The topic that chaps. 2–5 treat with respect to individuals is here discussed with relationship to nations, mainly Israel and Egypt. Whereas chaps. 2–5 are concerned with judgment after death, chaps. 10–19 focus on history (especially the Exodus) and this world as the arena of God's activity. Within this arena God is operative through intrinsic, natural phenomena and causation rather than through extrinsic, transcendent intervention.[59] Wisdom, the pervading force in the universe, is God's agent, both the teacher and savior of the righteous and the executor of his vengeance on the ungodly. Powerful critiques of paganism constitute an essential part of the exposition in these chapters.

Chapter 10, which illustrates the last verse of Solomon's prayer (9:18), catalogs notable examples of Wisdom's activity in the lives of the prominent saints and sinners of old: Adam, Cain and Abel, Noah, Abraham, Lot and the people of the Five Cities, Jacob, Joseph, Moses, Israel and the Egyptians. In each section Wisdom is the subject of verbs that denote salvation. The objects of Wisdom's activity are unnamed, like the hero and villains of chaps. 2–5, because they are construed as types of the righteous or the ungodly. The list culminates in a relatively lengthy reference to the Exodus, which is the subject matter of a large portion of the chapters that follow.

In 11:4–14 we have the first of seven comparisons that contrast God's dealings with Israel and the Egyptians.[60] The *synkrisis* was a common device in Greek literature. The first comparison shows how God slaked the thirst of the Israelites by giving them water from the rock, while he punished the Egyptians by turning the water of the Nile into blood. These examples illustrate how God uses nature as a means of effecting his judgment—a motif also found in the next verses and in the other comparisons.

God's mercy and forbearance are a central motif in 11:15–12:22. The subject of pagan idolatry, which is of great importance in these chapters, is introduced in 11:15. Because the Egyptians worshiped animals, God appropriately punished them through plagues of frogs, flies, lice, and locusts (vv. 15–16). Nonetheless, he showed his mercy by not loosing on them the more ferocious beasts that were at his disposal as Creator (vv. 17–20). In 11:21–12:2 the author generalizes on God's mercy and his use of discipline rather than outright punishment. In 12:3–11 he illustrates this with the case of the Canaanites. After stressing God's power and righteousness he applies the topic of God's chastisement to Israel, contrasting it with his punishment of their enemies (cf. above, pp. 32–33, 119; below, pp. 210–12).

In 12:23–27 the author returns to the subject of animal worship, which leads up to the extensive critique of idolatry and paganism that stands in the center of this part of the Wisdom of Solomon.[61] Chapters 13–15 are structured in a concentric pattern (A-B-C-B'-A') that comes to focus in 14:21. This verse identifies the heart of the problem: falsely ascribing to idols the name that belongs to God.

I.	13:1–9:	The vanity of the philosophers, who divinized nature
II.	13:10–15:9:	The misery of those who worship idols, wrongly calling them gods
	A. 13:10–19:	Idols of gold, silver, and especially wood; the role of the woodcutter
	B. 14:1–10:	The invocation of God, reference to salvation, transition
	C. 14:11–31:	The punishment of idols, the invention and consequences of idolatry, the punishment of idolaters
	B'. 15:1–6:	Invocation of God, reference to salvation, transition
	A'. 15:7–13:	Idols of clay, the role of the potter
III.	15:14–19:	The greatest folly is that of the Egyptians, who reckoned all the idols of the nations to be gods and who worship animals.

This section, then, is a scorching polemic against idolatry in general and Egyptian paganism in particular. In many of its observations and arguments it parallels the prophetic corpus and such writings as Bel and the Dragon, the Epistle of Jeremiah, and the *Apocalypse of Abraham*. In combining a polemic against idolatry with an attack against sexual immorality, the author parallels book 3 of the *Sibylline Oracles* and *Aristeas*.

In chaps. 16–19 the author takes up his series of comparisons between God's dealings with Israel and Egypt. According to 16:1–4 God satisfied the hunger of the Israelites by providing them with quail, while he ruined the appetites of the Egyptians by turning a multitude of odious animals loose on them. He provided deliverance from the fiery serpents, but the Egyptians found no healing from the bites of locusts and flies (16:5–14). In v. 12 God's "word" appears to be the functional equivalent of Wisdom (cf. 18:15 and 9:1b–2a). In the next comparison (16:15–29) fire, water, ice, and snow worked for both the benefit and the detriment of Israel and Egypt. The fifth comparison deals with darkness (17:1–18:4). The slaughter and protection of children are the subject of the sixth comparison (18:5–25). While the firstborn of Egypt were being slain God protected his people, whom the Egyptians had to acknowledge as his son (18:13; cf. 5:5). The final comparison contrasts Israel's passage through the Red Sea with the drowning of the Egyptians (19:1–8). Here again nature becomes the medium of God's deliverance (v. 6). The final verses of chap. 19 conclude the subject of God's judgment and stress his use of animate and inanimate creation (19:9–21). The book closes on a note of praise to God who has exalted, glorified, and helped his people (19:22).

Cumulative evidence in the Wisdom of Solomon points to its composition in Egypt. In chaps. 10–19 the author focuses on the Exodus and God's judgment of Egypt, the enemy par excellence. He labels the Egyptians' idolatry as the height of pagan folly. Parallels between this work and the religious and philosophical thought of Philo of Alexandria are many and close.[62]

The date of the book's composition is debated. Linguistic evidence may point to the first decades of the Common Era.[63] The prominence of the story of the persecuted righteous one and the theme of Egypt's oppression of Israel may indicate that the book was written during the reign of Caligula (37–41 C.E.), when Jews in Alexandria suffered severely under Roman rule.[64]

The author may have intended his book for a mixed audience. On the one hand the theme of chaps. 2–5 and its extension in the discussion of God's contrasting judgments on Israel and Egypt (chaps. 10–19) would serve to comfort the Jews (thus esp. 19:22). On the other hand the detailed attack on idolatry may well be directed to a Gentile audience. A similar indication is to be found in the exhortations to kings and rulers. The second of these exhortations clearly implies that these readers are to avoid the excesses of the ungodly rich. Both the Israel/Egypt contrast in chaps. 10–19 and the Dispersion setting of the work make it likely that these ungodly persecutors of the righteous are Gentiles rather than Jews.

The Wisdom of Solomon is of importance for the study of both early Judaism and early Christianity. As we have seen, it is an interesting example of a creative Hellenized Judaism. Aspects of the book also illuminate the New Testament. Its story of the persecuted righteous one was probably known by the author of the Gospel according to Matthew (cf. Wis 2:13, 18 and Matt 27:43). Paul's argument against paganism in Romans 1:18–27 bears important similarities to Wisdom of Solomon 13–15. Likewise Paul's doctrine of the Holy Spirit as a witness as well as God's power for the godly life (e.g., Rom 8) parallels this author's understanding of Wisdom. These similarities do not prove Paul's direct dependence on Wisdom of Solomon, but they do suggest a common milieu in Hellenistic Judaism. Whatever one makes of these parallels, the book enjoyed great popularity in Christianity of the patristic era, and the story of the persecuted righteous one was interpreted to refer to Jesus.[65]

2 ENOCH

"The Secret Book about the Rapture of Enoch the Righteous"[66] has been preserved in Church Slavonic in two recensions, or versions. The shorter of these is the more original[67] and is a translation from Greek, in which language the book was most likely composed.[68] Our discussion will be based on the short recension, although we shall occasionally make reference to expansion in the long recension.[69]

Second Enoch divides into three major sections, which correspond to important blocks of material in *1 Enoch*. Enoch's ascent to heaven, vision of God, and commissioning (chaps. 3–37) are the counterpart of *1 Enoch* 12–36. His return to earth and instruction of his children (chaps. 38–66) are analogous to *1 Enoch* 81, 91–105. The narrative about Melchizedek's miraculous birth[70] is the counterpart of *1 Enoch* 106–7.

Second Enoch is an apocalypse which has a testamentary setting. The purpose of Enoch's ascent is the acquisition and recording of cosmological and eschatological information that is of importance for Enoch's family and spiritual descendants. This information, which relates to the cosmos and God's creation of it as well as to eschatology, is obtained on the way up through the spheres and at the throne of God (chaps. 3–37). In its form—an ascent that culminates at the divine throne with a commissioning—this section corresponds to *1 Enoch* 12–16.[71] At the same time, Enoch's journey to places of cosmological and eschatological significance corresponds to the journeys described in *1 Enoch* 17–19 and 20–36 (and to the detailed accounts in chaps. 72–77); however, as we have seen, the journeys in *1 Enoch* 14–16 and 17–19 complement one another (see above, p. 54).

The cosmological and eschatological contents of the various spheres are described by means of the same literary forms employed in the descriptions of their respective counterparts in *1 Enoch*. Enoch's visions of the celestial phenomena in the first and fourth heavens (chaps. 3–6; 11–17), like their counterparts in *1 Enoch* 17–18:6; 33–36; and 72–77, are related in a straightforward manner. He sees (or the angels show him) certain heavenly phenomena, which he recognizes, names, and describes. On the other hand, when the seer describes the visions of eschatological import in the second, third, and fifth heavens (chaps. 7–10; 18),[72] he employs the form familiar from the visions in *1 Enoch* 18:6–19:2 and especially 21–27; 32: journey, vision, seer's comment or question, interpretation.[73] In his description of the rebel angels the seer distinguishes between two groups (as does *1 Enoch*): the *egrēgoroi* ("watchers"), who sinned with the women (chap. 18); and their "brethren" (18:7), called "apostates" (chap. 7), who may correspond to the angels as revealers.[74] Significant for this author's purpose are his descriptions of paradise and hell in the third heaven (chaps. 8–10). The complementary lists of sins and good deeds[75] correspond to similar lists in Enoch's instruction later in the book and reflect the strong ethical emphasis in the book.

Enoch's ascent terminates in the divine throne room in the seventh heaven (in the tenth heaven in the long recension, which adds 21:6–22:1a).[76] Although the scene closely parallels *1 Enoch* 14:15–16:4, here Enoch is commissioned not to take a book of indictment back to the "watchers" (*1 Enoch* 13:10–14:1) but to write books of cosmological and ethical teaching. After the seer has copied these 366 books, at the angel's dictation, the scene climaxes with God's lengthy account of creation— hitherto unknown even to the angels (chaps. 24–30). The account in the short recension appears to reflect Egyptian and Persian mythology,[77] while the elaborator of the longer recension has harmonized the account with Genesis 1–3. The climactic position of the creation narrative attests the centrality of creation in this author's theology. Commenting on his own narrative, God stresses his uniqueness as Creator and his total sovereignty in the heavens (chap. 33), and he reveals that the Flood will come because the human race refuses to acknowledge him as the one God (chap. 34). As a remedy for this situation God commissions Enoch to bring to earth books that stress creation as a rationale for ethics. The description of Enoch's ascent also emphasized God's creative power, which is evident in the cosmic phenomena and the places of eschatological significance that God has "prepared" (9:1; 10:4).

Enoch's instruction is an epitome of the books he has written, and it is divided into three parts. The first of these is addressed to his children (chaps. 39–56), although it has no formal introduction in the present state of the short recension.[78] Enoch asserts the divine origin and universality of his knowledge (39:1–40:1; cf. *1 Enoch* 93:2),[79] and he interweaves description of the celestial and eschatological phenomena he has seen with ethical exhortations in the form of blessings and curses that correspond to the Exhortations and Woes of *1 Enoch* 94–104.[80] In this section proper conduct is construed largely in terms of one's deeds toward others. Such conduct is based on the double rationale of creation and eschatology.[81] One dare not hold other human beings in contempt, for that is to hold God in contempt, since he created man in his image (44:1). Moreover, to do so invites God's wrath and great judgment (44:2). Elsewhere in this section the eschatological rationale is explicit (e.g., 49:2; 50:4–51:3), and it is implicit in descriptions of the places of judgment and reward and punishment (40:12–42:3) and in formulas of blessing and curse.

The second parenetic section is addressed to Methuselah's brethren and to the elders of the people (chaps. 57–63). An initial description of creation forms the basis for instruction about responsibility toward animals and human beings (chaps. 58–60).[82] The obligation to clothe the naked and feed the hungry (63:1) was mentioned as a touchstone of judgment in Enoch's descriptions of paradise and hell (chaps. 9–10) and in the previous parenetic section (42:8).

Enoch's final instruction is addressed to an assembly of two thousand. In it he combines creation and eschatology. The background of the author's thought here is the teaching of two ages: the present age of sorrow and trouble and the glorious age to come (cf. 66:6 and 50:2 and see the discussion of *2 Baruch* and *4 Ezra*, below, pp. 281–87, 288–94). For the author of *2 Enoch*, however, God created both the present time-bound and circumscribed age of creatures and "the great Age," the heavenly sphere, where every person goes at the time of death, whether to the place of reward or to the place of punishment. These two spheres— the heavenly and the earthly—continue to coexist until the time of the earthly and historical runs out, the great judgment takes place, and there exists only the one endless age.[83] This spatial dualism of heavenly and earthly is paralleled in such texts as the Wisdom of Solomon and the *Testament of Job* (see above, p. 178, and below, pp. 244–46), and it may have a counterpart in the eschatology of the Hymns of Qumran (see above, pp. 140–41). After this eschatological instruction and a final brief admonition (chap. 66) Enoch is taken to heaven (chap. 67).

The concluding narrative in *2 Enoch*, like some other testamentary works, is concerned with the problem of continuity.[84] The author seems to presume that Enoch was a priest (cf. 64:5), and the narrative traces the succession of the priesthood from Methuselah to Melchizedek. The story of Melchizedek's birth and assumption to heaven until after the Flood is remarkable in several respects. Its placement corresponds to the story of Noah's birth in *1 Enoch* 106–7. The miraculous circumstances attending his conception and birth are reminiscent of the Noah story, although the suspicion of Nir (his "father") is more closely paralleled in the version of the Noah story in the Genesis Apocryphon (see below, p. 264). Melchizedek's conception without benefit of a biological father and the motif of Nir's suspicion could indicate that this story is Christian in origin and dependent on Matthew as well as the Epistle to the Hebrews.[85] However, in view of Qumranic material about Melchizedek, the heavenly high priest, it is just as likely that the Christian and Jewish Melchizedek materials reflect a common tradition.[86]

Parallels to Egyptian mythological motifs and traditions in Philo of Alexandria suggest Egypt as the place of composition.[87] A date in the first century C.E. is often suggested,[88] but this is uncertain. We do not know in what circles it was composed. The closing narratives, however, indicate intense interest in the priesthood, and the emphasis on Melchizedek and on certain sacrificial practices may indicate a sectarian group.[89] Nonetheless, the author's purview is the world, and human beings in general as creatures of God are entitled to love and deeds of kindness. The focus on the history of Israel typical of sections of *1 Enoch* is lacking here, although the parenetic section touches on issues in the Torah as much as the corresponding section in *1 Enoch* 94–104 does.

For the brave who are prepared to work in ancient Slavic dialects, this little-studied work holds considerable promise. It is a remarkable transformation of older apocalyptic traditions and a testimony to the religious thought of some presently unknown sector of ancient Diaspora Judaism.

NOTES

1. On Elephantine and the papyri see E. G. Kraeling, "Elephantine Papyri," *IDB* 2:83–85. On the *Story of Ahikar* see above, p. 39, n. 14.

2. Victor A. Tcherikover and Alexander Fuks, *Corpus Papyrorum Judaicarum*, 3 vols. (Cambridge: Harvard University, 1957–64).

3. For bibliography see Emanuel Tov, "Jewish Greek Scriptures," in *Early Judaism and Its Modern Interpreters*, ed. R. A. Kraft and George W. E. Nickelsburg (Philadelphia: Fortress, 1986) 223–37.

4. For bibliography see Burton L. Mack, "Wisdom," in *Early Judaism and Its Modern Interpreters.*

5. Lanchester, *APOT* 2:368–71.

6. For a discussion of the time and place of origin of the other books see John J. Collins, "The Development of the Sibylline Tradition."

7. John J. Collins, *The Sibylline Oracles of Egyptian Judaism,* 24–25.

8. Ibid., 64–70.

9. Ibid., 80–87.

10. Ibid., 26.

11. On the similarities between this passage and Wis 5 see Nickelsburg, *Resurrection,* 92, n. 168. Note, however, the contrasting earthly and heavenly settings. On Wis 5 see below, pp. 176–79.

12. Collins, *Oracles,* 37–44.

13. Ibid., 53–55.

14. For the historical problems relating to Demetrius see Moses Hadas, *Aristeas to Philocrates,* 7–8.

15. Ibid., 28–32.

16. Ibid., 47–48.

17. Ibid., 121.

18. Ibid., 48–50.

19. Ibid., 42. Cf. also 1 Esdr 3–4:41.

20. Hadas, *Aristeas,* 40–43. On the place of God and the imitation of God in such treatises see Erwin R. Goodenough, "The Political Philosophy of Hellenistic Kingship," *Yale Classical Studies* 1 (1928) 65–78.

21. Hadas, *Aristeas,* 5–9.

22. See Elias Bickerman, "Zur Datierung des Pseudo-Aristeas," in his *Studies in Jewish and Christian History* (Leiden: Brill, 1976) 1:123–36; Hadas, *Aristeas,* 54; Jonathan A. Goldstein, "Jewish Acceptance and Rejection of Hellenism," in *Jewish and Christian Self-Definition,* vol. 2, ed. E. P. Sanders (Philadelphia: Fortress, 1981) 83.

23. Hadas, *Aristeas,* 54–59.

24. See ibid. 59–66; Goldstein, "Jewish Acceptance," 83. Victor A. Tcherikover ("The Ideology of the Letter of Aristeas") stresses the book's duality. Jews are to remain Jews, but they are to seek to participate in Greek culture.

25. Hadas, *Aristeas,* 66–84.

26. In addition to its abrupt beginning see 2:25, which presumes a part of the text now missing; see Moses Hadas, *The Third and Fourth Books of Maccabees,* 4–5.

27. Victor A. Tcherikover ("The Third Book of Maccabees as a Historical Source," 2–3) suggests dependence on a Ptolemaic historian.

28. On the background of this detail, see ibid., 3–5.

29. On the historical problems relating to this legend see Hadas, *Maccabees,* 10–11; Tcherikover, "Maccabees," 6–8.

30. Nickelsburg, *Resurrection,* 90–92.

31. Tcherikover, "Maccabees," 1–2.

32. Ibid., 25–26.

33. See the detailed argument of Tcherikover, ibid., 11–18.

34. Bacchisio Motzo, "Il Rifacimento Greco di Ester e il III Mac.," in his *Saggi di Storia e Letteratura Giudeo-Ellenistica,* CScA 5 (Florence: Le Monnier, 1924) 272–90.

35. Hadas, *Maccabees,* 8–10.

36. See ibid., 11–12.

37. For these parallels and similarities see Nickelsburg, *Resurrection,* 90–91, esp. nn. 157–66.

38. On the secondary character of these passages see Carey A. Moore, *Daniel, Esther, and Jeremiah: The Additions,* 153–54.

39. Ibid., 153.

40. See the literature cited in ibid., 155.

41. E. J. Bickerman, "The Colophon of the Greek Book of Esther," *JBL* 63 (1944) 339–62; but see Moore (*Daniel,* 250) for a dating in the reign of Ptolemy IX, ca. 114 B.C.E.

42. For a similar use of documents see above, p. 165, regarding *Aristeas.*

43. Comparisons with 3 Maccabees are based on Motzo, "Rifacimento," 275–80.

44. Nickelsburg, *Resurrection,* 50–51.

45. Motzo, "Rifacimento," 287–90.

46. James M. Reese, *Hellenistic Influence on the Book of Wisdom and Its Consequences,* 117–21.

47. James M. Reese, "Plan and Structure in the Book of Wisdom," *CBQ* 27 (1965) 391–99; Addison G. Wright, "The Structure of Wisdom 11–19," *CBQ* 27 (1965) 28–34; idem, "Numerical Patterns in the Book of Wisdom," *CBQ* 29 (1967) 524–38; idem, "The Structure of the Book of Wisdom," *Bib* 48 (1967) 165–84; Maurice Gilbert, "La structure de la prière de Salomon (Sg 9)," *Bib* 51 (1970) 301–31; idem, *La critique des dieux dans le Livre de la Sagesse,* AnBib 53 (Rome: Biblical Institute, 1973).

48. See C. Larcher, *Études sur le Livre de la Sagesse,* 179–261; Reese, *Influence*; John J. Collins, "Cosmos and Salvation: Jewish Wisdom and Apocalyptic in the Hellenistic Age," *HR* 17 (1977) 128–34.

49. Nickelsburg, *Resurrection,* 58–62.

50. See Collins, "Cosmos," 134–41.

51. Nickelsburg, *Resurrection,* 128–29.

52. Ibid., 62–82; see also Lothar Ruppert, *Der Leidende Gerechte,* Forschung zur Bibel 5 (Würzburg: Echter Verlag, 1972) 70–105.

53. Nickelsburg, *Resurrection,* 62.

54. Michael E. Stone, "Lists of Revealed Things in the Apocalyptic Literature," in *Magnalia Dei: The Mighty Acts of God,* ed. F. M. Cross et al. (Garden City, N.Y.: Doubleday, 1976) 436–37.

55. On the sophisticated structure of this prayer see Gilbert, "Structure."

56. See David Winston, *Wisdom of Solomon,* 31–32, 42.

57. See Reese, *Influence,* 46–49; Burton L. Mack, *Logos und Sophia,* SUNT 10 (Göttingen: Vandenhoeck & Ruprecht, 1973) 90–95.

58. See Winston, *Wisdom,* 182; Collins, "Cosmos," 133.

59. See Collins, "Cosmos," 125–28.

60. See Reese, *Influence,* 98–102; Winston, *Wisdom,* 227.

61. See Gilbert, *Critique,* esp. pp. 252–57.

62. On Wisdom of Solomon and Philo see Winston, *Wisdom*, 59–63.

63. Ibid., 22–23.

64. For a survey of proposed dates between 220 B.C.E. and 50 C.E. see ibid., 20–25, which argues for the date in Caligula's reign.

65. See Larcher, *Études*, 11–84.

66. The book's common title, drawn from inferior manuscripts, is "The Book of the Secrets of Enoch."

67. See A. Vaillant, *Le Livre des Secrets d'Hénoch*, xv-xxii; Ulrich Fischer, *Eschatologie und Jenseitserwartung im hellenistischen Diasporajudentum*, 37–38. Actually there is a third recension, and the textual relationships between the short and longer recensions are complex. See below, n. 69.

68. See Vaillant, *Hénoch*, xi-xiii; S. Pines, "Eschatology and the Concept of Time in the Slavonic Book of Enoch," 73; and Fischer, *Eschatologie*, 39, n. 12.

69. My authority for the original, short recension is the text printed by Vaillant, *Hénoch*. For the most part this corresponds to the B text printed by Charles in *APOT* 2. Nonetheless, significant parts of Charles's A text do appear in the short recension printed by Vaillant. The reader is best referred to Vaillant; however, for the convenience of those who do not read French, I have retained the chapter and verse numbering of *APOT*.

70. For the text of this narrative, which is omitted in *APOT*, see W. R. Morfill and R. H. Charles, *The Book of the Secrets of Enoch*, 85–93; and Vaillant, *Hénoch*, 65–85.

71. Cf. *2 Enoch* 1–2 with *1 Enoch* 12:1–3.

72. Vaillant (*Hénoch*, 19–21) prints the whole of chap. 18, although vv. 2–9 are not included in B in *APOT*.

73. The type of comment made by Enoch in *2 Enoch* 8:8 and 10:4 (wonderment rather than question) corresponds to *1 Enoch* 21:8, 22:2, 24:5, and 32:5, and the double question in *2 Enoch* 18:2 parallels *1 Enoch* 21:4.

74. On Enoch's intercession for the angels (*2 Enoch* 7:4–5) cf. *1 Enoch* 15:2.

75. See Fischer, *Eschatologie*, 48–49.

76. Vaillant (*Hénoch*, 25) includes in his text 22:1b–3, which does not appear in B in *APOT*.

77. See Marc Philonenko, "La Cosmogonie du 'Livre des Secrets d'Hénoch,'" in *Religions en Egypte hellenistique et romaine* (Paris: Universitaires de France, 1969) 113–16; and Pines, "Eschatology," 75–82.

78. See Vaillant, *Hénoch*, 37, nn. 17–19.

79. See especially the Aramaic of *1 Enoch* 93:2 (4QEn[g] 1 3:22, Milik, *Books of Enoch*, 264).

80. Cf., e.g., 50:4 and *1 Enoch* 95:5; 50:5 and *1 Enoch* 94:8; 53:1–3 and *1 Enoch* 98:7–8; 53:4–5 and *1 Enoch* 104:12–105:2.

81. See John J. Collins, "The Genre Apocalypse in Hellenistic Judaism," in *Apocalypticism in the Mediterranean World and the Near East*, ed. David Hellholm, Proceedings of the International Colloquium on Apocalypticism, Uppsala, August 12-17, 1979 (Tübingen: Mohr/Siebeck, 1983) 536.

82. For 59:2b–5 as part of the short recension see Vaillant, *Hénoch*, 59.

83. For details see Fischer, *Eschatologie*, 53–62.

84. Cf. *T. Mos.* 11:9–19; *2 Bar.* 31–33; 44–46; 77; *4 Ezra* 12:40–50.

85. See Arie Rubinstein, "Observations on the Slavonic Book of Enoch," *JJS* 13 (1962) 4–6, 11–12.

86. See the "Prolegomenon" by Jonas Greenfield in Hugo Odeberg, *3 Enoch* (reprinted New York: KTAV, 1973) xx–xxi. On the alleged Christian origin of 2 Enoch see Rubinstein, "Observations," 3–4, 10–15. On the most recent attempt to make *2 Enoch* a late, Christian writing see Milik, *Books of Enoch*, 107–12, and the refutation by Rainer Stichel in his review of Milik in *Byzantinoslavica* 39 (1978) 65.

87. See Charles, *APOT* 2:426; Philonenko, "Cosmogonie," 113–16; Fischer, *Eschatologie*, 40–41.

88. The date is asserted by Gershom Scholem (*Ursprung und Anfänge der Kabbala*, Studia Judaica 3 [Berlin: de Gruyter, 1962] 64), who is followed by Greenfield ("Prolegomenon," xviii), and by Fischer, *Eschatologie*, 40–41.

89. See Pines, "Eschatology," 74–75.

BIBLIOGRAPHY

HISTORY

Victor A. **Tcherikover** and Alexander **Fuks**, *Corpus Papyrorum Judaicarum* (Cambridge: Harvard University, 1957) 1:1–93. Menachem **Stern**, "The Jewish Diaspora," *CRINT* 1:1 (1974) 122–33. Peter **Fraser**, *Ptolemaic Alexandria*, 3 vols. (Oxford: Clarendon, 1972), a history of life, culture, and learning.

THE SIBYLLINE ORACLES

TRANSLATION: John J. **Collins**, *PsOT*.

TEXT AND OTHER TRANSLATION: J. **Geffcken**, *Die Oracula Sibyllina*, GCS 8 (Leipzig: Hinrichs, 1902), the Greek text, apparatus of textual variants and history of religions parallels. H. C. O. **Lanchester**, *APOT* 2:368–406, on books 3–5.

LITERATURE: John J. **Collins**, *The Sibylline Oracles of Egyptian Judaism*, SBLDS 13 (Missoula: Scholars Press, 1974), origin, contents, purpose of books 3 and 5. Idem, "The Development of the Sibylline Tradition," *Aufstieg und Niedergang der römischen Welt* 2:20 (forthcoming).

ARISTEAS TO PHILOCRATES

TRANSLATION: R. J. H. **Schutt**, *PsOT*.

TEXT AND OTHER TRANSLATION: Moses **Hadas**, *Aristeas to Philocrates*, JAL (New York: Harper, 1951), excellent introduction, Greek text and annotated translation.

LITERATURE: Victor A. **Tcherikover**, "The Ideology of the Letter of Aristeas," *HTR* 51 (1958) 59–85. Sidney **Jellicoe**, *The Septuagint in Modern Study* (Oxford: Clarendon, 1968) 29–58.

3 MACCABEES

TRANSLATION: *The Oxford Annotated Apocrypha, Expanded Edition* (New York: Oxford University, 1977).

Text and Other Translations: Robert **Hanhart**, *Maccabaeorum liber III*, Septuaginta, Vetus Testamentum Graecum 9:3 (Göttingen: Vandenhoeck & Ruprecht, 1960), critical edition of the Greek text. Moses **Hadas**, *The Third and Fourth Books of Maccabees*, JAL (New York: Harper, 1953), introduction, Greek text with facing annotated translation. Hugh **Anderson**, *PsOT*.

Literature: Victor A. **Tcherikover**, "The Third Book of Maccabees as a Historical Source," *Scripta Hierosolymitana* 7 (1961) 1–26.

ADDITIONS TO THE BOOK OF ESTHER

Translation: The Apocrypha.

Text: Robert **Hanhart**, *Esther*, Septuaginta, Vetus Testamentum Graecum 8:3 (Göttingen: Vandenhoeck & Ruprecht, 1966), critical edition of the Greek text.

Literature: Carey A. **Moore**, *Daniel, Esther, and Jeremiah: The Additions*, AB 44 (Garden City, N.Y.: Doubleday, 1977), annotated translation of the canonical Hebrew book, interwoven in order with a translation of the Additions and a commentary on them.

THE WISDOM OF SOLOMON

Translation: The Apocrypha.

Text: Joseph **Ziegler**, *Sapientia Salomonis*, Septuaginta, Vetus Testamentum Graecum 12:1 (Göttingen: Vandenhoeck & Ruprecht, 1962), critical edition of the Greek text.

Literature: David **Winston**, *Wisdom of Solomon*, AB 43 (Garden City, N.Y.: Doubleday, 1979), translation and detailed commentary. C. **Larcher**, *Études sur le Livre de la Sagesse*, EBib (Paris: Gabalda, 1969), encyclopedic study of the book's religious themes, its parallels in Jewish and pagan Hellenistic literature, and its influence on Christian theology. James M. **Reese**, *Hellenistic Influence on the Book of Wisdom and Its Consequences*, AnBib 41 (Rome: Biblical Institute, 1970).

2 ENOCH

Translation: Nevill **Forbes** and R. H. **Charles**, *APOT* 2:425–69.

Text and Other Translations: A. **Vaillant**, *Le Livre des Secrets d'Hénoch* (Paris: Institut d'études slaves, 1952), Slavonic text with facing French translation. W. R. **Morfill** and R. H. **Charles**, *The Book of the Secrets of Enoch* (Oxford: Clarendon, 1896), introduction, annotated translation of recension A, including the Melchizedek narrative. Francis **Andersen**, *PsOT*, two recensions in parallel columns, including the Melchizedek narrative.

Literature: S. **Pines**, "Eschatology and the Concept of Time in the Slavonic Book of Enoch," in *Types of Redemption*, NumenSup 18, ed. R. J. Z. Werblowsky and C. J. Bleeker (Leiden: Brill, 1970) 72–87. Ulrich **Fischer**, *Eschatologie und Jenseitserwartung im hellenistischen Diasporajudentum*, BZNW 44 (Berlin: de Gruyter, 1978) 37–70, eschatology and anthropology in *2 Enoch*.

6

The Romans and the House of Herod

THE HASMONEANS GIVE WAY TO ROME

The years 67–37 B.C.E. witnessed the fall from power of the Hasmonean house and the subjugation of Palestine to Roman authority. When she died, Queen Salome Alexandra was succeeded by her elder son, John Hyrcanus II, who had already been serving as high priest. Almost immediately Hyrcanus's ambitious brother, Judas Aristobulus, raised the flag of revolt and wrested both civil and religious power from the weak and irresolute Hyrcanus, who quietly resigned from office.

Other powers now came into play. The first of these was an Idumean named Antipater, who had served as governor of Idumea under Alexander Janneus and whose son, Herod, would later become king of Judea. Preferring to have Hyrcanus rather than Aristobulus as his king, Antipater used deceit and intrigue to convince Hyrcanus once more to seek the throne. Antipater and Hyrcanus found an ally in Aretas, the ruler of the Arabian kingdom of the Nabataeans. Aristobulus was severely defeated in battle, and when his army deserted him he fled to Jerusalem, where he was besieged in the Temple.

The resolution of the matter, however, lay in the hands of the Romans, who had long been a power to be reckoned with in the eastern Mediterranean. At this very time (65 B.C.E.) the armies of Pompey were busy extending Roman rule over western Asia. Pompey's commander, Aemilius Scaurus, was in Damascus. Both sides saw this as an opportunity to settle the dispute in their own favor. Bribe matched bribe. Scaurus decided in favor of Aristobulus. The siege was lifted.

The family quarrel was not yet at an end. Early in 63 B.C.E. both Hyrcanus and Aristobulus appeared before Pompey in Damascus and again pleaded their causes, while a third party of Jews brought complaint against both brothers. Pompey deferred a decision and asked that all concerned keep the peace. In a series of rash and unwise actions, Aristobulus defied Pompey's request and incited his anger. He was arrested, and the situation quickly passed out of his control.

Partisan dissension and Roman military might finally decided the issue. Jerusalem was under threat of Roman siege. The followers of Aristobulus and Hyrcanus disputed whether or not to capitulate. Hyrcanus's party won out and opened the city gates; however, the partisans of Aristobulus locked themselves into the Temple and prepared to resist. After a three-month siege in autumn 63, the wall was breached. Priests were slaughtered in the act of offering sacrifice, and according to Josephus some twelve thousand Jews perished. Pompey entered the holy of holies, but he took nothing and commanded that the cult be continued. The leaders of the resistance, however, were executed.

The Hasmonean dispute brought an end to Jewish independence. Much of the territory that had been won by Simon, John Hyrcanus I, and Alexander Janneus was removed from Jewish control and placed under the Roman governor of Syria. Jerusalem and the remainder of Judea were subject to Roman tribute. Hyrcanus was to govern them, but without the title "king." Pompey returned to Rome in triumph, accompanied by Aristobulus, who was in chains, his daughters and sons, and a large number of other Jewish captives, who were subsequently released in Rome.

Reappearing as if on a rotating stage, the principals of the Jewish civil war returned time and again to interact disastrously with the renowned figures of the last years of the Roman republic. In 57 B.C.E. Aristobulus's son Alexander, who had escaped on the way to Rome, gathered a sizable army and attempted to seize power in Palestine. He was defeated by Aulus Gabinius, the governor of Syria, and his lieutenant, Marc Antony. Hyrcanus, on the other hand, was stripped of his political authority, though he retained the office of high priest. The following year Aristobulus and his other son, Antigonus, escaped from Rome and made yet another abortive attempt to seize power. Alexander tried once again in 55 B.C.E. M. Licinius Crassus, who had joined Caesar and Pompey in Rome's "First Triumvirate," became governor of Syria in 54 B.C.E. and robbed the Temple of its treasures. He was succeeded in 53 by C. Cassius Longinus (later one of the conspirators against Caesar), who dealt with still another insurrection by selling thirty thousand Jews into slavery.

The year 49 saw the beginning of the Roman civil wars, which took their toll on the whole Roman world. Pompey fled Rome ahead of Caesar, who released Aristobulus so that he could lead an army against Pompey in Syria. This time the ever-resilient Hasmonean met his end. He was poisoned by Pompey's supporters before he could leave Rome. His son Alexander was beheaded in Syria at Pompey's command. The following year (48 B.C.E.) Pompey himself was defeated, slain, and decapitated.

As Julius Caesar now set out to make himself master of the eastern world, he found willing allies in Hyrcanus and Antipater. Their loyalty was rewarded. In 47 Hyrcanus was nominated as hereditary "ethnarch," thus receiving once again the political power he had lost. In point of fact the real power was given to Antipater, who was nominated governor of Judea. He in turn nominated his sons Phasael and Herod as governors in Jerusalem and Galilee.

After the assassination of Caesar in 44 B.C.E. Brutus and Cassius fled east. For two years Cassius once more ruled Syria. Antipater and Herod sought his favor and helped raise the heavy taxes he demanded of Judea. Violence followed upon violence. In 43 Antipater was poisoned by a rival named Malichus, who in turn was murdered at the instigation of Herod and with the connivance of Cassius.

With the defeat of Cassius and Brutus at Philippi in 42, the balance of power swung again. Marc Antony was now master of Syria. Although they had previously supported Cassius, and in spite of formal complaints that an embassy of Jews brought against them, Phasael and Herod were able to secure Antony's favor. He nominated them as "tetrarchs" of the Jewish territory, while Hyrcanus remained nominal head of state with the title of "ethnarch."

During Antony's absence from Syria in 40 B.C.E. the Parthians swept across the East, took Syria, and marched into Jerusalem, plundering as they went. They were supported by Antigonus, the remaining son of Aristobulus, who sought the title of "king." Phasael and Hyrcanus were betrayed to the Parthians, but Herod escaped with his family. Phasael and Hyrcanus were turned over to Antigonus. Phasael committed suicide. Hyrcanus's ears were cut off, thus physically disqualifying him permanently from the high priesthood. The Parthians named Antigonus "king."

By diverse routes Herod eluded his enemies and arrived in Rome, where with the support of Antony and Octavian (Augustus) the Roman senate named him "king" of Judea. He returned to Syria the following year. While the Romans were engaged in defeating the Parthians, Herod moved on into Palestine. The army of Antigonus was defeated. In the

spring of 37 Jerusalem was captured. At Herod's request and with Antony's permission, Antigonus, the last of the Hasmonean kings, was
beheaded.

HEROD THE GREAT

The career of Herod the Great is a study in opposites and extremes.
What was already evident in the record of his years as a general and
governor is written in boldface type through the annals of his reign.
High intelligence and an instinct for the appropriate action at the oppor-
tune moment combined and conflicted with incredible cruelty and ruth-
lessness and an irrepressible desire for revenge. In the political arena he
maneuvered with shrewdness, skill, and resourcefulness; on the battlefield he fought with courage and distinction. He loved with passion and
ruled with terror and cruelty. Although he went to great lengths to curry
the favor of his subjects, in their eyes he remained an Idumean—an outsider, despised and hated. Not only among his people but also in his own
family he was the object of opposition and conspiracy. Paranoia and conspiracy formed a vicious cycle that rapidly spiraled toward the end of
his career. Although he had lived in splendor and style he died in agony
—unloved and unmourned.

During the first decade of his reign Herod consolidated his power.
Already on the eve of his victory over Antigonus (spring 37 B.C.E.) he
had married Mariamme, the granddaughter of Hyrcanus II. This alliance
with the Hasmonean family was, however, of little political benefit to
Herod, and it became the source of numerous and tragic problems. The
many adherents of Antigonus were a threat to him, and he executed
forty-five of the most prominent and confiscated property and wealth.
Within his own family he had to deal with Alexandra, the mother of
Mariamme. Both mother and daughter pressured Herod into appointing
Mariamme's seventeen-year-old brother, Aristobulus, as high priest. When
the young Hasmonean's popularity among the people became a threat to
Herod, the king had him "accidentally" drowned after a banquet at
Herod's palace in Jericho. In spite of Alexandra's pleas through Cleo-
patra, Herod was acquitted by Marc Antony.

Herod's next problem was Cleopatra. When she successfully demanded
that Antony make her a present of sizable and rich parts of Herod's
kingdom, Herod was forced to rent his own land from her. Then she
attempted to seduce Herod, and the king sent her back to Egypt deftly

and with great ceremony. In September 31 Augustus defeated Antony in the battle of Actium. In spite of his close relationship to Antony, Herod convinced Augustus that he would be a good ally, and he was confirmed as king. The following year, after Cleopatra's suicide, Augustus returned Herod's territory to him.

Other domestic tragedy marred Herod's reign during these years. A victim of his own suspicions and of the intrigue of his family, he executed his uncle, Joseph, who was also married to Herod's sister, Salome; the aged Hasmonean, Hyrcanus II; his own most beloved wife, Mariamme; and Salome's second husband, an Idumean named Costobar, who was making common cause with some distant relatives of the Hasmoneans.

The middle years of Herod's reign (25–13 B.C.E.) offered some respite from this domestic strife. It was a time for splendid building projects and the importation of the trappings of high culture. The borders of the kingdom were secured with fortresses and palaces—most of them on the sites of Hasmonean citadels. Cities were embellished through great public works. On the Mediterranean coast, Straton's Tower was converted into a magnificent harbor city named Caesarea in honor of Julius Caesar. Samaria was renamed Sebaste, after the Greek form of Augustus's name, and a temple was erected there in his honor. Yet another pagan temple was built at the Panion, at the headwaters of the Jordan. The citadel in Jerusalem had already been rebuilt and named Antonia, in honor of Herod's patron Antony. In Hebron, at the reputed burial site of the patriarchs, Herod erected a magnificent memorial to Abraham, Isaac, and Jacob which still towers sixty feet into the air. The greatest of his public works, however, was in Jerusalem, where he greatly extended and rebuilt Zerubbabel's Temple, making it one of the architectural marvels of its time. Work on it ceased only a few years before its destruction in 70 C.E.

Herod's monuments to the Jewish religion did little to win the people's favor. To the contrary, the pagan shrines he erected and the dedication of other buildings and cities to prominent Romans probably exacerbated the opposition created by his Idumean origins and abetted by his cruel deeds and his flouting of Jewish custom.

The last nine years of Herod's reign were the worst. Domestic strife—Herod's constant demon—led to conspiracies, and conspiracies brought on a string of executions that whittled down the list of Herod's heirs. Early in his reign Herod had repudiated his Idumean wife Doris and her son Antipater. Herod's two sons by Mariamme, Alexander and Aristobulus, quarreled with Herod's sister Salome, who countered by making accusations against them. Herod brought back his son, Antipater, who fed the fires of suspicion. In 7 B.C.E., after alternating accusations and reconciliations, Alexander and Aristobulus were convicted of treason and executed. Meanwhile Antipater was plotting to seize the throne. Eventually he was found out and was imprisoned. Antipas, Herod's youngest son, by his Samaritan wife Malthace, was named his heir. The seventy-year-old king was gravely ill, and a rumor of his impending death circulated. Two scribes named Judas and Matthias stirred up some of their followers to pull down a golden eagle that Herod had erected over one of the main gates of the Temple. The instigators and executors of the deed were burned alive. Herod's illness became worse. In vain he sought a cure at the hot baths of Callirrhoe, east of the Dead Sea. A few days before he died Herod had his son Antipater executed. He rewrote his will, making his sons Archelaus and Philip coheirs with Antipas. His painful death came in the spring of 4 B.C.E.

THE HOUSE OF HEROD

In the months following Herod's death, Jerusalem and to some extent the wider Jewish territory were the site of a number of uprisings. Archelaus put down one rebellion stemming from the incident of the golden eagle. Thereafter Archelaus, Antipas, and Philip left for Rome, each pressing his case against the other for the title of "king." During their absence Varus, the governor of Syria, quelled a rebellion in Jerusalem. Shortly thereafter his general Sabinus put down yet another uprising there and burned some of the buildings around the Temple and plundered its treasury. Varus returned from Antioch, dealt with a rebellion in Galilee, and settled matters in Jerusalem. Two thousand rebels were crucified. In Rome, Augustus confirmed Herod's will in all its essential points.

Philip, the son of Herod and Cleopatra of Jerusalem, was named Tetrarch of Batanaea, Trachonitis, Auranitis, Gaulanitis, and Panias, north and east of the Sea of Galilee, where he reigned quietly from 4 B.C.E. to 34 C.E. He is remembered for his development of the area of Caesarea Philippi, around the shoulder of Mount Hermon, where he rebuilt the shrine at the Panion. He was married to Salome the daughter of Herodias.

Herod Antipas was appointed Tetrarch of Galilee and Perea. He is the Herod most frequently mentioned in the Gospels, especially Luke. An appreciator of fine architecture like his father, he built a splendid capital on the west shore of the Sea of Galilee, naming it Tiberias in honor of Augustus's successor, the emperor Tiberius. Antipas is notorious for having taken as his wife Herodias, the wife of his half-brother, Herod,[1] and for having executed John the Baptist when he reproved him for this deed. Antipas's alliance with Herodias proved to be his downfall. When his first wife heard that he planned to divorce her she fled to her father, the Nabataean king Aretas IV, whose army dealt Antipas a severe defeat. Subsequently, Tiberius's successor, Caligula, appointed Antipas's nephew, Agrippa, "king" over the tetrarchy of Philip. The ambitious Herodias prodded her husband to seek the same title. Charges were brought against Antipas. He was deposed and banished to Gaul in 39 B.C.E.

Archelaus had the worst reputation of the sons of Herod (cf. Matt 2:22), and his reign was the shortest. He ruled as ethnarch of Judea, Idumea, and Samaria from 4 B.C.E. to 6 C.E., when he was accused before Augustus, deposed, and banished to Gaul.

THE ROMAN GOVERNORS OF JUDEA

With the deposing of Archelaus, Judea, Samaria, and Idumea were placed under the direct rule of a Roman governor known first as a "praefect" and later as a "procurator." Holding both military and civil authority, these governors were beholden primarily to the emperor himself. In cases of emergency the legate of Syria could intervene. The arrangement was typical for provinces presenting special problems to the empire.

At the beginning of this direct Roman rule over Judea, Quirinius, the Roman legate of Syria, conducted a census of the people (cf. Luke 2:2).[2] A rebellion of uncertain proportions led by a Galilean named Judas was quickly put down.

Six or seven Roman governors ruled Judea from 6 to 41 C.E. Of these the most famous, or infamous, was Pontius Pilate. From the very beginning of his rule he showed insensitivity and contempt for Jewish customs and desires, and on several occasions during his ten years as praefect he met protests with force of arms. In this context his capitulation to the crowd at the time of Jesus' trial is odd and out of character, to say the least. A few years later, in 36 C.E., after an ill-advised attack on a group of Samaritans, Pilate was removed from office by Vitellius, the legate of Syria, and sent to Rome to answer for his conduct.

Other trouble erupted during the reign of the emperor Caligula (37–41 C.E.). In Egypt the Jewish community in Alexandria suffered bloody persecution, which was allowed if not abetted by the Roman governors. As for Judea, the emperor, taking claims of his own divine status seriously, ordered that his statue be erected in the Jerusalem Temple. The Roman legate of Syria, Petronius, knowing that the Jews would violently oppose this action, hesitated and attempted to negotiate. Through the intercession of Agrippa, who was in Rome at this time, Caligula temporarily rescinded his order. In January 41 he was murdered before he could enforce a second such demand.

AGRIPPA I

Agrippa was the grandson of Herod the Great. He was born in 10 B.C.E., just three years before the execution of his father, Aristobulus. In Rome he became an intimate of Tiberius's son and of Caligula. Although he was later imprisoned by Tiberius, Caligula released him after the old man's death and appointed him "king" of the tetrarchy of Philip, who had died in 34 C.E. When Herod's son Antipas sought the same title for himself and was removed from office his territories were also given to Agrippa. After the murder of Caligula, Agrippa helped to secure the succession of Claudius as emperor, and for this service his territory was extended to include Judea and Samaria. Thus from 41 to 44 C.E. Agrippa ruled as king over the realm that had once belonged to his grandfather. He was known as a pious and observant Jew. During the few years of his reign he strengthened and extended the fortifications of Jerusalem. According to the book of Acts he beheaded James the son of Zebedee and imprisoned the apostle Peter. After his sudden death his territories were placed under the direct supervision of Rome. Later his son, Agrippa II, would receive back some of the family territories. Those grants and concessions notwithstanding, the pervading Herodian influence had come to an end.

DOMINATION—OPPOSITION—EXPECTATION

Roman presence and domination were an overshadowing fact of life in Palestine during the century we have been discussing. Although Roman rule was exercised directly only in Judea and Samaria, and then only for thirty-five years, Jewish rulers held their power by permission of the Roman government, and positions and appointments were constantly subject to a succession of Roman governors, generals, and emperors.

To many, Roman rule doubtless appeared as just and as a relief from the infighting of the Hasmonean house in its waning years. Nonetheless, the advent of Roman power brought its own set of problems, burdens, oppression, and disastrous interaction with the population or segments of it. In the process of squelching Hasmonean power, Pompey desecrated the Temple and slaughtered some of the population, and Cassius sold thousands into slavery. Gabinius practiced extortion. Crassus plundered the Temple. Antony extracted heavy taxes. Among the governors of Judea, Pilate was notorious for his cruelty. Only Caligula's murder prevented a terrible disaster. While Herod and his sons were nominally Jews, Herod the Great, at least, was viewed as an outsider, and his cruel and ruthless life-style could be oppressive to the extreme.

There were periods during this century when oppression begat revolt and vice versa. The names of a few revolutionary leaders have been preserved. To what extent the uprisings they led were messianic in a strict sense, religious in a more general sense, or simply reactions without ideology is a question we cannot discuss here. The fact is that the times were harsh and tense. Within this charged atmosphere, well attested by the writings of Josephus and Philo, were spawned the documents that we discuss in this chapter, with their messages of messianic hope and apocalyptic cataclysm and their exhortations to courage and resistance to death if necessary. To them must be added those writings from Qumran that date from this period, at least the Habakkuk Commentary and the War Scroll.

Finally, we must note, this was the context for the appearance of John the Baptist and Jesus of Nazareth. With the fire of a prophet and the certitude of an apocalyptist, John appealed for wholesale repentance in the face of an imminent judgment. The message of Jesus is more difficult to extract, for it is interwoven in the Gospels with the church's testimony to him. But it is evident that he spoke of the coming of God's kingdom and that he saw it breaking in through his own words and actions. Little that he said and little that the church said about him can be understood apart from the times we have sketched and those Jewish theologies that we have discussed in our previous chapters and that we take up here in the documents that were written and expanded in the years that encircle the turn of the era.

THE PSALMS OF SOLOMON

The psalms in this collection date largely from the middle decades of the first century B.C.E., and they appear to have emanated from circles closely related to the Pharisees. The titles of the psalms attribute them to

King Solomon. This pseudonymous ascription may be late, and its rationale is not altogether clear. The last part of psalm 2 is reminiscent of Wisdom of Solomon 6, and the hope for an heir to the Davidic throne (*Ps. Sol.* 17) provides a superficial connection with Solomon, but there appears to be nothing uniquely Solomonic in any of the psalms.

The most striking feature of these psalms which differentiates them from their canonical counterparts is their didactic character. The author not only petitions or praises God for deliverance from distress but also explicates how this distress serves as chastening or punishment for sin. God's chief function according to the psalms is that of judge, dispensing reward and punishment to Israel and the Gentiles or to the righteous and sinners within Israel.

Psalms of the Nation

The psalms are of two categories, dealing respectively with the nation and its fate and with personal piety. Psalms in the first category either reflect upon events in the immediate past—the Roman conquest and related matters—or express Israel's eschatological hopes—the restoration of the Davidic monarchy and the return of the Dispersion.

Psalm 1

The speaker is Mother Jerusalem. When she first heard of the approach of the Roman army she was certain she would be spared. She had interpreted her prosperity as an indicator of the piety of her children, a reasonable deduction from Deuteronomic theological presuppositions. In point of fact, however, God was preparing to punish his people for their secret sins, which exceeded the transgressions of their Roman conquerors. The people had polluted the sanctuary. This psalm may have been written as an introduction to the collection. Its last line provides a transition to the beginning of psalm 2.

Psalm 2

The author plays a number of variations on the theme of sin and judgment, weaving them into a kind of narrative.

A.	Introduction: The Roman attack	vv. 1–2
B.	Reason: Israel's sin	v. 3
C.	Result: Judgment	vv. 4–13a
D.	Cause: Israel's sin	vv. 13b–15

E. Result: God's judgment	vv. 16–23
F. Prayer for deliverance	vv. 24–29
G. Answer: Pompey's judgment	vv. 30–31b
H. Reason: His arrogance	vv. 31c–35
I. Exhortation and summary	vv. 36–40
J. Doxology	v. 41

Pompey is able to breach the Temple walls, and his army can trample on the altar because the Jews themselves have already defiled the sanctuary in their conduct of its cult (A–B). Here the mode of punishment corresponds to the nature of the sin. Verses 6–9 suggest that more Jews than just the family of Aristobulus were taken captive to Rome. Reference to sexual sins (vv. 13–15) is repeated in 8:10–13. Typical of these psalms is the stress on the impartial nature of God's judgment (vv. 16–19). The author borrows imagery from Second Isaiah to describe the degradation of Jerusalem (vv. 20–22; cf. Isa 52:1–2). Employing a theme reminiscent of Deuteronomy 32:19ff. he describes how the agent of God's judgment grows arrogant and is himself punished (G–H). Pompey's arrogance is similar to that attributed to Antiochus and his prototype, the king of Babylon (see above, pp. 86, 88), and the language here seems to be informed by the parallel passage in Ezekiel 28:1–10. The description of Pompey as a "dragon" is a reference to the mythological motif of the chaos monster. A similar combination of the dragon motif with the arrogant anti-God figure occurs later in Revelation 12:7ff., where it is applied to Satan. The author implies that Pompey's judgment is an answer to prayer.

Verses 34–39 contain a number of motifs that are reminiscent of Wisdom of Solomon 1–6 (see above, pp. 175–79): the persecution (v. 39) and exaltation of the righteous (v. 35); the arrogance and punishment of the oppressor (v. 35); an address to the mighty, informing them of God's judgment (v. 36; cf. v. 34). Certain elements in vv. 36–40 stand in tension with the rest of the psalm. Previously we have heard of God's punishment of the whole of Israel for their sins. Here a distinction is made between the righteous and the sinner within Israel, who will be judged "according to their deeds" (v. 38).

Psalm 8

Again the pattern of sin and punishment governs the structure of this psalm.

A. Introduction: The coming of judgment   vv. 1–7
B. Israel's sins described   vv. 8–14
C. Pompey, the agent of divine judgment   vv. 15–24
D. Reprise: Sin, judgment, doxology   vv. 25–29
E. Prayer: That judgment turn to mercy   vv. 30–39
F. Doxology   v. 40

The author describes his terror at the approach of the Roman army. At first he thought that Jerusalem would be spared because of the righteousness of its inhabitants (v. 7a; cf. 1:3–5), but this righteousness was a fiction. As in 1:8 and 2:3 the cardinal sin involved defilement of the sanctuary and the cult (vv. 12–14, 25).

The events of 63 B.C.E. are clearly reflected in vv. 16–28. The party of Hyrcanus opens the gates of Jerusalem to the conqueror (vv. 16–20). When he finally breaches the walls of the Temple, great slaughter ensues (vv. 21–23, 28). The family of Aristobulus (at least) is taken captive to Rome (v. 24).

The prayer in vv. 30–39 corresponds to 2:24–29 but with several significant differences. Here, as throughout this psalm, there is no reference to the arrogance of the conqueror. Foremost in the author's mind is his understanding of this conquest as God's righteous judgment. Second, the prayer is broader in scope. The author looks for a return of the Dispersion and a general turn of God's wrath to mercy. Because of the nature of the petition, the author still awaits its fulfillment. Logically, this psalm is prior to psalm 2.

Psalm 7

This psalm is difficult to place in sequence with the others. Verses 2–3, 5 imply that the conquest has not yet taken place. The psalm reflects none of the panic or anguish that one would expect in the face of imminent conquest (cf. 8:1–6). Perhaps it was composed when Rome first came on the horizon and before the parties of Aristobulus and Hyrcanus had invited disaster.

Psalm 11

The author expresses his hope for a return of the Dispersion. The psalm is a pastiche of phrases and imagery from Second Isaiah (cf., e.g., Isa 40:1–5; 41:19; 43:5–6; 49:6; 52:1–2; 60:1ff.). A passage very closely connected with this psalm occurs in Baruch 4:36–5:9 (see above, p. 113).

Psalm 17

A. God is King	vv. 1–4
B. The sons of David were to be the human agents of this kingship	v. 5
C. Israel sinned	v. 6a
D. Their punishment was the rise of the Hasmonean dynasty	vv. 6b–8a
E. God punished their arrogance through the agency of Pompey	vv. 9–22
F. Prayer: Restore the Davidic dynasty	v. 23
G. Description of the Messiah and messianic times	vv. 24–50
H. Final petition	v. 51ab
I. God is King	v. 51c

God's kingly power is the central concept and underlying theme that runs like a thread through this psalm. God is Israel's king forever (v. 1). His kingdom extends forever over the Gentiles as well (v. 4). He chose David and his descendants to be the human agents exercising that reign (v. 5). The Hasmoneans usurped the privilege of this monarchy (vv. 6–8). The Romans have deposed them (vv. 8bff.). Let now the Davidic heir arise, thrust off the yoke of foreign domination, and reign in Israel (vv. 23ff.), for God is Israel's king forever (v. 51c).

The pattern of sin and punishment that is typical of psalms 1, 2, and 8 appears here with its own peculiar emphases. The Roman presence and the events surrounding it are construed as punishment for Israel's sin (vv. 17–22). More central, however, is the place of the Hasmonean house in this pattern. This dynasty arose as punishment for Israel's sin (v. 6), and the primary reason for the appearance of the Romans was not to punish Israel in general but to recompense the Hasmoneans for their usurpation and perversion of the monarchy (vv. 7ff.). The messianic removal of the Romans is not so much punishment for their sins as restoration of God's kingly presence in Israel and over the rest of the world.

The prayer for deliverance (vv. 23ff.) here takes a very specific form: that God would send an heir to the Davidic throne, the anointed of the Lord (v. 36, Gk. *christos*, reflecting the Hebrew, *meshiah*). The major portion of this psalm is devoted to a description of this Messiah and the messianic era in Israel, and it presents us with the most detailed description of what at least some Jews of this period expected in such a figure.

The Messiah is a human being, a member of the family of David. He is a latter-day fulfillment of God's ancient promise that the sons of David would rule over Israel *in perpetuum* (2 Sam 7:14; Ps 89:19–37). The continuity of that line had been broken with the Exile. Thus, during the years of Persian and Hellenistic rule the biblical oracles about the Lord's anointed and promises of the restoration of the dynasty were applied to a king yet to come. Now the usurpation of the monarchy by the Hasmonean house and the Roman domination of Israel are sufficient to bring these hopes to full and rich expression in this psalm. The author alludes to the biblical oracles, especially Psalm 2:9 and Isaiah 11:2–5 (vv. 26–27, 42).

Although the messianic king will be a human being, the author attributes to him certain semidivine characteristics that are typical of the older (especially Isaianic) oracles. As God's vicar and agent on earth the king shares in, or embodies, divine qualities. He is the presence of wisdom, strength, and righteousness (vv. 25, 29, 42, 44) and is pure from sin (v. 41). His word has power that is reminiscent of the mighty, creative, and effective power of God's word (vv. 37–39; cf. Isa. 11:4). He is the source of blessing (v. 40). The Messiah cannot be seen apart from God. God himself is Israel's king, and he is the Messiah's king (v. 38). However, the Messiah is the agent by whom and through whom God's reign and its consequences are actualized in this world. Thus God endows the Messiah with his own divine characteristics, and the author may speak of the Messiah in divine superlatives.

The messianic king has a variety of functions. God's reign means the removal of foreign domination; he will drive the Romans out of Palestine, the promised inheritance of God's people (vv. 24–27, 41, 51). He will gather the dispersed (vv. 28, 50) and restore the old tribal boundaries (v. 30). This implies the expansion of the nation to its former borders during the united monarchy—an expectation not surprising for a superlative, latter-day manifestation of the Davidic dynasty. He will reign in Israel as ruler, judge, and shepherd of the flock of the Lord (cf. Ezek. 34). However, because the Lord is king over all the world he will exalt Israel over all the Gentiles, who will flow to Jerusalem to bring their tribute (cf. Isa 60 and Dan 7:27).

The days of the Messiah will be ideal times. Israel will be cleansed of sin (vv. 29–30, 36, 45), and God's kingly power will become evident in Israel and over all the world. The psalmist's prayer may be summarized pithily: "Thy kingdom come; thy will be done on earth as it is in heaven."

In its assertion of the final, total kingship of God, the eschatology of this psalm closely parallels many manifestations of apocalyptic eschatology, but with important distinctions. There is here no concept of two corresponding levels of reality: the heavenly and earthly, the mythical and the historical. The author appeals for judgment against his enemies and the manifestation of God's kingly power in the form of a human agent, who will yet appear on the horizon of history. Finally, he awaits the messianic king "at the time which God sees" (v. 23). That time is fixed, we may suppose, yet there is no indication that it will be in the imminent future. We miss here the white heat of apocalyptic expectation.

Psalm 18

The author speaks mainly of Israel's present relationship to God and her future hope. The nation is described as God's firstborn, only-begotten son (cf. Exod 4:22). In connection with this metaphor the present suffering is interpreted as God's fatherly chastisement or discipline. The same interpretation occurs in 7:8 and 17:47 and especially in 3:4. The author stops short of calling the present calamity outright punishment for sin, and he presumes a relationship between God and his people which is different from that of judge and defendant. The bitter tragedy of 63 B.C.E. is somewhat muted. The emphasis is on God's close relationship to his people and the hope for the blessed days of the messianic age. The psalm forms a fitting conclusion to the collection and may have been composed for that purpose.

Verses 11–14 appear to belong to a different psalm, which has not been preserved in its entirety. Its theme is reminiscent of the hymn in col. 10 of the Qumran Community Rule.

Psalms of the Righteous and the Pious

A second category of psalms depicts two groups, their relationships to God, their deeds, and their fates at the hand of the divine Judge. The groups are the sinners (also called transgressors, lawless, and wicked) and the righteous (also called the pious [of the Lord], those who fear the Lord, and those who love the Lord). True religion is expressed in the proper observance of Torah, that is, in righteous conduct. Nonetheless, the author's choice of names for the righteous also implies an internalizing of religion. The righteous are those who *fear* and *love* the Lord and who do so "in truth" (10:4; 14:1). They stand in opposition to the "men-pleasers" or hypocrites, who take their place in the company of the pious while their hearts are far from God (psalm 4). Deeply in-

fluencing the portrait of the righteous in these psalms is a sense of covenant, although the word itself is rarely used (9:17–18). The righteous are
the pious *of the Lord,* those who fear *the Lord,* those who love *the Lord.*
They are his children: beloved, firstborn (13:8). Thus he deals with them
in special ways, chastising and correcting rather than punishing, cleansing them and forgiving their sins. The righteous, for their part, express
this relationship not only by striving to obey Torah but also through those
acts of personal piety which explicitly enact the relationship, namely,
prayer, praise, and thanksgiving.

Psalm 3

In two parallel sections the author contrasts the righteous and the sinners (vv. 3–10; 11–15). The righteous are not sinless or perfect. They are
"righteous" because they are concerned with their sins and because they
take the proper steps to atone for them. Thus God "cleanses" them
(v. 10). They live in awareness of and openness to God (vv. 3–6). The
sinner, by contrast, shows no concern for God. He accumulates sin upon
sin with no attempt to put himself right with God. Thus his "destruction" is eternal (vv. 13–14). Those who fear the Lord, however, will rise
to eternal life in the presence of the eternal glory of the Lord (v. 16).

Psalm 4

Participation in the externals of the religious life is no barometer of
true inward piety. Even among the congregation of the pious (v. 1) who
utter the Torah (v. 10) there are those whose lust and greed lead to
secret sins that blatantly and intentionally contradict public profession.
Again it is this willful and continuous sinning (vv. 15, 28) that characterizes "the sinner." God's judgment is sure to ensue.

Psalm 6

In all but two lines (vv. 4–5) God is mentioned either as the object
of piety and devotion, as the subject of a verb of deliverance, or as both.
Because the author fears and loves God and has experienced his saving
activity he can stand fast in trouble (vv. 4–5).

Psalm 9

The psalm depicts the activities of God, who is both the righteous
judge and the forgiver of those who repent. When Israel sinned, God

judged them through the Exile (vv. 1–4). God can judge righteously because of his perfect knowledge of the sins and righteous deeds of all (vv. 5–6). The presupposition for his judgment is the person's freedom to choose good or evil (v. 7), and "the doer of righteousness" and "the doer of iniquity" bring upon themselves eternal life and destruction, respectively, because of God's righteous judgment (vv. 8–10). Nevertheless, there is forgiveness with God (vv. 11–15). The doer of righteousness is not sinless, but when he repents and confesses his sin he is forgiven. The psalm concludes with an appeal for God's mercy on Israel, which is threatened by the Gentiles. The appeal is based on election and covenant (vv. 16–19).

Psalm 10

God's judgment on the righteous is of a special sort. He judges not in order to punish but in order to chastise, to purge, to discipline them, that they might be kept within the covenantal relationship (v. 5). The proper stance for the pious is to "endure" this discipline and to give thanks to God, who thus deals mercifully with them.

Psalm 13

The author contrasts God's dealings with the righteous and the sinners. In a recent calamity God punished the sinners but spared the righteous. Again the righteous is one who commits sins and who is indeed fearful that he will be punished for them. Nevertheless, his misdeeds and sins committed in ignorance have not nullified his covenantal status as a child of God, dear and beloved. In keeping with this relationship God disciplines and corrects his pious ones. Not only is God's judgment evident in this life, but life and destruction of the righteous and the sinners are eternal.

Psalm 14

This psalm is a paraphrase of the canonical Psalm 1. It contrasts the pious of the Lord, who endure God's chastening and follow his commandments, with the sinners, who spend their time sinning and ignoring God. As Judge, God has full knowledge of these things, and in consequence of his judgment both the pious and the sinners will receive their just deserts: life and destruction.

Psalm 15

Here, as in psalm 13, calamity enacts the judgment of God on the wicked, whereas the righteous escape. It is unclear whether vv. 13–15 refer to a future day of judgment or to God's perennial judgmental activity, exemplified in the recent calamity. The idea that the righteous and the wicked have on them "a sign," which marks them for salvation or destruction, is reminiscent of such passages as Genesis 4:15, Exodus 12: 21ff., and Revelation 14:9–11.

Psalm 16

Again we hear of the foibles of the righteous. It is not clear whether the author actually fell into an overt sexual sin (so vv. 7–8) for which God has forgiven him or whether he avoided committing the deed. In either case he gives thanks to God who has chastised him and thus brought him to his senses so that he might escape the consequences of gross sin.

These psalms are often attributed to Pharisaic circles. Many items in them point in that direction: the assertion of human responsibility for actions (9:7); the belief in a resurrection (although it is not specified as a resurrection of the body; 3:16); a deep concern for the righteous life and piety; and a conscious distinction between righteous and sinner. Lacking are references to such specific Pharisaic concerns as Sabbath laws and rules for table fellowship, but such argument from silence is scarcely convincing. Conversely, there is little if anything that characterizes them as non-Pharisaic. Among the Jewish sects known to us at this time, it is the Pharisees whom they most closely approximate. Assertions of the profanation of the Temple may rest on halakhic distinctions between Pharisees and Sadducees (cf. 8:13).

THE TESTAMENT OF MOSES—REVISED

The expectation of an imminent judgment was an essential feature of Jewish apocalyptic eschatology. When this judgment did not happen as expected, the apocalyptic literature and traditions were revised and updated in a variety of ways. Daniel 12:12 revises the timetable announced in 12:11. Reinterpretations of the vision in Daniel 7 are found in Revelation 13, *1 Enoch* 46–47 (see below, pp. 216–17), and 4 Ezra 11–13 (see below, p. 292). The *Testament of Moses* is an example of revision through interpolation.

As we have seen (above, pp. 80–82), the *Testament of Moses* was composed during the persecution by Antiochus Epiphanes. Chapter 5 refers to the events leading up to the persecution. Chapter 8 describes the persecution itself. According to chap. 9 the innocent deaths of Taxo and his sons will trigger God's vengeance and bring in the end-time described in chap. 10. In point of fact the persecution did cease and the Gentile oppressor met his end, although not in the kind of apocalyptic catastrophe depicted in chap. 10.[3] The apocalypse was shelved, but it was not forgotten.

Almost two centuries later the work was dusted off and revised to make it relevant for new times. The editor's method was to insert between chaps. 5 and 8 a sketch of events that would bring the reader to the present time. In chap. 6, v. 1 refers to the Hasmonean high priests, whom the editor obviously despised. The rest of the chapter makes reference to events in the reigns of Herod the Great and his sons.[4] Since v. 7 predicts that Herod's sons will rule for shorter periods of time than his thirty-four years (v. 6), the latest date for the revision would be 30 C.E., after which the reigns of both Antipas and Philip exceeded that of their father. The last identifiable events mentioned are in v. 9: the burning of the buildings around the Temple by Varus's commander, Sabinus, and Varus's crucifixion of the Jewish rebels in the months following Herod's death. The descriptions in chap. 7 are too stereotyped to be identifiable.

The net result of this interpolation is the transformation of the description of Antiochus's time into a kind of "eschatological tableau"[5] that would recapitulate the earlier events that transpired during the terrible times of the 160s. The repetition of such events would usher in the end-time.

There appears to be one final revision in 10:8. In the original version of the *Testament* this verse was most likely an allusion to Deuteronomy 33:29: Israel would tread on the necks of its enemies.[6] The reference to the wings of the eagle looks like an expansion that alludes to the incident of the golden eagle at the end of Herod's reign and perhaps to the eagle as symbol of the Roman Empire.[7]

In the months or years following Herod's death an apocalyptist with the same pacifist ideology expressed by the author of the *Testament* updated and reissued this work to encourage and exhort his comrades during the difficult years at the beginning of the Common Era.[8] For him, as for the writers of Revelation and *4 Ezra*, the great enemy was no longer the Seleucid kingdom but the Roman Empire; the apocalyptic message, however, remained essentially the same.

1 ENOCH 37–71
(THE PARABLES OF ENOCH)

These chapters of *1 Enoch* were originally a separate Enochic writing[9] that announced the coming of the great judgment, in which God would vindicate his "elect and righteous ones" and punish their oppressors, "the kings and the mighty." The book divides into three major sections called "parables" or "similitudes" (chaps. 38–44; 45–57; 58–69). As this term is employed in this book, it reflects the usage of biblical prophetic literature and denotes a revelatory discourse.[10] Since the expression occurs also in *1 Enoch* 1:2–3 and 93:1, 3 (Aram.), it is less distinctive of chaps. 37–71 than the universal scholarly designation "the book of parables" might indicate. The author's introduction entitles the work Enoch's "vision of wisdom" (37:1).[11]

Running through the parables are four major types of material, which parallel other parts of *1 Enoch*. The book as a whole depicts a journey or series of journeys. The seer ascends to the heavenly throne room (39:2–41:2). Then he visits the astronomical and other celestial phenomena (chaps. 41–44; 59–60) and the places of punishment (esp. 52–56:4). The literary form that describes segments of these journeys is familiar from *1 Enoch* 17–32: journey, vision, seer's question, interpretation by accompanying angel (see above, pp. 54–55). The second set of materials includes narratives about Noah and the Flood (especially chaps. 65–68). As in chaps. 6–11 and 106–7 the Flood is a type of the final judgment. The third group of materials consists of a series of heavenly tableaux, scenes in a developing drama that depicts events leading up to the final judgment. Intermingled with these tableaux and often introduced by the words "in those days" are a series of anticipatory allusions to the judgment. The closest Enochic parallels to the tableaux are the heavenly scenes in *1 Enoch* 9–10 and 89:70–71, 76–77; 90:14, 17. Chapters 92–105 also presume such heavenly activity but do not present it in vision form. The anticipatory allusions have formal counterparts in chaps. 92–105.[12]

Before turning to the drama itself, we must introduce the cast of char-

acters. On the one side are God, his heavenly entourage, the agents of his
judgment (primarily "the Elect One," but also certain of God's angels),
and God's people ("the elect," "the righteous," and "the holy"). On the
other side are the chief demon Azazel, his angels, and the kings and the
mighty. God is usually called "the Lord of Spirits," a paraphrase of the
biblical title "Lord of Hosts" (cf. 39:12 and Isa 6:3)[13] or "the Head of
Days," a title drawn from Daniel 7:9. The Elect One combines the titles,
attributes, and functions of the one like a son of man in Daniel 7, the
Servant of the Lord in Second Isaiah, and the Davidic Messiah. "Son of
man" is not a title. It is a Semitic way of saying "man," and it is almost
always qualified: "that son of man," "the son of man who has righteousness."[14] In the parables the term is ambiguous. On the one hand it cannot
be excluded that the author has in mind a human being glorified in
heaven, with a face "like one of the holy angels" (46:1).[15] In chap. 71,
which is probably an appendix, this figure is in fact identified with Enoch
himself. On the other hand the usage of Daniel 8:15, 9:21, 10:5, and
12:6 indicates that an angel can be called "a/the man" or described as
having "the appearance of a man." The Elect One is the agent of God's
judgment and as such is depicted with imagery that the early chapters
of *1 Enoch* ascribe to God himself. Related to his judgmental function is
his role as the champion of God's people, and his titles "the Elect One"
and "the Righteous One" correspond to the titles "the elect" and "the
righteous ones." The salient features of God's people are their status as
his chosen ones, their righteousness, and their suffering. Named among
God's angels are Michael, Raphael, Gabriel, and Phanuel, who correspond
to the four archangels in chaps. 9–11. Azazel and his hosts are the counterparts of 'Asael and of Shemiḥazah and his hosts in chaps. 6–16. Here, as
in chaps. 12–16, Shemiḥazah is never mentioned. His function as arch-
demon is ascribed to the other angelic chieftain. Different from chaps.
12–16, the angels' major sin here is the revelation of secrets rather than
the spawning of bastard offspring. Although the parables speak of "sinners," the references are usually very general. Where they are specific they
seem to identify "the sinners" with "the kings and the mighty," the real
villains of the piece (46:4; 62:2). The latter are notorious for denying
the name of the Lord of Spirits and the heavenly world and for oppres-
sing and persecuting the righteous. Their common destiny with the
wicked angels suggests that they are agents of the latter.[16]

The Unfolding Drama

The first parable is the shortest of the three. It introduces most of the dramatis personae, as well as the theme of judgment, which will be elaborated in the rest of the book. Together with the introduction to the book (chap. 37), it follows roughly the structure of the first chapters of *1 Enoch.* Chapter 37 corresponds to *1 Enoch* 1:1–3. The repeated formula "I lifted up and said" (37:2, 5) parallels the repetition of "he (I) lifted up his (my) parable and said" in 1:2, 3 (and 93:1, 3). Also similar to 1:2 is the contrast between present and future in 37:2–3. Chapter 38 opens the first parable by introducing the subject of the coming judgment. Corresponding to the theophany predicted in 1:3–9 is the epiphany of "the Righteous One" (38:2).[17] The story of the descent of the angels (chaps. 6–7) is summarized in 39:1. Enoch is introduced in 39:2 (cf. 14:1).[18] Verse 3 mentions his ascent, which is described in chap. 14. After seeing the dwellings of the angels and the righteous, Enoch beholds the one whose coming he has anticipated (38:2), here called "the Elect One" (39:6–8). He is then caught up in the praises of the heavenly entourage (39:9–14). Enoch's vision of the divine throne room in chap. 40 corresponds to chap. 14, and the author here employs for the first time the format of vision, question, and interpretation. Enoch views the judgment process and then moves on to the places of the celestial phenomena. There may be a literary displacement in chaps. 41–44. In the present order 41:3–8 and 41:9 are both separated from the sections to which they are naturally related. The original order may have been 41:1–2, 9; 42; 41:3–8; 43–44. The little Wisdom poem in chap. 42 suggests a parody on Sirach 24 and Baruch 3:9–4:4. Wisdom does not dwell in Israel; unrighteousness drove her back to heaven—a pithy and telling summary of the apocalyptic world view (cf. 94:5).

The second parable, like the first, begins with a poetic introduction that anticipates the judgment and its consequences and makes reference to the Elect One (chap. 45). Verse 3 is the first of several anticipatory references to the enthronement of the Elect One. In spite of the heavenly setting of the parables, the place of eternal life will be on earth, which will be purged of sinners (vv. 4–6; cf. *1 Enoch* 10:16–11:2 and 91:14).

Chapters 46–47 present the first tableaux in the developing drama about the Elect One and the judgment. In 46:1–3 the author draws on Daniel

7:9, 13, identifying his protagonist with the one like a son of man who is presented to the Ancient of Days in Daniel 7. The angelic answer to Enoch's inquiry employs or alludes to three of the four names of the protagonist. He is the son of man who has righteousness (son of man, the Righteous One) and whom God has chosen (the Elect One). In 46: 4–8 the angel anticipates the judgment scene in chaps. 62–63, which has been constructed from an exegetical tradition that combined Isaiah 52–53 with Isaiah 13–14. Here the deeds and fate of the kings and the mighty are depicted in language drawn from Isaiah 14.[19] Verse 7 suggests that these rulers are pagan since they worship idols. Chapter 47 strikes a familiar Enochic theme. The blood of the righteous will be avenged. The interceding angels will relay the prayer of the righteous and thus trigger God's judgment.[20] Verse 2g alludes to Daniel 7:22 and introduces another tableau in v. 3, which paraphrases Daniel 7:9–10.

Chapter 48 presents yet another tableau, the naming of "that son of man." Because it follows the enthronement of "the Head of Days," it may correspond to the presentation in Daniel 7:13 (cf. 49:2d; the Elect One now stands in the presence of the Lord of Spirits). The scene, however, expands on the call of the Servant in Isaiah 49,[21] thus drawing on this strand of the author's tradition. That son of man is both a helper of the righteous and a light to the Gentiles. The latter term is drawn from Isaiah 49:6 but is also consonant with the openness to the salvation of the Gentiles in *1 Enoch* 10:21, 90:38, and 91:14. Language about the preexistence of that son of man and his name (vv. 3, 6), read in the context of the many references to wisdom in chaps. 48–49, may indicate that this figure is in some sense identified with or related to preexistent Wisdom.[22] This would fit with the usage of the Servant tradition in Wisdom 2, 4–5, where the righteous man is the bearer of preexistent Wisdom.[23] Linked to the tableau in 48:1–7 is a section that describes the coming judgment of the kings and the mighty in language drawn from Exodus 15:7, 10 (the destruction of Pharaoh and his host).

The unique expression "kings of the earth" and the reference to "the Lord of Spirits and his Anointed" (48:8, 10) are drawn from Psalm 2:2 and indicate the third source of this author's description of the Elect One —biblical language about the Davidic Messiah.[24] In 49:1–2 the author returns to the theme of Wisdom introduced in 48:1 and links it in v. 3 to a paraphrase of the messianic oracle in Isaiah 11:2. Because of his wisdom the Elect One can penetrate lies and judge rightly (v. 4, anticipating 62:3). Verse 4c paraphrases Isaiah 42:1, the source of the Servant title "the Elect One."

Chapters 50–51 anticipate future events connected with the judgment. Chapter 50 mentions a third group in addition to the righteous and the sinners, who will be saved by repentance (cf. *1 Enoch* 100:6). Chapter 51 includes a resurrection in the events of the end-time, and v. 3 makes another anticipatory reference to the enthronement of the Elect One. Verses 4–5 again designate earth as the locus of salvation and eternal life.

The journey and visions described in chaps. 52–56:4 are related to the myth of the angels and to the journey traditions in *1 Enoch* 6–11 and 17–21. The vision of the mountains in chap. 52 contains several literary problems. Verse 1 refers back to Enoch's ascent (39:3). The double angelic interpretation in v. 4 and in vv. 5–9 suggests that two traditions have been conflated, the first referring to a variety of things which Enoch saw and which will serve the Anointed One (vv. 1–2a, 3–4), then a separate vision of the mountains (v. 2b), which is interpreted in vv. 6–9. The mountains are reminiscent of the six mountains that flank the mountain of God in chap. 18. The interpretation of some of the metals as materials for warfare (v. 8) suggests 'Asael's revelation of metallurgy in 8:1. Unlike 8:1, however, silver and gold are here (futile as) a means of buying deliverance (cf. 63:10). Verse 6 is of special significance. As in 38:2, the author has replaced the theophany of chap. 1 with an epiphany of the Elect One, before whose presence the mountains and hills will melt (see also 53:6–7 and cf. 1:6). As in chap. 18, the mountains are located by a deep abyss which will serve as a place of eternal punishment. Chapter 53 describes the place of punishment for the kings and the mighty. The futility of bringing gifts and tribute parallels the motif in 52:7. A comparison of chaps. 53 and 54 indicates that 54:2 has probably been displaced from chap. 53. In the respective valleys Enoch sees instruments of punishment being prepared (53:3; 54:3). He questions the angel (53:4; 54:4), who answers him (53:5; 54:5). As in 54:6, we expect in chap. 53 a reference to the actual punishment of the respective culprits. Thus 54:2 belongs after 53:5 and is out of place in chap. 54. As in chap. 18, there is a second abyss of punishment, this one for the hosts of Azazel (chap. 54). Verses 5–6 reflect 10:4–6. The description of the angels' place of punishment appears to have been interpolated by a tradition about the

Flood (54:7–55:2). Thus 55:3 picks up where 54:6 left off, with a reference to the angels' "taking hold of" the hosts of Azazel, and the passage concludes, as do chaps. 52 and 53, with mention of the judgment by the Elect One. The whole section ends as the angels of punishment set out after certain "elect and beloved ones," perhaps the kings and the mighty, less likely the giants, who have otherwise not been mentioned in the parables.

The reference to the Parthians and the Medes in 56:5 is the only explicit historical reference in the entire book. The author may well be referring to the invasion in 40 B.C.E., just before the beginning of the reign of Herod the Great. This poetic passage describing the horror of the end-time is followed by a vision of the Return of the Dispersion or the coming of the Gentiles to worship in Jerusalem.

The third parable is the longest of the three. Like the other two it begins with a poetic section, which in this case anticipates the glorious theophanic light that will envelop the righteous after the judgment (chap. 58). The material in chaps. 59–60 appears to have suffered a displacement. On the one hand 60:1–10 separates two blocks of astronomical lore (59:1–3 and 60:11–23). At the same time 60:24 and its reference to the two monsters is separated from 60:7–10, which deals with the same subject. By placing 60:11–23 after chap. 59 we solve both problems and arrive at what may well have been the original order: 59; 60:11–23; 60: 1–10, 24–25. The reference in 60:8 to "my grandfather who was taken up, the seventh from Adam" (i.e., Enoch) indicates that 60:1–10 + 24–25 is a tradition originally ascribed to Noah that is now placed in this Enochic book.[25]

In chaps. 61–63 the drama of the judgment moves to its denouement. In 61:1–5 the angels prepare for the resurrection. Verses 6–13 are held together by the common theme of angelic praise. In v. 8 the event occurs toward which the whole book has been pointing, the enthronement of the Elect One. First he will judge the angels (v. 9).

Chapters 62–63 describe the great judgment and its aftermath, which form the climax of this work. For this tableau the author has employed a traditional judgment scene, attested also in Wisdom 4–5 (see above, pp. 178–79), which expanded Isaiah 52–53 with material from Isaiah 13 and 14.[26] The Servant figure in Wisdom is the persecuted righteous man, now exalted, who judges his former persecutors, who are depicted in language drawn from Isaiah 14. These persecutors recognize him, react in terror, confess their sins, and anticipate their punishment, from which their riches cannot deliver them.

The present text begins with the exaltation of the Elect One (a Servant title). Before him stand the kings and the mighty, the counterpart of the audience in Isaiah 52–53, whom the tradition transformed into the enemies of the righteous man. The recognition referred to in 62:1 suggests that the kings and the mighty are to recognize in the Elect One the elect ones whom they have been persecuting.[27] Verse 2bc draws on the language of Isaiah 11:2, 4 and hence the messianic strand of the Elect One tradition (cf. 49:3). Verse 3ef provides a further counterpart to 49:4, and v. 7 to chap. 48. The kings and the mighty petition for mercy without success and are driven from the presence of the Lord and delivered to the angels of punishment (vv. 9–12; cf. 53:3–5). The author then shifts his focus to the righteous and elect and to their coming deliverance and fellowship with their helper and champion, that son of man (62:13–16). Verses 15–16 interpret Isaiah 52:1 and its reference to Mother Zion to refer to the community of the elect. Chapter 63 is the counterpart of the confession in Isaiah 53:1–6 and Wisdom 5:6ff. The section ends with the banishment of the kings and the mighty, described in terms of the banishment from Eden (63:11; cf. 62:10, 12d and Gen 3:24). Chapter 64 and its reference to the angels has no clear connection with its context.

Chapters 65–68 are a collection of Noachic traditions. The story in chap. 65 is closely related to *1 Enoch* 83–84 and 106–7 and presumes a typology between the Flood and the last judgment. God's oracle to Noah (67:1–3) is related to both 10:1–3 and 84:5. In chap. 66 and 67:4 Noah appears to be a visionary guided by his grandfather Enoch, and 67:4 refers back to chap. 52, where Enoch had been guided by an angel. The parallel between the punishment of the angels and that of the kings and the mighty has been prepared for already in chaps. 53–54. The description of that punishment in 67:5–13 has led many scholars to see here an allusion to the attempts of Herod the Great to find healing at the hot springs of Callirrhoe.[28] The reference to "the Book of Parables" in the book itself (68:1) suggests that the Noachic traditions have been interpolated into an already extant work. The list of rebel angels in 69:2–3 is essentially the same as 6:7, while vv. 4–12 present an alternative version. The precise meaning of 69:13–25 is uncertain. Reference to the oath that holds the earth together may be connected with the Flood (see vv. 17–19). If so, this passage may be related to the Noachic traditions in chaps. 67–68 (cf. also the presence of Michael in 67:12–68 and 69:14–15).

After the materials in chaps. 64–69:25 the scene in 69:26–29 comes as something of a surprise. Clearly, it belongs with the judgment scene in chaps. 62–63. It is an acclamation by the elect and the righteous, who have witnessed the appearance of that son of man, his enthronement, and his judgment and banishment of the wicked. This connection is consonant with our previous conjecture that the Noachic materials, and indeed all of 64–69:25, are an interpolation.

In its present form the book of parables has two conclusions. The first describes Enoch's final removal from earth in rather straightforward prose (chap. 70). The second conclusion (chap. 71) is an ascent vision that interprets *1 Enoch* 14–16 and 46 in terms of one another. Enoch's ascent and commissioning as prophet of judgment (chaps. 14–16) are here interpreted as his presentation as "the son of man who was born for righteousness" (chap. 46; 71:14). In the present form of the book this final tableau provides a climax and key to the work as a whole. The author of this chapter repeats the material in chaps. 46–47 but identifies that son of man. He is Enoch, the righteous man par excellence, "the son of man born for righteousness." His ascent to heaven and his exalted status are a promise of the deliverance and vindication of the righteous in the coming judgment. This second conclusion is very likely a later appendix to the book of parables. The descriptions of Enoch's visions of the secrets of heaven (71:3–4) repeat in capsule form what has occurred previously in the book. This may indicate that chap. 71 once stood apart from the book of parables.

Date

The parables of Enoch are notoriously difficult to date. Arguments for a late date based on the fact that only these chapters of *1 Enoch* are not found in Qumran are inconclusive.[29] The earlier parts of *1 Enoch* that formed the basis for this work were not authored at Qumran and were not the sole property of that community. Not every Jewish apocalyptic work authored before 68 c.e. found its way into the Qumran collection. The absence of the parables proves nothing about the date of the work.[30] On the other hand the passages usually cited as evidence for a relatively early date are suggestive but not unambiguous.[31] The end of chap. 56 may refer to the invasion of Judea by the Parthians and the Medes in 40 b.c.e., or it may be a prediction of a future invasion written at some later time. Similarly, the punishment of the kings and the mighty in 67:8–13 may have as much to do with mythic geography in general as with Herod's treatment at Callirrhoe.

Several other considerations may indicate, however, that *at least the traditions now collected in this book* were known around the turn of the era. In the first place the judgment scene in chaps. 62–63 is a reworked form of the tradition that occurs also in Wisdom 2, 4–5, the story of the persecuted righteous man, who is exalted as judge over his enemies. Wisdom 4:10–15 identifies Enoch as the prototype of this righteous one. This may indicate that the author of the Wisdom of Solomon knew that this tradition existed in an Enochic context and perhaps that the Elect One was there identified with Enoch.

A second type of evidence comes from the New Testament. In the Gospels the passages that pertain to the eschatological Son of Man appear to presume that he will function as judge. Such a role contradicts Daniel 7, which these passages usually quote or allude to. In Daniel the one like a son of man appears *after* the judgment. The parables offer us the exegetical basis for such a transformation: the conflation of Daniel 7 with the Isaianic tradition of the exalted righteous one and thus the identification of the one like a son of man with the Servant figure. Moreover, in Matthew 24:37–44/Luke 17:22–27 the typology between the days of Noah and the days of the Son of Man recalls the frequent Enochic typology of Flood and final judgment and connects this judgment with the figure of the Son of Man, who is mentioned in *1 Enoch* only in the parables. Finally, the judgment scene in Matthew 25:31–46 may well reflect *1 Enoch* 62–63. For Matthew the touchstone of judgment is the manner in which people have treated the brethren of the Son of Man and hence the Son of Man himself. In *1 Enoch* 62–63, as we have interpreted it, the solidarity between the Elect One and the elect ones enables the kings and the mighty to recognize in the Elect One the elect ones whom they have persecuted. That Matthew refers to the Son of Man as "the king" (25:34) is consonant with the title "the Anointed One" in the parables.

It has been argued that the parables of Enoch are a Christian composition based on the Gospels.[32] Several factors tell against this hypothesis. There is nothing explicitly Christian in the parables. To the contrary, in their present form the parables identify the Elect One with Enoch himself. It is unlikely and indemonstrable that Jews would have taken up such a Christian eschatological work and transformed it so as to identify the Elect One (originally Jesus) with Enoch, as is presently the case. Finally, the traditions in the parables give all indications of being earlier than those in the Gospels. They show us the exegetical steps by which the one like a son of man came to be judge. Moreover, the sheer repetition of the term "son of man" provides an intermediate step toward the usage of "the Son of Man" as a title and technical term in the Gospels. Conversely, the parables employ the more Semitic and original meaning of the term in a nontitular sense (= "man"). It is unlikely that this usage is a secondary resemiticizing of the titular use of the term.

If this appraisal of the evidence is correct the parables are a Jewish writing produced around the turn of the era. Within that period the kings and the mighty would have had their counterparts among the many Roman generals, governors, triumvirs, and monarchs whose activities in Judea are well documented in the sources. The author might also have had in mind the late Hasmoneans and the Herods.[33]

We can no longer determine from what group this document stems. However, its eschatology was compatible with the views of early Christianity, and the one like a son of man came to be identified with the risen and exalted Christ, whose imminent coming as judge the church awaited. It is noteworthy that both this document and the early church conflated the originally separate figures of the Servant, the one like a son of man, and the Messiah.[34]

The parables of Enoch were most likely composed in Aramaic, and there is some evidence that they may have been translated directly into the Ethiopic version in which they are now extant.[35]

4 MACCABEES

Transformations of Jewish religious traditions are of many sorts. In *4 Maccabees* the stories of the martyrs in 2 Maccabees 6–7 have been transposed into the key of Greek philosophy and embodied in a discourse that demonstrates—mainly on the basis of these stories—that "religious reason is sovereign over the emotions" (Hadas).[36]

In his introduction the author presents his thesis (1:1) and summarizes his argument (1:2–12). This thesis, a "thoroughly philosophical subject" (1:1), was a standard doctrine of the Platonic and Stoic schools, and the author's enumeration of the four cardinal virtues (prudence, temperance, justice, courage, 1:3–4), which stand in opposition to the emotions, is similarly Platonic and Stoic.

In his definition of terms (1:13–30a) the author both agrees with his non-Jewish predecessors and sets himself apart from them. Reason is for him "the intellect choosing with correct judgment the life of wisdom," and he agrees with the Stoics that "wisdom is the knowledge of things human and divine" (1:15–16).[37] What defines his philosophy as Jewish is the assertion that "this wisdom is education in the Law," that is, the Torah (1:17). His exposition will demonstrate how religious reason informed by the Law governed and subdued those emotions that would have led the martyrs to violate the Law.

Before turning to the story of the martyrs the author illustrates his thesis with a number of examples, most of them from biblical history (1:30b–3:18). The citing of biblical figures as examples of abstract virtues (and vices) is typical of the Jewish didactic literature of this period. In the *Testament of Joseph*, as here, the young patriarch exemplifies temperance (*sōphrosynē, 4 Macc* 1:30–2:6; *T. Jos.* 3–9; see below, p. 240).

The author places his discussion of the martyrs in the context of the events that led to their martyrdom (3:20–4:26; cf. 2 Macc 3:6–11). Although the heavy emphasis on divine judgment which runs through 2 Maccabees is here toned down, the persecution is still seen as punishment for Hellenization (4:19–21), and the resistance of the innocent is contrasted with this sin (4:24–26). The deaths of the martyrs are described as three separate but closely linked episodes: Eleazar (chaps. 5–7); the seven brothers (8:1–14:10); their mother (14:11–17:6).

Chapters 5–7 retell the story in 2 Maccabees 6:18–31. Here the graybeard is not only an expert in the Law (cf. 2 Macc 6:18, "a scribe") but also a priest and a distinguished philosopher (5:4, 35). The discussion between Eleazar and Antiochus (who is not mentioned in 2 Macc 6) takes the form of a philosophical debate (chap. 5). The king derides Judaism as folly and nonsense, unworthy of a philosopher. Even if the Law is divine, sin committed out of necessity will be forgiven. Eleazar maintains that a Jew's prime necessity is to obey the Law in all its commandments. Far from being unreasonable, Judaism teaches temperance, courage, justice, and piety. Because God is Creator his Law is fitting to the nature of his people and appropriate to their souls. Now reasoning gives way to straightforward refusal. Eleazar will not violate the Law, and in good Stoic-Cynic fashion he asserts that the tyrant cannot lord it over his reason. And so he faces death by torture. Unlike 2 Maccabees 6, Eleazar's tortures are here described in detail (6:1–11, 24–26), providing evidence for the old priest's claim that his philosophy furnishes him with the virtue of courage, which overcomes bodily pain (7:22–23; cf. 5:23). In the midst of his pain Eleazar continues to philosophize, declaring that his refusal to play the hypocrite is reasonable (6:12–22; cf. 2 Macc 6: 21–23). His final words are an appeal to God to accept his death as an expiation for the sins of the nation (6:26–29). Both this motif and the reference to eternal life in 7:19 are drawn from the story of the seven brothers and their mother in 2 Maccabees 7. By using them here and by other means the author welds the two stories together. Employing a variety of images typical of Greek rhetoric (7:1–7) and reasserting his thesis—now demonstrated by Eleazar's actions—the author concludes this section by singing the praises of his hero.

Chapters 8–12 narrate the martyrdom of the seven brothers and thus correspond to 2 Maccabees 7. The introduction connects the story with the martyrdom of Eleazar (8:1–2; see also 9:5–6 and cf. 2 Macc 6:28, 31). In its outline the story approximates 2 Maccabees 7, connecting similar words and tortures with the respective brothers. The major omission is the material about the mother, which is gathered in the next section. The descriptions of the tortures are expanded, probably to emphasize the brothers' courage (see 8:16). The brothers' speeches are also lengthened and modified. Retained from 2 Maccabees 7 are the motifs of dying for the Law and the punishment of Antiochus. References to Israel's suffering for their sins are deleted, and the theme of resurrection—here immortality and eternal life—is mainly deferred until later. Additions in the narrative, the speeches, and the author's comments interpret the story as evidence of the book's thesis. This application is spelled out at length in the author's conclusion to the story in 13:1–14:10. Like chap. 7 it employs rhetorical imagery, sings the praises of the heroes (and of reason), and appeals to the audience to draw the proper conclusion from the story.

The mother of the seven brothers, whose speeches are integrated into the narrative of 2 Maccabees 7, is here treated in a separate section (14:11–17:6). She is the ultimate example of the author's thesis. In encouraging her sons to die for the Law she demonstrates how reason triumphed over the deepest of the emotions—mother love. Even her suicide to avoid defilement is applauded as a courageous religious act. The remainder of the work rounds off the discourse with a series of observations and applications (17:7–18:24): The thesis has been proven; the courageous deaths of the martyrs have expiated the sins of the people and purified the land; the audience is exhorted to emulate their example and to give praise to God.

Although the author's purpose was to demonstrate a philosophical thesis for the edification of his audience, he has significantly transformed and emended his tradition in other ways. Future resurrection of the body (2 Macc 7) is here replaced by immortality and an eternal life that begins at the moment of death (7:3; 9:22; 13:17; 14:5–6; 15:3; 16:13, 25; 17:12, 18–19). God's creative power is cited as a reason for obedience (11:5; 13:13) rather than as a guarantee of resurrection, as it is in 2 Maccabees 7. Eternal life is God's reward for obedience to the Torah not his vindicative restoration of that which the martyrs have lost (i.e., their limbs, as in 2 Macc 7). In 2 Maccabees the placement of the stories of the martyrs enables them to serve as a turning point that changes God's wrath to mercy (see above, p. 119). This function of the martyrs' deaths is made explicit in *4 Maccabees,* which employs categories of expiation and cleansing that may find their closest analogies in pagan Greek literature (1:11; 6:28–29; 9:24; 12:17–18; 17:19–22; 18:4–5).[38] The actions of the martyrs are likened to a battle in behalf of virtue or an athletic contest to be endured (9:8, 24; 17:11–16). This imagery and conception has parallels in traditions about Abraham, Job, and Joseph, and in Hebrews 10–12,[39] and it suggests that martyrdom is seen (here also) as the extreme example of the human striving for virtue.

Even if our author has been heavily influenced by Greek philosophical, religious, and rhetorical categories he remains in his own self-understanding a Jew. Judaism is the true philosophy. Right reason takes its stand on wisdom, which is the Torah. The martyrs were true children of Abraham (6:17, 22; 7:19; 9:21; 13:17; 15:28; 16:20; 17:6; 18:23) who took their place with other heroes of Israelite history as examples to be emulated by "the seed of Abraham, the children of Israel," who constitute the author's audience.

Fourth Maccabees may well have been written around the year 40 in response to Caligula's attempt to have his statue erected in the Jerusalem Temple.[40] Apollonius's title as "governor of Syria, Phoenicia, and Cilicia" (4:2) suggests the time period between 20 and 54 C.E., when Syria and Cilicia were associated administratively in the Roman Empire.[41] The book was composed in Greek, possibly in Syrian Antioch.[42]

We cannot be certain whether the book was written to be delivered orally or to be read. Reference to "the season" (3:19) may indicate that it was composed to be delivered as an edifying discourse at a festival commemorating the deaths of the martyrs.[43]

The accounts of the martyrs' deaths have strongly influenced both Jewish and Christian piety and tradition. In rabbinic tradition the death of a mother and her seven sons is dated to the time of Hadrian.[44] The church fathers made use of this book, and although it was not canonized by the Eastern churches it has continued to influence their preaching and piety.[45]

NOTES

1. According to Mark 6:17 Herodias was first married to Antipas's brother, Philip, presumably the Tetrarch. Josephus indicates, however, that Herodias's first husband was Herod, the son of Herod the Great, and that Philip the Tetrarch was married to Salome, the daughter of Herod and Herodias; see Schürer, *History*, 1:344.

2. On the difficulties of dating this census see ibid., 399–427.

3. For an example of the historicizing of an apocalyptic tradition about Antiochus's judgment see Nickelsburg, *Resurrection*, 79–80.

4. It is possible that most of chap. 6 is a revision of materials that originally described Antiochus rather than a wholesale interpolation; see Jonathan A. Goldstein, "The Testament of Moses: Its Content, Its Origin, and Its Attestation in Josephus," in *Studies on the Testament of Moses*, SBLSCS 3, ed. George W. E. Nickelsburg (Cambridge: Society of Biblical Literature, 1973) 45–47.

5. For this expression see E.-M. Laperrousaz, "Le Testament de Moïse," *Sem* 19 (1970) 122.

6. On the *Testament of Moses* as an interpretation of Deuteronomy see above, pp. 80–81.

7. A. Y. Collins, "Composition and Redaction of the Testament of Moses 10," *HTR* 69 (1976) 179–86.

8. For a detailed discussion of the place of the revised *Testament* in the time after Varus's campaign see the articles by John J. Collins in *Studies on the Testament of Moses*, 28–30, 38–39.

9. See R. H. Charles, *The Book of Enoch* (Oxford: Clarendon, 1912) 66, for some significant differences from the rest of *1 Enoch*. For chaps. 37–71 as a late addition to an earlier collection see above, pp. 150–51.

10. Cf. Isa 14:4; Mic 2:4; Hab 2:6; and Num 23:7, 18; 24:3, 15, 20, 21, 23. See above, p. 49, for the dependence of 1:2–3 on the Balaam oracles.

11. The title "book of parables" occurs in 68:1, a later addition to the work.

12. E.g., 99:4–5; 100:1–6; 102:1–3.

13. The phrasing of the title may derive from Num 16:22.

14. The unqualified term appears in 62:7 and 69:27.

15. See Maurice Casey, "The Use of Term 'Son of Man' in the Similitudes of Enoch," *JSJ* 7 (1976) 11–29.

16. Cf. the parallelism between chaps. 53 and 54 and cf. 55:4.

17. Some manuscripts read "righteousness" for "the Righteous One," but cf. 52:9.

18. According to Charles (*APOT* 2:210) 39:1–2 is an interpolation. The parallel with the early chapters of *1 Enoch* suggests rather that the last line of 39:2 has been displaced from the end of 38:6.

19. Nickelsburg, *Resurrection*, 74–75.

20. Cf. 7:6; 8:4; 9:1–11; 10:1ff.; 89:69–71, 76–77; 90:14, 17; 97:5; 99:3; 104:1.

21. Nickelsburg, *Resurrection*, 74, n. 103.

22. See above, pp. 59–61.

23. See Dieter Georgi, "Der vorpaulinische Hymnus Phil. 2:6–11," in *Zeit und Geschichte*, Fs. R. Bultmann, ed. E. Dinkler (Tübingen: Mohr, 1964) 277–78.

24. Johannes Theisohn, *Der auserwählte Richter*, 55–59.

25. See below, p. 220, on 68:1.

26. For details see Nickelsburg, *Resurrection*, 70–74.

27. Ibid., 72.

28. See Jos. *Ant.* 17.168–72 (17.6.5).

29. For these and other arguments see Milik, *Books of Enoch*, 91–98. For a critique see Jonas C. Greenfield and Michael E. Stone, "The Enochic Pentateuch and the Date of the Similitudes," and the review of Milik by the present writer in *CBQ* 40 (1978) 417–18. Michael Knibb ("The Date of the Parables of Enoch: A Critical Review") disputes Milik at many points but finds the silence of Qumran significant and accepts a date near 100 C.E.

30. David Flusser has suggested that the parables are not found in the Qumran library because the book's astronomical views were not compatible with those of the Qumran community; Greenfield and Stone, "Pentateuch," 56–57.

31. The Herodian dating of both passages is accepted most recently by Greenfield and Stone ("Pentateuch," 58–60), who argue convincingly against attempts to date 56:5–8 in the time of Trajan.

32. Milik, *Books of Enoch*, 91–92. John J. Collins ("The Son of Man Who Has Righteousness," 126) suggests that the parables' identification of that son of man with Enoch may be a Jewish response to Christian belief. On the likely dependence of Matt 25:31–46 upon the tradition in *1 Enoch* 62–63 see, however, David R. Catchpole, "The Poor on Earth and the Son of Man in Heaven: A Re-appraisal of Matthew xxv.31–46," *BJRL* 61 (1979) 378–83.

33. The reference to idols in 46:7 allows the possibility that the author could have had *some* Jewish rulers in mind when he used the generic category.

34. The writer of the Fourth Gospel may reflect a tradition that conflates the figures of the Son of Man and the Servant. Cf. John 13:31 with Isa 52:13 and see C. H. Dodd, *The Fourth Gospel* (Cambridge: University Press, 1965) 246–49.

35. See the discussion by M. Knibb (*The Ethiopic Book of Enoch* [Oxford: Clarendon, 1978] 41–42) and the bibliography cited by him (p. 38, nn. 2–3).

36. It is not impossible that this author used the history of Jason of Cyrene rather than its epitome, 2 Maccabees. See, however, Moses Hadas, *The Third and Fourth Books of Maccabees*, 92–95.

37. For the passages see ibid., 149.

38. Sam K. Williams, *Jesus' Death as Saving Event*, HDR 2 (Missoula: Scholars Press, 1975) 137–61.

39. See below, pp. 247–48.

40. See Hadas, *Maccabees*, 95–96.

41. Urs Breitenstein (*Beobachtungen zu Sprache*) cites other linguistic and rhetorical usage in the book as evidence for its composition between 100 and 135 C.E.

42. See Hadas, *Maccabees*, 109–13.

43. Ibid., 103–9.

44. Ibid., 127–35.

45. Townshend, *APOT* 2:658–62. With an eye toward the usage of Eastern Orthodoxy it is now included in editions of the RSV.

BIBLIOGRAPHY

HISTORY

Schürer, *History*, 1:233–454. E. Mary **Smallwood**, *The Jews under Roman Rule*, SJLA 20 (Leiden: Brill, 1976) 1–200. David M. **Rhoads**, *Israel in Revolution: 6–74 C.E.: A Political History Based on the Writings of Josephus* (Philadelphia: Fortress, 1976) 47–68. A. H. M. **Jones**, *The Herods of Judaea*, 2d ed. (Oxford: Clarendon, 1967). Abraham **Schalit**, *König Herodes: Der Mann und sein Werk* (Berlin: de Gruyter, 1969).

THE PSALMS OF SOLOMON

TRANSLATION: Robert B. **Wright**, *PsOT*.

TEXTS, OTHER TRANSLATIONS, LITERATURE: For the Greek text see an edition of the Septuagint. G. Buchanan **Gray**, *APOT* 2:625–52. H. R. **Ryle** and M. R. **James**, *Psalmoi Solomōntos: Psalms of the Pharisees, Commonly Called the Psalms of Solomon* (Cambridge, 1891), introduction, Greek text, annotated translation. J. **Viteau**, *Les Psaumes de Salomon* (Paris: Letouzey & Ané, 1911), introduction, Greek text, facing annotated French translation.

THE TESTAMENT OF MOSES—REVISED

See the bibliography for Chapter 3. Adela Yarbro **Collins**, "Composition and Redaction of the Testament of Moses 10," *HTR* 69 (1976) 179–86.

1 ENOCH 37–71

TEXT AND TRANSLATIONS: See the bibliography for Chapter 2.

LITERATURE: The literature on the parables of Enoch and the son of man is vast. A classic treatment of the latter is Erik **Sjöberg**, *Der Menschensohn im Äthiopischen Henochbuch*, Acta Reg. Societatis Humaniorum Litterarum Lundensis 41 (Lund: Gleerup, 1946). Recent treatments include: Johannes **Theisohn**, *Der auserwählte Richter*, SUNT 12 (Göttingen: Vandenhoeck & Ruprecht, 1975); Barnabas **Lindars**, "Re-Enter the Apocalyptic Son of Man," *NTS* 22 (1975) 52–72; John J. **Collins**, "The Son of Man Who Has Righteousness," in *Ideal Figures in Ancient Judaism: Profiles and Paradigms* (ed. John J. Collins and George W. E. Nickelsburg, SBLSCS 12 [Missoula: Scholars Press, 1980]) 111–33. On the date of the parables see Jonas C. **Greenfield** and Michael E. **Stone**, "The Enochic Pentateuch and the Date of the Similitudes," *HTR* 70 (1977) 51–65; Michael **Knibb**, "The Date of the Parables of Enoch: A Critical Review," *NTS* 25 (1979) 344–57.

4 MACCABEES

TRANSLATION: *The Oxford Annotated Apocrypha, Expanded Edition* (New York: Oxford University, 1977).

TEXTS AND OTHER TRANSLATIONS: For the Greek text see an edition of the Septuagint. R. B. **Townshend**, *APOT* 2:653–85. Hugh **Anderson**, *PsOT*.

LITERATURE: Moses **Hadas**, *The Third and Fourth Books of Maccabees*, JAL (New York: Harper, 1953), introduction with bibliography, Greek text with facing annotated translation—a good starting point. Urs **Breitenstein**, *Beobachtungen zu Sprache, Stil und Gedankengut des Vierten Makkabaerbuches* (Basel: Schwabe, 1976).

7

The Exposition
of Israel's Scriptures

The biblical stories about the patriarchal era were the fountainhead of
a lively and imaginative tradition, as we have already seen in the *Book
of Jubilees* (see above, pp. 73–80). In this chapter we shall look at other
evidences of that tradition. Almost all the writings that we shall consider
have come down to us in the Greek language and through Christian
hands. However, it is probable that they originated in Jewish circles,
often in more or less their present form. However one resolves this question in individual cases, these writings are interesting from two perspectives. They are examples of a kind of narrative interpretation of the
Bible that became popular in the haggadic exegesis of the rabbis, and
indeed certain individual traditions among them were known and used
in the rabbinic literature. At the same time, for a variety of reasons, circles
in the Byzantine and medieval church found it profitable to preserve and
transmit these writings. The time and place of their composition are
difficult to ascertain, and we must therefore interpret them without reference to these data.

THE TESTAMENTS OF THE
TWELVE PATRIARCHS

The testamentary form is found already in the Bible. Genesis 49 depicts
Jacob's deathbed scene. The old patriarch gathers his twelve sons around
him and makes a series of predictions about them and their descendants.
The passage ends with Jacob's death and burial. In the last chapters of
Deuteronomy, Moses announces his death and commissions Joshua as his
successor (chap. 31). He predicts the course of Israel's future in his
"Song" (chap. 32) and then pronounces his final blessing on the nation in

the form of a series of predictions about eleven of the twelve tribes (chap. 33; Simeon is not mentioned). Then he dies and is buried by God (chap. 34).

We have seen the expansion of these testamentary models in the *Testament of Moses*, which details the events that Moses foretold (see above, pp. 80–83); in the testaments of Abraham in *Jubilees* 20, 21, and 22, which are more concerned with ethical instruction and thus parallel the broader framework of Deuteronomy; and in *1 Enoch*, which subsumes a wide variety of material under the category of Enoch's farewell instructions to his sons and descendants.

The *Testaments of the Twelve Patriarchs* is a collection of twelve self-contained units. Each of these describes one of Jacob's sons on his deathbed (or just before his death), gathering his sons and making his testament in their presence. Following the biblical model, each *Testament* contains a prediction about the future of the tribe and sometimes of Israel in general. Similar to the testaments in *Jubilees* 20, 21, and 22, the contents of the *Testaments of the Twelve Patriarchs* (with the exception of the *Testament of Levi*) are controlled by ethical considerations. This emphasis is provided by the insertion of two interrelated elements into the biblical model. First, the patriarch narrates an event or events from his life. The narrative illustrates a particular virtue or vice, which is repeatedly mentioned. Then the patriarch addresses his sons, exhorting them to emulate his virtuous conduct or to avoid the example of his wickedness.

The common outline for most of the *Testaments* is as follows:[1]

A. Introduction, setting the scene
B. Narrative from the patriarch's life
C. Ethical exhortation
D. Prediction of the future
E. A brief second exhortation
F. Patriarch's death
G. His burial

In the introduction to each *Testament*, the patriarch is either on his deathbed or advanced in age. He summons his sons. Narrative and exhortative sections are sometimes interwoven and sometimes duplicated. Where the Bible provides details about an individual patriarch, these are employed and elaborated in the respective *Testament*. Other of the

Testaments draw upon elements in the biblical story of Joseph. Occasionally a detail in the blessing of Jacob or the blessing of Moses is elaborated into narrative. Only the *Testament of Asher* has no narrative.[2] Some of the narrative sections are undoubtedly older than the particular *Testament*. Others appear to have been created ad hoc. The exhortatory sections often employ themes, language, and forms typical of wisdom literature. The predictive sections are often designated as revelation. In some cases they employ the sin-punishment-repentance-salvation scheme that we have met in earlier apocalypses, usually specified as sin-exile-repentance-return.[3] These sections of the *Testaments* are perhaps the most stereotyped and contain many parallels to one another. They can be very short, and their content can be very general. More than any other section they give the impression of being ad hoc creations, inserted because the element is expected in the genre.

Certain themes and theological conceptions pervade the *Testaments* as a whole. Presumed throughout is the opposition of the two spirits.[4] Sometimes they function judicially as accuser and advocate. More often they influence human behavior for the better or for the worse. Apocalyptic sections describe the *eschaton* as the time when "Beliar" and his spirits will be bound. Another central theme is the priority of the tribes of Levi and Judah and of their eschatological leader(s). This pairing is reminiscent of Zechariah 3–4 and is related to the Qumranic hopes regarding the Messiah(s) of Aaron and Israel. The figure of Joseph is also prominent throughout the *Testaments* as an example of virtue and the avoidance of vice. Common eschatological hopes include not only the appearance of an anointed priest and/or king, the binding of Beliar, the return from Dispersion, and the salvation of the Gentiles, but also resurrection from the dead and life in a new Jerusalem and/or in paradise.[5]

The present form of the collection of the twelve *Testaments* is clearly Christian, and they contain more explicit references to the Christian Messiah than any parallel documents. How these testaments came into this final form is a hotly debated issue.[6] Among the scrolls of Qumran have been found fragments of a number of documents related to the *Testaments*: an Aramaic testament of Levi, considerably longer than the Greek *Testament* and in some sense one of its sources; evidently an Aramaic testament of Kohath, the son of Levi; an Aramaic testament of Amram, the father of Aaron, Moses, and Miriam; and, according to its editor, a

Hebrew testament of Naphtali.[7] The Levi, Kohath, Amram group may point to a collection of priestly testaments. On the other hand, it can be argued that the existence of a testament of Naphtali would almost require the conception of a collection of twelve testaments, given the relative obscurity of that patriarch. In such a case the present Greek collection has been interpolated with explicit christological references and in other ways expanded, compressed, and edited by Christians. Alternatively one may posit an early Jewish collection of testaments of several of the patriarchs, which later Christian and/or Jewish editors rounded out to a collection of a full twelve testaments.[8] We shall not attempt here to decide among these alternatives.

In this section we shall discuss six testaments that exemplify the formal characteristics of these writings, as well as their narrative technique and their ethical and eschatological contents.

The Testament of Reuben

The major portion of this *Testament* consists of alternating narrative and related exhortation. In recounting Reuben's incest with Bilhah (Gen 35:22) the author combines the tradition also found in *Jubilees* 33:1–9 with the idea that Bilhah was drunk and hence unaware of the deed (cf. Gen 9:20–22; 19:30–35, of Noah and Lot). The motif of drunkenness leading to sexual misconduct parallels the *Testament of Judah* 13–16. In the *Testament of Reuben* the catchword in narrative and exhortation is "fornication." The spirits of Beliar work this vice in men. However, the basic problem is with women themselves, who are particularly prone to the vice and who use their wiles and beauty to seduce men. To prove his case the author cites the example of Potiphar's wife (cf. *T. Reub.* 4:9–11; *T. Jos.* 6) and utilizes that element in the Enochic tradition about the rebel watchers which implicitly blames the women (*T. Reub.* 5:6–7; cf. *1 Enoch* 8:1–2). Bilhah's drunkenness is also consonant with this viewpoint. This author's low estimate of women is paralleled but probably unequaled in the literature of his time.[9] The connection between fornication and idolatry is traditional (cf. *Jub.* 20:6ff.). Joseph is cited as a positive example—one who resisted seduction to fornication (4:8–11), and the author's description links this *Testament* to that of Joseph (cf. *T. Jos.* 6). The fact that jealousy is a second vice mentioned (6:5) connects this *Testament* with the *Testament of Simeon*. The final section of the *Testament* asserts the primacy of the tribes of Levi and Judah, from whence come the high priests and the royal line. The higher position clearly belongs to the priestly line, the members of which function as officiants at the cult and as teachers. The prediction that Reuben's sons will rebel against Levi is paralleled in the *Testament of Simeon* (5:4) and the *Testament of Dan* (5:5–6).

The Testament of Simeon

The catchwords in this *Testament* are jealousy and envy. The jealousy toward Joseph which the Bible attributes to his brothers in general (Gen 37:11) is here a characteristic of Simeon in particular. Simeon's specific complicity in the plot against Joseph is probably deduced from the fact that Joseph held Simeon hostage (Gen 42:24; cf. *T. Sim.* 4:2–3).[10] Simeon's jealousy is attributed to the influence of "the prince of deceit" and his "spirit of envy" (2:7; 3:1). Simeon contrasts himself with Joseph, "a good man" in whom "the spirit of God" was present and who was characterized by "compassion," "pity," and "love" (4:4–7). Mention of Joseph's love links this *Testament* to the second Joseph story in the *Testament of Joseph* (see below). The use of Joseph's virtue as a foil to Simeon's vice and the mention of a second vice (fornication, 5:3–4) link this *Testament* to the *Testament of Reuben*. The predictive section mentions the tribe's futile war against the sons of Levi (5:4–5). Eschatological blessing to Simeon's tribe will appear when his sons put away the envy of which he has spoken at length (6:2). Final salvation means the destruction of the "spirits of deceit," which are the cause of the wickedness that infected Simeon's life and would continue to plague his sons (6:6). The poem in which Simeon predicts the future shows a number of parallels to ben Sira's hymn in praise of the high priest Simon (Sir 50) and may indicate a relationship between the two. Particularly interesting is the derogatory reference to the Samaritans in Sirach 50:26. Simeon's action against the Shechemites is hinted at in the *Testament of Simeon* 5:6 (cf. Gen 49:6–7).

The closing part of the *Testament of Simeon* asserts the dual sovereignty of Levi and Judah (7:1), and in a passage that is patently Christian in its present form it "predicts" salvation in one who will be priest and king, God and man (7:2).

The Testament of Levi

The divine origin of the priesthood and God's resolution of its abuses are the primary considerations in this *Testament*.

Levi's first vision appears to be based on the account of Enoch's vision in *1 Enoch* 14–16.[11] In its attachment to Levi the tradition has gone through several stages of development, as is evident from its ambiguous relationship to the fragments of the longer Aramaic testament of Levi.[12] In the present form of the vision, an angel escorts Levi up through the heavens to the divine throne room, where God commissions him to be his priest until the *eschaton*. The angel, who later identifies himself as Israel's intercessory angel, returns Levi to earth and gives him a second commission—to destroy Shechem for the rape of Dinah. The remainder of this section describes Levi's and Simeon's sack of Shechem and contains some polemics against the Samaritans that are paralleled in ben Sira's hymn in honor of the high priest Simon (Sir 50).[13] The connection between Levi's commission as high priest and his action against Shechem is paralleled in *Jubilees* 30:18, where the priestly office is bestowed on him as a consequence of his destruction of the Shechemites.[14]

In his second vision (chap. 8) Levi is invested with the garb and equipment of the high-priestly office. This section parallels *Jubilees* 32: 1–9 and its context. Chapter 10 describes the sins of Levi's descendants, which will be the focus of the apocalypse in chaps. 14–18. As it now stands the section is Christian in form. Chapters 11–12 contain the genealogy of Levi's sons, dating their births to specific years of his life. Levi's exhortation to his sons (chap. 13) is particularly appropriate to their priestly office. Lacking are the vices and virtues typical of the exhortative sections of the other *Testaments*.

Chapters 14–18 are a historical apocalypse which was in some form a part of the Aramaic testament of Levi.[15] Chapters 14–17 describe the wicked deeds of the priesthood, and chap. 18 presents the resolution of the situation: the appearance of "a new priest" and the inception of the *eschaton*. The first part of the apocalypse appears to be conflating two sources or traditions, each describing priestly abuses (chaps. 14–15; 16–17).

As is evident from chap. 18 the new priest is, for this author, the chief eschatological functionary. Precisely how the original tradition depicted him is uncertain, because the present form of the passage is almost certainly Christian. However, parallels between the prayer of Levi in the Aramaic testament of Levi[16] and the present Greek form of 4:2–6 and 18:1ff. indicate that the Jewish author of this tradition colored his description of the eschatological priest with language traditionally applied to the Davidic king,[17] thus combining two traditional eschatological figures into one. In its present form chap. 18 is perhaps unmatched for its attribution of superlatives to a human figure.[18] For example, unlike *Psalms of Solomon* 17, it describes a cosmic reaction to the appearance of the new priest. He will reopen paradise, disarm the cherubim, and give the holy ones the tree of life. He will fulfill the angelic function of binding Beliar. With this passage the *Testament of Levi* moves to its logical conclusion: from the initial commissioning and ordination of Levi to the appearance and "investiture" of the last priest, who functions as the one who brings the earth back to its primordial state. This glorification of the eschatological high priest must be read as the background for the rest of the statements in the *Testaments* regarding the latter-day descendant of Levi.

The Testament of Judah

This is the longest of the *Testaments*. It contains all the elements typical of the *Testaments*, though sometimes in an order that suggests either displacement or later accretion:

A.	Introduction	1
B.	Narrative I: Judah's military exploits	2:1–7:10
C.	Narrative II: Judah's sexual misconduct	8:1–3
D.	Narrative I concluded	9:1–8
E.	Narrative II continued	10:1–12:12
F.	Exhortation based on Narrative II	13:1–17:1
G.	Forecast	17:2–18:1
H.	Exhortation continued	18:2 – 19:4
I.	Instruction on the two spirits	20:1–5
J.	Exhortation to obey Levi	21:1–5
K.	Forecast	21:6–25:5
L.	Conclusion	26:1–4

Central to this *Testament* is Judah's status as the patriarch of the tribe from which the royal dynasty will arise and whose latter-day heir will be the messianic king. The theme is introduced in the first section (1–6). The lengthy narrative about Judah's military exploits shows that Judah himself acted as a king. This narrative appears to have originally ended in chap. 7, and the reference to Judah's age (7:10) parallels the similar reference at the end of the next narrative (12:12). Chapter 9, which describes Judah's exploits against the sons of Esau, breaks the continuity between 8:3 and 10:1 and may be a secondary interpolation from *Jubilees* 37–38 or its source.

The second narrative develops the story of Judah, his marriage to Bathshua and its consequences (Gen 38). The motif of Judah's drunkenness may be drawn from Genesis 49:11–12 (but cf. *T. Reub.* 3:13 and its combination of drunkenness and fornication). Two exhortatory sections are based on this narrative (13:1–17:1; 18:2–19:4). In form they weave together first-person narrative and second-person exhortation. Although the author places some implicit blame on Bathshua, his emphasis differs considerably from that in the *Testament of Reuben.* Here Judah gets drunk and is thus carried away to fornication—on two occasions. The *Testament* advocates not teetotalism but only a proper limit to one's drinking, a motif typical of the wisdom literature. A secondary but important motif in the narrative and exhortation is the evil that arises from the love of money. The motif of Judah's kingship appears in these sections in 12:4 and 15:5–6. The forecast in 17:2–18:1 looks like a secondary interpolation breaking apart two narrative-exhortatory sections that warn against fornication and the love of money.

Chapter 20 internalizes the eschatological battle between the two spirits and is reminiscent of col. 4 of the Qumran Community Rule (see above, pp. 135–36).[19] The spirit of truth, who prods the righteous to good deeds, will also function as eschatological witness—interceding for the righteous and accusing the wicked. In chap. 21 the authority of Levi is superior to that of Judah. The final section, an eschatological forecast, follows the typical pattern of sin-punishment-repentance-salvation. Chapter 24, which may be modeled partly on the *Testament of Levi* 18 (or an earlier form of it), describes the kingly Messiah, accreting to him many biblical titles. Here the kingly nature of Judah and his descendants reaches its climax in this *Testament.* The appearance of the Messiah will be followed by the resurrection and the *eschaton* (chap. 25).

The Testament of Issachar

This *Testament* celebrates *haplotēs* ("simplicity" or "uprightness"), an all-encompassing virtue especially consonant with hard labor and the agricultural life and contrasted with such vices as envy, slander, being a busybody, and lust.[20] The *Testament* is particularly noteworthy for its thoroughgoing stress on ethics, even in its brief, pro forma eschatological section.

After the typical introduction (1:1) there follow a pair of narrative sections. The first of these (1:2–2:5) elaborates the biblical story about Rachel, Leah, and the mandrakes (Gen 30:14–18). Rachel is cited as an example of sexual "continence" who eschews the love of sexual pleasure (chap. 2). In the second section (chap. 3) Issachar speaks of his own life, effectively providing the reader with a catalog of virtues. That he was a farmer has been deduced from the blessing of Jacob (Gen 49:14–15).[21] Verses 7–8 stress that God blesses such upright conduct.

Chapters 4–5 are mainly exhortation, built on themes set forth in chap. 3. Issachar's sons are to emulate him and his virtues, and for this they are promised the rewards that he (and Judah and Levi) received. Typical of the late wisdom tradition are the initial address (4:1a; cf. Sir 6:23), the command "to walk" in the right way, the stress on Torah, and the promise of blessing for righteous conduct. The cataloglike form of the description of the righteous person in 4:2–6 is reminiscent of the description of love in 1 Corinthians 13:4–7. In chap. 4, as well as in chaps. 6–7, the spirits of Beliar are the cause of sin and straying and are to be avoided.

Chapter 6 is the typical predictive section, presented as a revelation of the last times. Verses 1–2b are a reversal of the catalog in chaps. 4–5. Issachar's sons will disobey his exhortation and will "forsake" all the virtues he has recommended and "cling" to all the vices he has denounced. For these sins they will be punished until they repent and are returned to their land (vv. 2c–4).

Chapter 7 recapitulates briefly the form of the first part of the *Testament*: a description of some of Issachar's virtues, with "simplicity" notably missing (vv. 1–6), a one-line exhortation to follow his example (v. 7a), and the promise of God's blessing (v. 7b–f), which provides a reversal of the prediction in chap. 6. After a final reference to "simplicity of heart" (v. 7f) the *Testament* concludes typically with a description of the patriarch's death and burial.

The Testament of Joseph

The biblical story of Joseph is a tale of the persecuted and exalted courtier, an early example of the type of story we have seen in Daniel 3 and 6 (see above, pp. 22–24). In keeping with these later developments of this genre, the *Testament of Joseph* depicts the patriarch as a *righteous* man, persecuted but delivered, rewarded, and exalted.[22] To make this point the author greatly elaborates the incident of Joseph and Potiphar's wife and expounds the theme of Joseph's self-effacing love.

The typical testamentary introduction (1:1) is followed by a poetic summary of Joseph's life (1:2–2:7), which contrasts the patriarch's troubles with God's deliverance.[23] The style is reminiscent of biblical psalms of individual thanksgiving.[24] The repetition prepares us for the reference in 2:7 to Joseph's patience and endurance "in ten temptations," as well as for the episodic nature of the narrative that follows.

This narrative describes Joseph's chastity or moderation (*sōphrosynē*) in the face of the seductive wiles of "the Egyptian woman" (chaps. 3–9). The author does not tell a plotted story but relates a series of episodes, which may have originated as a homiletical elaboration of Genesis 39:10, ". . . and she spoke to Joseph day after day."[25] Several of these incidents suggest the influence of Hellenistic literature and tradition and of the Phaedra story in particular.[26] Depicted in this series of episodes is the struggle between two able, wily, and resourceful opponents (cf. 2:2)— the one driven by incessant lust, the other contending for chastity. The summary that follows (10:1–4, here not in the form of the usual direct, second-person imperative) stresses Joseph's patience and endurance (cf. 2:7). These virtues also characterize Abraham in the *Book of Jubilees* (see above, pp. 75–76) and Job in the *Testament of Job* (see the next section). The endurance of the spiritual athlete contending for virtue is a typical feature of Hellenistic moral philosophy and of Jewish martyr traditions,[27] and this virtue is important also in some apocalyptic literature.[28] Under this canon the worlds of the persecuted martyr and the virtuous hero are seen in a similar light.

The second narrative in the *Testament* (10:5–16:6) relates events that chronologically precede those in the first narrative. Also episodic in nature, it describes how on a number of occasions Joseph's self-effacing love led him to keep his silence lest he put others (especially his brothers) to shame. The motif is particularly striking in view of Genesis 40:14–15, where Joseph *reveals* how he had been kidnapped. Chapter 17 combines exhortation with narrative and underscores the theme of brotherly love, which vv. 5–8 tie to Genesis 50:15–21. Such love leads one not to exalt oneself (17:8; cf. 10:5). This characteristic of Joseph led to God's exaltation of the patriarch (cf. 10:3–5; 17:8–18:1), which is of course an essential part of the biblical story. Chapter 18 interweaves exhortation and narrative, presenting the idea that God does reward righteousness.

Joseph's revelation about the future comes in the form of a dream that is clearly Christian as it stands (chap. 19). The conclusion of the *Testament* (chap. 20), which develops motifs in Genesis 50:24–26, is atypically long.

THE TESTAMENT OF JOB

The testamentary genre described in the previous section provides the outline and external form within which the biblical story of Job is here retold.

A. Introduction	1:1–5
B. Narrative I: Job's combat with Satan	1:6–27:10
C. Narrative II: Job's debate with the kings	28–43
D. Resolution of the tale	44
E. Exhortation	45:1–4
F. Eschatological section: Job distributes his inheritance	45:5–51:3
G. Conclusion	52–53

Central to the book as a whole is the contrast between heavenly realities and this world, which is the arena of Satan's activities. Job gains insight into this distinction and is contrasted with other characters who lack the insight. The plot unfolds Job's insight in various stages and describes the movement of certain of the other characters from ignorance to knowledge, from unfaith to salvation, with Job always playing the key and mediating role.[29]

The book begins with the typical testamentary setting (A): the dying father gathers his children around him to relate to them the events of his life and to exhort them on the basis of his example. Different from the *Testaments of the Twelve Patriarchs*, the narrative sections of the *Testament of Job* (B–D) predominate almost to the exclusion of other sections.

Job's Combat with Satan

The first narrative section (B) depicts a contest or battle between Satan and Job, who is here the king of Egypt. "Patience," "endurance," and "perseverence" are the key words. The initial episode in this section describes Job's conversion from paganism, his commission to raze the idolatrous temple, and his execution of this task (1:6–5:3). The episode has many of the features typical of angelophanic commissioning scenes. Job's pondering over "who this God is"—the functional equivalent of a prayer—is answered by the appearance of an angel who reveals the truth to Job and at his request (3:5b) authorizes him to destroy the temple. The episode is, however, much more than a commissioning scene. The angel is primarily a revealer. He exposes Satan as a deceiver who puts himself forward as God. By means of this revelation, Job is set apart from the rest of humankind, who remain subject to Satan's deceptions (3:4b, 5b). Job responds to this revelation by requesting permission to destroy the temple and thus to end Satan's cult and his deceptive spell over Job's countrymen and subjects. The angel warns Job that he is entering into a struggle with Satan in which no holds are barred, but he assures Job that if he endures he will, like a true athlete, receive his reward and win his crown. God will equip him for the struggle. Job solemnly responds that he will endure until death, and he challenges Satan by demolishing his temple.

In the next episode Satan appears in the first of several disguises (chaps. 6–8). As a beggar he should be welcome at Job's door (see chaps. 9–10). The servant girl is deceived, but Job, with his newfound wisdom, penetrates the disguise. The burnt loaf that Job offers Satan is symbolic of Job's refusal henceforth to participate in the cult, of which the offering of bread seems to have been a part, and it may also imply Job's burning of the temple (see above, p. 75, regarding the closely related story in *Jub.* 12). Satan turns the imagery back on Job: the bread symbolizes Job's body—soon to be destroyed like the loaf. Job reasserts his readiness for the contest. At this point the narrative links up with the biblical story. Satan receives authority to attack Job (cf. 8:1 and Job 1:6–12).

We now move to the heart of the contest, ultimately derived from Job 1:13–21 and 2:7–10 but here greatly elaborated and divided into four distinct episodes. The first episode (chaps. 9–16) begins with a lengthy description of Job's deeds of charity. In both form and literary function this section is the counterpart of the narrative sections of certain of the *Testaments of the Twelve Patriarchs* (e.g., *T. Iss.* and *T. Zeb.*). It defines pious conduct: looking after the poor, giving alms, not withholding wages, etc. Satan directs his fury at the livestock of Job that were set aside for charitable purposes. Job loses the rest of his livestock. He responds to this first onslaught of Satan by praising God and refusing to blaspheme. He has won the first round.

In the next episode (chaps. 17–19) Satan assumes another disguise and deceives Job's countrymen. By distorting reality he enlists them against Job. Satan destroys Job's children, and his erstwhile subjects drive him away and plunder his house. Although Job is greatly distressed, he contemplates the goal of this contest. The heavenly city is of far greater worth than all that Job has given up by his voluntary entrance into battle with Satan. In spite of his deep distress over his children's death, Job blesses the name of the Lord. Satan has lost round two.

Now Satan turns his attacks on Job's person (chap. 20). In short order Job, who had been sitting on his throne, finds himself sitting on a dung heap, his body infested with worms. He responds not with complaint but by making certain that he suffers this affliction to the full (20:10). Again Satan has been bested, and we are now ready for the final round (chaps. 21–27).

Satan attempts to get at Job through Job's wife, Sitidos. He dons yet another disguise and deceives Sitidos. Roles are reversed from the first scene. The wife is a beggar, and Satan is the seller of bread. Whereas Job had freely given bread to the poor, his wife must now have herself sheared in public in order to pay for the bread. The lament in chap. 25 underscores the reversal of situations. His wife's public degradation completes Job's humiliation. She comes to him with the tale of woe, mocks his hopes for salvation, and urges him "to speak some word against the Lord and die." All this is of course a cleverly contrived plan of Satan, who is using Sitidos as his unwitting accomplice (23:13). Job responds to his wife with a word of encouragement. Then he unmasks Satan, who is comically depicted hiding behind Sitidos. Job challenges him to come out into the open and do battle. But the deceiver cannot fight in the open, and so with tears the spirit must concede defeat to Job, the human being, who has shown himself superior and victorious in the contest (27:3–8). The narrative, which began with the dialogue in chap. 4, is now resolved. Satan must withdraw, defeated—at least for the time being. The section concludes with the typical testamentary admonition that the children emulate the father's virtue, here his patience (27:10). This is the last we hear of this virtue.

Job's Debate with the Kings

This second narrative section of the book (C) corresponds to the poetic section of the biblical book and describes Job's debate with his friends, here depicted as four kings. Once again Job's superior insight is pitted against others' lack of perception. The primary opposition is between Job and Elious, who is "filled with Satan" (41:7) and is his representative in this debate (cf. 27:9).

The brief narrative at the end of the prose section of the biblical book (2:11–13) is here developed into a lengthy scene describing the kings' reaction to Job's situation (chaps. 28–30): astonishment, disbelief, and doubt as to his identity. This leads to Elious's lengthy lament (chap. 32), which contrasts Job's former glorious state with his present degradation: "Are you the one who . . . ? Where now is the splendor of your throne?" Some of the verses contrast Job's former charity and generosity to others with his present deprivation (vv. 2a, 3a, 4a, 8a). To the repeated rhetorical question "Where now is your throne?" (chap. 33) Job responds, "My throne is in heaven." In this exchange Job's superior insight is once more evident. Elious and his colleagues, as we shall see, misperceive reality. Job's present suffering does not prove that he has lost his kingdom, for this world is essentially transitory and changing, and prosperity may fade. But Job understands that he will be exalted in heaven, the place of unchanging, permanent realities, and the present existence of his throne there guarantees that exaltation. Eliphaz rejects this assertion out of hand, mocks his claim, and suggests that the kings leave. Baldas adopts a mediating position: Job may be "mentally disturbed." The next interchange is intended to test this hypothesis (chaps. 35–38). Again Job contrasts heavenly and earthly things. The earth and its inhabitants are unstable— witness his present predicament. His heart is fixed on heavenly things. He will not disavow God, who has permitted his present situation. Baldas, with his human mind-set, is incapable of understanding heavenly things (38:8). He does not perceive Job's throne in heaven, nor can he see God's hand in Job's affliction. Sophar reasserts Job's mental derangement and offers the help of his physicians, which Job refuses because his "healing and treatment are from the Lord," who is superior to the physicians whom he created (38:13).[30]

At this point the narrative is broken by the reappearance of Job's wife (chaps. 39–40). Because the debate picks up again in chap. 41 it is likely that chaps. 39–40 have been interpolated into the present context, albeit for a specific purpose. When Sitidos appears, the kings fail to recognize her, and she identifies herself in the mode of the lament that had been raised for her in the marketplace (39:2–3; cf. chap. 25). The interchange between Job and his wife again contrasts his superior insight with the lack of perception on the part of others. Previously his wife had failed to perceive the identification of Satan. Here her lack of perception parallels that of the kings (one reason for its placement here). For Sitidos the death of her children is reality, and she asks that they might have a memorial in the form of a proper burial. The kings agree. Job disputes their ignorance of reality—which is in heaven. The "tomb" (the house that fell on them) is empty. The children have been taken to heaven by the Creator, their king (cf. 2 Macc 7:11, 22–23, 27–29). Sitidos and the kings think Job is mad. Now Job *proves* the reality of his assertion. His wife and the kings are given a vision of the heavenly realities: God on his throne and the children crowned alongside him. Sitidos is convinced. She has the memorial she has sought—in heaven. In a wordplay the author has her say, "I shall arise and enter the city . . ." (40:7). She departs to die in peace. The story about Sitidos has two functions in its present context. Having likened Sitidos's lack of perception to that of the kings, the author uses the vision to bring her from ignorance to knowledge, from disbelief to faith. The kings have also had the vision and thus are responsible for their knowledge. Elious is culpable for his action in what follows.

Elious denies what he knows to be true. He takes up the conversation that had been broken off, specifically Job's assertion of a throne in heaven. With words that are not recorded in the text here,[31] he exposes Job's "nonexistent portion." He does so as a spokesman of Satan, employing the satanic device of deception and confusing and contradicting reality.

Now God himself intervenes to resolve the plot (chap. 43). Eliphaz, Baldas, and Sophar have sinned by speaking falsely against Job, but they will be forgiven through Job's sacrificial intercession. With Elious it is a different matter. The heavenly reality he has denied is now refused him.

His kingdom has passed away and his throne has decayed. His miscon-
strual of Job's situation becomes the reality of his own case. Job's relationship to his compatriots is restored, as is his fortune (chap. 44).

With the major elements in the story now resolved we have arrived at
the end of the biblical story. Job must now die (Job 42:17). To tell this
story the author returns to the testamentary framework. The final ethical
exhortation is brief and *pro forma* (45:1–4). Job does not exhort his children to the endurance and patience of which we heard so much in the
first narrative section. Rather, he paraphrases the double commandment
in terms consonant with the content of the book: Job had not forgotten
God, and his life had been a model of charity to the poor and helpless.
The stricture against marrying foreign wives is frequent in the literature
of this time.

Job Distributes His Possessions

This section (F) brings to a climax and resolution a number of elements in the book as a whole. Job apportions his earthly possessions
among his sons, as was the custom, but he bequeaths a better inheritance
to his daughters. The magical bands with which he invests them will lead
them to a better world. Moreover, the bands transform the daughters'
minds. They are no longer concerned with or troubled by earthly things
but are enabled here and now to participate in the heavenly level and to
join in the praise of the heavenly chorus. Thus Job transfers his special
powers to his daughters.

This transfer is remarkable in light of the rest of the book. In three
different cases Job's insight has been contrasted with misperceptions by
women (chaps. 7; 22–27; 39–40). Now Job's daughters become the knowl-
edgeable ones, the true heirs of their father. This episode resolves clearly
and definitively the inferior role of women in the book. Against the background of his earlier distinction between the earthly and the heavenly,
Job distributes his earthly possessions to his sons and his heavenly gifts to
his daughters. This action ascribes a higher religious status to women
than to men, surely a reversal of values in the contemporary world.

This section adds a twist to the testamentary genre. Job's highest "virtue," his insight, is not recommended in a typical exhortatory section but
is bequeathed by means of certain magical apparatus, which also acts as
an amulet against the power of the enemy (47:11). The section is also
the counterpart of the eschatological section of the testamentary genre,

providing entrée to heaven and eternal life and knowledge of "things present and future" (47:11).

Message and Origin

The *Testament of Job* is in the first place an exhortation to patience and endurance in a troubled and unstable world. Permanence and stability are to be found only in heaven (33:2–9; 36:4–6). The world, by contrast, is in a state of flux. More than that, it is the arena in which Satan perpetrates his deceptions and illusions as he engages in combat with the believer. Salvation involves a revealed perception of these facts and of the present existence of one's reward in heaven. At the same time, this perception enables one to endure in the combat and thus obtain the reward (18:5–7). Endurance for Job is almost tantamount to faith or faithfulness. When Job was rich, charity and generosity were appropriate as piety. When he is cast into dire straits true religion is that endurance which resists the satanic temptation to despair by cursing God and accepting the present miserable situation as ultimate reality. The lonely spiritual athlete, locked in mortal combat with Satan, is persistent and victorious. At the same time, he is the true "martyr," testifying—to friend, onlooker, and antagonist—to the spiritual realities which he knows to exist in spite of his predicament. Through this testimony he wins others to his side.

The place and date of the *Testament of Job* cannot be fixed with certainty. The description of Job as a king of Egypt does suggest that country as a place of origin. The personal mysticism depicted and the tendency toward ecstasy on the part of women in the last section may support an origin among the Therapeutae in Egypt.[32] If the book presumes a situation of persecution, the first century C.E. may be a proper date.[33]

Related Literature

Although the *Testament of Job* is one of the less familiar of the Pseudepigrapha, its traditions and its theology are related to a wide variety of Jewish and Christian literature. The first episode closely parallels traditions about Abraham in *Jubilees*. Abraham comes to a knowledge of the true God and recognizes the folly of idols. He defeats Satan's attempt to destroy the crops, and he burns down the local idolatrous temple (11:15–12:15; cf. *Apoc. Abr.*, below, pp. 294–95). The story of the sacrifice of Isaac in *Jubilees* 17:15–18:19 is set in the framework of a heavenly con-

flict between the prince of *mastēmā* and the angel of the Presence which
is reminiscent of the prologue of the book of Job. In this story Abraham
is depicted as a model of patience and endurance, a characteristic attached to him through ten different trials (19:8). The *Testament of
Joseph,* on the other hand, speaks of Joseph's patience and endurance
through ten trials. Common to these works is the idea of life as a struggle
to be endured and the use of patriarchal examples to make the point.
The *Testament of Job* is unique among these in its emphasis on Job's
knowledge of heavenly realities.[34]

The second narrative in the *Testament of Job* (chaps. 28–43) has af-
finities with the Wisdom of Solomon, which sets the story of the suffering
and exalted hero in the midst of a debate over the existence of heavenly
reality, specifically immortality. As in the case of Elious the antagonists
lose the immortality they have denied.[35]

Jewish apocalyptic literature and the Qumran corpus provide other
parallels that can be only mentioned here. The appeal to a revealed
knowledge of heavenly realities as a dynamic for endurance under stress
is essential to the message of *1 Enoch* 92–105 (see above, pp. 145–49).
Salvation both as knowledge and as a present reality is typical of the
Qumran Hymns.[36] The ecstatic angelic liturgy of Job's daughters has
parallels in the Qumran literature.[37]

On the Christian side the closest parallel is perhaps the Epistle to the
Hebrews, particularly chaps. 10–12. Life is a struggle to be endured, and
the victor's crown is promised as reward. The author encourages his
readers by citing the example of past heroes of faith, the last of these
being Jesus. The ground of one's hope is in the realities of the heavenly
world. Revealed knowledge brought down from heaven as salvation from
a world under the spell of Satan is essential to the theology of the Fourth
Gospel.

THE TESTAMENT OF ABRAHAM

This didactic but entertaining story about the last day of Abraham's
life is preserved in two recensions (editions). The longer of the two is by
far the more interesting and probably preserves a more original form of
the outline of the story.[38] The time for Abraham's death has arrived. Out
of special consideration for his "friend," God dispatches Michael to announce his death and to command the patriarch to put his affairs in order,
that is, to make his testament. At first Abraham refuses to follow Michael,

but then he agrees when God promises that he can have a trip through the whole universe. During this chariot ride Abraham calls down divine punishment on certain sinners whom he sees in the act of transgression. Fearing that sinless Abraham will annihilate the whole human race, God orders the patriarch up to heaven to see the judgment process and learn mercy. When Abraham successfully intercedes for a soul whose righteous deeds and sins are equally balanced in the judgment scale, he decides that he should also intercede for the sinners whom he had previously condemned. They are brought back to life, and he has learned about the compassion of a long-suffering God. Michael escorts him back to earth and again orders him to make his testament. Once more he refuses, and then God sends Death, who relentlessly presses the patriarch despite his protests and finally takes his soul by a subterfuge. Abraham never does make his testament.

The book is neatly divided into two parallel and symmetrical parts. Each begins as God summons the messenger of death and ends with Abraham in the typical testamentary situation, on his bed surrounded by his household.

Part I		Part II	
Chap.		Chap.	
1	God summons Michael: Go, tell Abraham he will die, so that he makes testament.	16	God summons Death: Go, bring Abraham to me.
2	Michael leaves, goes to Abraham, who sits at Mamre.		Death leaves, goes to Abraham, who sits at Mamre.
	Abraham sees, rises to meet him.		Abraham sees, rises to meet him.
	Michael greets honored father, righteous soul, friend of God.		Death greets honored Abraham, righteous soul, friend of God.
	Abraham returns the greeting, notes Michael's glory and beauty. Whence are you?		Abraham returns the greeting, notes Death's glory. Who are you, and whence?
	Michael replies elusively.		I tell you truth: I am Death.
	———		Abraham contradicts him, then refuses to follow.
2–3	They go to his house, conversing.	17	They go in the house: Death is silent.

	The talking tree: a hint.		———
	Isaac, Abraham wash his feet.		(Abraham's sullen inhospitality)
4	They prepare the room. Michael returns to heaven.		Death stays.
5	They eat, go to bed.		Abraham goes to bed, orders Death away.
5–7	Isaac's dream, interpretation; Michael reveals identity, mission.		Are you Death? Discuss how Death comes to different people.
7	Abraham refuses to go.		———
8–9	Michael's ascent, return: Make testament!		Death stays.
9	Abraham asks to see all the world.		Show me all your rottenness.
10	Abraham sees, calls down various kinds of death.		Death unmasks, shows Abraham various kinds of death; servants die.
11–13	Sees Judgment; Michael explains.		———
14	They pray for the dead; revived.	18	They pray for dead; revived.
		19	Further delays, refusal; Death explains vision.
	———		
15	Michael returns Abraham to Sarah, Isaac, servants, who rejoice.	20	Isaac, Sarah, servants, mourn.
	Make your testament! No! Michael returns to heaven.		Abraham is suddenly taken. Michael takes soul to heaven.

Binding these two parts together is a double narrative thread: God's command that Abraham prepare for death and Abraham's refusal to do so. The plot line moves through the two parts from God's initial command to its fulfillment with Abraham's death. Each of the two parts has its own pace and tone, corresponding to its relative place in the development of the plot. Part I is lengthy and rambling, and it has more than its share of humorous touches: the double entendre in Michael's identification of himself (chap. 2), the picture of the disturbed patriarch afraid to admit that he hears trees talking and sees teardrops turning to pearls (chap. 3),

Michael unable to cope with Abraham's repeated refusals and making repeated trips to the divine throne room for new orders (chaps. 4, 8, 9, 15). When Michael fails in his mission, we move to Part II, where a totally different pace and tone pervade. The divine messenger is "merciless, rotten Death." His identification of himself is quick and to the point. Abraham's continued refusals are met not by repeated trips to the throne room but by Death's pursuit of Abraham into the inner chambers of his house, right to his bed. This time Abraham's request for a revelation results in a fierce vision that strikes terror in the patriarch's heart, and he falls into "the faint of death." Again Abraham's family gathers around his bed, not to rejoice over his return but to mourn his imminent death. Now there is no command to make his testament, only the sudden, unexpected death about which he had inquired moments before. God's command is finally fulfilled. The plot is resolved.

Whereas the testaments we have previously discussed use the deathbed situation as a setting for ethical and eschatological instruction that is not essentially connected with this setting, the *Testament of Abraham* focuses on the problem of death itself and right and wrong attitudes about its relationship to God's judgment. By means of his plot line the author underscores the inevitability of death while at the same time dealing sympathetically with the universal human fear of death and aversion to it. He employs the figure of Abraham to both ends. Abraham's righteousness could not save him from death:

> Even upon [pious, all-holy, righteous, hospitable Abraham] there came the common, inexorable, bitter cup of death and the uncertain end of life (chap. 1; Stone, adapted).

Although the author ascribes to the patriarch some of the virtues traditionally attributed to him (righteousness, hospitality), he has glaringly omitted the most celebrated of these: Abraham's obedient faith. Indeed, he has created a veritable parody on the biblical and traditional Abraham. He fears God's summons to "go forth" (cf. *T. Abr.* 1 and Gen 12:1), and his haggling with God (contrast Gen 18:22–32) takes on the character of disobedience.[39] Through this parody the author transforms the exceptional patriarch into a character who stands in solidarity with the rest of humanity and with whom his readers can empathize.

Not only has our author reversed the traditional theme of Abraham's obedient faith, but he has also used the motif of Abraham's righteousness to counter wrong (and self-righteous) ideas about the relationship between death and divine judgment.[40] Because he has not sinned, Abraham has no sympathy for sinners, and he invokes divine judgment on them in the form of sudden death (chap. 10). The Bible itself describes the prophets doing this, and contemporary Jewish literature is replete with wishes, prayers, and statements about God's judgment of sinners. God responds to this traditional attitude by reference to Scripture, namely, Ezekiel 18. The righteous one not only fails to understand sinners, he also fails to comprehend the long-suffering mercy of the Creator, who does not desire the death of his creatures but grants them time to repent. When Abraham has learned his lesson by viewing the judgment process and has repented and prayed (this time for the restoration of those whose death he had invoked) God makes yet another point. Persons who suffer an untimely death are not punished after death.[41] Thus, to call down sudden death on sinners in the hope of catching them in their sins before they have a chance to repent is not only contrary to God's merciful intent but also counterproductive. The act itself prevents its intended result.

In the corresponding section of Part II, our author treats the problem of death in a more programmatic fashion. At Abraham's request Death unmasks himself, and this causes the untimely demise of seven thousand(!) of Abraham's servants (chap. 17). In the discussion that follows, Death reveals himself as the universal devastator of humanity. What Abraham did in an ad hoc manner is Death's occupation. Moreover, these deaths are untimely at the rate of seventy-one to one (chap. 22). This very fact, however, mitigates Death's effectiveness and validity, for as we learned in the corresponding section of Part II such deaths deliver one from postmortem judgment.

Abraham must die, as must all human beings. Nonetheless, Death's self-description, when read in the light of God's previous revelation, neutralizes Death's sting. Premature death saves one from postmortem judgment and eternal destruction. When such judgment takes place God's mercy is operative. On the basis of these consoling principles our author sweetens "the bitter cup" and tempers the first part of his message, which asserted the inevitability of death.

In his trip to heaven Abraham receives a double vision of the judgment process: the separation of the souls into the two gates leading to life and destruction (chap. 11) and the judgment before Abel (chaps. 13–14). Both scenes imply that the soul goes to its eternal destiny shortly after death. A bodily resurrection is not envisioned, and the references to the second and third judgments look like interpolations into the text.[42] The main judgment scene is probably a piece of tradition. Its description of the two angelic scribes and the book is paralleled in a number of other Jewish writings.[43] The stated rationale for Abel's position as judge is that he is the son of Adam, and therefore he judges all of Adam's subsequent progeny. However, the ascription to him of judicial powers may in fact derive from his status as protomartyr.[44] The balancing of righteous deeds versus sins may reflect Egyptian ideas attested in the *Book of the Dead*.[45]

This recension of the *Testament of Abraham* probably originated in Egypt[46] at a time that cannot be precisely determined.[47]

THE APOCALYPSE OF MOSES

The story of Adam and Eve inspired a considerable volume of Jewish and early Christian literature.[48] Two recensions of one such work are entitled the *Apocalypse of Moses* and the *Life of Adam and Eve*. The shorter and simpler of the two recensions, the *Apocalypse of Moses*, is primarily an account of Adam's death, its cause and its cure. Chapters 1–4 retell Genesis 4:1–25: the birth of Cain and Abel, the murder of Abel, and the birth of Seth.[49] The main function of the section is to introduce Seth, who will be the recipient of important traditions and in other ways a central figure in the action that follows. Once Seth has appeared the author moves quickly to Adam's terminal illness (5:1–2) and devotes the remainder of his book to the events surrounding Adam's death. Most of the elements of the testamentary genre occur in these chapters, but they are incorporated into a broader plot that embodies the author's message.

When Adam sees that he is going to die he summons his children (5:2). Because they do not understand what death is (5:4–6:3) Adam recites briefly the story of the Temptation, the Fall, and the expulsion from paradise (chaps. 7–8). Unlike the typical testamentary narrative, this recital does not present Adam's conduct as example but explains the reason for his present plight. He has sinned and therefore must die. As we shall see, the necessity of Adam's death is an essential part of the author's message.

The author now interrupts the testamentary form with a narrative sequence that dramatizes his message (9:3–13:6). Seeking to put off the time of his death, Adam dispatches Eve and Seth to paradise in search of the oil of mercy, which will bring him relief (9:3). On the way Seth is attacked by a beast (chaps. 10–12). God's curse in Genesis 3:15 is in effect. When Seth and Eve pray for the oil of mercy the angel Michael responds,

> [The oil of mercy] *will be yours not now but at the end of the times.* Then will arise all flesh from Adam to that great day. . . . Then all the joy of paradise *will be given to them* (13:2–4).

This twofold assertion—not now but at the end—is central to the message of the book and will be repeated later.

Having eliminated the possibility that Adam can escape death, the author returns us to the testamentary form he had temporarily abandoned in chap. 5. Knowing that he is going to die, Adam bids Eve to gather the children and to recount to them the story of the Temptation, the Fall, and the expulsion from paradise (chap. 14). Like its briefer counterpart in chaps. 7–8, this lengthy and artful elaboration of the events in Genesis 3 explains to Adam's children the reason for his death. The detailed account of the expulsion from the garden repeats the earlier sequence of Adam's petition and God's response (cf. chaps. 27–29 and 9–13). Adam seeks mercy (27:2; cf. 9:3; 13:1 and the request for the oil of mercy). God commands the angels to continue with the expulsion (27:4–28:1). When Adam pleads for access to the Tree of Life (28:2) God repeats the twofold assertion of chap. 13:

> You shall *not* take from it *now.* . . . If you keep yourself from all evil as one about to die, when again the resurrection comes to pass *I shall raise you up.* And then *there shall be given to you* [fruit] from the tree of life (28:3–4).

Now Adam pleads for herbs from paradise to offer incense. God allows him to take these and seeds to grow food, and then Adam and Eve are expelled from the garden (chap. 29). The section concludes with the stereotyped testamentary exhortation that the children not follow their parents' example (chap. 30; contrast 5:4–6:3).

The author's narration of the deathbed events continues to focus on Adam's fate. After giving instructions about the disposal of his body Adam asks Eve to pray because he is not yet certain of God's mercy (31:3–4). Her repetitious confession of sin is typical of the book's emphasis on Eve's primary responsibility for the Fall (32:1–2).[50] Through this confession she is presumably lessening Adam's fault in the hope that

God will have mercy on him. In answer to her prayer she is given a vision of the heavenly throne room and of the salvation of Adam's spirit (chaps. 33–37). God then summons his heavenly entourage and gives instructions for the burial of Adam and Abel (38:1–41:2). God's last word repeats the now familiar double formula:

> Adam, Adam, . . . I told you that you are earth and *to earth you will return* [cf. Gen 3:19]. Again I promise you the resurrection; *I shall raise you up on the last day* in the resurrection with every man who is of your seed (chap. 41).

Adam's burial completes those events relating to his death and shaped by the testamentary genre.

Chapters 42–43 describe Eve's death and burial. Seth receives special instructions for her burial, together with the command "Lay out in this manner every man that dies until the day of the resurrection, . . . and do not mourn beyond six days" (43:2–3). Eve's death and burial close the narrative.

Speculation about the salvation of Adam and Eve is central to this book. Will God have mercy on the people responsible for the presence of sin and death in this world? The answer is twofold. Death is an inevitable consequence of Adam's (and Eve's) sin. No amount of bargaining and praying can alter this fact (cf. the *Testament of Abraham*, above, pp. 248–52). Adam has been cut off from the Tree of Life, and the most he can take from paradise are seeds to grow food and incense to accompany his prayer. In the latter is a bridge from condemnation to ultimate salvation, which is the author's second point. In spite of Adam's death, God responds to the prayers that have been offered by Adam, Eve, Seth, and the angels and has mercy on the first father. He receives his spirit and promises the resurrection of his body. Thereafter he will have access to the joy and the eternal sustenance he left behind in the garden.

The author's interest, however, is broader. Adam and Eve will participate in a general resurrection. The specifications for burial in chaps. 38–43 apply to "every man who dies." If the death and trouble Adam and Eve brought into the world are a universal malady, the resurrection provides a remedy for all "the holy people" who descend from him. Proper burial is performed in the hope of the resurrection and as a sign of it. Because of this hope, mourning must give way to joy. It must not extend beyond six days, because the seventh day is symbolic of the eternal rest.[51]

In summary, our author admits the inevitability of death for everyone but expresses his faith in the resurrection. As Adam was the creature of God and his image, so it is with all humanity; and the Creator will redeem his creature in the resurrection.[52]

THE LIFE OF ADAM AND EVE

Approximately one half of the *Life of Adam and Eve*[53] overlaps with a similar portion of the *Apocalypse of Moses*:

		Life	*Apoc. Mos.*
1.	Penitence, devil's narrative, Cain's birth	1:1–22:2	———
2.	Birth of (Cain) Abel, Seth, et al.	22:3–24:2	1:1–5:1a
3.	Adam's revelations to Seth	25–29	———
4.	Adam's sickness, journey to paradise, testamentary situation	30–44	5:1b–14:3
5.	Eve's narrative, exhortation	———	15–30
6.	Adam's death, Eve's vision, Adam's burial	45–48	31:1–42:2
7.	Eve's testament	49:1–50:2	———
8.	Eve's death, burial	50:3–51:3	42:3–43:4

The material found in the *Life of Adam and Eve* but not in the *Apocalypse of Moses* occurs in three blocks (1, 3, 7).

The narrative thread that binds together chaps. 1–22 of the *Life* is Adam and Eve's quest for food, although other episodes and themes are interspersed. When Adam and Eve are driven from paradise they find the earth devoid of food (1:1–4:2). They hope that acts of penitence will obtain divine favor and bring them the gift of food (4:3–6:2). While Eve is standing in the waters of the Tigris, Satan appears in the guise of an angel (cf. *Apoc. Mos.* 17) and again deceives Eve (7:1–10:4). When she asks him why he has tricked them he tells the story of his expulsion from heaven.[54] The story of Cain's birth is narrated as a separate incident (chaps. 18–21). After Cain's birth God sends Adam seeds to grow the food for which he has been searching (22:2). Seen as a whole this narrative sequence is a very elaborate version of Adam's request and receipt of herbs and seeds at the end of Eve's narrative in the *Apocalypse of Moses* 29:3–7.

In chaps. 25–29 of the *Life*, Adam transmits secret knowledge to Seth. In the first part of this instruction (25:1–29:1) he relates his ascent to the heavenly paradise and his vision of God after his expulsion from the garden. Its theme (God's threat of death, Adam's petition, God's promise of mercy) parallels the last part of Eve's narrative in the *Apocalypse of Moses* 27–29, and it would appear that a major part of Eve's narrative in the *Apocalypse of Moses* has been transformed into a heavenly throne vision. The second part of Adam's instruction to Seth is a historical apocalypse that transmits eschatological secrets Adam learned after eating of the Tree of Knowledge (29:2–10). The content of this part has no parallel in the *Apocalypse of Moses*.

In the *Apocalypse of Moses* 14 Adam bids Eve to recount the story of the Fall, and Eve's narrative follows. In the corresponding place in the *Life* (chap. 44) Adam tells Eve to recount the story *after his death,* and so Eve's long narrative is dropped at this point. After Adam's death and immediately before her own, Eve gathers her children. However, instead of telling the story of the Fall she repeats Michael's instructions that the children should write the story of their parents' lives on stone and clay tablets so that it survives two judgments by water and fire (chaps. 49–50). This section is also unparalleled in the *Apocalypse of Moses.*

The precise relationship between the *Apocalypse of Moses* and the *Life of Adam and Eve* is a complex literary problem that can be solved only by a study of yet other recensions of this work, some of them still unpublished. With some caution, however, we may make a few suggestions.[55]

Chapters 1–22 of the *Life* are most likely an expansion of the end of Eve's narrative in the *Apocalypse of Moses* 29. In the *Life* this section stands in its proper chronological relationship to the rest of the book. It is told as third-person narrative before the time of Adam's final days rather than retrospectively in the first person as a piece of testamentary biography. The penitence of Adam and Eve doubtless has a theological rationale, and their bathing in the Jordan and Tigris rivers may be connected with ritual ablutions that may have been practiced by the Jewish and/or Christian groups that generated and transmitted this literature.[56] The role played by the devil in this section dramatizes the continuing problem of temptation after the Fall. The transformation of the heart of Eve's narrative into a heavenly throne vision may have been due to a theology of a transcendent God, which preferred to depict a theophany in the heavenly paradise rather than his descent to earth à la Genesis 3.[57] Adam's second revelation to Seth and Eve's testament (*Life* 29:2–10; 49–50) comprise the kind of apocalyptic material that is at home in testamentary literature. These sections may have been drawn from an earlier testament attributed to Adam.[58]

JOSEPH AND ASENETH

Although the patriarch Joseph is cited in much of Jewish literature as a paragon of virtue, one item in the biblical stories about him was bound to raise theological problems. Contrary to the patriarchal admonitions of Genesis,[59] Joseph married a foreign woman—the daughter of an Egyptian priest (Gen 41:45). The story of *Joseph and Aseneth* deals with this problem constructively, describing Aseneth's conversion from idolatry and attributing to her the status of prototypical proselyte.[60]

Aseneth is introduced as a virgin of peerless beauty whose hand in marriage is sought by suitors from far and near, among them Pharaoh's son (chap. 1). She scorns them all and lives in virginal isolation in a great tower (chap. 2). When Joseph announces his intention to dine with her father Pentepheres, the priest informs Aseneth that Pentepheres wishes her to marry Joseph (chaps. 3–4). Aseneth scornfully refuses to have anything to do with this "alien and fugitive . . . this son of the shepherd from the land of Canaan . . . who lay with his mistress" (4:9–10; Brooks, adapted).

When Joseph appears Aseneth retreats to her tower (chap. 5). As she peeks through her window, however, she is shocked at his resplendent appearance and repents her rash words (6:3–6).

Pentepheres describes Aseneth to Joseph, who agrees to see her and to "love her from today as my sister" (chap. 7). But when Aseneth appears he refuses to kiss her. It is improper for a man who with his mouth blesses the living God and partakes of sacred food to kiss a strange woman who with her mouth blesses dead and deaf idols and partakes of the polluted food of their cult (8:5). Aseneth is deeply chagrined at her rejection, but Joseph prays for her conversion, promising to return in a week (chaps. 8–9).

Aseneth retreats to her tower, where she mourns, fasts, and repents for seven days. She exchanges her royal robes for sackcloth and destroys her idols, casting them out the window, together with her rich foods (chaps. 9–10).

Aseneth is alone, forsaken by her parents and hated by all because of her repudiation of her idols. Gradually she comes to the decision to seek "refuge" with the God of Joseph, who, she has heard, is merciful, filled with pity, long-suffering, not reckoning the sin of the humble (chap. 11). In her lengthy prayer (chaps. 12–13) she confesses her sin of idolatry and asks to be delivered from the devil, the "father of the gods of the Egyptians," who pursues her like a lion. She points to her acts of penitence and repudiation as signs of her true repentance and asks forgiveness for her idolatry and her blasphemy against God's "son," Joseph.

In answer to her prayer the angel Michael appears and commands Aseneth to replace her mourning garments with bridal array. God has accepted her confession. Her name has been written in the book of life, and from this day she will be renewed and requickened and will partake of the blessed food of immortality. God will give her to Joseph as a bride, and her name will be changed to "City of Refuge," symbolizing her status as the prototypical proselyte (15:2–7).

Michael then commands Aseneth to bring a honeycomb that mysteriously appears in her storehouse. He places his hand on her head, thereby transmitting to her "the ineffable mysteries of God," and he bids her eat of the honeycomb, which is the spirit of life, made by the bees of paradise from the roses of life. Now she has eaten the bread of life and drunk the cup of immortality and has been anointed with the unction of incorruption. Henceforth her flesh and bones will flower and she will never die. When Aseneth turns her back momentarily Michael vanishes.

The structure of the first part of the narrative is now repeated with significant changes (cf. chaps. 18–20 with chaps. 3–8). The servant announces that Joseph will come to dine. Aseneth orders the meal prepared. She adorns herself with special bridal array and her face is gloriously transfigured. Joseph arrives once again. Aseneth goes out to meet him. They embrace and kiss three times, and Aseneth receives "the spirit of life," "the spirit of wisdom," and "the spirit of truth." She is fit to be Joseph's bride. Her parents return, astonished at her beauty. Amid glorious ceremonies and feasting Joseph and Aseneth are married by Pharaoh (chap. 21).

Chapter 22 is an interlude that describes Aseneth's meeting with Jacob. Simeon and Levi are introduced as Aseneth's friends and protectors. This provides the transition to the last part of the story (chaps. 23–29). Pharaoh's son reappears as Joseph's rival, madly in love with Aseneth. He vainly seeks the help of Simeon and Levi in murdering Joseph. Finally he enlists the help of the sons of Bilhah and Zilpah. Their attempted kidnapping of Aseneth and murder of Joseph are stymied because of the efforts of Simeon, Levi, and Benjamin. The prince is mortally wounded. Later, when Pharaoh dies, Joseph becomes sole ruler of Egypt.

Integrated into the present literary work is a legend, known from other Jewish sources, which identified Aseneth as the daughter of Dinah and Shechem (cf. Gen 34).[61] This story solved the problem of Joseph's marriage to an Egyptian woman by maintaining that she was in reality an Israelite. The story replayed the events at Shechem, but the chastity of Dinah's daughter was preserved. The role of Shechem was played by Pharaoh's son, with Levi and Simeon assuming their biblical roles as the young woman's protectors.

This story of Aseneth's Israelite descent has been edited into a story that solves the problem of Genesis 41:45 in a different way. Aseneth is an Egyptian who is converted to the religion of Israel before she marries Joseph. This story governs the present form of *Joseph and Aseneth* and dominates the reader's attention. The story about Pharaoh's son (introduced in chap. 1) is employed mainly as a short second act (chaps. 23–29) that draws motifs from the main story[62] and serves the didactic purposes of the final author or editor. It demonstrates how God protects his new convert, and in the actions of Simeon, Levi, and Benjamin it exemplifies the conduct that "is proper for a man who worships God."

Aseneth's conversion is twofold. Chapters 4–6 depict her change in attitude toward Joseph. At first she spurned "the son of the shepherd from the land of Canaan," saying she would marry the king's firstborn son. However, when she sees Joseph she acknowledges him to be "son of God" and likens his advent to a solar epiphany.[63] By describing Joseph in language appropriate for the Pharaoh's son[64] she is not only making a marital choice but also adumbrating her conversion from the gods of Egypt to the God of Joseph. This conversion and its implications are the main subject of chaps. 2–23.

Aseneth's status as an idolatress constitutes a twofold problem for her. First, because she worships "dead and deaf idols" she is cut off from "the living God."[65] She exists in the realm of death and corruption, deprived of eternal life and incorruptibility (8:5, 9). Moreover, her idolatry has defiled her. For seven days she does not dare to open her polluted mouth to address the living God (11:2–3, 9; 12:5).[66] Second, her state of defilement imperils her relationship to Joseph. A man who has blessed the living God and has partaken of the food and drink of immortality may not kiss the polluted mouth of an idolatress (8:5). The marriage of Joseph and Aseneth is forbidden.

Through her conversion Aseneth passes from death to life (8:9).[67] After she has destroyed her gods and their sacrificial food and drink (10:12–13) she engages in a mourning ritual, evidently lamenting her sojourn in the realm of death (10:8–17).[68] When Michael announces that God has accepted her acts of repentance and that her name is now written in the book of life (15:2–4) he enacts certain rituals that dramatize this fact and confer on her a new status that reverses her former deprivation. She receives the mysteries of God (16:13–14) in the place of the ignorance of her idolatry (12:4–5). She partakes of the food and drink of immortality (16:13–16). Her investiture in bridal array transfigures her appearance and beauty beyond recognition, testifying to the eternal life that is now hers (18; 19:4–5).[69] Joseph may now kiss her, thus conferring on her the spirit of life, wisdom, and truth (19:11). Their marriage resolves the plot of chaps. 2–23.

Aseneth's is no ordinary conversion, for she does not marry an ordinary man. Joseph is the prototype of the persecuted and exalted righteous man (see above, pp. 23, 240). Imbued with a special measure of God's spirit, he is mighty, wise, and clairvoyant (4:8–9; 6:1–7). Glorious in appearance and resembling Michael,[70] he is called by the angelic title "son of God" and is set apart from mere mortals (6:5–7).[71] For such a one a special bride is required. Aseneth becomes a very special person. The angelophany has its typical commissioning function. Michael announces Aseneth's change of name. As in parallel biblical epiphanies the name change denotes a change from individual to collective and matriarchal or foundational status.[72] Aseneth, who sought refuge, will be a city of refuge (13:12; 15:7). The first proselyte is the prototype of future proselytes. She is both woman and city, proselyte and congregation of proselytes. The immortality she has gained is promised to all who follow her example and thereby become citizens of her city.

Although *Joseph and Aseneth* has more than its share of obscure passages, certain of its peculiar features and contours suggest a context and function. Different from the conversion stories in Daniel 1–6 and Bel and the Dragon (see above, pp. 19–28), *Joseph and Aseneth* makes explicit reference to the author's own time. Aseneth of old is the prototype of proselytes now. What the author says about idolatry and about conversion applies to his own time. Immortality and eternal life are to be found only through the worship of the God of Israel, the living God, and idolaters must completely forsake their idols and turn to him if they would obtain it. Both Pentepheres and Pharaoh acknowledge Joseph's God (4:

6–7; 21:4), but it is noteworthy that the author does not relate their conversion, though the analogy of the Danielic stories might lead us to expect it. It is Aseneth's conversion which is described, specifically as it removes the impediment to her marriage to Joseph. The author may intend to forbid all contact between Jews and idolatrous Gentiles on the grounds that it pollutes. In point of fact, however, he construes pollution from idols in a very specific way. Marriage to an idol-worshiper is contaminating.

Was *Joseph and Aseneth* written with a Jewish or a Gentile readership in mind? An answer is not easy. Surely there are clear implications for Jews: abstain from idolatry; do not marry an idolater. Two considerations suggest, however, that the author may have had a Gentile readership in mind. First, the story is written entirely from Aseneth's viewpoint. She is the central figure, and the author describes her thoughts and emotions: her suffering over the loss of Joseph; her distress at being abandoned by her family—an element that ill befits the plot (11:3–5; cf. 20:1–2); her uncertainty about whether God will accept her repentance (11:7–15); her joy and relief when he does. The author has recounted a proselyte's progress *from the point of view of the proselyte.* This in itself might be understandable in a book directed to new converts (cf. Eph 2:11–22). However, the book's syncretism adds another dimension. Aspects of the story are reminiscent of the tale of Cupid and Psyche.[73] The rituals of Aseneth's conversion almost certainly betray the influence of descriptions of non-Jewish initiatory rites.[74] Similarities between Aseneth and the goddesses Isis and Neith have also been noted.[75] In view of the book's explicit and repeated polemic against idolatry, this blatant religious syncretism is strange, to say the least. If it is directed to Gentiles, however, it is understandable. Although the God of Israel alone is the living God, the source of life, and although idolatry is forbidden, Judaism is made attractive and understandable through the use of motifs and elements to which Gentiles are accustomed.

The author has written what is functionally a religious myth that explains the origins of proselytism. Its kerygmatic content is simple. Eternal life and immortality are to be found only in the God of Israel, whose worship excludes idolatry. This God is, as he had revealed himself to Moses, "a merciful God and compassionate, and long-suffering and full of mercy and gentle, and not reckoning the sin of a humble man" (11: 10 [Brooks, adapted]; cf. Exod 34:6). He accepts the repentant idolater.

Aseneth's marriage to a son of God reflects biblical imagery about the marriage of Yahweh and Israel and may be parabolic of the covenantal relationship between the proselyte and God.[76] In accepting proselytes God promises deliverance from the fury of the devil, who is piqued by the conversion (12:9–11). The second part of the story underscores this by demonstrating that God "is with" his new convert, protecting her in mortal danger (26:2; 27:10–11).

In creating his myth the author portrays Joseph and Aseneth as larger-than-life figures with special characteristics that befit their archetypal status. The elaborate rituals may also function to underscore the special, prototypical nature of Aseneth's conversion and need not imply that such rituals were employed in the author's community.[77] In view of these ad hoc explanations we may ask whether other specific features in the story belong to the essence of the author's message or whether they are necessary trappings of the plot. In light of the Yahweh-Israel analogy, is the author really making a statement about Jewish-Gentile marriage? The specific construal of the nature of idolatrous pollution as an impediment to marriage and the author's use of a popular erotic literary genre suggest that he is making such a statement.[78]

The place of writing is disputed.[79] If it was written in Egypt, as has often been suggested, its message would have a special bite. Pharaoh and an Egyptian priest acknowledged the God of Israel. Aseneth deserted her Egyptian gods and rejected Pharaoh's son in order to embrace the religion of Israel and marry an Israelite. What better precedents? The particular circle in which *Joseph and Aseneth* was written is uncertain.[80] The time of its composition was perhaps around the turn of the era.[81] It was composed in Greek.[82]

THE GENESIS APOCRYPHON

This compilation of narratives about the patriarchs is one of the original Dead Sea Scrolls found in Qumran Cave 1. Because the stories indicate no certain influence from Essene beliefs,[83] we are treating the document here with other examples of biblical interpretation rather than in the context of the sectarian writings (see above, Chapter 4).

The extant portion of this scroll covers the period from Lamech (Noah's father) to Abraham; however, the scroll's badly deteriorated condition allows us to reconstruct a substantial portion of only five of its twenty-two extant columns (cols. 2, 19–22). The narratives are versions of the biblical accounts, freely reworked in Aramaic and largely in the first-person singular. In places the actual wording of the Bible is reproduced; more often it is paraphrased. There are also a number of substantial additions, some of which parallel other contemporary written sources.

Columns 2–5 contained a version of the same story of Noah's birth that is preserved in *1 Enoch* 106–7. Some of the peculiarities of the present version are paralleled elsewhere in the scroll and may well be the work of the author of this compilation. In keeping with the usual technique in the scroll the narrator is the person immediately concerned, that is, Lamech rather than Enoch. Moreover, Lamech's suspicion that Noah's conception was of angelic origin (cf. *1 Enoch* 106:6) leads to a lengthy and emotional scene—totally absent in *1 Enoch*—in which Lamech adjures his wife to reveal the truth of the matter (2:3–18). The scene parallels other emotionally oriented additions to the biblical accounts in this document.[84] Finally *1 Enoch* stresses the child's miraculous appearance by a double repetition of the initial description, first by Lamech to Methuselah (106:5–6), then by Methuselah to Enoch (106:10–12). Because the child's appearance suggests to Lamech that Noah is a portent of things to come (106:6), this repetition is consonant with the interest in eschatology in *1 Enoch* as a whole.[85] In the Genesis Apocryphon 2:2 no reference is made to the things that may happen, and in 2:19 Lamech's speech is omitted. Whether the bottom of col. 2 contained Methuselah's repetition of the description of the child is uncertain.[86] The differences noted suggest, however, that the author of the Genesis Apocryphon may have omitted eschatological material that was not of interest to him.

Columns 6–17 described the Deluge and its aftermath. The legible parts of these columns reveal significant parallels (including chronological details) to nonbiblical material in the *Book of Jubilees*.[87]

The story of Abram probably began in col. 18. Columns 19–22 retell the events in Genesis 12:8–15:4. The fragmented beginning of col. 19 (ll. 7–10a) appears to parallel the slightly expanded version of Genesis 12:8–9 in *Jubilees* 13:8–10.[88]

The story of Abram's sojourn in Egypt (Gen 12:10–20) is extensively elaborated in cols. 19:10–20:32 but reveals only chronological parallels to *Jubilees* 13:11–15. Novelistic devices are employed, and independent literary forms are introduced to create a story richer and more complex than its biblical counterpart. Abram's dream provides divine justification for his subsequent lie.[89] The lengthy description of Sarai's beauty, suggested by Genesis 12:15, follows a traditional genre.[90] A third addition is Abram's prayer for judgment, which triggers the plague on Pharaoh and his household. Later Abram himself functions as the divinely empowered healer. Pharaoh's inability to consummate his marriage to Sarai has moral or apologetic overtones.[91] Through these additions the biblical story is transformed to underscore the providence of God and his power over the Egyptian king. Abram is his agent—seer and interpreter of dreams, wise man, speaker of efficacious prayer, and a healer, set in opposition to the magicians and physicians of Egypt. Thus he assumes characteristics associated with Joseph and Daniel. The storyteller's skill is evident in his development and resolution of the plot and in his portrayal of the relevant reactions and emotions of his characters.

Columns 20:33–21:7 retell the story of Abram and Lot (Gen 13:1–13) in compressed form. God's promise and command to Abram (Gen 13: 14–18) are reproduced almost in their entirety, with additions containing geographical information (21:10–12, 15–19). Genesis 14 is paraphrased in somewhat compressed form (21:23–22:26). The scroll breaks off midway through an expanded version of Genesis 15:1–4 (22:27–34).

In retelling the biblical stories the author of this work has employed techniques akin to those in the *Book of Jubilees,* parts of *1 Enoch,* and the *Testaments of the Twelve Patriarchs.* Similar to *Jubilees,* and probably using *Jubilees* as a source,[92] he has compiled a running narrative that parallels a sizable part of Genesis. His wording is a much freer paraphrase of Genesis than is generally the case in *Jubilees.* Unlike *Jubilees* and the *Testaments,* the extant sections indicate little interest in halakhic matters or moral exhortation. Considerable notice is given to geographical details,[93] and there is some emphasis on prayer.[94] The author's treatment of his characters is marked by a sensitivity to the emotions and reactions that reflect their humanity.

The Genesis Apocryphon appears to have been composed in Aramaic[95] around the turn of the era.[96]

THE BOOK OF BIBLICAL ANTIQUITIES ("PSEUDO-PHILO")

This lengthy chronicle retells biblical history from Adam to the death of Saul.[97] The treatment of the ancient material varies widely. Lengthy portions of Scripture are briefly summarized or completely bypassed. Other sections are paraphrased, with occasional verbatim quotations. Still others are interpolated with prayers, speeches, or narrative expansions. In a few cases whole new stories have been inserted or old ones have been radically revised.

Among the sections deleted are Genesis 1–3; Genesis 12–50 (its contents are briefly summarized in *LAB* 8); Exodus 3–13; all the legal material in Exodus except chap. 20; almost the entire book of Leviticus; all the legal material in Numbers; Deuteronomy 1–30; the descriptions of the conquest in Joshua (chaps. 3–21); and parts of 1 Samuel.

The book of Judges is a notable exception to the author's technique of excision and compression. Only chaps. 1–3 have been deleted; however, they have been replaced by the lengthy story of Cenez (*LAB* 25–28). According to Judges 1:13 Cenez was the father of Othniel; here he assumes Othniel's place as the first judge (Judg 3:7–14).[98] The stories of Deborah, Gideon, Abimelech, Jephthah, Samson, Micah, the Levite, and the war between Benjamin and Israel have all been retained, though with many revisions. The section corresponding to Judges comprises one third of the entire work (*LAB* 25–49).

Two tendencies in the *Antiquities* are consonant with this concentration on the book of Judges. The first relates to the historical pattern of Judges: sin, divine punishment by means of an enemy, repentance, salvation through a divinely appointed leader. The pattern (or references to it) appears in many of the (interpolated) speeches in the *Antiquities*.[99] In presenting this theme the author often raises the question of Israel's survival of the present onslaught of its enemies.[100] His affirmative answer is rooted in Israel's status as the chosen covenant people of God[101] and is sometimes spelled out in a recitation of Israelite history, including the patriarchal history he bypassed earlier in his narrative.[102]

A second tendency in the *Antiquities* relates to Judges' orientation of history around great Israelite leaders.[103] The story of Abraham is radically revised (*LAB* 6). The patriarch was present at the building of the Tower of Babel. He and eleven others refused to participate in the idolatrous enterprise. Even among these twelve Abraham is set apart as the only one who rejected the possibility of escape and confronted death in a fiery furnace (cf. Dan 3). The story of Moses' birth is prefaced by a lengthy episode involving his father, Amram (*LAB* 9), a leader of Israel who convinces the elders of God's protection of the nation and leads a mass disobedience of the Pharaoh's decree. The other parts of the Pentateuch that are reproduced center mainly on the figure of Moses and his functions as mediator of the covenant, intercessor for his people, and spokesman of God and executor of his judgment (*LAB* 10–19). Clearly he maintains his preeminent position in Israelite history (*LAB* 19:16). The author's treatment of the book of Joshua centers on the figure of Moses' successor (*LAB* 20–24). Cenez is introduced as a leader par excellence (cf. *LAB* 49:1). The treatment of Judges makes specific moral judgments about Israel's leaders, often adding a motif of retribution lacking in the biblical text. Gideon, who dies unpunished for his idolatry (Judg 8:22–32), will be punished after death (*LAB* 36:4).[104] Jephthah's loss of his daughter is punishment for a wicked vow (*LAB* 39:11), and she is said to be wiser than her father (*LAB* 40:4). Samson is blinded because his eyes went astray (*LAB* 43:5). Judges 17–20 is unified around the theme of Micah and his idolatry (*LAB* 44–47). His punishment, not mentioned in Judges, is explicit (*LAB* 47:12). Israel's initial defeat by Benjamin is punishment for those who do not oppose Micah's idolatry (*LAB* 47). The birth of Samuel is set against a vacuum of leadership in Israel, and he is designated as a leader like Cenez (*LAB* 49:1). The treatment of 1 Samuel centers mainly on the figures of Samuel, Saul, and David, which is quite consonant with the biblical book.

The message of Pseudo-Philo is perhaps to be found in the two tendencies we have just described. The content of the many speeches put on the lips of the leaders of Israel appears to function as a kind of kerygma. Israel is God's people, chosen already before creation (60:2). Therefore even when their very existence is threatened God's covenant fidelity will deliver them. The specific interpretation of foreign oppression as a threat to Israel's continued existence suggests as a historical setting a time when conditions made this a relevant question. The device of interpolated speeches has analogies in Greek historiography and in the book of Acts, and it may be only a literary device. On the other hand its net result is to add a particular dimension to the biblical portraits of these leaders and to undergird their significance. They are often set in contrast to the people, and the frequent use of the first-person singular in their speeches stresses their individuality.[105] Perhaps Pseudo-Philo sees good or bad leadership as an important constituent in the strong or weak religious and moral fiber of the nation. The book can easily be read in this way.

The *Biblical Antiquities* has usually been dated shortly before or after the fall of Jerusalem in 70 c.e. (see the next chapter).[106] Similarities to *2 Baruch, 4 Ezra,* and traditions in Josephus's *Antiquities* may support that contention.[107] A query about Israel's continued existence in the face of powerful Gentile opposition and conquest would fit well in the post-70 period. Such a query would present another facet of the problem raised in *2 Baruch* and *4 Ezra*, which ponder Israel's defeat as it relates to God's justice (see below, pp. 281–94). The emphasis on the necessity of good leaders would be especially appropriate during or after the chaos of the years 66–70.[108] If the *Antiquities* are dated to the earlier part of the first century[109] their precise setting and function are less clear.

The *Antiquities* is extant only in Latin, which is generally thought to be a translation of a Greek translation of a Hebrew original.[110] Its author is unknown, but the work came to be attributed to Philo of Alexandria perhaps because it was transmitted with genuine works of Philo.[111]

NOTES

1. On the possible relationship between this outline and the biblical covenant forms see Klaus Baltzer, *The Covenant Formulary* (Philadelphia: Fortress, 1972) 141–63.

2. In *T. Asher* the narrative section is replaced by a didactic section on the two ways and the two spirits. See Nickelsburg, *Resurrection*, 161–62.

3. On this pattern see M. de Jonge, *The Testaments of the Twelve Patriarchs: A Study of Their Text, Composition, and Origin*, 83–86.

4. On this opposition see Nickelsburg, *Resurrection*, 158–59.

5. On resurrection in the *Testaments* see ibid., 34–37, 141–42; and H. C. C. Cavallin, *Life after Death*, ConB N.T. Series 7:1 (Lund: Gleerup, 1974) 53–57.

6. For a critical discussion of the possibilities see M. de Jonge, "The Testaments of the Twelve Patriarchs: Central Problems and Essential Viewpoints," IV.

7. On the fragments of *T. Levi* see J. T. Milik, "Le Testament de Lévi en araméen"; idem, *Books of Enoch*, 23–24. On the fragments of *T. Napht*, see idem, *Ten Years of Discovery in the Wilderness of Judaea*, SBT 26 (E.T.; London: SCM, 1959) 34. For fragments of the Testaments of Kohath and Amram see idem, "4Q Visions de 'Amram et une citation d'Origène," *RB* 79 (1972) 77–97. Problematic is Milik's claim to have found Aramaic fragments of a testament of Judah and a testament of Joseph, "Écrits préesséniens de Qumrân," in *Qumrân: Sa piéte, sa théologie et son milieu*, ed. M. Delcor, BETL 46 (Leuven: University, 1978) 95–104.

8. For one possibility of such a collection see A. B. Kolenkow, "The Narratives of the TJ and the Organization of the Testaments of the XII Patriarchs," in *Studies on the Testament of Joseph*, ed. George W. E. Nickelsburg, Jr., 37–45.

9. But see above, Chapter 2, n. 46.

10. Cf. also *Tg. Ps.-J.* Gen 42:24, where Simeon is specified as the one who plotted Joseph's death.

11. Connections between the two passages are suggested by Milik, "Le Testament de Lévi," 404–5. See also George W. E. Nickelsburg, "Enoch, Levi, and Peter: Recipients of Revelation in Upper Galilee," *JBL* 100 (1981) 588–90.

12. For this text see above, n. 7, and the discussion of de Jonge, "The Testaments . . . Central Problems," II.

13. For a possible historical setting for Sir 50:26 and *T. Levi* 7:2–3 see James Purvis, *The Samaritan Pentateuch and the Origins of the Samaritan Sect* (Cambridge: Harvard University, 1958) 119–29.

14. On the relationship between priestly office and zealous action see above, p. 153, n. 48.

15. See Milik, *Books of Enoch*, 23–24.

16. For this prayer see Milik, "Le Testament de Lévi," 400–403.

17. See Jonas C. Greenfield and Michael E. Stone, "Remarks on the Aramaic Testament of Levi from the Geniza," *RB* 86 (1979) 45.

18. Chapter 18 itself does not say that the new priest will be a descendant of Levi, but the implication can be drawn from the context of the other *Testaments*, which speak of a descendant or descendants from Levi and Judah. That this priest will receive revelation (18:2) indicates that he is not purely a divine figure.

19. Nickelsburg, *Resurrection*, 36–37, 158.

20. See J. Amstutz, ΑΠΛΟΤΗΣ: *Eine begriffsgeschichtliche Studie zum jüdisch-christlichen Griechisch*, Theophaneia 19 (Bonn: Hanstein, 1968), and the summary by de Jonge in *Studies on the Testaments of the Twelve Patriarchs*, 302–5.

21. See esp. LXX 49:15, where he is called *geōrgos* as he is in *T. Iss.* 3:1.

22. See Nickelsburg, *Resurrection*, 49.

23. The passage 2:1–3 is not poetic in form but has the same pattern.

24. See H. W. Hollander, "The Ethical Character of the Patriarch Joseph," in *Studies on the Testament of Joseph*, 47–60.

25. Richard I. Pervo, "The Testament of Joseph and Greek Romance," in *Studies on the Testament of Joseph*, 17–18.

26. Ibid., 15–28.

27. See Hollander, "Ethical Character," 50–58.

28. Cf., e.g., Rev 1:9; 2:2, 3, 19; 3:10; 13:10; 14:12.

29. My approach to this book is largely indebted to John J. Collins, "Structure and Meaning in the Testament of Job."

30. Cf. Sir 38:1.

31. It is possible that 41:7 alludes to the lament now at 32:1–12; Robert A. Kraft, *The Testament of Job*, 74, n. on 41:7.

32. See Collins, "Structure," 50–51.

33. Ibid., 50.

34. Cf. also the discussion of *4 Maccabees*, above, pp. 223–26.

35. In Wisdom the wise man knows the mysteries of God whereas his enemies do not (2:22). He is exalted to heaven in spite of his suffering. His life is described as *mania* (5:4; cf. *T. Job* 35:6; 49:1–3). The enemies propose a test to see whether he is the servant of God (2:17; cf. *T. Job* 36–37). Great emphasis is placed on the recognition (5:4; cf. *T. Job* 30), where the situation of

Wisdom is reversed, and one thinks of Isa 14, which stands behind Wisdom; see above, p. 179.

36. On the presence of eternal life see above, pp. 140–41. On salvation as knowledge see W. D. Davies, " 'Knowledge' in the Dead Sea Scrolls and Matthew 11:25–30," in his *Christian Origins and Judaism* (Philadelphia: Westminster, 1962) 124–34.

37. For a translation see Vermes, *Scrolls*, 210–13; for a translation and thorough discussion see John Strugnell, "The Angelic Liturgy at Qumran," in *Congress Volume*, VTSup 7 (Leiden: Brill, 1960) 318–45.

38. On the relationship of the two recensions see the articles by G. Nickelsburg, F. Schmidt, R. Martin, and R. A. Kraft in *Studies on the Testament of Abraham*, 23–137.

39. There are seven refusals of one kind or another: chaps. 7, 9, 15, 16, 17, 19, 20.

40. On this aspect of *T. Abr.'s* message see A. B. Kolenkow, "The Genre Testament and the Testament of Abraham," in *Studies on the Testament of Abraham*, 143–47.

41. The idea is not unique here; cf. *1 Enoch* 22:12–13.

42. On the judgment scene see George W. E. Nickelsburg, "Eschatology in the Testament of Abraham," in *Studies on the Testament of Abraham*, 29–37.

43. Ibid., 37–39; cf. Nickelsburg, *Resurrection*, 39–40.

44. Cf. *1 Enoch* 22:7, where he is the advocate of all the persecuted righteous; and *Tg. Neof.* Gen 4:8, which may presume an identification of Abel with the persecuted righteous man in Wis 2, 4–5, who judges his persecutors (see above, pp. 177–79).

45. See Schmidt, "Le Testament d'Abraham," 1:71–78 (summarized by Nickelsburg in *Studies on the Testament of Abraham*, 32–34). A judgment scene like the present one may be presupposed in *1 Enoch* 41:1–2, 9; 61:8; *2 Enoch* 49:2B; 52:15–16. For the metaphor of God's weighing the human spirit and heart cf. Prov 16:2; 21:2; 24:12.

46. See Schmidt, "Testament," 1:71–76, 101–10, 119; Mathias Delcor, *Le Testament d'Abraham*, 67–69.

47. See Schmidt, "Testament," 1:115–17; Delcor, *Testament*, 73–77.

48. See A.-M. Denis, *Introduction aux Pseudépigraphes grecs d'Ancien Testament*, SVTP 1 (Leiden: Brill, 1970) 7–14; M. E. Stone, "Adam, Other Books of," *EncJud* 2:245–46.

49. Elements in Eve's dream (*Apoc. Mos.* 2:2–3 and esp. in the form in *Life* 22:4) suggest an exegetical development from Gen 4:11.

50. Cf. *Apoc. Mos.* 9:2; 10:1–2; 14:2; 21:6.

51. The idea is clearer in *Life* 51:2.

52. See J. L. Sharpe, "The Second Adam," *CBQ* 35 (1973) 35–46. For the relationship of creation and redemption with reference to resurrection cf. 2 Macc 7:11, 22–23, 27–29.

53. See below, n. 55.

54. This section is based ultimately on Isa 14, which is an important source of Jewish demonic speculation. See Nickelsburg, *Resurrection*, 69–82, for some examples.

55. For a detailed discussion of the possible literary relationships among the *Apocalypse of Moses,* the *Life of Adam and Eve,* and other forms of this work see George W. E. Nickelsburg, "Some Related Traditions in the Apocalypse of Adam, the Books of Adam and Eve, and 1 Enoch," 524–25.

56. Ibid., 538. Cf. *Life* 29:10; 42:2–5; *Apoc. Mos.* 37:3.

57. On the possible relationship of *Life* 25:1–29:1 to *1 Enoch* 14–16, see Nickelsburg, "Some Related Traditions," 526–28.

58. Ibid., 525.

59. See Gen 24:3–4, 37–38; 27:46; 18:1 and the expansion of these admonitions in *Jub.* 20:4; 22:20; 30:7–16. See also Tob 4:12–13.

60. The Greek text of *Joseph and Aseneth* is extant in a long form and a short form. For a convincing argument supporting the originality of the longer text see Burchard, *Untersuchungen,* 45–90, and "Joseph et Aséneth," 78–84. Versification is that of P. Riessler, *Altjüdisches Schriftum ausserhalb der Bibel* (Heidelberg: Kerle, 1928) 497–538.

61. For the parallel sources see Aptowitzer, "Asenath," 243–56; and Philonenko, *Joseph* 32–43. For a somewhat longer discussion see Nickelsburg, "Stories," 65–71.

62. Cf. 23:10, "son of God"; 27:10–11, Aseneth's appeal to her conversion; the many references to "(what is proper for) one who worships God," 22:13; 23:9, 10, 12; 28:7; 29:3; cf. 4:7; 8:5–7.

63. He comes from the east (5:2). The solar language is explicit in 6:5. The contrast of Aseneth's former scorn of Joseph with her present acclamation of him as a "son of God" is reminiscent of the wicked's change of mind in Wis 2 and 5. On the relationship of Wis 2, 4–5 and Gen 37ff. see above, pp. 23, 176.

64. For Egyptian texts describing the Pharaoh as the son of Re, the sun god, see J. B. Pritchard, *Ancient Near Eastern Texts,* 3d ed. (Princeton: Princeton University, 1969) 234, 254, 370–71.

65. For the contrast see 8:5; cf. also 11:8–10; 12:1, 5. The expression "living God" is traditional (see Bel and the Dragon, above, p. 27).

66. Other references to Aseneth's mouth are 8:5 and 11:15; cf. 13:13.

67. Cf. 15:4–5; 16:16. The language of realized eschatology in these formulations is most closely paralleled in the hymns of Qumran (1QH 3:19–23; 11: 3–14 [see above, pp. 140–41]; cf. *Jos. As.* 15:12) and Philo's description of Therapeutic belief (*De Vita Contempl.* 13 [see Nickelsburg, *Resurrection,* 169]).

68. Suggested by Prof. Jonathan Z. Smith in correspondence. It fits the author's death/life polarity.

69. For the imagery cf. Sir 24:13–17; 50:8–12.

70. Chapters 5–6 are an epiphany scene. On the resemblance of Joseph and Michael see 14:9.

71. On Joseph's and Aseneth's supernatural beauty see O. Betz, "Geistliche Schönheit," in *Die Leibhaftigkeit des Wortes,* Fs. A. Köberle (Hamburg: Im Furche, 1958) 76–79.

72. See Christoph Burchard (*Untersuchungen,* 112–21), who cites such passages as Isa 62:4–5; Gen 17:5, 15; 32:28; Matt 16:17–19.

73. See Christoph Burchard, *Der Dreizehnte Zeuge,* 64–83; "Joseph et Aséneth," 84–96.

74. Ibid.

75. See Burchard, *Der Dreizehnte Zeuge,* 85; and M. Philonenko, *Joseph et Aséneth,* 61–79.

76. See Isa 52:1–2; 54:1–13; 61:10–11; 62:1–2, where the imagery of re-marriage and reinvestiture is prominent and the imagery fluctuates between woman and city. Cf. also Eph 5:22–23; Rev. 21:1–2.

77. Christoph Burchard, "Joseph et Aséneth," 96–100.

78. On the literary genre of *Joseph and Aseneth* see Richard I. Pervo, "Joseph and Asenath and the Greek Novel."

79. Burchard, *Untersuchungen,* 140–43.

80. See ibid., 99–112.

81. Ibid., 143–51.

82. Ibid., 91–99.

83. See Joseph A. Fitzmyer, *The Genesis Apocryphon of Qumran Cave I,* 11–14.

84. Cf. 2:25; 7:7; 19:21; 20:8–16; 21:7; 22:5.

85. The typology of flood and last judgment is typical of the book as a whole. On this thrust in *1 Enoch* 106–7 and parallel stories see Nickelsburg, "Bible," 93–95.

86. The bottom of col. 2 may have described the confrontation between Lamech and his wife or the appearance of the child, or it may have contained other discourse between Methuselah and Enoch.

87. See the references cited by Fitzmyer, *Genesis Apocryphon,* 99–105.

88. Ibid., 105.

89. Ibid., 110. Cf. *T. Levi* 5 for a similar justification. On the dream see B. Dehandschutter, "Le rêve dans l'Apocryphe de la Genèse," in *La littérature juive entre Tenach et Mischna,* ed. W. C. van Unnik, RechBib 9 (Leiden: Brill, 1974) 48–55. For a parallel to the dream, cf. *T. Abr.* 7.

90. See Fitzmyer, *Genesis Apocryphon,* 119–20.

91. Ibid., 131–32.

92. See the discussion by Fitzmyer, ibid., 16–17.

93. Cf. 2:23; 12:13; 16; 17; 19:11–12; 21:8–12, 15–19.

94. Cf. 12:17; 19:7; 20:12–16, 28; 21:2–3.

95. See Fitzmyer, *Genesis Apocryphon,* 25.

96. See the discussions and opinions in ibid., 16–19.

97. M. R. James (*The Biblical Antiquities of Philo,* 60–65) and John Strug-nell ("Philo [Pseudo] or Liber Antiquitatum Biblicarum," 408) believe that the ending of the *Antiquities* has been lost. Feldman (in James, *Biblical Antiquities,* lxxvii) and Perrot (*Pseudo-Philon: Les Antiquités Bibliques,* 2:21–22) contest this hypothesis.

98. So also Jos., *Ant.* 5.182 (3.3), noted by James, *Biblical Antiquities,* 146.

99. L. Cohn, "An Apocryphal Work Ascribed to Philo of Alexandria," 322.

100. E.g., 9:3; 12:8; 18:10–11; 19:9; 30:4; 35:3; 49:3.

101. See Perrot, *Pseudo-Philon,* 2:43–47.

102. 18:5–6; 23; 32:1–10.

103. George W. E. Nickelsburg, "Good and Bad Leaders in Pseudo-Philo's *Liber Antiquitatum Biblicarum," Ideal Figures in Ancient Judaism: Profiles and Paradigms,* ed. John J. Collins and George W. E. Nickelsburg, SBLSCS 12 (Missoula: Scholars Press, 1980) 49–65.

104. For other references to postmortem judgment cf. 3:10; 16:3; 23:13; 25:7.

105. E.g., 6:11; 9:3–6; 24:1 (cf. Josh 24:15).

106. Cohn, "Apocryphal Work," 327; James, *Biblical Antiquities*, 30–33; Strugnell, "Philo," 408; Harrington in *Pseudo-Philon*, 2:78. Bogaert (in *Pseudo-Philon*, 2:66–74) suggests wider limits for the date.

107. For the parallels to *4 Ezra* and *2 Baruch*, see James, *Biblical Antiquities*, 46–58; but cf. Feldman, in James, *Biblical Antiquities*, liv–lv. For the many parallels to Josephus see ibid., lviii–lxiv.

108. The chaos and crises of leadership during these years are detailed by David M. Rhoads, *Israel in Revolution* (Philadelphia: Fortress, 1976).

109. Bogaert (*Pseudo-Philon*, 2:66–74) suggests wide limits for the date that would permit composition in this period.

110. James, *Biblical Antiquities*, 28–29; Strugnell, "Philo," 408; Harrington in *Pseudo-Philon*, 2:75–77.

111. See James, *Biblical Antiquities*, 26–27; and Feldman, in James, *Biblical Antiquities*, xxii–xxiv.

BIBLIOGRAPHY

THE TESTAMENTS OF THE TWELVE PATRIARCHS

TRANSLATION: Howard C. **Kee**, *PsOT*.

TEXTS: M. **de Jonge**, *The Testaments of the Twelve Patriarchs*, PVTG 1:2 (Leiden: Brill, 1978), critical edition of the Greek text. J. T. **Milik**, "Le Testament de Lévi en araméen: Fragment de la grotte 4 de Qumrân," *RB* 62 (1955) 398–406, publication of the fragments of one Qumran manuscript of the Aramaic Testament of Levi.

LITERATURE: M. **de Jonge**, *The Testaments of the Twelve Patriarchs: A Study of Their Text, Composition, and Origin* (Assen: Van Gorcum, 1953), marked the beginning of renewed research on the *Testaments*. Idem, ed., *Studies on the Testaments of the Twelve Patriarchs*, SVTP 3 (Leiden: Brill, 1975), articles on textual criticism, exegesis, and the history of research. George W. E. **Nickelsburg**, Jr., ed., *Studies on the Testament of Joseph*, SBLSCS 5 (Missoula: Scholars Press, 1975), collection of working papers. For bibliographies and the history of research see: Jürgen **Becker**, *Untersuchungen zur Entstehungsgeschichte der Testamente der Zwölf Patriarchen*, AGJU 8 (Leiden: Brill, 1970) 129–58, an important contribution in its own right to this history; and M. **de Jonge**, in *Studies on the Testaments of the Twelve Patriarchs*, 183–92. Forthcoming and of importance is idem, "The Testaments of the Twelve Patriarchs: Central Problems and Essential Viewpoints," in *Aufstieg und Niedergang der römischen Welt* (Berlin: de Gruyter), a critical and constructive approach.

THE TESTAMENT OF JOB

TRANSLATION: Russell P. **Spittler**, *PsOT*.

TEXTS AND OTHER TRANSLATIONS: S. P. **Brock**, *Testamentum Iobi*, PVTG 2 (Leiden: Brill, 1967) 1–59, critical edition of the Greek text. Robert A. **Kraft**,

The Testament of Job, SBLTT 5, Ps. Ser. 4 (Missoula: Scholars Press, 1974), Greek text with apparatus, translation, and annotated bibliography by Russell Spittler.

LITERATURE: John J. Collins, "Structure and Meaning in the Testament of Job," SBLASP (1974) 1:35–52.

THE TESTAMENT OF ABRAHAM
TRANSLATION: E. P. **Sanders**, *PsOT*.

TEXTS AND OTHER TRANSLATIONS: M. R. **James**, *The Testament of Abraham*, TextsS 2:2 (Cambridge: University Press, 1892), introduction, critical edition of the Greek texts of the long and short recensions, summary of the Arabic version, translation of the related Coptic testaments of Isaac and Jacob. Michael E. **Stone**, *The Testament of Abraham*, SBLTT 2, Ps. Ser. 2 (Missoula: Scholars Press, 1972), reprint of James's Greek texts with a facing translation.

LITERATURE: Francis **Schmidt**, "Le Testament d'Abraham," 2 vols. (Diss. Strasbourg, 1971), introduction, edition of the Greek of the short recension, translation of both recensions. Mathias **Delcor**, *Le Testament d'Abraham*, SVTP 2 (Leiden: Brill, 1973), introduction, commentary on the long recension, translation of the long recension and of the Greek and the versions of the short recension, translation of the testaments of Isaac and Jacob. George W. E. **Nickelsburg**, Jr., ed., *Studies on the Testament of Abraham*, SBLSCS 6 (Missoula: Scholars Press, 1976), articles mainly on the recensional problem and parallel traditions, annotated bibliography, translations of the Coptic and Slavonic versions of the short recension.

THE APOCALYPSE OF MOSES AND THE LIFE OF ADAM AND EVE
TRANSLATIONS: M. D. **Johnson**, *PsOT*; L. S. A. **Wells**, *APOT* 2:123–54.

TEXTS: Konstantin von **Tischendorf**, *Apocalypses Apocryphae* (Hildesheim: Olms, 1966; reprint of 1866 ed.) 1–22, critical edition of the Greek text of the *Apocalypse of Moses*. Wilhelm **Meyer**, "Vita Adae et Evae," in *Abhandlungen der königlichen bayerischen Akademie der Wissenschaft: Philosophisch-Philologische Classe* 14:3 (1878) 187–250; and J. H. **Mozley**, "Documents: The 'Vita Adae,'" *JTS* 30 (1929) 121–49, Latin text of the *Life*.

LITERATURE: George W. E. **Nickelsburg**, "Some Related Traditions in the Apocalypse of Adam, the Books of Adam and Eve, and 1 Enoch," in *The Rediscovery of Gnosticism*, vol. 2: *Sethian Gnosticism*, Studies in the History of Religions 41, ed. Bentley Layton (Leiden: Brill, 1980) 515–39.

JOSEPH AND ASENETH
TRANSLATION: Christoph **Burchard**, *PsOT*.

TEXTS AND OTHER TRANSLATIONS: P. **Batiffol**, "Le livre de la Prière d'Aséneth," in *Studia Patristica* 1–2 (Paris: Le Roux, 1889–90) 1–115, introduction, long Greek text. M. **Philonenko**, *Joseph et Aséneth*, SPB 13 (Leiden: Brill, 1968), introduction, short Greek text, annotated French translation. E. W. **Brooks**,

Joseph and Asenath (New York: Macmillan, 1918), introduction, translation of the long text, with variants from the versions.

LITERATURE: Victor **Aptowitzer**, "Asenath, the Wife of Joseph," *HUCA* 1 (1924) 239–306. Christoph **Burchard**, *Untersuchungen zu Joseph und Aseneth*, WUNT 8 (Tübingen: Mohr, 1965). Idem, *Der Dreizehnte Zeuge*, FRLANT 103 (Göttingen: Vandenhoeck & Ruprecht, 1970) 59–88. Idem, "Joseph et Aséneth," *La Littérature juive entre Tenach et Mischna*, RechBib 9, ed. W. C. van Unnik (Leiden: Brill, 1974) 77–100. Richard I. **Pervo**, "Joseph and Asenath and the Greek Novel," SBLASP (1976) 171–81.

THE GENESIS APOCRYPHON

N. **Avigad** and Yigael **Yadin**, *A Genesis Apocryphon* (Jerusalem, 1956), *editio princeps*, introduction, text, translations, plates. Joseph A. **Fitzmyer**, *The Genesis Apocryphon of Qumran Cave I*, BibOr 18a, 2d ed. (Rome: Biblical Institute, 1971), introduction, text, translation, detailed commentary, bibliography.

THE BOOK OF BIBLICAL ANTIQUITIES
("PSEUDO-PHILO")

TRANSLATION: Daniel J. **Harrington**, *PsOT*.

TEXTS, OTHER TRANSLATIONS, LITERATURE: Daniel J. **Harrington**, Jacques **Cazeaux**, Charles **Perrot**, Pierre-Maurice **Bogaert**, *Pseudo-Philon: Les Antiquités Bibliques*, SC 229–30 (Paris: Le Cerf, 1976), introduction, critical text of the Latin with a facing French translation, commentary, extensive bibliography. M. R. **James**, *The Biblical Antiquities of Philo* (London: SPCK, 1917), extensive introduction, translation, reprinted in 1971 with a lengthy prolegomenon by Louis H. Feldman. L. **Cohn**, "An Apocryphal Work Ascribed to Philo of Alexandria," *JQR*, O.S. 10 (1898) 277–332. John **Strugnell**, "Philo (Pseudo-) or Liber Antiquitatum Biblicarum," *EncJud* 13:408–9.

8

Revolt—Destruction—Reconstruction

THE EVENTS

Events in Palestine in the second half of the first century c.e. threatened Jewish life and religion as they had not been threatened since the persecution by Antiochus IV some two centuries earlier. More exactly, these events paralleled the situation in the sixth century b.c.e. Chaos and revolt brought on the devastation of Judea and the destruction of Jerusalem and the Temple. This in turn spawned a period of religious reflection and reconstruction.

After the death of Agrippa I in 44 c.e., his kingdom was constituted a province of the Roman Empire, governed by a procurator who was responsible to the legate of Syria. The land was relatively quiet during the rule of the first two of these procurators, but tensions with Rome were evident. The first procurator, Cuspius Fadus (44–±46), attempted to place the vestments of the high priest in Roman custody (as they had been before the time of Agrippa I), but Jewish protest prevented this. Fadus acted decisively when a prophet named Theudas led a large following to the Jordan River, where, he claimed, he would part the waters. Evidently suspecting political motives, Fadus sent his cavalry. Some of the crowd were killed and captured. Theudas was executed.[1] Fadus was succeeded by Tiberius Julius Alexander (±46–48 c.e.), the nephew of the Jewish philosopher Philo of Alexandria. He ordered the crucifixion of two sons of Judas the Galilean, who had led an uprising in 6 c.e.

During the procuratorship of Ventidius Cumanus (48–52 c.e.) events took a turn for the worse. One altercation in the Temple, caused by a Roman soldier's obscene gesture, cost the lives of a host of Passover pilgrims. Some time later some Galilean Jews journeying to Jerusalem for a festival were murdered in a Samaritan village. When Cumanus accepted a bribe from the Samaritans and refused to take action, a band of Jewish brigands, led by a certain Eleazar, avenged the murders by burning several Samaritan towns and killing their inhabitants. Cumanus then attacked the Jews, killing some and capturing others. Quadratus, the legate of Syria, intervened, and both Jews and Samaritans were punished. Eventually a hearing was held in Rome, and Claudius removed Cumanus from office because of his inept handling of the affair.

Cumanus's successor was a freedman named Felix ($52-\pm60$ c.e.). The appointment of a freedman as governor was unprecedented, and Felix's misdeeds were due in part to the fact that he was ill-qualified for the office. That he was appointed and that his conduct was tolerated is attributable to the influence which his brother, Pallas, exercised in the court of Claudius. During his rule conditions in Judea continued to deteriorate. He took strong action against the brigands who ravaged the countryside, crucifying many of them and punishing their sympathizers. One of their leaders, the aforementioned Eleazar, was captured and sent to Rome for trial. The *sicarii*, so named for the daggers (*sicae*) they carried, mingled with crowds in Jerusalem and assassinated their opponents, including the high priest Jonathan. Others sought freedom from Rome in less violent ways. Among these was an Egyptian Jew[2] who gathered a large number of followers in the desert and prepared to march on Jerusalem, whose walls he expected to crumble before him. Felix's soldiers attacked them, slaughtering and capturing many. At the end of Felix's rule the country was infested with brigands and rebels.

Felix was succeeded by Porcius Festus ($\pm60-62$ c.e.), a good man, who was unable, however, to reverse the conditions that had been exacerbated by his predecessor. The *sicarii* continued their terroristic activities.

When Festus died in office Nero appointed Albinus as procurator. His rule was worse than that of Felix. He plundered public and private funds, accepted bribes, and allowed criminals, notably the *sicarii*, to be ransomed from prison. When he left office he emptied the prisons, thus filling the country with brigands.

According to Josephus, Gessius Florus ($64-66$ c.e.) made his predecessor, Albinus, look like "the most righteous" of people. He plundered whole cities and cooperated with brigands, accepting a share of their booty. His robbery of the Temple treasury led to an uprising in Jerusalem, which accelerated to the point of no return. The Roman troops were driven from

Jerusalem, and the revolution began to spread to other cities. Cestius Gallus, the legate of Syria, marched on Judea with a sizable army, but he was unable to take Jerusalem. During the winter of 66/67 c.e. preparations were made for war.

Nero delegated the task of waging this war to his general Vespasian. The conflict began in Galilee. One city and fortress after another fell to the armies of Vespasian and his son Titus. By winter 67 the north of Palestine was again in Roman hands.

The war in Judea might have been short. In June 68 Vespasian was ready to besiege Jerusalem. The news of Nero's assassination, however, caused Vespasian temporarily to suspend his military operations. In January 69 Nero's successor Galba was assassinated. New uprisings in south Judea brought an end to Vespasian's inactivity. During the spring of 69 he reestablished the occupation of Judea. Meanwhile, Galba's successor, Otho, had committed suicide, and Vitellius had been acclaimed emperor by his troops. In July 69 Vespasian's army acclaimed their general as emperor. As Vespasian set out for Rome, where he would begin a ten-year reign, he entrusted the completion of the war to Titus. Only Jerusalem and the fortresses of the Herodium, Machaerus, and Masada remained to be conquered.

The siege of Jerusalem lasted some four months. Within the city, the people were divided into factions. This had been the case for two and a half years since a certain John of the city of Gischala in Galilee had fled to Jerusalem, where he precipitated a civil war during the winter of 67/68. During the siege, factions fought not only the Romans but one another. In stages the Romans broke through the fortifications that ringed the city. On the 17th of Tammuz (June/July) the daily offering was suspended in the Temple. On the 10th of Ab (July/August) the Romans broke into the Temple. The sanctuary was set ablaze, and the Romans slaughtered everyone in sight. John of Gischala and his followers escaped across the central valley to the "Upper City," where they withstood further assault until the 8th of Elul (August/September), when the last bastions of the city fell. Titus ordered the entire city and the Temple leveled, leaving only the three towers of Herod's citadel standing as a memorial of the dimension of the Jewish fortifications and hence of the Roman victory. The following year Rome acclaimed the joint victory of Vespasian and Titus. A triumphal arch—built after Titus's death—still stands in the Forum in Rome, with a relief depicting the altar of shew-bread and the Menorah (seven-branched candelabrum) being carried in triumphal procession.

Following the destruction of Jerusalem, Lucilius Bassus, the governor of Judea, subdued the fortresses of the Herodium and Machaerus. The siege of Masada, which was held by the *sicarii,* lasted until spring of 74.

The great war with Rome left Palestine in ruins and its people in shock. Leadership had failed. Large segments of the population had been killed. Cities had been demolished. Institutions were destroyed. Jerusalem and its Temple were no more.

As had been the case in 587 B.C.E. the tragedy spawned reflection about the ways of God and soul-searching about the human situation. The agony of this process and the shock waves of the year 70 which set it in motion can still be felt in the writings that we shall discuss in this chapter.

If Judaism was to survive the events of the year 70, reflection had to be accompanied by reconstruction. Since the Temple was not rebuilt, as it had been in the sixth century, the nature of reconstruction was radically different. The Torah, its study, definition, and observance, began to fill the vacuum created by the annihilation of the Jewish cultic center. In the city of Jamnia, or Yavneh, on the Mediterranean coast, the rabbi Yoḥanan ben Zakkai gathered an assemblage of scholars and students around him and began the process of crystallizing the interpretations of the Torah which were their heritage. This crystallization of the tradition led to new definition and interpretation. Generations of rabbis would follow one another. The literary deposits of their activities are to be found in the bulky collections that we know as the Mishnah, the Tosefta, the Palestinian and Babylonian Talmudim, and the rabbinic commentaries.

APOCALYPTIC RESPONSES TO THE FALL
OF JERUSALEM

The problems created by the destruction of Jerusalem are addressed in four apocalypses: *2 Baruch, 4 Ezra,* the *Apocalypse of Abraham,* and *3 Baruch.* While all four works stem from a common tradition, the relationship between *2 Baruch* and *4 Ezra* is especially close.

"Why?" and "Whither?" are the questions raised by these writers as they ponder the events of 70 C.E. The first question refers to the problem of theodicy: why has a just God allowed the sinful Gentiles to defeat his covenant people and devastate their land and his Temple? The second question relates to reconstruction: what will take the place of the Temple as the people attempt to pick up the broken pieces of their life and their religion? The two apocalypses differ in their answers to the first question, but they agree that the immediate remedy for the plight of Judaism lies in the Torah. In this respect they are in accord with developments in rabbinic circles.

Both *2 Baruch* and *4 Ezra* use the fall of Jerusalem in 587 B.C.E. as their fictional setting. Their alleged authors are two famous scribes: Baruch, the secretary of Jeremiah, and Ezra, the scribe who brought the Torah to Jerusalem in the fifth century. The literary structure of the two works depicts the brokenhearted and troubled scribes challenging God's justice and disputing with him or his angels, receiving apocalyptic visions, and eventually becoming the agents of God's consolation of his people.

2 BARUCH[3]

Chapters 1–9 describe the fall of Jerusalem, thus providing a setting for the rest of the apocalypse. The section interweaves narrative, possibly drawn from an earlier source,[4] with the kind of dialogue that will recur throughout the work. Baruch is depicted as a prophet (1:1) who is surprisingly the superior of Jeremiah (2:1; 5:5; 9:1; 10:2).[5] God announces that he is going to destroy the city because of the sins of the people, and he commands Baruch and Jeremiah to depart because their good deeds and prayers protect the city from destruction (2:2). The distraught Baruch responds with a flurry of questions, which reduce to three: the future of Israel and hence the honor of God (3:4–6); the future of the world and of the human race (3:7–8); the validity of God's promises to Moses (3:9). God's initial response is brief (4:1). The destruction of the city and the captivity of the people are temporary. God has not canceled his promises or stripped Israel and his city of their status. The captivity is, moreover, chastisement rather than final punishment. The present crisis is not a sign of the coming annihilation of world and humanity. As for the present city, it is a mere shadow of the heavenly Jerusalem, which God revealed to the patriarchs and which he holds in reserve for the future (4:2–7). When Baruch worries that the enemy's victory will threaten God's name, God announces that he himself will destroy the city (chap. 5). The ensuing narrative describes this destruction (chaps. 6–8). As in Ezekiel 8–11, God abandons his Temple before it is captured. Both the opening of the city and the voice from the Temple are mentioned in Josephus's account (*J.W.* 6.293–300 [6.5.3]).[6] The section concludes as Baruch and Jeremiah engage in the first of several seven-day fasts, which are prelude to revelation. The motif of lamentation, repeated throughout this section (5:6; 6:2; 9:2), is typical of *2 Baruch* and may be related to the biblical Jeremiah tradition (i.e., the book of Lamentations).

The next major section of the book begins with a lament by Baruch, depicts the seer in dialogue with God, and ends with Baruch addressing the distressed complaints of the people (chaps. 10–34).

After Jeremiah has left for Babylon, Baruch goes to the Temple to lament over Zion and to await a revelation about what will happen "at the end of days" (10:1–5), a subject about which he had earlier expressed concern (cf. 3:7–8). Baruch's lament begins with a beatitude for those who have not been born or who died before the destruction of Jerusalem (10:6–7; cf. 11:6–7). He then appeals to nature and humanity to join his lament. Under the circumstances, business as usual is inappropriate (10:8–19). Chapters 11–12 deal mainly with the paradoxical situation that Babylon prospers while Israel suffers, and Baruch warns the Gentile nation of God's coming wrath. Another seven-day fast anticipates the revelation that follows (12:5).

Chapters 13–20 are a lengthy and complex dialogue between God and Baruch on the subject of theodicy. The seer misperceives the present contrasting circumstances of Israel and the Gentiles (chap. 13). Because the Gentiles fail to appreciate their prosperity as God's blessing, they will fall victim to God's future wrath. On the other hand, Israel's present misfortune is divine chastisement which will later turn to mercy (cf. also 1:4; 4:1).[8] Baruch responds with a series of objections (chap. 14). Few of the nations that now prosper will still exist at the time of God's wrath (vv. 1–3). The righteous, by contrast, have been carried off; God has not forgiven Zion for their sake but has punished her for the evil deeds of the wicked (vv. 4–7). Obviously God's judgments cannot be known by mere mortals (vv. 8–11). Although the righteous who die await eternal life (vv. 12–13), those who remain suffer (vv. 14–15). God's promise to Israel goes begging. The world remains, but Israel—on whose account the world was made—passes away (vv. 16–19). Although God's response in chap. 15 makes allusion to Baruch's objections, it does not answer all of them. Verses 1–6 assert human responsibility on the basis of an assumed knowledge of the Torah; hence divine judgment is to be expected. Verses 7–8 contrast this world and the world to come. In the place of the present world, which as a result of Adam's sin (56:6) is characterized by labor and misery, God has prepared for the righteous another world and a glorious crown. Significant in the dialogue in chaps. 17–20 are the mention of Moses (17:4) and the covenant and Torah. God again asserts responsibility under the Torah (19:1–4). He then turns to a consideration of the end. What is important is not present distress but future glory. The time is near, and the destruction of Zion is God's way of hastening the end (19:4–20:2). God promises new revelation, and he commands Baruch to fast for seven days in preparation for it (20:3–6).

This next revelation and dialogue provide details about "the consummation of the times" (chaps. 21–30). Chapter 21 is one of several lengthy prayers in the book. The extended doxology (vv. 4–12) touches on those qualities of God that are the ground for Baruch's expectation that his petition will be heard (vv. 8, 12). Baruch's complaint about the misery and instability of "this life" (vv. 13–17) leads to a twofold petition which dwells on the problem of mortality. First is the question "How long will the corruptible and the mortal continue?" (vv. 18–19). More important is Baruch's repeated and impassioned plea that God hasten the time of the end (vv. 20–26). God answers the double petition in reverse order. Using parabolic illustrations (chap. 22) he states that he cannot hasten the time of the end which he has already decreed. Mortality must continue until the foreordained number of humanity have been born (23: 1–5). Nonetheless, in answer to Baruch's first query he promises that his redemption is near (23:6–24:2). In the dialogue that follows, God discusses how near the time is and the nature and extent of the woes that will come on the world (24:3–29:2). After the woes the Messiah will appear and the earth will blossom like paradise (29:3–30:1).[9] Then when the Messiah has returned to heaven the event awaited by Baruch will occur. The dead will rise and mortality will come to an end (30:2–5; cf. 21:22–26). On the basis of these revelations Baruch gathers the people for instruction (chaps. 31–34). The times are bad and will get worse before the renewal of creation (32:3–5), but the people are to prepare their hearts by faithful adherence to the Torah (32:1–2). Now Baruch announces that he must leave the people for the present, and they lament his absence (32:7–33:3). He assures them that his departure is only temporary for the purpose of receiving new revelation (chap. 34). The scene as a whole foreshadows chaps. 45–46 and 77 and raises in a preliminary way the problem of a vacuum of leadership.

Chapters 35–47 parallel chaps. 10–34. After a seven-day fast Baruch returns to the Temple and laments over Zion (chap. 35; chaps. 10–12). God responds here with a vision and its interpretation (chaps. 36–40). The vision itself, like *4 Ezra* 11–12:3, may represent older tradition. Its imagery is paralleled in Daniel 2, 4, 7 and *4 Ezra* 4:13–18. In common with the Danielic visions it predicts the destruction of a great power. Chapter 39 interprets the vision in terms of the four kingdoms of Daniel 7, with the last kingdom being Rome (cf. *4 Ezra* 11–12). As in chaps. 29–30 (and 72) the time of the Messiah precedes the end of the corruptible world. After another exchange about the final fate of apostates and proselytes (chaps. 41–42) God informs Baruch that he must soon leave this world, and he commands the seer to gather the people for some testamentary instruction (chap. 43). The scene parallels chaps. 31–34, except that now Baruch tells the people he is leaving them permanently (chaps. 44–47). His speech is a reprise of themes now familiar to the reader. Adherence to the Torah will bring the consolation of Zion (44:3–7). This will mean the end of corruption and mortality and the beginning of a new world that will not pass away (vv. 8–15). The people again object, protesting that there will be no one to teach them the Torah and to lead them on the paths of life (46:1–3). Baruch assures them that there will be no lack of leadership. The wise will be there, and the people should prepare to submit to their wisdom and to obey the Law (46:4–5). Then the good things he announced will come to pass (46:6). Now Baruch sets out for Hebron, where he fasts seven days in preparation for a final revelation (chap. 47).

Chapters 48–52 consist of a prayer and ensuing dialogue. The extended doxology focuses on God as Creator and Lord of the times (48:1–10; cf. 21:4–12). The complaint in vv. 11–17 parallels 21:13–17 somewhat. The petition in vv. 18–24 suits Baruch's situation admirably. Like John 17 it is a departing leader's intercessory prayer in behalf of his people. They are God's people, his "little ones," in need of his compassionate help. They will find this in the divine Wisdom that is resident in the Torah. As in chaps. 25–27 God responds with reference to the coming woes and the judgment (48:25–41). Verses 38–47 focus on the fate of the wicked, and vv. 48–50 focus on the hope of the righteous, who will be relieved

of the labors of this world. This motif leads to a discussion of the resurrection and the resurrection body (chaps. 49–52). Baruch's question in
chap. 49 follows naturally from the context and indeed from much of the
previous discussion. In the resurrection will the righteous be rid of those
bodies that have partaken of the weakness and evil of this world (chap.
49)? God states that after recognition has taken place (chap. 50)[10] he
will separate the righteous and the wicked (51:1–6). Those who have
been faithful to the Torah and have trusted in its wisdom will be transformed into the likeness of the stars and the angels (cf. Dan 12:3) and
will enjoy the blessings of paradise and the world—now invisible—which
does not die (51:1–13). Thus is resolved the problem of mortality and
corruptibility so central to this author. After some further observations on
the unhappy fate that awaits those who have turned from Torah and
denied their future (51:14–52:3), the author returns to the future reward
of the righteous, which allows them to rejoice in their present sufferings
(52:3–7).

This dialogue is followed by a final vision and its lengthy interpretation (chaps. 53–74). As in chaps. 36–40 Baruch responds to his vision
(chap. 53) with a prayer (chap. 54). The doxology acknowledges God
as omniscient and the revealer (54:1–5). On these grounds Baruch asks
for an interpretation (vv. 6, 20). The major part of the prayer is, however, a hymn of praise. As such it stands in striking contrast to the laments that have pervaded previous chapters (contrast esp. v. 10 with
10:6). Turning to the subject of theodicy Baruch affirms what God has
asserted on a number of occasions, namely, human responsibility (vv.
14–19; contrast 54:15 with 48:42–43). Baruch's second request for an
interpretation is followed by the appearance of the interpreting angel
Ramiel (54:20–55:8). The interpretation divides the history of Israel into
alternating periods of righteousness and wickedness. The sin of Adam
was foundational and brought to the world all the evils that Baruch is
experiencing in his own time (56:5–6). The alternating periods of good
and evil focus on covenant, Torah, and Zion; judgment, eternal reward,
and eternal punishment—topics central to Baruch's exposition throughout
the book. The interpretation of the last black waters describes again the
woes to come (chap. 70). According to chap. 72 the Messiah will function
as judge over the Gentiles. The detailing of the criterion for salvation or
destruction of the Gentiles is unique to this literature, and the references
to "those who have trodden down Israel" speaks to Israel's defeat by

Rome. After the Messiah has subdued all things, the consummation will take place, the evils that Adam brought will be reversed (chap. 73), and the age of incorruptibility will begin (chap. 74). Baruch responds with a doxology of God's unsearchable goodness, compassion, and wisdom (75:1–6). In two parallel verses (vv. 7–8) he lays out the two alternatives before Israel: to obey the God of the Exodus (and his Torah) and thus to remember his chastisement and to rejoice; or to reject him (and his Torah) and thus to revert to previous wickedness and the grief that characterizes Israel's present existence.

Baruch is now ready for his farewell (chaps. 76–77). In keeping with the heavy stress on the Torah and the previous references to the Exodus, the section is reminiscent of the last chapters of Deuteronomy. Baruch is to instruct the people so that they can survive the last times. Then after forty days he will receive a vision of the world and depart (chap. 76). Baruch's farewell is reminiscent of chaps. 31–34 and 44–47. The motif of sin and punishment is repeated. The issue of leadership is discussed, and Baruch assures the people that the Torah will spawn its interpreters in spite of the evident darkness of the present situation. At the request of the people he writes two epistles to the exiled tribes and sends them via eagle.[11]

Chapters 78–87 purport to be the epistle that Baruch sent to the tribes exiled in Assyria. In their content, themes, and wording they have much in common with chaps. 1–77. Chapters 78–80 recapitulate the narrative in chaps. 1–9. Chapters 81–82 offer consolation, largely with reference to the coming judgment of the Gentiles. Chapters 83–84 contain admonitions to prepare for the imminent judgment by obeying the Torah. Chapter 85 stresses the nearness of the end and the finality of the judgment. The author's dispersion situation (vv. 2–4) may indicate that this chapter is not an original part of the epistle.

Second Baruch focuses on two poles: Temple and Torah. The Gentiles' destruction of the Temple raises the question of God's justice, and the author presents some answers: God was chastising his people; he will punish the Gentiles; the present Jerusalem is only a shadow of that to come. The judgment and the age of incorruption are near. However, between destruction and the hope of a new age lie the lamentable facts of life in the present. It is not by accident that this author speaks so often of "sorrow, grief, and lamentation" and that his book contains a number of laments. Reality as the author perceives it is a world burdened down with trouble, grief, and death—an understandable position in the wake of the Jewish War. The root of the situation was Adam's sin. Nevertheless his transgression is constantly repeated, and sinners are wholly responsible for their deeds. The accumulation of such sin had to be judged, and this happened in the destruction of Jerusalem. But the God who chastens will have mercy: the age of sorrow will give way to the age that does not die; mortality will surrender to incorruptibility; death will be overcome by life—all this in God's good time. The author encourages his people to obey the Torah, which the nation has forsaken, in the meantime. Such obedience, taught by leaders whom God will provide, will fill the vacuum left by the desolation of Zion and prepare the souls of God's people for the joys of the world to come. In this way the manifold crisis felt so acutely by this author and the people for whom and to whom he speaks will be finally resolved.

The precise dating of the apocalypse is uncertain. Arguments based on its relationship to *4 Ezra* are tenuous,[12] since that relationship is uncertain. We may simply suggest that it was written toward the end of the first century C.E.[13] The author is still deeply grieved by the events of the year 70. Unlike the author of *4 Ezra,* however, he has not produced studied speculations on theodicy. His interest is primarily "pastoral" and practical. His own grief has given way to consolation. His admonitions to "prepare your souls" are part of that consolation, and together with his exhortations to heed God's sages and teachers they focus on the practical task of reconstruction.

Second Baruch is extant in one Syriac manuscript, which is translated from the Greek, which itself may be a translation of a Semitic original.[14]

4 EZRA

Second Esdras in the Apocrypha is in its present form a Christian writing which contains within it (chaps. 3–14) a Jewish apocalypse commonly known as *4 Ezra.*[15] This apocalypse has its fictional setting in Babylon in the thirtieth year after the destruction of Jerusalem, that is, in 557 B.C.E. It is ascribed to a certain Salathiel (Shealtiel), whom the Bible names as the father of Zerubbabel, the builder of the second Temple.[16] In *4 Ezra,* however, Salathiel is identified with Ezra the scribe, who in reality lived during the following century.[17] Evidence that we shall consider below indicates that the book should be dated at the end of the first century C.E., that is, approximately thirty years after the *Roman* destruc-

tion of Jerusalem. Many of the images, themes, and traditions in *4 Ezra*
have counterparts in the *Biblical Antiquities* of Pseudo-Philo and *2
Baruch,* and its outline and structure parallel *2 Baruch* at many points.

Fourth Ezra divides into seven sections, each centering around a revelation. The first three sections are dialogues about theodicy, sometimes reminiscent of the book of Job. Each begins with a prayer in which Ezra takes
up the theme of divine justice. An angel appears and responds to Ezra.
The two engage in a disputation. The section ends with Ezra fasting in
preparation for another revelation.

The first section is 3:1–5:20. Together with the next section it corresponds roughly to *2 Baruch* 10–34. Ezra's prayer in 3:4–36 is less a petition
than a complaint. Through his recital of history from Adam to the present
he blames Israel's present plight on the state of the human heart. Since
the first father and his transgression, humanity has been burdened with
"an evil heart." The problem is more acute with Israel. Although God had
chosen them as his people (vv. 12–17) and given them his Torah, he did
not remove the evil heart and thus allow the Torah to bear fruit (vv.
20–22).[18] Moreover, the nation is now in ruins because God has punished
his people for the sins their evil hearts led them to commit (vv. 25–27).
Carrying his complaint a step further he observes that the deeds of the
Babylonians are no better than those of the Jews. He concludes by challenging God to compare the deeds of Israel and those of the Gentiles
(vv. 28–36; cf. *2 Bar.* 11–12; 14). Thus the problem of theodicy is clearly
outlined. Since Adam, humanity has had a propensity to sin. The Creator
has not removed this tendency even from his chosen people. Nonetheless,
he holds them responsible for their deeds, and he punishes them at the
hands of Gentiles whose deeds are worse than those of the Jews.

The angel Uriel appears and challenges Ezra to explain certain phenomena in this world. When the seer is unable to do so, the angel asks
how he expects to understand the way of the Most High. Such compre-
hension lies beyond human capacity (4:1–21). Ezra objects that he is not
interested in fathoming *heavenly* things. Israel's suffering at the hands of
the Gentiles is a matter of the *here and now.* Why does God permit it,
and what will he do about it (4:22–25)? This last question shifts the
discussion in the direction of eschatology, which provides Ezra with the
only solution that he will receive in his confrontation with the Almighty.
Presumed is a teaching of two ages. The present age is marked by sadness

and infirmities (4:27; cf. *2 Bar.* passim) which are caused by the evil seed that was sown in Adam's heart from the beginning (4:30–32). Deliverance from this situation lies in the *eschaton* and the beginning of the age to come, and so Ezra asks the perennial apocalyptic question, "How long?" (4:33). This section corresponds to *2 Baruch* 21–24, and the answer is basically the same. The time has been predetermined by God and cannot be rushed (4:34–37). By the same token, when the time has arrived not even human sinfulness can hold it back (4:38–43). The angel assures Ezra that more time in the history of the world has passed than is yet to come, and he enumerates some of the signs of the end (4:44–5:13; cf. *2 Bar.* 25–30). The section concludes as Ezra speaks with one of the Jewish leaders and fasts for seven days in preparation for the next revelation (5:13–20; cf. *2 Bar.* 31–34).

Ezra's second discourse (5:21–6:35) parallels somewhat the first one, although the focus is not on the anthropological problem of the human heart but on the dilemma of Israel's subjugation to the Gentiles. In his prayer Ezra stresses Israel's unique status as God's chosen people and asks why God has delivered the one to the many rather than himself punishing Israel (5:23–30). Uriel's responses again take the form of a challenge. Do you love Israel more than its Maker? (5:33). When Ezra protests that he wishes to understand God's ways and judgment, Uriel responds that it is not possible to understand God's judgment or the goal (*finis*) of his love for his people (5:34–40; contrast *2 Bar.* 14:8–9; 15:3–5). As in the first discourse the focus shifts to eschatology and the question of who will be present at the end (*finis*, 5:41). Ezra wants to know whether God could not have arranged things so that the end would come sooner, and the angel again stresses that God has his own time (5:44–49). After further discussion of the nearness of the end and the signs of its coming (5:50–6:28) the section closes with Ezra fasting for another seven days (6:29–35).

The third discourse is the longest of the three (6:36–9:26). In it the question of theodicy is pressed to its unanswerable limits. Ezra's prayer deals again with Israel's plight. After a lengthy description of creation (6:38–54) the seer asks, If the world has been created for Israel, why is Israel dominated by the nation^ rather than in possession of its inheritance, and how long will this continue? (6:55–59; cf. *2 Bar.* 14:18–19). As in the first discourse, the angel expounds the teaching of the two ages. The sorrow and toil of this age, caused by Adam's transgression, will be overcome in the age to come, and it is to this that Ezra should direct his attention (7:1–16).

A new motif now appears. The hope for an age to come is fine for the righteous, but what about the wicked, who can only anticipate punishment? (7:17–18). The angel asserts human responsibility. God gave his covenant and his Torah, and the wicked will be judged according to their deeds, for they are responsible for these deeds (7:19–25). Then follows a description of the last days—a four-hundred-year reign of the Messiah, the expunging of all life and a week when the earth returns to its primordial silence, the resurrection, and the great judgment over which God will preside (7:26–44). Judgment will be on the basis of deeds, and even the Gentiles will be punished for not having served the Most High and obeyed his commandments.[19] Ezra now pursues a question that will occupy him through much of this discourse: who has not sinned? Thanks to the evil heart, the delights of paradise will be enjoyed by few, while many will be tormented (7:45–48). The angel dismisses the question. Things that are rare (here "the few" to be saved) are more precious than those in great quantity. God will rejoice over the few who are saved and will not grieve over the multitude that perish (7:49–61). Ezra laments the fate of humans, who are equipped with a mind to understand their future torment (7:62–69). Again the angel asserts human responsibility for sins knowingly committed (7:70–74). There now follows a lengthy excursus on the "intermediate state," the situation of souls between death and the judgment (7:75–101). It is the most detailed discussion of the subject in our literature.[20] Returning to the subject of the righteous and the wicked, Ezra inquires whether the wicked might be saved at the judgment through the intercession of the righteous (7:102–3). The angel's negative answer (7:104–5) leads to another lament over the human plight caused by Adam (7:116–26; cf. 7:62–69). According to the angel, Adam is not to blame. Life is a contest in which people must make the choice that Moses put to them (7:127–31). Ezra pleads the compassion of God, revealed to Moses (7:132–40; cf. Exod. 34:6–7), which would pardon more than just a few; but the angel asserts that only a few will be saved (8:1–3). The seer now addresses God, pleading for his mercy (8:4–19, 20–36). The disputation continues but reaches an impasse. God assures Ezra, who doubts his own salvation, that he is among the righteous (8:48–54), but he cuts short any more questions about the many who will perish (8:55). Ezra cannot love the creation more than the Creator does (8:47). The angel states that the judgment is near. Ezra asks when it will come. Signs are again enumerated (8:61–9:6) and the judgment again predicted. The angel forbids any more questions about the punishment of the wicked (9:7–22) and commands Ezra to fast for another seven days (9:23–26).

The fourth and middle section (9:27–10:59) partakes of the characteristics of the first and second halves of the book and serves as a transition between them. It begins with a prayer, which leads us to expect another dialogue on theodicy. Instead, Ezra receives a vision and its interpretation, which are the revelatory medium in chaps. 11–13 (the fifth and sixth sections). In his prayer Ezra laments Israel's inability to bring forth the fruit of the Law which has been sown within them (9:29–37). His complaint is met by the vision of the lamenting woman, who is transformed into the glorified Zion (9:38–10:27). A comparison of the vision and Ezra's response to it with the angelic interpretation (10:29–59) indicates how this section functions in the seer's own progress from complaint to consolation.[21]

Vision and Response	*Interpretation*	*Ezra's Progress*
The woman grieves	The woman is Zion	Ezra grieves over Zion
Ezra consoles her with promise of resurrection		Ezra's consolation can be applied to himself
The woman is transformed into a glorious city	The new Zion	because of the revealed promise of the new Zion

A hint of the pivotal function of this section is given in Ezra's repeated statement that he dismissed the thoughts with which he had been engaged (9:39; 10:5). In spite of his own grief he begins to console the woman, promising mercy and her son's resurrection (10:15–17, 24). Although Ezra continues to speak of the desolation of Zion (10:6–14, 20–23), for the first time in the book he utters words of hope. Similarly, the angel finally acknowledges the genuine character of Ezra's distress (10:39, 50), speaks words of encouragement to him, and bids him view the glory and vast dimensions of the new Zion (10:55–57). In it and in its promise he will find the consolation for the grief with which the book began. He will now receive visions of what God will do in the last days

(10:58). The linkage between inquiring complaint and eschatological answer, internal to the three discourses, is now made externally between the discourses as a group and the visions as a group, and it is explicated within section four, where God answers Ezra's complaint with a vision of the glorious Zion.

Chapters 11–13 (sections 5 and 6) contain two visions of the end-time together with their interpretations. The visions are traditional, based in part on Daniel 7. The interpretations also include traditional material, though in their present form they reflect the thought of the author of *4 Ezra*.[22]

Chapters 11–12 (section 5) are an exposition of the four-kingdom vision in Daniel 7. Like *2 Baruch* 36–40 and Revelation 13 they understand the last kingdom to be the Roman Empire. The three heads of the eagle represent the three Flavian emperors (Vespasian, Titus, and Domitian) and thus indicate a date around the end of the reign of Domitian (±96 c.e.). The last kingdom is confronted by the Messiah, here depicted as the Lion from the tribe of Judah (cf. *2 Bar.* 36:7–11; 40:1–2). Although he comes from the family of David, the Messiah is thought to be pre-existent (12:32). He functions as accuser and judge of Rome (11:38–46; 12:32–33), bringing that empire and its oppression to an end. Conversely, he is the helper and deliverer of Israel. In these functions he differs from the one like a son of man in Daniel 7 but parallels the Elect One in the parables of Enoch. After receiving this vision and its interpretation, Ezra gathers the people and speaks words of comfort to them (12:40–50; *2 Bar.* 44–47). This consolation is again in marked contrast to Ezra's grief in the first half of the book.

The vision of the man from the sea and its interpretation comprise section 6 (chap. 13). The central figure is called "man" in the vision and "(my) son or servant" (*filius*) in the interpretation. Although he is never called "Messiah," his characteristics and functions parallel those attributed to the Messiah in chaps. 7 and 11–12. He is preexistent (v. 26), protector of the righteous remnant (vv. 23–29), judge (vv. 37–38), and warrior (vv. 9–11, 49). The section ends with the seer's doxology (v. 57), a feature typical of some apocalyptic visionary material (e.g., *1 Enoch* 21–36) but again in notable contrast to Ezra's earlier complaints.

The seventh and final section of *4 Ezra* (chap. 14) parallels the end of *2 Baruch*. The seer is depicted as a second Moses, and his scribal functions are stressed. At God's behest, Ezra admonishes the people to be obedient, promising them mercy and eternal life if they do so (vv. 34–35). The section is remarkable in view of Ezra's previous complaints that only a few are able to be righteous. For this reason some scholars take it to be a later addition to the book.[23] As it stands, however, it resolves Ezra's previous skepticism. After this admonition, Ezra receives special divine inspiration, which enables him to dictate for future preservation the writings of Moses and the rest of the Hebrew scriptures (which had evidently been lost in the destruction of Jerusalem, 14:21), as well as seventy esoteric books received by Moses, which are to be read only by the wise (vv. 5–7, 23–26, 44–48). Thus the portrait of the seer is brought into line with the historical Ezra, who, we are told, brought the Torah to Jerusalem. With this emphasis on Ezra's admonition that the people obey the Torah and his transmission of that Torah for future generations, the apocalypse concludes (14:37–48).

"Ezra," like his colleague "Baruch," has been badly scarred by the events of the year 70. The fall of Jerusalem, he agrees, was the result of Israel's sins, but he draws deductions more radical than Baruch's. So massive was the disaster that it must be a fact that the number of the sinners vastly exceeds that of the righteous. The nature of the predicament is even deeper. Israel's sinfulness stands side-by-side with the nation's election and the gift of the Torah, which are unable to overcome the evil heart that has been with the human race since Adam. Given these circumstances, Israel's punishment at the hands of sinful Gentiles is the more incomprehensible. Taken together, these observations and speculations—which move far beyond *2 Baruch*—constitute an indictment of the God who is Creator and initiator of the covenant.

The writer of this apocalypse finds two answers to this line of questioning. The first, which is not totally different from the book of Job, is no answer at all. God simply pulls rank, maintaining that no human can hope to understand his ways, asserting his love for his creation, and finally forbidding any further questions by the seer. In his second answer God takes up the traditional apocalyptic response. He does not explain *why* he tolerates sin but rather directs the seer's attention to his *solution* of the problem: the coming judgment and the beginning of a new age which is free from the troubles Adam brought into the present age. The function of the visions in chaps. 9–13 is to assure the seer that this age is coming and that it will come soon. At the same time, material in the dialogues reminds the reader that the time until the *eschaton* cannot be shortened.

For all his agonized probing of the questions of theodicy, the author indicates by the structure of his book that the present grief is to be overcome by consolation—just as Ezra was so moved. God's answer is not an explanation, but it is a promise. Moreover, since the Judge holds people responsible for their deeds, obedience to the Torah is a possibility, and to that end Ezra published the Scriptures. As the age moves toward its end and the Roman eagle is on the verge of faltering in its final flight, God's people are called to faith and obedience while they await the glory of the new Zion.

Fourth Ezra was most likely composed in Hebrew and then translated into Greek and from Greek into a variety of languages.[24] Perhaps as early as the second century, a Christian editor prefaced the Greek apocalypse with two chapters, which radically alter its tone. The basic shift is evident in the repeated assertion that God has forsaken Israel and given his name to other nations (1:24–26, 33–38; 2:10–11). Mother Zion must take leave of her children permanently (2:1–7). In her place is Mother Church, who awaits her sons in the resurrection (2:15–17, 30–32).[25] Ezra's admonition to the people failed (cf. 2:33 with chap. 14). His publication of the Scriptures was ineffectual. God will give his prophets to his new people, the church (1:38–40; 2:18). It is they and "the Son of God" who will inherit Mount Zion (2:42–47). This dramatic Christian transformation and reinterpretation of a Jewish document reflects the same theology that governs another literary product of the post-70 period, the Gospel according to Matthew (see below, pp. 303–5).

THE APOCALYPSE OF ABRAHAM

Like the book of Daniel, this seldom-read apocalypse divides into two major sections. The narrative section describes Abraham's conversion from idolatry, and the apocalyptic section depicts his ascent to heaven, where he is granted a vision of the enthroned deity and revelations of the cosmos and of the future.

Chapters 1–8 recount Abraham's progress from his search for the true identity of the Mighty God to God's revelation of himself to Abraham. A series of three incidents demonstrates the helplessness of idols (chaps. 1–5). The story focuses on Abraham's cogitations on these episodes, which begin with perplexity and end with inner laughter over the folly of idol-atry. This folly is exemplified by Abraham's father, Terah the idol-maker. In the climax of the story Abraham chides his father for foolishly resist-ing the obvious lesson of their experience, and he calls on the Creator to reveal himself (chaps. 6–7). God answers the prayer of the seeker and commands him to go out from his father's house (cf. Gen 12:1), which is immediately reduced to ashes (chap. 8). This story draws on older tra-ditions about Abraham's conversion from idolatry (cf. *Jub.* 11:16–12:31) and his escape from Ur (Heb. for "the fire") of the Chaldeans (cf. *Jub.* 12:12–14; *LAB* 6). The author expounds Genesis 12:1 and casts into nar-rative form traditional polemics that stress the helplessness of idols and the folly of idolatry.[26]

The theophany and sacrifice in' Genesis 15 provide the occasion for Abraham's visions in the *Apocalypse*. Chapters 9–13 describe this occa-sion. God reveals himself as Creator and promises visions because Abra-ham has searched for God and has been named as his "friend" (chap. 9). Appropriately, Abraham's helper and guide to the heavenly regions is the archangel Yahoel, who bears the name of God (YHWH)[27] and is most closely associated with the divine throne (chaps. 17–18). He appears to Abraham, strengthens him after his confrontation with God, and instructs him about the sacrifice (chaps. 10–12). The devil, here called Azazel (cf. *1 Enoch* 6–16), appears as a bird of prey (cf. Gen 15:11; *Jub.* 11:11) and attempts by deceit to dissuade Abraham from offering the sacrifice (chaps. 13–14). His intention is blocked by Yahoel, who commands him to leave and gives Abraham the necessary words of exorcism. The scene is reminiscent of other stories in which the angel of the Lord confronts Satan, who is attempting to frustrate God's purposes by disqualifying or annihilating his agent.[28] At stake here is Abraham's future as patriarch, for it is only in chap. 20 that he receives the promise of progeny.

Chapters 15–18 describe Abraham's ascent to heaven and his vision of God. The sacrificial birds, which Abraham has not slaughtered (chaps. 12, 15; cf. Gen 15:10), transport Abraham and Yahoel to heaven. The fire of the divine presence (Gen 15:17) increases and defines itself as the angelic entourage and finally the divine Glory itself (chaps. 16–17). The hymn of praise that Yahoel has taught Abraham is the song of the angelic attendants of the throne (chap. 17; cf. chap. 10). Its repetitious recitation of divine names and attributes is paralleled in the angelic songs of later ascent texts of Jewish mysticism.[29] To the extended doxology is appended a brief petition that God accept the prayer and sacrifice of him who "sought" God and that he grant Abraham the revelation that was promised him. The description of God's throne in chap. 18 is drawn from Ezekiel 1.

God now grants Abraham a series of visions, which God himself interprets. From the highest heaven Abraham looks down on the seventh, sixth, and fifth heavens, which are inhabited by various classes of angels (chap. 19). Abraham's vision of the "powers of the stars" in the fifth heaven leads to God's command that he count them and to the promise that Abraham's innumerable descendants will be God's chosen people (chap. 20; Gen 15:5). God's reference to Azazel's presence in the world causes the patriarch to inquire about the problem of evil.

Abraham's question leads to a second vision, which is divided into a number of segments. Structuring the whole are the format of vision, question, and answer and the device of a divine-human discourse about the problem of evil (cf. *2 Baruch* and *4 Ezra*). Abraham looks through the heavens to the earth beneath them and to the underworld and the place of torment (chap. 21; cf. *1 Enoch* 17–32). Within the frame of this cosmic view Abraham sees like a great picture the events of history played out as a series of vignettes.[30] The picture is divided into a left side and a right side, which are inhabited by the Gentiles and by Israel, whom God has set apart as his people (chap. 22). In effect the author has built the distinction between Jews and Gentiles into the cosmic structure.

The first vignette depicts the Fall (chaps. 23–24). Abraham asks why God has permitted Azazel to rule over the wicked. God explains that he has delivered those who *will* to do evil into the power of the devil, who prods them to do evil. Abraham presses the question further: why does God permit sin to be willed? The answer at the beginning of chap. 24 is obscure, perhaps due to textual corruption; however, it makes reference to the Gentiles' ill-treatment of Israel—one of the author's special concerns.

Abraham witnesses the murder of Abel. Then he sees human actions representing impurity, theft, passion, and desire, as well as their punishment (chap. 24; cf. *T. Abr.* 10).

The last segments of Abraham's vision center around the Temple and its cult. In the first of these segments (chap. 25) he sees an idealized vision of the Temple and its altar, which correspond to their heavenly counterparts beneath the throne of God.[31] This vision is marred, however, by the presence of cultic abominations: an idol like those that Terah made, which provokes God's jealousy or wrath (cf. Ezek 8:3, 5); a man who "incites" child sacrifice (cf. 2 Kgs 21:4-7; 2 Chr 33:4-6, of Manasseh). Abraham asks why God permits this to happen and then condemns it (chap. 26). God cites the examples of Terah and Abraham, who freely chose to continue in idolatry and to abandon it. God's will, however, is reserved for the coming days.

Chapters 27–29 are the main eschatological section of the *Apocalypse of Abraham*. Abraham sees the Gentiles destroy Jerusalem and burn the Temple (chap. 27). God has permitted this as punishment for cultic abominations that Abraham had earlier witnessed. Abraham asks, "How long?" (chap. 28). God responds in terms of Genesis 15:16. The precise chronology of this section is obscure. The division of the present age into twelve parts is, however, reminiscent of a similar division in *4 Ezra* 14:12 and *2 Baruch* 27; 53:6. The central part of chap. 29 appears to be Christian in its present form. It describes the coming of Jesus and the varied responses to him on the part of Jews, Gentiles, and Azazel.[32] The last part of chap. 29 describes the *eschaton*. Abraham's descendants will judge the lawless Gentiles. God will bring ten plagues on the world. The righteous among Abraham's descendants, whose number is predestined, will come to the Temple, where they will offer righteous sacrifices and gifts in the new age. Their enemies will be destroyed. With this promise God concludes Abraham's vision and dismisses him.

Although Abraham has returned to earth he continues to communicate with God, who presents something of an eschatological scenario (chaps. 30–31). The ten plagues are enumerated. They will be followed by the appearance of "my Elect One," who will bear God's authority and will gather the dispersed Israel from the nations that have despised them.[33] These Gentiles and those who have mocked God will be delivered to eternal punishment. The *Apocalypse* ends with a prediction of Israel's slavery and the Exodus (chap. 32), thus making final contact with Genesis 15:13-14.

The purpose of the author of the *Apocalypse of Abraham* may be discerned in two themes that run through the book and unify it. The first of these is the tension between Israel's status as God's people and its fate at the hands of the Gentiles. The ascription of the book to Abraham is related to his status as patriarch. Israel is repeatedly identified as Abraham's descendants, a conception that is at the heart of Genesis 15. The distinction between Israel and the Gentiles is fundamental to the book, as is evident from the graphic division of the picture of the world into a left side and a right side. Also stressed on several occasions are the Gentiles' defeat, mistreatment, and ridicule of Israel. The apocalyptist asks why God has permitted this state of affairs, and, like the authors of *2 Baruch* and *4 Ezra*, he traces the roots of the problem to the Fall.

The author explains the dilemma of Israel's suffering by means of a second theme that runs through the book, namely, the practicing or the rejection of idolatry. The narrative section of the *Apocalypse* climaxes in God's initial appearance to Abraham. God chooses Abraham and commands him to leave Chaldea because he has searched after God and has rejected the idolatry of his father Terah. He is given the promise of descendants after he has parried the satanic temptation to cease from the sacrifice commanded by God. In connecting Israel's latter-day idolatry with that of Terah the author indicts the people for reversing Abraham's decision which led to his election, and the reference to "devilish idolatry" (chap. 26) suggests capitulation to Azazel. This leads quite naturally to Israel's punishment, ironically at the hands of the Gentiles.

Like "Ezra" and "Baruch," this author finds his solution in the future: in appropriate judgments, a restored Temple and sacrificial system, and eschatological joy for Israel.

Among the apocalypses we have studied in this chapter, the *Apocalypse of Abraham* is unique in its explicit indictment of the cult. With respect to this theme, what is the relationship between the author's narrative world and his real world? Is the author simply following biblical tradition, namely, that the fall of Jerusalem in 587 B.C.E. was punishment for Manasseh's sin (2 Kgs 21:10–15)? Arguing against such a conclusion is the centrality of right and wrong cult in this work. It provides content for the crucial elements in the plot. It is the cause for Abraham's election, the means of his ascent, the reason for the destruction of Jerusalem, and a key element in the author's hope for the future. Thus it is likely that the author believes the events of 70 C.E. were caused by some sort of wrong cultic activity, which he construes as idolatry.

The *Apocalypse of Abraham* parallels *2 Baruch* and *4 Ezra* at many points, indicating that it shares with these works a common apocalyptic tradition that was crystallized after 70 C.E. in response to that crisis.[34] These similarities notwithstanding, the *Apocalypse* has its own peculiarities and emphases. The common concern for the disparity between Israel's election and its present circumstances is here tied very naturally to the figure of the patriarch. The emphasis on cult is missing in *4 Ezra* and for the most part in *2 Baruch* (cf., however, *2 Bar.* 1–8; 64–66). Abraham's ascent and throne vision stand in a tradition that stretches from *1 Enoch* 12–16 to the medieval mystical texts. The tradition is only alluded to in *2 Baruch* 4:4 and *4 Ezra* 3:13–14. On the other hand emphases in *2 Baruch* and *4 Ezra* are played down in the *Apocalypse of Abraham*. The extended discussions of theodicy have only brief counterparts in the *Apocalypse*. Totally lacking in the *Apocalypse* is a concern for Torah and teachers as indispensable constituents for reconstruction. In the place of a Davidic Messiah, this author awaits God's Elect One.

The *Apocalypse of Abraham* is extant in Church Slavonic, which translates a Greek text, most likely made from a Hebrew original.[35]

3 BARUCH

This apocalypse attributed to Baruch is set in an unspecified place[36] at the time of Nebuchadnezzar's destruction of Jerusalem. The lamenting scribe asks God,

> Why have you burned your vineyard and made it desolate? Why did you not requite us with another discipline? But you delivered us to nations such as these, so that they might reproach [us] and say, "Where is their God?" (1:2).

The circumstances and type of questioning are familiar to us from *4 Ezra* and especially *2 Baruch* (see above, pp. 281, 288). As we might expect, an angel appears in response to Baruch's complaint. If the scribe will cease provoking God the angel will show him "other mysteries greater than these" (1:6). Baruch takes an oath to be silent if he is shown these things (1:7). The "mysteries of God" are then shown to Baruch in a guided tour of the five heavens (chaps. 2–16).[37] The book concludes as the seer returns to earth and offers praise to God (chap. 17). This progress from lamentation and questioning to praise is, as we have seen, a feature also of *2 Baruch* and *4 Ezra*. To understand its dynamic here, we must look closely at the contents of Baruch's vision of the heavens.

In the first two heavens, Baruch sees the respective punishments of the builders of the Tower of Babel and of those who took counsel to build it. This distinction derives ultimately from the two introductions to the biblical story in Genesis 11:3 and 4, treated here in reverse order. In the first heaven are the builders, who made war on God and were transformed into animals with the faces of oxen, the horns of stags, the feet of goats, and the haunches of lambs (chap. 2). In the second heaven (chap. 3) are those who planned to build the tower and who forced a multitude of men and women to make bricks for it (cf. Gen 11:3). Their excessive cruelty is mentioned, as well as their attempt to pierce heaven with a gimlet. These men have been transformed into animals with the appearance of dogs and the feet of stags. The tradition that distinguishes two groups in Genesis 11:3 and 4 is reflected also in chaps. 6 and 7 of the *Biblical Antiquities* of Pseudo-Philo. Chapter 6 conflates Genesis 11:3, 4b with Daniel 3, another story about an idolatrous structure erected on a plain in Babylon. The would-be builders of the tower try to force Abraham and his friends to take part in the brick-making process. When the latter refuse because they worship one Lord, they are consigned to death in the brick kiln. They are rescued and their enemies slain by the fire. Chapter 7 is a separate story in which the building of the tower is actually begun (cf. 7:1 and Gen 11:4a). God sentences the builders to live "like the beasts of the field," and he "changes their appearance" as well as their languages (7:3, 5).

In *3 Baruch* 4, most probably in the third heaven,[38] Baruch sees a serpent, or dragon, and a monster that is identified with Hades.[39] The dragon eats the bodies of the wicked. Between the angel's description of the gluttonous appetite of Hades (4:6) and Baruch's question about it (5:1) there occurs a lengthy discussion about the vine, which was the tree that caused Adam to sin (4:8–17). Verse 15 is patently Christian, at least in its present form. It describes how the cursed vine will be turned to a blessing, when its fruit becomes "the blood of God," that is, of "Jesus Christ, Emmanuel." Scholars debate how much of vv. 8–17 was interpolated by a Christian editor.[40] If we eliminate only v. 15, Baruch's question in v. 9 ("Why has the cursed vine been allowed to continue to exist?") and Noah's prayer ("Shall I replant the vine?" [v. 14]) are not answered. Perhaps the whole section was originally Jewish, and in v. 15 a Christian editor has revised a passage that previously described the transformation of the vine into the Tree of Life.[41] Speaking for the originality of the vine digression are similarities between it and a problem raised in both *2 Baruch* and *4 Ezra*. Reference to the punishment of the wicked and to Hades (*3 Bar.* 4:1–7) leads Baruch to inquire about the cause of Adam's sin (cf. *4 Ezra* 7:117–18). The seer's question in v. 9 and the story that follows may be compared with "Ezra's" puzzlement as to why God continues to allow the evil seed, planted in man's heart, to remain (*4 Ezra* 3:20–22). The story about Noah becomes more specific. How did sin, which God judged in the Flood, survive the Flood? That the author is concerned with sin in general and not just with drunkenness is evident from the catalog in v. 17, which corresponds closely to other catalogs in 8:5 and 13:4. In some way, which is now obscure, this whole section appears to have been a parabolic treatment of the problem raised and discussed variously by *4 Ezra* and *2 Baruch*: the cause of Adam's sin is the cause of the sins of humanity after him;[42] his descendants sin as he sinned and, being responsible, are liable to punishment for their sins.[43]

Chapters 6–9 are primarily cosmological in content. Baruch learns the mechanisms by which God governs the heavenly bodies, and from the Phoenix he learns how God protects all humanity from the lethal rays of the sun (6:1–12). The section, however, is not lacking in the ethical dimension. The sun's rays are defiled by the sins of humanity. Nonetheless, God both renews the light and graciously protects humanity from its scorching heat (chap. 8).

The author returns to the subject of retribution in chap. 10. In the fourth heaven (the text reads "third") Baruch sees the dwelling place of the souls of the righteous, who are depicted as choruses of birds praising God.[44] Again cosmology and eschatology are combined, for this heaven is also the source of "the dew of heaven."

Chapters 11–16 climax the apocalypse. Michael descends from the fifth heaven with a gigantic vessel to collect the virtues of the righteous and present them to God. The angels assigned to the human race appear in three groups. The first have large baskets filled with flowers, which are the virtues. The second group lament that their baskets are only half full. The third group weep and wail because their baskets are empty. They have been assigned to wicked and foolish men, who are guilty of all the vices mentioned in 4:17 and 8:5 (here listed mainly in the order of the Decalogue, with numerous additions).[45] When these angels ask to be assigned to other people, Michael ascends to the divine throne room for instructions.[46] He returns bearing oil, with which he fills the containers of the first group of angels. This is the hundredfold reward of "our friends," who have labored to do good deeds (15:1–2).[47] The second group are given an (unspecified) appropriate reward for "the sons of men" (15:3).[48] The third group hear God's answer to their request (chap. 16). They are commissioned to go and punish the wicked for not listening to God's voice and not keeping his commandments. The finality of the decision is emphasized with the words "the gate was closed" (17:1).

What then are the revealed mysteries of God that transform Baruch's grief over Jerusalem (chap. 1) into the praise of God (chap. 17)? The seer has been given an entrée to a hidden world. In this world he learns that God exercises beneficent control over his creation. He also learns that God rewards his "friends" and punishes the wicked "sons of men." Herein lies "the glory of God," which the seer is told to await (6:12; 7:2; cf. 7:6). On the basis of this glory he can "glorify God" and encourage others to do so (17:3–4). Rewards and punishments are dispensed individually and at the time of death, rather than on a final day of judgment.[49]

But what of the specific questions raised in chap. 1 (see above, p. 299)? That the author has not sidestepped these issues is evident from a close reading of 16:2–4. Verse 2 is a paraphrase, verging on a quotation, of the LXX of Deuteronomy 32:21. Reference to punishment at the hands of a "*non-nation*" and a "foolish *nation*" responds to the seer's question in 1:2, "Why did you deliver us to *nations* such as these?" Moreover, the two verbs in 1:2 ("recompense," *apodidōmi*; "deliver," *paradidōmi*) occur in parallelism in Deuteronomy 32:30. Both 32:21 and 30 refer to God's delivering his people to the Gentiles for punishment. The question "Where is their God?" (1:2) is placed in the mouths of the Gentiles several times in the Bible.[50] In Deuteronomy 32:37 it is presumed in God's ironic query "Where are their [the Gentiles'] gods?" This question is ironic because the nations had made the fatal and "foolish" mistake of assuming that their victory over Israel was due to their own power rather than by permission of the God whom they thought they had defeated (32:27–31). Thus the language of Deuteronomy 32 in both the sage's complaint and the divine sentence indicates that the author answers Baruch's question by interpreting the destruction of Jerusalem and the scattering of the people as punishment for their sins. It is possible that the quotation of Deuteronomy 32:21cd implies 32:21ab and its reference to God's jealousy with Israel's idolatry (cf. *Apoc. Abr.*).

In light of the quotation from Deuteronomy, we may look more closely at chaps. 2–3. Who are the builders of the Tower of Babel and those who planned to build it? The parallel story in the *Biblical Antiquities* 6, and its use of Daniel 3, suggests that the figure of Nebuchadnezzar (Dan 3), mentioned in *3 Baruch* 1:1, may still be in the author's mind in

3 Baruch 2–3. Furthermore, in 2 Maccabees 7:19, 5:21, and 9:10 the motifs of waging war against God (*3 Bar.* 3:7) and of storming heaven are applied to Antiochus Epiphanes's actions against Jerusalem, within an account that is informed by the last chapters of Deuteronomy (see above, pp. 118–21). If we take these parallels into consideration we may have a second answer to Baruch's lament and query. The arrogant victors will be punished, again as Deuteronomy 32:34–43 informs us.[51]

The author's third answer to the problems raised in chap. 1 has been suggested above. The souls of the righteous will receive their reward in heaven.

Thus the author responds to the questions raised in chap. 1 with a triad of answers that parallel those given in *2 Baruch, 4 Ezra,* and the *Apocalypse of Abraham*: the destruction of Jerusalem is punishment for the people's sin; the arrogant victors will be punished; the righteous will receive their reward. A major and significant difference from these other apocalypses lies in this author's silence about a future age and a glorified Jerusalem. The angel's command in 1:3 is never rescinded. The question "Where is their God?" is answered in two ways. He is present in judgment. He is enthroned in his heavenly temple. The hope for a nation reconstituted around Land and Temple is here replaced by an individualized, heavenly eschatology.

Similarities with *2 Baruch* and *4 Ezra* suggest that *3 Baruch* was written around the end of the first or the beginning of the second century C.E. Similarities with one tradition about Titus also may indicate a connection with the Roman destruction of 70.[52] Parallels with Egyptian mythology and with *2 Enoch* suggest that Egypt was the place of composition.[53]

The author speaks to the troubles of his people's hearts. The angel's warning that the seer not "provoke" God (1:6, *paroxynō*) may be yet another allusion to Deuteronomy 32 (vv. 16–19). To complain to God and question his ways is to continue the provocation that led to his punishment of the nation. Conversely, the revelation of God's mysteries—his control of the universe and his judgment—provides the dynamic that opens the mouths of his people (1:7) to speak his praise (17:3–4).

THE GOSPEL ACCORDING TO MATTHEW[54]

The authors of *2 Baruch, 4 Ezra,* the *Apocalypse of Abraham,* and *3 Baruch* concur that the destruction of Jerusalem was punishment for Israel's sin. Only the *Apocalypse of Abraham* appears to emphasize the precise nature of that sin. The Christian author of the First Gospel makes another such specification.

The Gospel according to Matthew, written toward the end of the first century c.e., is the most Jewish of the Gospels. For the author of Matthew, Jesus was the teacher of the Torah par excellence. He was indeed the fulfillment of the Torah and of God's promises through the prophets (5:17–20). More than that, he was God's promised Messiah, the "Son of David" (e.g., 1:1; 9:27; 12:23; 15:22), born "king of the Jews" (2:2). His mission was to "the lost sheep of the house of Israel" (15:24; cf. 10:5–6). This mission, however, was met by Jewish rejection. In 21:28–22:10 Matthew juxtaposes three parables which have in common the idea of reversal. Israel has been stripped of its status as God's people, and the church—largely Gentile in its constituency—has been raised to this position (see esp. 21:43). Climaxing a long history of rejecting the prophets the Jewish leaders have crucified Jesus (21:35–39), and by their assent "the people" have brought a curse upon themselves and their descendants (27:25). The burning of Jerusalem was punishment for this sin (22:6–7). The scenario is foreshadowed in chap. 2, where the Gentiles worship the newborn king of the Jews, whom the reigning monarch seeks to eradicate. The Gospel concludes with the risen Christ commissioning his apostles to make disciples of "all nations" (28:16–20; contrast 10:5–6).

Matthew writes at a time when his Christian community has broken with the synagogue. Although he despises what he perceives to be the hypocritical piety and "lawlessness" of the Pharisees (chap. 23), different from the apostle Paul and his successors, he does not declare the Torah to be null and void. His quarrel with Judaism relates to the nation's rejection of God's superlative envoy, the Messiah, his Son. This rejection notwithstanding, Matthew does not offer an anguished and extended lament, as do 2 *Baruch* and 4 *Ezra*, nor does he write with an eye toward the problem of theodicy, as do all the contemporary apocalyptists in their own ways. Moreover, he does not hope for restoration and reconstruction, nor does he presume at the very least the continued existence of the Jews as God's people. For him as for the Christian editor of 2 Esdras the future lies with God's *new* people, the predominantly Gentile church, and his apocalyptic hope centers around Jesus' return as the exalted Son of Man. In these contrasting hopes and differing appraisals of the year 70 we see the dividing of the ways: the tragic splitting of Christianity from Judaism, the children leaving one Mother for another.

NOTES

1. According to Acts 5:36 Theudas preceded Judas of Galilee.

2. According to Acts 21:38 this Egyptian was a contemporary of Paul.

3. My analysis is indebted to the work of my student, Gwendolyn B. Sayler, *Have the Promises Failed: A Literary Analysis of 2 Baruch* (SBLDS 72; Chico: Scholars Press, 1984).

4. See the discussion of the *Paraleipomena of Jeremiah*, below, pp. 313–16.

5. In the parallel version of this narrative in the *Paraleipomena of Jeremiah* the roles are reversed, as they seem to be in *2 Bar.* 33:1–2.

6. In *Par. Jer.* 4:2 God does not destroy the walls but opens the gate.

7. See Krister Stendahl, "Hate, Non-Retaliation, and Love: 1 QS x, 17–20 and Romans 12:19–21," *HTR* 55 (1962) 343–55.

8. For this formula see above, pp. 32–33 and 210–12. Cf. *Ps. Sol.* 3, which contrasts God's chastisement of the righteous and his punishment of the sinner.

9. Cf. *1 Enoch* 10:16–11:2.

10. See Nickelsburg, *Resurrection*, 84–85.

11. Cf. *Par. Jer.* 7.

12. See, e.g., G. H. Box, "IV Ezra," *APOT* 2:553–54.

13. Pierre-Maurice Bogaert (*Apocalypse de Baruch*, 1:294–95) suggests the year 96.

14. For arguments in favor of a Semitic original see Charles, *APOT* 2:472–74. Bogaert (*Apocalypse*, 1:378–80) favors Greek as the original language and suggests that the book was written for circulation in the Dispersion.

15. Esdras is the Greek form of the Hebrew name Ezra. Because Saint Jerome included 2 Esdras in his Latin translation of the Bible (the Vulgate) it has come to be included in the Apocrypha. The Latin manuscripts generally separate the Jewish core of this work from its Christian additions, giving each its own enumeration, which is often as follows:

The canonical Ezra-Nehemiah	= 1 Ezra
2 Esdras 1–2 of our Apocrypha	= 2 Ezra
1 Esdras of our Apocrypha	= 3 Ezra
2 Esdras 3–14 of our Apocrypha	= 4 Ezra
2 Esdras 15–16 of our Apocrypha	= 5 Ezra

16. Cf. Ezra 3:2 and 5:2; Neh 12:1.

17. The identification is explicit in *4 Ezra* 3:1, but this may be an explanatory gloss by a scribe. Ezra's name is mentioned in 6:10; 7:2, 25; 8:2, 20; and 14:2, 38, as well as in the Christian addition in 1:1 and 2:10, 33, 42.

18. For a thorough discussion of this problem see Wolfgang Harnisch, *Verhängnis und Verheissung der Geschichte*, passim.

19. On this passage see Nickelsburg, *Resurrection*, 138–40.

20. One brief treatment of the subject occurs in *1 Enoch* 22, on which see Nickelsburg, ibid., 134–37.

21. My observations here are indebted to the important article by Earl Breech, "These Fragments I Have Shored against My Ruins: The Form and Function of 4 Ezra."

22. On the messianic teaching of *4 Ezra* see Michael Stone, "The Concept of the Messiah in IV Ezra."

23. See, e.g., E. P. Sanders, *Paul and Palestinian Judaism* (Philadelphia: Fortress, 1977) 409–18, who stresses the difference between *4 Ezra*'s view of the few and the many and the covenantal theology that was typical of Palestinian Judaism.

24. These versions include the Syriac, Ethiopic, Arabic, Armenian, and Georgian, as well as the Latin of the Vulgate.

25. The author's imagery about the mother sending her children off and the mother receiving her children back draws on the Jewish traditions about Mother Zion, attested in Baruch and 2 Macc 7, on which see above, pp. 112–13, 121. The immediate contextual reference, however, is *4 Ezra* 9–10.

26. Cf. Isa 44:9–20, Bel and the Dragon, and Ep Jer.

27. Gershom Scholem, *Major Trends in Jewish Mysticism* (New York: Schocken, 1971) 68–69.

28. Cf. Zech 3; *Jub.* 17:16–18:16; 48; Mark 1:12–13; 8:32–33.

29. Scholem, *Major Trends,* 61.

30. Cf. *1 Enoch* 85–90; see above, pp. 91–93.

31. On the heavenly temple and throne see above, pp. 52–53.

32. Since chap. 27 blames the destruction of Jerusalem and the Temple on idolatrous cult, and since the present section makes no connection between the Jewish rejection of Jesus and the destruction, it is unlikely that this section is original to the *Apocalypse,* which would then by definition be of Christian origin.

33. On the Elect One see above, pp. 215–21.

34. G. H. Box (*The Apocalypse of Abraham*) mentions many of these parallels in his notes.

35. On the recensions of the Slavonic text see Émile Turdeanu, "L'Apocalypse d'Abraham en Slave." On the Greek see Box, *Apocalypse,* xv. On the Hebrew see Arie Rubinstein, "Hebraisms in the Slavonic 'Apocalypse of Abraham.'"

36. Verse 2 of the prologue, which alludes to the tradition about Agrippa's garden in *Par. Jer.* (see below, pp. 313–14), is probably a later interpolation; see Hughes, *APOT* 2:528.

37. Origen (*De princip.* 2.3.6) mentions an apocalypse of Baruch with seven heavens. Our discussion here has not dealt with the indemonstrable possibility that *3 Baruch* is a truncated version of the apocalypse mentioned by Origen. See J.-C. Picard, *Apocalypsis Baruch Graece,* 77.

38. Baruch speaks of the third heaven in 10:1 and the fifth in 11:1. Evidently 10:1 should read "fourth." The formula in 4:1–2, compared with 2:1–2 and 3:1–2, suggests entrance to a new (third) heaven at 4:1–2.

39. On the problems of the identification and relationship between these two

monsters see Ulrich Fischer, *Eschatologie und Jenseitserwartung im hellenis-tischen Diasporajudentum*, 80–82.

40. See the discussion in ibid., 72–74.

41. See Picard, *Apocalypsis*, 76. For a parallel see the difficult and not unrelated passages in *Adam and Eve* 42:1–5 and *Apoc. Mos.* 13:3–5.

42. Cf. *4 Ezra* 3:20–22.

43. Cf. *4 Ezra* 7:117–18; *2 Bar.* 48:42–43; 54:15. It is also possible that Baruch's question in *3 Bar.* 5:2 is related to the discussion in *2 Bar.* 21:19–23:7. J.-C. Picard ("Observations sur l'apocalypse grecque de Baruch") thinks that the author still has Jerusalem *qua* vineyard (1:2) in mind here. However, for the vine as the tree that caused Adam's sin cf. *Apoc. Abr.* 23, *b. Ber.* 40a, *b. Sanh.* 70, and *Gen. Rab.* 19:5.

44. A comparison of 10:5 and 7 suggests that the birds are the souls, although the equation is not explicit.

45. The lists combine specific sins against the Decalogue with vices at home in such catalogs as Gal 5:19–21.

46. This feature is a frequent structuring device in *T. Abr.*

47. Cf. the motif of the eschatological gift of the oil of mercy in *Apoc. Mos.* 13:1–5.

48. 15:4 is a Christian interpolation based on Matt 25:21–23, quite understandable in view of the threefold division in the Matthean parable.

49. See Fischer, *Eschatologie*, 76–84.

50. Cf. Ps 42:10; 79:10; 115:2; Joel 2:17; Mic 7:10, cited by Picard, "Observations," 78, n. 2.

51. That the enemies should be in a special place of punishment is paralleled in *2 Enoch*, where the two groups of rebel angels are located in places of punishment different from the wicked in general.

52. Cf. *b. Giṭ.* 56b, where Titus quotes Deut 32:37, blasphemes heaven, and slashes the Temple curtain with his sword.

53. On the Phoenix and Egyptian mythology, as well as on parallels in Greek mythology, see Hughes, *APOT* 2:527. Parallels with *2 Enoch* include the ascent through the heavens, the combined cosmic and eschatological contents of these spheres, the heaven-earth dualism of the two apocalypses, and the specific references to the mythology of the Phoenix.

54. In this section I briefly summarize my article "Good News/Bad News: The Messiah and God's Fractured Community," *CurTM* 4 (1977) 324–32.

BIBLIOGRAPHY

HISTORY

Schürer, *History*, 1:455–528. David M. Rhoads, *Israel in Revolution: 5–74 C.E. A Political History Based on the Writings of Josephus* (Philadelphia: Fortress, 1976) 68–181. E. Mary Smallwood, *The Jews under Roman Rule*, SJLA 20 (Leiden: Brill, 1976) 256–355. Jacob Neusner, "The Formation of Rabbinic Judaism: Yavneh (Jamnia) from A.D. 70–100," in *Aufstieg und Niedergang der römischen Welt* (Berlin: de Gruyter, 1979), 2:19, 2, pp. 3–42.

2 BARUCH

TRANSLATION: A. F. J. **Klijn**, *PsOT*.

TEXTS, OTHER TRANSLATIONS, LITERATURE: Antonius M. **Ceriani**, "Apocalypsis Baruch Syriace," *Monumenta Sacra et Profana* (Mediolani: Bibliotheca Ambrosiana, 1871) 5:113–80, *editio princeps* of the Syriac text of chaps. 1–87. S. **Dedering**, "Apocalypse of Baruch," *The Old Testament in Syriac*, 4:3 (Leiden: Brill, 1973) 1–50, the Syriac text of chaps. 1–77. R. H. **Charles**, *The Apocalypse of Baruch* (London: Black, 1896), introduction, annotated translation, the Syriac text of chaps. 78–86. Idem, *APOT* 2:470–526. Pierre-Maurice **Bogaert**, *Apocalypse de Baruch*, SC 144–45 (Paris: Le Cerf, 1969), introduction, French translation, commentary.

4 EZRA

TRANSLATION: The Apocrypha.

TEXTS: Bruno **Violet**, *Die Ezra-Apokalypse*, I: *Die Überlieferungen*, GCS 18 (Leipzig: Hinrichs, 1910), critical edition of the Latin; German and Latin translations of the other versions. Robertus **Weber**, ed., *Biblia Sacra Iuxta Vulgatam Versionem* (Stuttgart: Würtembergische Bibelanstalt, 1969) 2:1931–74, critical edition of the Latin based on Violet.

LITERATURE: G. H. **Box**, *APOT* 2:542–624, translation with text-critical and exegetical notes. Bruno **Violet**, *Die Apokalypsen des Esra und des Baruch in deutscher Gestalt*, GCS 32 (Leipzig: Hinrichs, 1924), extensive introduction German translation, commentary. Wolfgang **Harnisch**, *Verhängnis und Verheissung der Geschichte*, FRLANT 97 (Göttingen: Vandenhoeck & Ruprecht, 1969), a study of the interpretation of time and history in *4 Ezra* and *2 Baruch*. Earl **Breech**, "These Fragments I Have Shored against My Ruins: The Form and Function of 4 Ezra," *JBL* 92 (1973) 267–74. Alden L. **Thompson**, *Responsibility for Evil in the Theodicy of IV Ezra*, SBLDS 29 (Missoula: Scholars Press, 1977). Michael **Stone**, "The Concept of the Messiah in IV Ezra," in *Religions in Antiquity*, ed. Jacob Neusner, Fs. E. R. Goodenough (Leiden: Brill, 1968) 295–312.

THE APOCALYPSE OF ABRAHAM

TRANSLATION: R. **Rubinkiewcz**, *PsOT*.

TEXT, OTHER TRANSLATION, LITERATURE: On the Slavonic text and manuscripts, see Emile **Turdeanu**, "L'Apocalypse d'Abraham en Slave," *JSJ* 3 (1975) 153–80. G. H. **Box**, *The Apocalypse of Abraham* (London: SPCK, 1919), introduction, translation, textual and exegetical notes. Arie **Rubinstein**, "Hebraisms in the Slavonic 'Apocalypse of Abraham,'" *JJS* 5 (1954) 108–15.

3 BARUCH

TRANSLATION: Harry E. **Gaylord,** *PsOT*.

TEXTS AND OTHER TRANSLATIONS: Montague Rhodes **James,** *"The Apocalypse of Baruch,"* TextsS 5:1 (Cambridge: University Press, 1897) li-lxxi, 84–102, detailed introduction, Greek text, and English translation of the Slavonic version by W. R. Morfill. J.-C. **Picard,** *Apocalypsis Baruch Graece,* PVTG 2 (Leiden: Brill, 1967) 61–96, critical edition of the Greek text. H. M. **Hughes,** *APOT* 2:527–41.

LITERATURE: J.-C. **Picard,** "Observations sur l'apocalypse grecque de Baruch," *Sem* 20 (1970) 77–103, a hermeneutical discussion prelude to a commentary on *3 Baruch*. Ulrich **Fischer,** *Eschatologie und Jenseitserwartung im hellenistischen Diasporajudentum,* BZNW 44 (Berlin: de Gruyter, 1978) 71–84, discussion of eschatology with careful attention to critical problems.

9

The Second Revolt

THE EVENTS

Sources provide relatively little information about events in Palestine during the fifty-five years after the fall of Masada (74–129 C.E.). Palestine was ruled by Roman governors, but we know little more than the names of some of them. Religious authority resided in the academy that Yoḥanan ben Zakkai had established in Jamnia. Yoḥanan's successor, Rabban Gamaliel II, appears to have received Roman permission for the academy to function also as a civil court.

In the last years of the reign of Trajan, 115–117 C.E., revolt against Rome flared up in the Jewish communities in the western Mediterranean. The sources mention Egypt, Cyrene, Cyprus, and Mesopotamia. Palestine, however, appears to have remained quiet, but the country would have one last, ill-fated turn at rebellion.

The causes of the Second Revolt are disputed.[1] In the years 129–131 the emperor Hadrian traveled through the East. In conjunction with his travels, cities were "founded," buildings were constructed, coins were struck, and games and cults were instituted. Up to this time Jerusalem lay in ruins, serving as the location of a Roman army camp. In connection with Hadrian's trip through Syria in 130, the site was refounded as "Aelia Capitolina," after Hadrian's family name, Aelius. Although the Jews must have bitterly resented the establishment of their former capital as a Roman colony, the storm did not break until 132 C.E.

Sometime in the latter half of his reign Hadrian issued a ban against circumcision, which he considered to be a barbaric custom. The prohibition was not directed against the Jews in particular; others in the Near East practiced the rite. For the Jews, however, the ban struck at the heart of their religion; it forbade the sign of the covenant. While the

311

date of Hadrian's decree is uncertain, we may reasonably deduce from the sources that the ban was a major precipitating cause of the Revolt.[2]

The leader of the Revolt was Simeon bar Kosibah. He was acclaimed *nasi* (prince) of Israel. According to Christian sources his nickname was bar Kokhba—"son of the star," a messianic title drawn from Balaam's prophecy in Numbers 24:17, "a star shall come forth out of Jacob."[3] According to Jewish tradition it was the prominent contemporary rabbi Akiba who coined this nickname. Some Jewish sources after the Revolt called him bar Koziba, "son of the lie," thus mocking him as a pretender or deceiver.

Information about the conduct and extent of the Revolt is spotty. Some very specific information is provided by a series of letters from and to Simeon, which have been recovered from caves in Judea that served as refuges for the rebels in the last days of the war. These letters provide specific names and places, but they are very few. The war spread through the Roman province of Judea. The rebels fought guerrilla-style, operating from strongholds, forts, caves, and underground galleries. Whether they actually held Jerusalem is a disputed point.[4] That it was their goal is evident from the slogan on Simeon's coins, "For the freedom of Jerusalem."

After three years of fighting, the rebels made their last stand at Beth Ter, a stronghold some ten kilometers west-southwest of Jerusalem, where a protracted siege brought the war to an end. Thereafter followed the mop-up work of searching out those rebels who had fled into remote caves. Many starved to death, leaving their possessions and documents to be found by archeologists in the present century.

The war was bitter and costly. According to Dio Cassius, the Roman historian,

> fifty of their most important outposts and nine hundred and eighty-five of their most famous villages were razed to the ground. Five hundred and eighty thousand men were slain in the various raids and battles, and the number of those that perished by famine, disease and fire was past finding out. Thus nearly the whole of Judea was made desolate.[5]

Even allowing for considerable exaggeration the war was a disaster, striking a second terrible blow in sixty years.

As part of his reprisals for the Revolt, Hadrian forbade the Jews access to Jerusalem. The city was, however, rebuilt in style as a Roman colony. Pagan temples marked the city that had once been the site of the sanctuary of the God of Israel. The ban on circumcision continued through Hadrian's reign but was lifted by his successor, Antoninus Pius, perhaps near the beginning of his reign (138 C.E.). By the beginning of the fourth century Jews were permitted to enter Jerusalem once a year to mourn the loss of the capital and sanctuary. Despite this loss and through these tears—neither of them atypical of the centuries we have been discussing —the rabbis preserved, transformed, and passed on to future generations the religion of their ancestors.

THE PARALEIPOMENA OF JEREMIAH
("THE THINGS OMITTED FROM JEREMIAH")

This writing is based on those parts of Jeremiah that describe the last days of Jerusalem. The action begins on the eve of Nebuchadnezzar's conquest. The Lord addresses Jeremiah, commanding him and Baruch to leave the city because he is about to deliver it to the Chaldeans on account of the sins of its inhabitants. At Jeremiah's request God agrees to open the gates, lest the enemy boast of their ability to conquer "the holy city of God" (1:4–11).[6] As Jeremiah and Baruch await a divine sign confirming the impending destruction, they see angels descend from heaven with torches ready to set fire to the city. Again at Jeremiah's request God commands the prophet to commit the sacred vessels to the earth "until the gathering of the beloved [people]" (3:4–11; cf. 4:9).[7] When Jeremiah asks that Abimelech (*Ebed-melech*) be spared the sight of the city's destruction God bids the prophet to send Abimelech into the vineyard of Agrippa, where he will be hidden "until I cause the people to return to the city" (3:12–14; cf. Jer 39:15–18). Jeremiah and Baruch consign the sacred vessels to the earth, which swallows them up. In the morning Jeremiah sends Abimelech to Agrippa's property to gather figs. There the servant falls asleep for sixty-six years. Meanwhile the Chaldean army surrounds Jerusalem. The city gates are found open. Jeremiah hurls the Temple keys at the sun, exhorting it to take custody of them "until the day that the Lord asks for them" (4:4–5). Jeremiah is taken captive to Babylon while Baruch is left behind in the environs of Jerusalem.

After sixty-six years Abimelech wakes from his sleep and, finding the figs still fresh, supposes that he has taken a brief siesta. A local inhabitant informs him that sixty-six years have passed since the people were taken captive. Abimelech shows him the fresh figs, and they conclude that a miracle has occurred because it is not the season for figs. An angel appears to Abimelech, in answer to his prayer, and leads him to Baruch, who interprets the miracle as proof that the time has come for the people to return to the city. (It is also a sign of the resurrection of the body; 6:6–10.) In response to Baruch's prayer an angel appears and dictates a letter Baruch is to send via eagle to Jeremiah in Babylon:

> . . . Let the stranger . . . be set apart and let fifteen days go by; and after this I will lead you into your city. . . . He who is not separated from Babylon will not enter into the city; and I will punish them by keeping them from being received back by the Babylonians (6:16–17; Kraft-Purintun).

Moreover, Baruch writes,

> you will test them by means of the water of the Jordan; whoever does not listen will be exposed—this is the sign of the great seal (6:25; Kraft-Purintun).

The divinely sent eagle carries the letter to Jeremiah, who reads it to the exiles and sends a reply to Baruch, describing the terrible plight of the exiles. In their despair they even pray to a foreign god for deliverance (7:24–29).

Jeremiah exhorts the people "to abstain from the pollutions of the Gentiles of Babylon" (7:37; Kraft-Purintun). Soon he receives God's command to lead the people out of Babylon to the Jordan, where they must "forsake the works of Babylon" (8:1–3). Specifically, they are to abandon foreign spouses. Those who refuse to do so are forbidden entrance into Jerusalem. Returning to Babylon they are rejected there, and so they found the city of Samaria. Jeremiah once more calls on them to repent (8:7–12).

In the Temple, after Jeremiah has offered special sacrifices and prayer, he appears to die; however, in three days he is revived, and he begins to describe a vision about "the son of God, the Messiah, Jesus." The people attempt to stone him for blasphemy, but he is miraculously protected until he has transmitted the entire contents of his vision to Baruch and Abimelech. Then he is stoned to death,[8] and Baruch and Abimelech bury him.

Essential to this story are the problem of destruction and exile and the hope of return and restoration. The author takes up his narrative on the eve of destruction and exile, and he concludes it when the return has

taken place and the problem with which the story began has been resolved.[9] Moreover, at a number of points in the first part of the story,
return and restoration are the last events in the author's purview (3:11,
14, 15). The literary function of the Abimelech incident is to provide a
transition from exile to return.

This emphasis in the story suggests that the author is concerned with
some similar problem in his own time. In the apocalypses of *4 Ezra* and
2 Baruch Nebuchadnezzar's destruction of Jerusalem was viewed as a
prototype of the destruction of 70 C.E. (see above, pp. 281, 287). A similar
typology seems to be operative here.[10] Within this context the author uses
the Abimelech story to assert that there will be a second return and
restoration sixty-six years after the second destruction, that is, in 136 C.E.
Quite possibly he expects this return to be "the gathering of the beloved"
people of God, that is, the return of the Dispersion and the final restoration of Jerusalem.

In preparation for this return the readers are to purify themselves of
the works of the places of their exile (here called Babylon). They are to
abstain from Gentile defilement and to divorce foreign spouses, a require-
ment enforced by Ezra and Nehemiah after the first return (Ezra 9–10;
Neh 13:23–27). Since Jerusalem is a holy city and Israel is a holy people,
defilement caused by contact with pagan spouses cannot be tolerated.[11]
Samaria is thus identified as the home of a half-breed people. The author's
attitude is not, however, wholly unconciliatory, and he may be making an
appeal to the Samaritans. An important event in the end-time, according
to some traditions, was to be the reunification of the twelve tribes.[12]

The precise date of writing is uncertain. The year 136 C.E. is one year
after Hadrian crushed the Second Revolt and issued an edict forbidding
Jews to enter Jerusalem. There is no explicit reference to the war in this
writing, although it is possible that that author intends Nebuchadnezzar's
destruction to be typical of the defeats of both 70 and 135. In such an
event the writing would have been composed between 135 and 136. It is
also possible that it was written a short time before the Second Revolt.

Scholarly opinion is divided on whether the writing was originally
Jewish or Christian. In its present form it is clearly Christian, as is evident from Jeremiah's revelation in chap. 9. On this level the ordeal at the
Jordan is to be interpreted as Christian baptism. Only the baptized can
enter the holy city. It has been suggested that the writing was composed

as an eirenicon, or peace offer, from Christians to Jews, exhorting the latter to accept baptism and thus to renounce the Jewish faith that prevented them from returning to their home city.[13] According to a variation on this hypothesis the book was written by Jewish Christians to other Jewish Christians.[14] These interesting possibilities notwithstanding, there is much to commend the view that the *Paraleipomena of Jeremiah* is a Jewish composition.[15] The sign of the great seal at the Jordan (6:25) could be circumcision.[16] The author likens the return from Babylon to the Exodus, and Jeremiah's role is analogous to those of Moses and Joshua.[17] The ordeal at the Jordan may be intended as a parallel to the circumcisions at Gilgal (Josh 5:2–9). Supporting the hypothesis of Jewish composition is the total lack of clear Christian allusions in the references to the *eschaton* in chaps. 1–8. The author awaits the gathering of Israel and the reconstitution of the Jerusalem cult, not the appearance of Jesus the Messiah. This latter idea occurs only in chap. 9, which probably does not belong to the original form of the book. Thematically and structurally, the plot is resolved when Jeremiah leads the people back to Jerusalem. The story of his "second death" appears to be influenced by other traditions, including the *Martyrdom of Isaiah*[18] (see above, pp. 142–43). If we accept the hypothesis of a Jewish origin the book appears to be an appeal to the Jews to prepare themselves for a return to Jerusalem by divesting themselves of Gentile practices and associations: mixed marriages, perhaps uncircumcision, perhaps some form of idolatry or participation in pagan cult.[19]

Our author has made use of earlier traditions. Parallels with *2 Baruch* suggest that this apocalypse may have been the source in question.[20] There is, however, some evidence that the authors of the *Paraleipomena of Jeremiah* and *2 Baruch* have used a common source, which was written in the name of Jeremiah and explained the events leading up to the destruction of Jerusalem in 587.[21] Second Maccabees 2:1–8 makes reference to such a written tradition. It is one of two stories in 2 Maccabees 1–2 that are concerned with the cessation of the Jerusalem cult in 587 and its reinstitution after the Exile and that are recounted in connection with the celebration of Judas's purification of the Temple after its defilement by Antiochus IV. It is altogether possible that a pseudo-Jeremianic account of the fall of Jerusalem originating during the time of Antiochus formed the basis for the narratives in *2 Baruch* and the *Paraleipomena of Jeremiah.*

NOTES

1. See Joseph A. Fitzmyer, "The Bar Cochba Period," 317–24; Schürer, *History*, 534–43; Yigael Yadin, "Bar Kochba," 90; E. Mary Smallwood, *The Jews under Roman Rule*, 428–38; Glen W. Bowersock, "A Roman Perspective on the Bar Kochba War."

2. See Schürer, *History*, 536–40; Bowersock, "A Roman Perspective," 138.

3. For the "messianic" use of this passage see Fitzmyer, "Bar Cochba," 315–16.

4. That the rebels took Jerusalem is generally assumed. See Schürer, *History*, 545–46; Yadin, "Bar Kochba," 90; Smallwood, *The Jews*, 443–45. See, however, the arguments presented by Bowersock, "A Roman Perspective." These arguments do not take into consideration the *possible* reading, "Jerusalem," in two of the bar Kokhba letters; see DJD 2:205, cited by Fitzmyer, "Bar Cochba," 335.

5. *Rom. Hist.* 69.14.1–2; translation by Earnest Cary, *Dio's Roman History*, Loeb Classical Library, vol. 8 (Cambridge: Harvard University, 1925).

6. Chapter and verse numbering and translations follow the edition of R. A. Kraft and A.-E. Purintun.

7. On the meaning of this expression see Gerhard Delling, *Jüdische Lehre und Frömmigkeit in den Paraleipomena Jeremiae*, 65–67.

8. Cf. *Vita Ieremiae* 1; cf. Heb 11:37.

9. See the discussion of Baruch above, pp. 110–13, for a similar pattern.

10. For a date early in the second century C.E. see J. Rendel Harris, *The Rest of the Words of Baruch*, 1–25; Delling, *Lehre*, 2–3; Pierre-Maurice Bogaert, *Apocalypse de Baruch*, 1:220–21.

11. On the problem of mixed marriages in our literature see Delling, *Lehre*, 42–44.

12. Cf., e.g., *4 Ezra* 13:39–45; *2 Bar.* 78; *T. Napht.* 6–7.

13. Harris, *Baruch*, 13–17.

14. Bogaert, *Apocalypse*, 1:216–21.

15. Delling, *Lehre*, 68–74; Michael E. Stone, "Baruch, Rest of the Words of," 276–77.

16. Stone, "Baruch," 276. On this use of "seal" as a designation of circumcision see G. Fitzer, "σφραγίς," *TDNT* 7:947.

17. For parallels to the Exodus cf. 6:23–25; 7:20. The crossing of the Jordan and entrance into the city are reminiscent of the book of Joshua. Other Exodus reminiscences occur in another form of the tradition of the temple vessels in 2 Macc 2, on which see below, n. 21. Cf. also *Vita Ieremiae* 11–15.

18. Delling, *Lehre*, 14–16.

19. Ibid., 42–53.

20. Bogaert, *Apocalypse*, 1:177–221.

21. Nickelsburg, "Narrative Traditions in the Paraleipomena of Jeremiah and 2 Baruch," 60–68.

BIBLIOGRAPHY

HISTORY

Schürer, *History*, 1:529–57. E. Mary **Smallwood**, *The Jews under Roman Rule*, SJLA 20 (Leiden: Brill, 1976) 389–466. Joseph A. **Fitzmyer**, "The Bar Cochba Period," in *Essays on the Semitic Background of the New Testament*, SBLSBS 5 (Missoula: Scholars Press, 1974) 305–54. Yigael **Yadin**, *Bar Kochba* (New York: Random House, 1971). Idem, "Bar Kochba," *IDBSup* 89–92. Glen W. **Bowersock**, "A Roman Perspective on the Bar Kochba War," *Approaches to Ancient Judaism* 2 (Brown Judaic Series 9; Missoula: Scholars Press, 1980) 131–41.

THE PARALEIPOMENA OF JEREMIAH

TRANSLATIONS AND TEXTS: Robert A. **Kraft** and Ann-Elizabeth **Purintun**, *Paraleipomena Jeremiou*, SBLTT 1, Ps. Ser. 1 (Missoula: Society of Biblical Literature, 1972), Greek text with a facing translation, extensive annotated bibliography. J. Rendel **Harris**, *The Rest of the Words of Baruch* (London: Clay, 1889), introduction, critical edition of the Greek text. S. E. **Robinson**, *PsOT*.

LITERATURE: Gerhard **Delling**, *Jüdische Lehre und Frömmigkeit in den Paraleipomena Jeremiae*, BZAW 100 (Berlin: Töpelmann, 1967), theology and other contents. Pierre-Maurice **Bogaert**, *Apocalypse de Baruch* 1, SC 144 (Paris: Le Cerf, 1969) 177–221, *Par. Jer.* and its relationship to *2 Baruch*. Michael E. **Stone**, "Baruch, Rest of the Words of," *EncJud* 4:267–77. George W. E. **Nickelsburg**, Jr., "Narrative Traditions in the Paraleipomena of Jeremiah and 2 Baruch," *CBQ* 35 (1973) 60–68.

Charts

MAJOR FIGURES IN THE SELEUCID DYNASTY

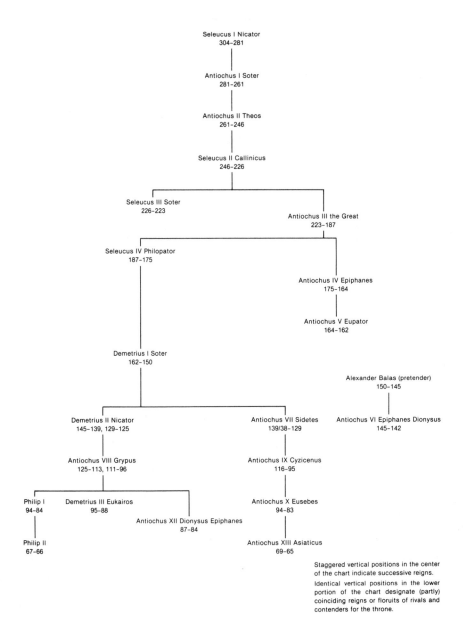

Seleucus I Nicator
304–281

Antiochus I Soter
281–261

Antiochus II Theos
261–246

Seleucus II Callinicus
246–226

Seleucus III Soter
226–223

Antiochus III the Great
223–187

Seleucus IV Philopator
187–175

Antiochus IV Epiphanes
175–164

Antiochus V Eupator
164–162

Demetrius I Soter
162–150

Alexander Balas (pretender)
150–145

Demetrius II Nicator
145–139, 129–125

Antiochus VII Sidetes
139/38–129

Antiochus VI Epiphanes Dionysus
145–142

Antiochus VIII Grypus
125–113, 111–96

Antiochus IX Cyzicenus
116–95

Philip I
94–84

Demetrius III Eukairos
95–88

Antiochus X Eusebes
94–83

Antiochus XII Dionysus Epiphanes
87–84

Philip II
67–66

Antiochus XIII Asiaticus
69–65

Staggered vertical positions in the center
of the chart indicate successive reigns.

Identical vertical positions in the lower
portion of the chart designate (partly)
coinciding reigns or floruits of rivals and
contenders for the throne.

THE HASMONEAN HOUSE

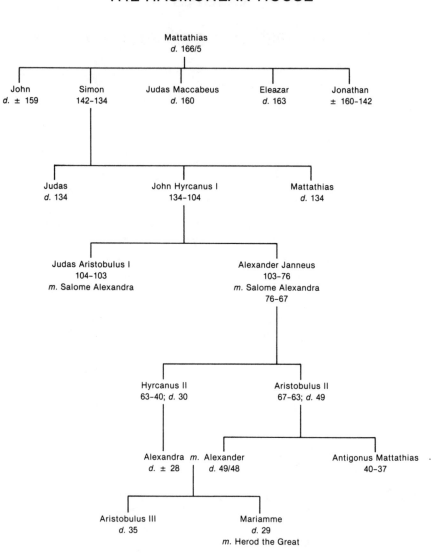

Mattathias
d. 166/5

John
d. ± 159

Simon
142–134

Judas Maccabeus
d. 160

Eleazar
d. 163

Jonathan
± 160–142

Judas
d. 134

John Hyrcanus I
134–104

Mattathias
d. 134

Judas Aristobulus I
104–103
m. Salome Alexandra

Alexander Janneus
103–76
m. Salome Alexandra
76–67

Hyrcanus II
63–40; *d.* 30

Aristobulus II
67–63; *d.* 49

Alexandra   *m.* Alexander
d. ± 28   *d.* 49/48

Antigonus Mattathias
40–37

Aristobulus III
d. 35

Mariamme
d. 29
m. Herod the Great

d. = died
m. = married

THE HOUSE OF HEROD

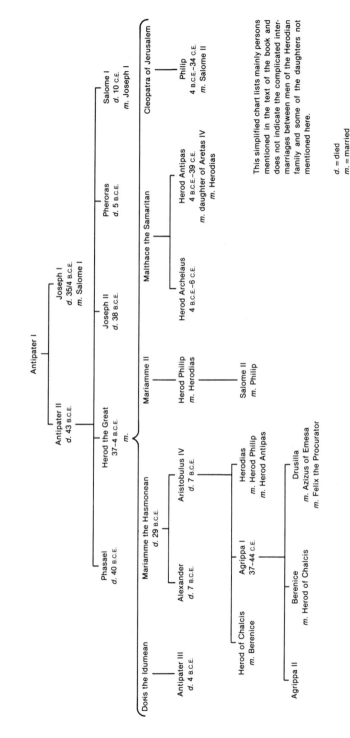

Index of Subjects

Boldface type indicates works treated in this book and page numbers of the major discussions of these works. A few citations enclosed in parentheses ( ) indicate that the subject is mentioned not on the book page but in a text referred to on that page.

Abel, 182, 252–53, 255, 256, 270 n. 44, 296
Abraham, 74, 75–76, 77, 91, 95 n. 5, 124, 146, 163, 182, 199, 226, 232, 240, 247–48, 263–65, 266, 300
Abraham, Apocalypse of, 183, 294–99, 303
Abraham, Testament of, 248–53, 255
Adam, sin of, 283, 285–87, 290, 293, 300–301
Adam (and Eve), 74, 93, 182
Adam and Eve, Life of, 256–57. *See also* Moses, Apocalypse of
Agrippa I, 201–2, 277
Agrippa II, 202
Ahikar, Story of, 23, 39 nn. 14–15, 161
Akra, 72, 103
Albinus, 278
Alcimus, 101–2, 113, 116
Alexander (son of Aristobulus II), 196–97
Alexander Balas, 102, 116
Alexander Janneus, 104, 117, 121, 130–31, 149, 195, 196
Alexander the Great, 16, 43–44, 45–46, 52, 85, 163–64
Alexandra, Salome, 104, 195
Alexandria, 46, 165–66, 170, 172, 184, 201–2
Amram, 233–34, 266
Angels, 18 n. 5, 40 n. 41, 84, 86, 88–89, 177; agents of judgment, 36, 76, 88–89, 91, 119, 215, 218–20, 254, 301, 313; chorus, 216, 248, 270 n. 37, 295; fall of, 49–54, 76, 91, 93, 146, 186, 215, 218–20, 264; guides, interpreters, revealers, 30–32, 34, 47, 54–55, 75, 91, 97 n. 46, 146, 151, 185–86, 214, 216–20, 236, 242, 249–51, 254–55, 285, 288–91, 295–96, 299–301, 314; intercessors, scribes, helpers, or patrons,

30–32, 36, 50, 75, 84–85, 88–89, 91, 92, 148, 150–51, 217, 236, 253, 301; of God's presence, 73, 75; opposition of two angels, 75, 88–90, 237, 248 (*see also* Dualism, angelic); presence at Qumran, 126, 140–41; priests, 53–54; Gabriel, 50, 84, 86, 91, 215; Michael, 50, 88–89, 91, 92, 215, 248–51, 254; 257, 259, 261, 301; Phanuel, 215; Raguel, 91; Ramiel, 285; Raphael, 30–32, 34, 50, 91, 215; Remiel, 91; Sariel, 50, 91; Uriel, 47, 75, 91, 150–51, 288–89; Yahoel, 295. *See also* Satan
Anointed One, 12, 13–14, 18 n. 3 (defined), 86, 207, 217, 222. *See also* Messiah
Antigonus (son of Aristobulus II), 196–98
Antioch (Syria), 101, 200, 226
Antiochus III, 45, 71, 88, 169
Antiochus IV, 64, 71–73, 80, 84, 101, 120, 164, 205; persecution of, 10, 28–29, 35, 72–73, 77, 79, 81–82, 85–86, 88–90, 92–94, 113, 114–15, 118–19, 133, 143–44, 178–79, 213, 224–26, 277, 316
Antiochus V, 101, 113
Antipas, 200, 213
Antipater (father of Herod the Great), 195, 197
Antony, Marc, 196–97, 199, 203
Apocalypse of Abraham. See Abraham, Apocalypse of
Apocalypse of Moses. See Moses, Apocalypse of
Apocalypse of Weeks. See *1 Enoch* 9͟2–105
Apocalyptic eschatology, 13, 15, 18 n. 5, 95, 126–27, 203, 208–9
Apocalyptic literature, 46–55, 73–95,

323

137–41, 204–12. *See also* Conversion;
Exaltation; Future life; Judgment;
Restoration
Samaria: city, 9, 44, ʾ03, 199, 314–15;
territory, 46, 109, 201, 202; Samaritans,
9, 40 n. 43, 103, 201, 236, 277, 315
Sariel. *See* Angels
Satan, 78, 82, 90, 123, 143–44, 205, 241–
46, 256; ʿAsael, 52, 91, 215, 218;
Azazel, 52, 215, 218–19, 295, 297–98;
Belial, 125, 138, 140; Beliar, 142–43,
163, 233, 234, 237, 239; demons, 52,
157 n. 133; devil, 257, 259, 263; evil
spirits, 53, 76; *masṭēmā*, prince of, 75,
248; Shemiḥazah, 50, 52, 91, 215
Scribes, 15, 52, 55, 60, 66 n. 24, 292
Sectarianism, 123, 128–29, 133–34, 140–
42, 188
Seleucids, 20, 45, 71, 88, 92, 103, 214
Seleucus I, 45
Seleucus IV, 71, 101
Septuagint, ix, 161, 165–68
Servant of the Lord, 12, 13, 14, 89, 121,
138, 179, 217, 219–20, 222, 223, 228
n. 34
Seth, 253–57
Sexual relations, 50, 59, 62, 74–75, 162,
166, 177, 183, 186, 205, 212, 234, 238,
239, 240
Shechem, 75, 103, 235, 236, 260
Shemiḥazah. *See* Satan
Sheol, 140, 148, 179. *See also* Hades
Sibyl, 162 (defined)
Sibylline Oracles, book 3, **162–65**, 183
Sicarii, 278, 280
Simeon (patriarch), 75, 107, 152 n. 10,
236, 268 n. 10, 260
*Simeon, Testament of. See Twelve
Patriarchs, Testaments of the*
Simon (Hasmonean), 73, 102–3, 114,
116–17, 121, 123, 129, 132, 196
Simon the Just (high priest), 62, 64,
169, 235, 236
Sinai, Mount, 73, 82
Sirach. *See* Jesus the Son of Sirach,
Wisdom of
Solomon, 14, 104, 175, 179–81, 203–4
Solomon, Psalms of, 113, **203–12**, 237
Solomon, Wisdom of, 161–62, 172, **175–
85**, 187, 205, 219–20, 222, 248
Song of the Three Young Men. *See*
Azariah, Prayer of
Son(s) of God, 164, (171), (174), 176–
77, 209, 261
Son of Man: in Dan 7, 83–84 (defined),
97 n. 43, 215, 217, 222, 292; in *1
Enoch* 37–71, 215 (described), 217,
220–21, 222–23 (*see also* Elect One);
in the NT, 222–23, 304; man from the
sea in *4 Ezra*, 292
Spirit, Holy, 143–45, 184. *See also*
Dualism, angelic
Story of Ahikar. See Ahikar, Story of
Susanna, 25–26
Syria, 197, 200. *See also* Seleucids

Taxo, 81–82, 115, 119–20, 155 n. 81, 213
Teacher of Righteousness, 123, 124–30,
132, 137, 144–45
Temple: destruction in 587 B.C.E., 10,
110, 281, 313; Ezekiel's vision, 11, 53;
Second Temple, its construction and
early days, 13–15, 34, 93–94; attempted
plunder by Heliodorus, 71, 88, 119;
plundered and desecrated during reign
of Antiochus IV, 72–73, 81, 86, 88,
89–90, 109, 119, 144, 316; rededicated
by Judas Maccabeus, 73, 90, 109, 113,
316; threatened by Nicanor, 101–2,
109, 120; in early Roman times, 195–
96, 199–200, 202–3, 204–6, 213, 226;
Herod's rebuilding, 199; destruction in
70 C.E., 277–80, 281–82, 284, 286, 297,
307 n. 52; attitudes toward Temple in
Egyptian Jewish literature, 162, 164,
166, 168, 169, 171, 174; centrality in
other literature, 81–83 (*T. Mos.*), 118–
21 (2 Macc); negative attitudes
toward, 93–94, 123, 125, 129, 130,
133, 144; site of Jeremiah's death, 314;
vessels and furnishings, 22, 72, 109,
110, 281, 313; Wisdom's residence, 60;
eschatological Temple, 18, 33–34, 164,
297–98; heavenly Temple, 29, 53–54,
303 (*see also* Heaven, heavenly court
or throne room). *See also* Jerusalem;
Priesthood
Testament(s): genre, 80, 231–33 (defined
and described); of Abraham (in *Jub.*),
74, 232; of Adam (in *Apoc. Mos.*),
253–55; of Baruch, 284, 286; of Enoch,
150–51, 185–87, 232; of Eve, 257; of
Hezekiah, 142–43; of Jacob (in Gen
49), 231–32; of Mattathias, 115; of
Moses (in Deuteronomy), 80–81, 231;
of Tobit, 31, 32, 33. *See also Abraham,
Testament of; Job, Testament of;
Moses, Testament of; Twelve
Patriarchs, Testaments of*
Testing, 75–76, 107, 176–77, 242–47
Theodicy, 280 (defined), 281–305 passim
Theophanies, 49, 82, 216, 218, 256–57.
See also Commissionings by God;
Epiphanies
Therapeutae, 247
Theudas, 277
Tiberius, 201, 202
Titus, 10, 279, 303, 307 n. 52
Tobit, 30–35, 62, 107–8
Torah, Law: and Prophets, 35, 56;
Antiochus III officially recognizes, 71;
Antiochus IV proscribes, 73, 85; Enoch
cites its violation, 147; eternity of, 75;
Ezra reads and enforces, 15–16, 17;
Idumeans forced to observe, 103;
increasing importance after 70 C.E.,
281, 284, 286–87, 293; Matthew's view
of, 304; Nehemiah enforces, 16, 17;
observance and violation during
Antiochan persecution, 71–73, 77, 81,
88–89, 114, 119, 224–26; patriarchs
observed, 74; peculiarity of, 170–72,

Index of Modern Authors

331